# System Forensics, Investigation, and Response

JOHN R. VACCA AND K RUDOLPH

JONES & BARTLETT
LEARNING

**World Headquarters**
Jones & Bartlett Learning
40 Tall Pine Drive
Sudbury, MA 01776
978-443-5000
info@jblearning.com
www.jblearning.com

Jones & Bartlett Learning Canada
6339 Ormindale Way
Mississauga, Ontario L5V 1J2
Canada

Jones & Bartlett Learning
 International
Barb House, Barb Mews
London W6 7PA
United Kingdom

Jones & Bartlett Learning books and products are available through most bookstores and online booksellers. To contact Jones & Bartlett Learning directly, call 800-832-0034, fax 978-443-8000, or visit our website, www.jblearning.com.

Substantial discounts on bulk quantities of Jones & Bartlett Learning publications are available to corporations, professional associations, and other qualified organizations. For details and specific discount information, contact the special sales department at Jones & Bartlett Learning via the above contact information or send an email to specialsales@jblearning.com.

**Production Credits**
Chief Executive Officer: Ty Field
President: James Homer
SVP, Chief Operating Officer: Don Jones, Jr.
SVP, Chief Technology Officer: Dean Fossella
SVP, Chief Marketing Officer: Alison M. Pendergast
SVP, Chief Financial Officer: Ruth Siporin
SVP, Business Development: Christopher Will
VP, Design and Production: Anne Spencer
VP, Manufacturing and Inventory Control: Therese Connell
Editorial Management: High Stakes Writing, LLC, Editor and Publisher:
 Lawrence J. Goodrich

Reprints and Special Projects Manager: Susan Schultz
Associate Production Editor: Tina Chen
Director of Marketing: Alisha Weisman
Sernior Marketing Manager: Andrea DeFronzo
Cover Design: Anne Spencer
Composition: Sara Arand
Cover Image: © ErickN/ShutterStock, Inc.
Chapter Opener Image: © Rodolfo Clix/Dreamstime.com
Printing and Binding: Malloy, Inc.
Cover Printing: Malloy, Inc.

ISBN: 978-0-7637-9134-6

6048
Printed in the United States of America
15 14 13 12    10 9 8 7 6 5 4 3

# Contents

# Preface

## Purpose of This Book

This book is part of the Information Systems Security & Assurance Series from Jones & Bartlett Learning (*www.jblearning.com*). Designed for courses and curriculums in IT Security, Cybersecurity, Information Assurance, and Information Systems Security, this series features a comprehensive, consistent treatment of the most current thinking and trends in this critical subject area. These titles deliver fundamental information-security principles packed with real-world applications and examples. Authored by Certified Information Systems Security Professionals (CISSPs), they deliver comprehensive information on all aspects of information security. Reviewed word for word by leading technical experts in the field, these books are not just current, but forward-thinking—putting you in the position to solve the cybersecurity challenges not just of today, but of tomorrow, as well.

Computer crimes call for forensics specialists—people who know how to find and follow the evidence. This book begins by examining the fundamentals of system forensics: what forensics is, an overview of computer crime, the challenges of system forensics, and forensics methods and labs. The second part of this book addresses the tools, techniques, and methods used to perform computer forensics and investigation. These include collecting evidence, investigating information-hiding, recovering data, scrutinizing e-mail, and searching memory in real time. Finally, the third part explores incident and intrusion response, emerging technologies and future directions of this field, and additional system forensics resources.

## Learning Features

The writing style of this book is practical and conversational. Each chapter begins with a statement of learning objectives. Step-by-step examples of information security concepts and procedures are presented throughout the text. Illustrations are used both to clarify the material and to vary the presentation. The text is sprinkled with Notes, Tips, FYIs, Warnings, and sidebars to alert the reader to additional helpful information related to the subject under discussion. Chapter Assessments appear at the end of each chapter, with solutions provided in the back of the book.

Chapter summaries are included in the text to provide a rapid review or preview of the material and to help students understand the relative importance of the concepts presented.

## Audience

The material is suitable for undergraduate or graduate computer science majors or information science majors, students at a two-year technical college or community college who have a basic technical background, or readers who have a basic understanding of IT security and want to expand their knowledge.

# Acknowledgments

The authors would like to thank the following individuals and organizations for granting permission to re-use materials in this book:

Matthew Braid, Carnegie Mellon Software Engineering Institute (SEI), Computer Forensic Services, Inc., Andreas Furuseth, Frank Y. M. Law, NTI/Armor Forensics, Dr. Thomas O'Connor, and Golden Richard III and Vassil Roussev (through IGI Global).

The publisher wishes to extend special thanks to Kitty Wilson, whose yeoman efforts made this book possible.

## About the Authors

**JOHN R. VACCA** is an information technology consultant and internationally known best-selling author based in Pomeroy, Ohio. Since 1982, John has written 62 books and more than 600 articles in the areas of advanced storage, computer security, and aerospace technology. John was also a configuration management specialist, computer specialist, and the computer security official (CSO) for NASA's space station program (*Freedom*) and the International Space Station Program from 1988 until his retirement from NASA in 1995. In addition, John is an independent online book reviewer. He was also one of the security consultants for the MGM movie *AntiTrust*, which was released in 2001.

**K RUDOLPH** is a Certified Information Systems Security Professional (CISSP) with a degree from Johns Hopkins University. She is the primary author of the chapter on security awareness from the *Computer Security Handbook, Vol. 5*, and is also the author of the chapter on security awareness in the *Handbook of Information Security* published in 2006 and 2009. K is a named contributor to and participant in the work group that created NIST Special Publication 800-16, *Information Technology Security Training Requirements: A Role- and Performance-Based Model*. K has presented at conferences that include the Computer Security Institute Security Exchange (CSI SX) Conference in 2008, the New York Cyber Security Conference (2006 and 2007), the Annual CSI Computer Security Conferences (2005, 2007), and Information Assurance and Security Conferences held by FISSEA, FIAC, and eGOV. In March 2006, K was honored by the Federal Information Systems Security Educators' Association (FISSEA) as the Security Educator of the Year.

# PART ONE

# The System Forensics Landscape

# System Forensics Fundamentals

**N**UMEROUS ELECTRONIC DEVICES are commonly used today. These devices include computers, global positioning system (GPS) receivers, personal digital assistants (PDAs), and mobile phones. Electronic devices record aspects of our lives and activities. An increasing number of conflicts and crimes exploit the data on these devices. Electronic evidence and information gathering have therefore become important issues. Collecting, preserving, analyzing, documenting, and presenting digital evidence are all facets of the field of system forensics.

System forensics can be studied several ways. For example, it can be studied by operating system, such as Windows, Macintosh, or UNIX. It can also be studied by the source and type of evidence collected. This book looks at system forensics in a step-by-step manner. Later chapters address topics such as collecting and protecting evidence, investigating information-hiding techniques, and recovering data. This book also covers special cases, such as investigating e-mail, performing network forensics, and working with memory in real time.

This chapter discusses the fundamentals of system forensics. It begins by providing an overview of forensics. Then it discusses how computers are used in crimes, the role of forensic specialists, evidence, and application of forensic analysis skills.

---

## Chapter 1 Topics

This chapter covers the following topics and concepts:

- What system forensics is
- How computers are used in crimes
- What system forensics specialists are and what they do
- What forensic evidence is, who uses it, and why it's important to handle it carefully
- How to apply forensic analysis skills

## Chapter 1 Goals

When you complete this chapter, you will be able to:

- Define *system forensics*
- Understand how computers are used in crimes
- Describe the role of a system forensics specialist
- Explain the importance of properly handling forensic evidence
- Describe some of the important points in forensic analysis

# Understanding System Forensics

Technological advances have resulted in a modern form of crime. Computer crime, or **cybercrime**, is criminal activity that pertains to any of the following:

- Wrongfully taking information
- Causing damage to information
- Causing an information system or resources to be unavailable to authorized users when needed

To combat cybercrime, computer and law enforcement professionals have developed new areas of expertise. They have also invented new avenues for collecting and analyzing evidence. This has developed into the science of system forensics. The process of acquiring, examining, and applying digital evidence is crucial in prosecuting a cybercriminal.

System forensics was originally called computer forensics because it focused on hard drives and storage devices. Today, system forensics is also referred to as *digital forensics, computer forensics analysis, electronic discovery, electronic evidence discovery, digital discovery, data recovery, data discovery, computer analysis*, and *computer examination*. **System forensics** is the process of methodically examining computer media as well as network components, software, and memory for evidence. A forensic investigator is likely to look for evidence on hard disks, tapes, compact disks (CDs) and other optical disks, flash drives, and other media. A skilled system forensics specialist may be able to conduct a thorough analysis to reconstruct a user's activities on a single device or across a network or the Internet. As discussed later in this chapter, system forensics now includes a number of specialties.

 **NOTE**

The term *computer forensics* was coined in 1991, in the first training session held by the International Association of Computer Specialists (IACIS) in Portland, Oregon. Since then, computer forensics has become a popular topic in computer security circles and in the legal community.

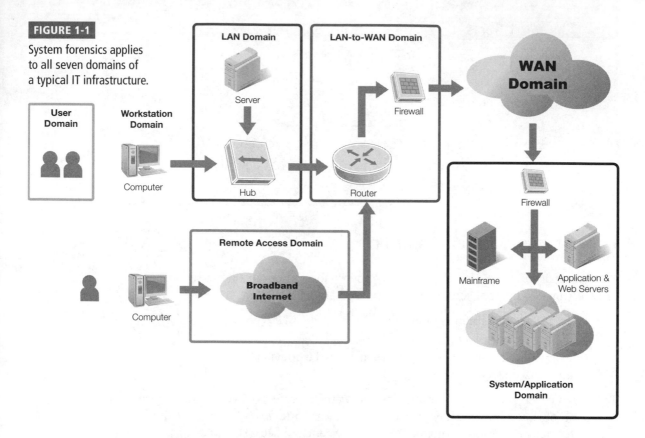

System forensics applies
to all seven domains of
a typical IT infrastructure.

A system forensics specialist uses evidence to reconstruct past events or activities. Forensic specialists also use evidence to gain a better understanding of a crime. They may use it to show possession and handling of digital data. They may use it as well to show use or abuse of information technology (IT) infrastructure and services and to prove policy violations or illegal activity.

System forensics applies to all the domains of a typical IT infrastructure, from the User Domain and Remote Access Domain to the Wide Area Network (WAN) Domain and Internet Domain. (See Figure 1-1.)

## Who Uses Forensics?

Forensics is important to many professions and organizations. The following are some examples:

- **Law enforcement**—Law enforcement uses forensics to gather digital evidence for a variety of crimes. These crimes include child pornography, fraud, terrorism, extortion, cyberstalking, money laundering, forgery, and identity theft. Forensic specialists can help law enforcement personnel prepare search warrants and handle computer equipment that has been seized.

- **The military**—The military uses forensics to gather intelligence information from computers captured during military actions.
- **Government agencies**—Government agencies use forensics to investigate crimes involving computers. These agencies include the Federal Bureau of Investigation (FBI), the U.S. Postal Inspection Service, the Federal Trade Commission, and the U.S. Secret Service. They also include the U.S. Department of Justice's National Institute of Justice (NIJ), the National Institute of Standards and Technology (NIST) Office of Law Enforcement Standards (OLES), and the Department of Homeland Security.
- **Law firms**—Law firms need experienced system forensics professionals to conduct investigations and testify as expert witnesses. For example, civil cases can use records found on computer systems that bear on cases involving fraud, divorce, discrimination, and harassment.
- **Criminal prosecutors**—Criminal prosecutors use digital evidence when working with incriminating documents. They try to link these documents to crimes, such as drug and embezzlement, financial fraud, homicide, and child pornography.
- **Academia**—Academia is involved with forensic research and education. For example, many universities offer degrees in digital forensics and online criminal justice.
- **Data recovery firms**—Data recovery firms use digital forensics techniques to recover data after hardware or software failures and when data has been lost.
- **Corporations**—Corporations use digital forensics to assist in employee termination and prosecution. For example, corporations sometimes need to gather information concerning theft of intellectual property or trade secrets, fraud, embezzlement, sexual harassment, and network and computer intrusions. They also need to find evidence of unauthorized use of equipment, such as computers, fax machines, answering machines, PDAs, and mobile phones.
- **Insurance companies**—Insurance companies can sometimes reduce costs by using digital evidence of possible fraud in accident, arson, and workers' compensation cases.
- **Individuals**—Individuals sometimes hire forensic specialists in support of possible claims. These cases may include, for example, wrongful termination, sexual harassment, or age discrimination.

The objective in system forensics is to recover, analyze, and present computer-based material in such a way that it can be used as evidence in a court of law. In system forensics, as in any other branch of forensic science, the emphasis must be on the integrity and security of evidence. A forensic specialist must adhere to stringent guidelines and avoid taking shortcuts.

Computers can be involved in both white-collar and violent crimes. The FBI recently conducted a survey to determine where it was focusing its system forensics efforts. The survey found that 79 percent of the FBI's workload is focused on white-collar crime.

> **The RCFL Program**
>
> The RCFL Program is a national network of forensic laboratories and training centers. The FBI provides startup and operational funding, training, staff, and equipment to the program. State, local, and other federal law enforcement agencies assign personnel to staff RCFL laboratories.
>
> Each of the 16 RCFLs examines digital evidence in support of criminal and national security investigations. The RCFL Program provides law enforcement at all levels of government with digital forensics expertise. It works with a wide variety of investigations, including terrorism, child pornography, fraud, and homicide.
>
> The RCFL Program conducts digital forensics training. In 2008, for example, the program trained nearly 5,000 law enforcement personnel in system forensics tools and techniques. For more information, see *http://www.rcfl.gov*.

This type of crime includes health care fraud, government fraud such as erroneous Internal Revenue Service and Social Security benefit payments, and financial institution fraud. Technology makes these high-dollar crimes easy. The other 21 percent of the FBI's forensic workload is focused on violent crime. This type of crime includes child pornography, interstate theft, organized crime such as drug dealing, counterterrorism, and national security.

Computer crime is widespread and has infiltrated areas unimaginable just a few years ago. In 1985, the FBI investigated zero cases of computer crime. In 2008, it investigated nearly 52,000 cases. The FBI's caseload is no doubt even higher today. The number of FBI system forensics personnel has gone from a few part-time scientists to thousands of personnel. These personnel work in and with Regional Computer Forensics Laboratories (RCFLs) throughout the country. Technology has made system forensics an important field.

## How Computers Are Used in Crimes

According to *http://www.internetworldstats.com/stats.htm*, more than 1.8 billion Internet users worldwide were online in mid-2010. This means a lot of data interchange. Unfortunately, many small businesses and even large organizations do not properly protect their sensitive data. In this way, they leave the door open to cybercriminals.

Many crimes today involve the use of computers and networks. According to Judd Robbins, a computer forensics expert, a computer or another device can play one of three roles in a computer crime:

- It can be the target of the crime.
- It can be the instrument of the crime.
- It can be an evidence repository that stores valuable information about the crime.

In some cases, a computer can have multiple roles. It can be the instrument of a crime and also serve as a file cabinet that stores critical evidence. For example, an attacker may use a computer as a tool to break into another computer and steal files. The attacker may then store the stolen files on the computer used to perpetrate the theft. When investigating a case, it is important to know what roles a computer played in the crime and then tailor the investigative process to those roles.

Applying information about how a computer was used in a crime also helps when searching a system for evidence. If a computer was used to hack into a network password file, the investigator should look for password-cracking software and password files. If a computer was the target of a crime, such as an intrusion, the investigator should check audit logs and look for unfamiliar programs.

Knowing how a computer was used in a crime helps narrow down the evidence collection process. Hard drives today are generally very large. Therefore, checking and analyzing every piece of data a computer and associated media contain can take a long time. Often, law enforcement officials need information quickly. Having a general idea of what to look for on a suspect computer speeds the evidence collection process.

> **NOTE**
>
> Like any other forensic science, system forensics deals with the application of law to a science. In this case, the science involved is computer science, sometimes referred to as *forensic computer science*. System forensics involves using specialized software tools and techniques to analyze the various levels at which computer data is stored.

Computers can be involved in a variety of types of crimes, including white-collar crimes, violent crimes such as murder and terrorism, counterintelligence, economic espionage, counterfeiting, child pornography, and drug dealing. A 2008 FBI survey reported that the average bank robbery netted $11,400. In contrast, the average computer crime netted $3.4 million. The Internet has made targets much more accessible, and the risks involved for criminals are much lower than with traditional crimes. From the comfort of home or some other remote site, a cybercriminal can hack into a bank and transfer millions of dollars to a fictitious account. In essence, the criminal can rob the bank without the threat of being physically harmed while escaping.

Cybercrime can involve modification of a traditional crime by using the Internet in some way. It can be as simple as the online illegal sale of prescription drugs or as sophisticated as cyberstalking. Pedophiles use the Internet to exchange child pornography and pose as children to lure victims into real-life kidnappings. Laws governing fraud apply with equal force, regardless of whether the activity is online or offline.

**FYI**

Not every crime involving a computer is considered cybercrime. A person who uses a stolen telephone code to make free calls, even though the number is processed by a computer, is engaging in toll fraud, not computer crime. A person who embezzles $700 from the automatic teller machine of a company he works for commits embezzlement, not cybercrime. A crime that involves the use of computers that is incidental to another offense is not cybercrime.

Cybercriminals are more aware of digital forensics today than they were in the past. Many are adept at destroying digital evidence to cover their crimes. Some use "anti-forensic" tools to foil investigations into their activities. Chapter 3, "Challenges of System Forensics," briefly discusses anti-forensic tools.

## System Forensics Specialists and What They Do

A **system forensics specialist** finds evidence, determines the significance of the evidence, and relates the evidence to a crime. The goal of a forensic specialist is to provide a better understanding of what happened, when it happened, and how it happened. Forensics involves research, experimentation, and analysis.

 **NOTE**

The American Academy of Forensic Science recognizes forensic computer crime investigation as a discipline. See *http://www.aafs.org* for more details.

The growth in the number of court cases that involve digital evidence has created a high demand for people with forensic skills. The field of digital forensics is challenging. Investigations may involve a single computer or a network with hundreds or thousands of nodes. As digital forensics technologies and methods have advanced, forensics has become a science as well as an art. A forensic specialist needs a sound knowledge of proven and accepted scientific methods, as well as a deep understanding of various technologies, hardware, and software. (Chapter 15, "System Forensics Resources," discusses some of the training and certification options in the field of system forensics.)

### Tasks of a Forensic Specialist

These are the two most important aspects of a forensic investigator's job:

- Ensuring that the evidence is what the investigator says it is
- Showing that the evidence hasn't been altered or substituted since it was collected

A system forensics specialist needs to know how to find and interpret clues. In some situations, files have been deleted, disks have been reformatted, or other steps have been taken to conceal or destroy evidence. Criminals may attempt to steal anything from customer databases to blueprints. No matter how careful they are, when people attempt to steal electronic information, they leave traces of their activities. Likewise, people may try to destroy incriminating computer evidence, such as harassing memos or stolen technology. When they do, they leave behind vital clues. Such traces can help win a court case. Thus, digital evidence is a reliable and essential form of evidence that should not be overlooked.

A system forensics professional does more than turn on a computer, make a directory listing, and search through files. Such a person needs to be able to successfully perform complex evidence recovery procedures. According to Judd Robbins, a forensic specialist may need to take the following measures to identify and attempt to retrieve evidence from a subject computer system:

### No Clues Left Behind

When looking for clues in a forensic investigation, an investigator should look for answers to the following questions:

- Which Web sites have been visited?
- Which files have been downloaded?
- When were files last accessed?
- Have attempts been made to conceal or destroy evidence?
- Have attempts been made to fabricate evidence?

An investigator should also keep in mind the following:

- The electronic copy of a document can contain text that was removed from the final printed version.
- Some fax machines can contain exact duplicates of the last several hundred pages received.
- Faxes sent or received via computer may remain on the computer indefinitely.
- People tend to write things in e-mail or text messages that they wouldn't consider writing in a memorandum or letter.
- E-mail is often backed up on tapes that are generally kept for months or years.
- Many people keep their financial records, including investments, on computers.
- Mobile devices, such as PDAs, mobile phones, and netbooks, contain evidence. For example, they carry records of whom the user spoke to. They also record what the user sent and received text messages about. In addition, they can contain photographs and calendars of what the users did and when.

- During the forensic examination, protect the subject computer system from any possible alteration, damage, data corruption, or virus introduction. (See Chapter 6, "Controlling a Forensic Investigation.")
- Discover all pertinent files on the subject system. This may include existing normal files, deleted yet remaining files, hidden files, password-protected files, and encrypted files. (See Chapter 7, "Collecting, Seizing, and Protecting Evidence," and Chapter 8, "Understanding Information-Hiding Techniques.")
- Understand how to use search and analysis tools to recover as many of the discovered deleted files as possible. (See Chapter 9, "Recovering Data.")

- Create an overall analysis of the subject computer system and a list of all possibly relevant files and discovered file data. A system forensics specialist should also provide an opinion of the system layout, the file structures discovered, and any discovered data and authorship information. The specialist should examine attempts to hide, delete, protect, or encrypt information. In addition, a specialist should try to find explanations for anything else that appears to be relevant to the overall computer system examination. (See Chapter 9, "Recovering Data.")

- Draw conclusions and provide expert consultation and testimony, as required. (See Chapter 9, "Recovering Data.")

**NOTE**

Although involving some of the same skills and software as data recovery, system forensics is a much more complex undertaking. In *data recovery*, the goal is to retrieve lost data. In *system forensics*, the goal is to retrieve the data and interpret as much information about it as possible.

A system forensics expert who helps during evidence discovery needs to have experience with a wide range of computer hardware and software. When files have been damaged, a system forensics expert can use advanced tools to recover even very small remaining fragments. Many methods can reveal data that resides in a computer system. An experienced investigator can recover deleted, encrypted, or damaged file information. This information may prove highly valuable during legal proceedings.

## How a Forensic Specialist Begins an Investigation

It's not sufficient to have the technical skills to locate evidence on computer media. In recovering evidence, system forensics experts must follow certain procedures to ensure that the evidence is preserved in its original form. The general principles are as follows:

- The scene of a crime has to be frozen. That is, the evidence must be collected as early as possible and without contamination.

- It must be possible to account for all that has happened to the evidence between its original collection and its appearance in court. This is called the *chain of custody*. In addition, the evidence should be unaltered, if possible.

- All procedures used in examination should be auditable. That is, a qualified independent expert should be able to track all the investigations carried out by the prosecution's experts.

**TIP**

Forensic investigation is most effective when conducted by an impartial third party who has the necessary technical and law enforcement background.

These topics are covered in more detail in Chapter 6, "Controlling a Forensic Investigation," and Chapter 7, "Collecting, Seizing, and Protecting Evidence."

In many cases, it is possible to produce reliable computer-derived evidence without using specialized tools. An investigator can get good results by using the standard disk repair, network testing, and other utilities and by keeping full records. In some cases, however, these methods may not be enough.

More-specialized tools are needed, for example, to recover previously deleted material or if a logic bomb or virus is suspected. The specialized tools themselves don't address all the problems of producing evidence that will stand up in court. Special training is also required. Thus, a forensic specialist must have the following key characteristics:

- Careful methodology of approach, including record keeping
- A sound knowledge of computing, particularly in any specialist areas claimed
- A sound knowledge of the law of evidence
- A sound knowledge of legal procedures
- Access to and skill in the use of appropriate utilities

Chapter 15, "System Forensics Resources," discusses training and certification programs for forensic specialists.

## System Forensics Evidence: Its Use and Handling

In the past, documentary evidence was primarily limited to paper documents. Copies were made with carbon paper or using a photocopy machine. Most documents today are stored on computer hard disk drives, CDs, flash drives, and other types of computer storage media. This is where **system forensics evidence** may reside. An investigator must find this evidence by using system forensics tools and methodologies. Paper documents are no longer always considered the best evidence.

Evidence gathered from computers is subject to the same standards as evidence gathered from any other type of crime scene. Like any other evidence, system forensics evidence must be authentic, accurate, complete, and convincing to juries. In addition, it must conform to all applicable laws to be admissible in court.

Almost any type of investigation and litigation today—criminal or civil—may rely on evidence obtained from computer systems. System forensics evidence, also known as *computer evidence* or *digital evidence*, can often make or break a case. Digital evidence can be used to establish that a crime has been committed. It can also be used to assert other points of fact in a court of law. For example, digital evidence can be used to identify suspects, defend the innocent, prosecute the guilty, and understand the motives and intents of individuals.

A computer's operating system can create digital evidence without the knowledge of the computer operator. Such information may actually be hidden from view. Special forensic software tools and techniques are required to preserve, identify, extract, and document hidden digital evidence. This evidence may include deleted e-mail messages or files, computer logs, spreadsheets, and accounting information.

> **NOTE**
>
> Criminal and civil litigation actions are relying more and more on digital evidence. Computer evidence helped identify the now-infamous blue dress in the Clinton impeachment hearings. Oliver North got into some of his trouble with the U.S. Congress when erased computer files were recovered as digital evidence. Digital evidence is also used to identify Internet account abuses.

## Digital Evidence Challenges

There are some special problems related to digital evidence. A significant problem, called **evidence dynamics**, refers to anything that changes or destroys digital evidence between the time the evidence is created and when the case goes to court. It doesn't matter whether the action that changed the evidence is accidental or deliberate. One common cause of evidence dynamics is a criminal attempting to cover his or her tracks. Or a victim may delete files or e-mails to avoid embarrassment. In addition, when someone uses a subject computer after a crime has been committed, evidence may be altered or destroyed. Other problems related to evidence include:

* Digital data changes moment by moment.
* Computer data is invisible to the human eye. It can be viewed only indirectly and only after appropriate procedures are followed.
* The process of collecting computer data may change it in significant ways. For example, the processes of opening a file and printing it are not always neutral.
* Computer and telecommunications technologies are always changing. Forensic processes must keep up with these changes.
* The laws haven't kept up with technology.

## Protecting Evidence

Protecting evidence is critical. Knowledgeable system forensics professionals should ensure that a subject computer system is carefully handled. According to Judd Robbins, the basic criteria are as follows:

* No possible evidence is damaged, destroyed, or otherwise compromised by the procedures used to investigate the computer
* No computer virus is introduced to a subject computer during the analysis process
* Extracted and possibly relevant evidence is properly handled and protected from later mechanical or electromagnetic damage
* A continuing chain of custody is established and maintained
* Business operations are not affected or are affected for only a limited amount of time
* Any client–attorney information that is inadvertently acquired during a forensic exploration is ethically and legally respected and not divulged

Chapter 6, "Controlling a Forensic Investigation," and Chapter 7, "Collecting, Seizing, and Protecting Evidence," discuss these issues in greater detail.

## Testing Forensic Evidence

The rules vary from legislation to legislation, but basically, the law distinguishes between real evidence, testimonial evidence, and hearsay. Real evidence comes from an inanimate object that can be examined by the court. Testimonial evidence is evidence that a live witness has seen and on which he or she can be cross-examined. The hearsay rule excludes any assertions other than those made by the witness who is testifying. The pure hearsay rule is extremely restrictive and has been extensively modified by various statutory provisions. (See Chapter 7, "Collecting, Seizing, and Protecting Evidence," for more information on these types of forensic evidence.)

> **▷ NOTE**
>
> In the United States, the seizure of computers containing evidence presents many problems. Law enforcement officers must comply with the Fourth Amendment to the U.S. Constitution. Chapter 6, "Controlling a Forensic Investigation," provides more information.

There are rules about the *proving* of documents and business books. Some of these rules apply explicitly to computers, but many do not. However, these rules may be interpreted to cover many situations in which computers are involved.

System forensics goes beyond procedures and methods of handling computer hardware and files. The ultimate aim of forensic investigation is use in legal proceedings. However, an obsession with law and judicial rules may inhibit an investigation. It might be a mistake not to commence inquiries simply because of fear of possible inadmissibility. Furthermore, a number of computer-investigatory methods may not be directly admissible but may nevertheless be useful in locating noncomputer evidence that is admissible.

Forensic evidence must undergo the following broad tests:

- **Authenticity**—Does the material come from where it purports to come from?
- **Reliability**—Is the story that the material purports to tell believable? Is it consistent? In the case of computer-derived material, are there reasons to doubt the correct working of the computer?
- **Completeness**—Is the story that the material purports to tell complete? Are there other stories that the material also tells that might have a bearing on the case?
- **Freedom from interference and contamination**—After forensic investigation and other post-event handling, are the levels of interference and evidence contamination acceptable?

## Applying Forensic Analysis Skills

An important component of the electronic discovery process is applying forensic analysis skills to recovered data. Forensic analysis is an art and a science. Each case presents unique challenges. The objective of system forensics analysis is to determine the facts of a case in an efficient and nonbiased manner. It involves following the chain of evidence as it unfolds. System forensics analysis goes beyond the initial investigation to include the following:

- Ensuring that electronic evidence is admissible in a court of law
- Searching for relevant information and determining the history, authentication, and origin of electronic documents
- Using electronic data to reconstruct events or substantiate allegations and claims
- Minimizing the impact of **spoliation**—that is, the withholding, hiding, alteration, or destruction of evidence relevant to a legal proceeding

- Linking evidence to prove the case
- Preparing evidence for litigation support, including deposition and expert witness testimony

## Following Proper Forensic Procedures

One of the fundamental principles of system forensics investigation is the need to follow established and tested procedures meticulously and methodically. At no point in an investigation is this more critical than during initial evidence capture. Reproducibility of evidence is the key. Without a firm base of solid procedures that have been strictly applied, a case as a whole will likely be weakened.

> **NOTE**
>
> One of the most difficult onsite skills is knowing when to ask for help. It is essential to create a sympathetic working environment. Otherwise, an investigator may not call for help because of peer pressure or fear he or she will lose status and respect.

In several high-profile instances, apparently solid cases have been weakened or thrown out because inappropriate consideration was given to the integrity and reproducibility of the digital evidence. This may happen for several reasons. Lack of training is a prime culprit. If the individuals involved have not been trained to the required standards, tainted or damaged digital evidence is the sad but inevitable result. Another frequent cause is lack of experience. Finally, sloppiness, pressure applied onsite, tiredness, and carelessness have been contributory factors in transforming solid digital evidence into a dubious collection of files. It is in everyone's best interest to ensure that the highest forensic standards are maintained.

## Types of System Forensics Analysis

Today, system forensics includes a number of specialties. The following are some examples:

- **Disk forensics**—The process of acquiring and analyzing data stored on physical storage media, such as computer hard drives, smartphones, and removable media. Disk forensics includes both the recovery of hidden and deleted data and also the process of identifying who created a file or message. (See Chapter 8, "Understanding Information-Hiding Techniques," and Chapter 9, "Recovering Data.")
- **E-mail forensics**—The study of the source and content of e-mail as evidence. E-mail forensics includes the process of identifying the sender, recipient, date, time, and origination location of an e-mail message. You can use e-mail forensics to identify harassment, discrimination, or unauthorized activities. (See Chapter 10, "Investigating and Scrutinizing E-mail.")
- **Network forensics**—The process of examining network traffic, including transaction logs and real-time monitoring, using sniffers and tracing. (See Chapter 11, "Performing Network Analysis.")

- **Internet forensics**—The process of piecing together where and when a user has been on the Internet. For example, you can use Internet forensics to determine whether inappropriate Internet content access and downloading were accidental. (See Chapter 11, "Performing Network Analysis.")

- **Software forensics** or **malware forensics**—The process of examining malicious code. (This topic is beyond the scope of this book but is briefly touched on in Chapter 8, "Understanding Information-Hiding Techniques.")

- **Live system forensics**—The process of searching memory in real time, typically for working with compromised hosts or to identify system abuse. (See Chapter 12, "Searching Memory in Real Time with Live System Forensics.")

Each of these types of forensic analysis requires specialized skills and training, as discussed throughout this book.

## Examples of Forensic Investigations

Consider two real-life examples of the type of material a system forensics specialist might have to work with:

- **The case of the flying laptop**—Police rushed to the ninth floor of a building. Almost immediately thereafter, a laptop flew out the window of the premises and toward the ground. The resultant bag of smashed laptop components arrived at a laboratory for forensic analysis.

- **The case of the burned tapes**—Sets of digital audio tapes (DATs) were caught in a fire that had engulfed a company's head office and wiped out the primary trading infrastructure. The company's IT systems had been at the center of the blaze and were destroyed. The DATs had, inadvisably, not been stored offsite. They were, however, not stored near the center of the blaze. The DATs arrived at a forensics lab in a rather sorry condition. The plastic casing had melted to, around, and onto the tapes, and the whole mechanism was fused into a homologous glob.

As you can see, a system forensics specialist faces a variety of situations. Gathering data and investigating cases provide exciting opportunities to learn new forensic skills.

## CHAPTER SUMMARY

When computer systems are involved in a crime, much work needs to be done to analyze the contents of those systems. System forensics is the collection, analysis, and presentation of computer-based evidence. A system forensics specialist must take careful steps to identify and attempt to retrieve possible evidence that may exist on a subject computer system. A system forensics specialist should be competent in data seizure, data duplication and preservation, data recovery, document searches, media conversion, and providing expert witness services.

This chapter describes the fundamentals of system forensics, how computers are used in crimes, the role of system forensics specialists, system forensics evidence, and application of forensic analysis skills. The following chapters expand on these ideas.

## KEY CONCEPTS AND TERMS

Cybercrime

Disk forensics

E-mail forensics

Evidence dynamics

Internet forensics

Live system forensics

Network forensics

Software forensics

Spoliation

System forensics

System forensics evidence

System forensics specialist

## CHAPTER 1 ASSESSMENT

**1.** To which domains of a typical IT infrastructure does system forensics apply?

A. User Domain
B. Workstation Domain
C. LAN Domain
D. WAN Domain
E. Remote Access Domain
F. All of the above

**2.** A computer can play one of three roles in a computer crime: It can be the target of the crime, it can be the instrument of the crime, or it can serve as an evidence repository that stores valuable information about the crime.

A. True
B. False

**3.** When people try to destroy incriminating evidence contained on a computer, they leave behind vital _____ .

**4.** System forensics is the same as data recovery.

A. True
B. False

**5.** A system forensics professional should be able to successfully perform complex evidence recovery procedures. Which of the following tasks should such a specialist be able to perform? (Select three.)

A. Expert witness services
B. Data recovery
C. Data dump
D. Document searches

**6.** Which of the following is *not* an important characteristic of a forensic specialist?

A. A sound knowledge of computing
B. Careful methodology of approach
C. Law degree
D. Access to and skill in the use of appropriate utilities

**7.** Which of the following refers to anything that changes or destroys digital evidence between the time the evidence is created and when the case goes to court?

A. Disk forensics
B. Evidence dynamics
C. Spoliation
D. Live system forensics

**8.** Which of the following is *not* a broad test that should be applied to forensic evidence?

A. Fairness
B. Authenticity
C. Reliability
D. Completeness
E. Freedom from interference and contamination

**9.** The system forensics specialty that involves acquiring and analyzing data stored on physical storage media, such as computer hard drives and removable media is called _____ .

**10.** _____ is an area of system forensics that is used to search memory in real time, typically for working with compromised hosts or to identify system abuse.

**11.** _____ is an area of system forensics that is most often used to examine malicious code.

# Overview of Computer Crime

I N CHAPTER 1, "SYSTEM FORENSICS FUNDAMENTALS," you learned that a computer can play one of three roles in a computer crime. It can be the target of the crime, it can be the instrument of the crime, or it can serve as an evidence repository that stores valuable information about the crime. As technology evolves, cyberattacks grow in sophistication and frequency. In recent years, these attacks have become more widespread, diverse, and financially damaging.

System forensics personnel fight computer crime, or cybercrime. They do so by identifying and analyzing evidence to put together a picture of what happened, when, where, how, and why. Forensic analysts may be directly involved in identifying offenders and in establishing a link between people and their computer or online activities.

On television, police detectives often catch criminals by determining who has the means, motive, and opportunity to commit a crime. System forensics analysts can view cybercrime by looking for the same three factors.

---

### Chapter 2 Topics

This chapter covers the following topics and concepts:

- What the various types of cybercrime are
- What sources of cybercrime threats exist
- What the means, motives, and opportunities of cybercriminals are
- Which cybercrimes to report and to whom
- What the role of system forensics is in solving crimes

## Chapter 2 Goals

When you complete this chapter, you will be able to:

- Describe some of the many types of cybercrime
- List various sources of cyberthreats
- Explain some of the means, motives, and opportunities of cybercriminals
- Recognize activities that should be reported and to which authorities
- Understand the role of system forensics in solving crimes

# Types of Cybercrime

Computers have become more and more numerous in recent years. In addition, access to the Internet is now widespread. At the same time, the number of crimes involving computers has risen dramatically. The U.S. Department of Justice (DOJ) defines computer crimes, or cybercrimes, as "any violations of criminal law that involve knowledge of computer technology for their perpetration."

In some cybercrimes, computers are used as tools. In other cybercrimes, evidence is left on computers. In many cases, computers serve both roles. Cybercrime can be either white collar or violent. It can focus on specific individuals or aim to harm entire companies or even countries. The goal of cybercrime can range from causing irritation or playing a prank, to stealing information or money, to committing violence against people.

 **NOTE**

Governments, individuals, and businesses incur huge costs due to cybercrime. A 2007 Government Accountability Office report estimates the total U.S. business losses due to cyberattacks exceed $117.5 billion per year. The Internet Crime Complaint Center (IC3) reported the total loss related to online fraud was $559.7 million in 2009, up from $265 million in 2008.

A cybercrime may be a traditional criminal act committed with the help of a computer. Some examples of these crimes are forgery, fraud, extortion, theft of intellectual property, drug trafficking, terrorism, child exploitation, and kidnapping. Cybercrime also includes offenses that the Internet and other technological advances have made easier. These crimes include denial of service attacks, identity theft, software piracy, and cyberwarfare. The following sections discuss a few of the most common types of computer crimes.

## DoS and DDoS Attacks

**Denial of service (DoS)** and **distributed denial of service (DDoS)** attacks are some of the most widespread cybercrimes. DoS/DDoS occurs when an attacker deprives people of the services they are entitled to access or provide. DoS/DDoS can occur when an attacker floods the bandwidth of the victim's network. It can also occur when an attacker fills an individual's e-mail box with spam mail. DoS/DDoS attacks have caused some of the largest commercial Web sites, including Yahoo!, eBay, and Amazon, to become inaccessible to customers, partners, and users. Attackers mounted large-scale DoS/DDoS attacks against Estonia in 2007 and Georgia in 2008.

## Intellectual Property Theft

Another common cybercrime is intellectual property theft. **Intellectual property theft** is theft of trade secrets, material that is copyrighted, or other information to which an individual or a company has a right. Intellectual property theft has resulted in increasing revenue losses worldwide. This theft is especially significant in the United States, which leads the world in the creation and sale of intellectual property products.

One common form of intellectual property theft is theft of trade secrets. Trade secrets are plans, methods, technologies, and other sensitive information that an individual or a company owns. **Trade secrets** are common in all types of industries, including manufacturing, financial services, and the computer industry. Examples of trade secrets are plans for the latest iPhone, designs for a fuel-efficient electric airplane, the recipe for a soft drink, or the spices in a fast-food chain's fried chicken. Theft of trade secrets damages a business's competitive edge.

**Piracy** is theft of copyrighted material through illegal copying of genuine programs or counterfeiting of products that are intended to pass as originals. Software, music, videos, and electronic games are commonly pirated. Piracy includes illegal end user copying, illegal hard disk loading, counterfeiting, and illegal downloading from the Internet.

## Child Exploitation, Abuse, and Pornography

Child exploitation includes crimes such as child pornography, luring, child-sex tourism, and child prostitution. Creating or possessing non-commercial child pornography is also illegal. According to the 2008 Annual Report published by the National Center for Missing & Exploited Children, child pornography is a multi-billion-dollar business.

## Identity Theft

**Identity theft**, also known as identity fraud, is a common cybercrime. An identity thief wrongfully obtains and uses another person's personal data in some way that involves fraud or deception. Criminals typically commit identity fraud for economic gain. One common method criminals use to obtain others' identities is phishing.

**Phishing** involves using e-mail or Web sites to get confidential information by deceptive means. Through phishing, a criminal can obtain a victim's Social Security number, bank account number, credit card number, passwords, and other valuable identifying data.

With enough information about an individual, a criminal can take over that person's identity and conduct many different crimes. For example, a criminal may submit false applications for credit cards, or withdraw funds from bank accounts. A savvy criminal

---

### The Child Exploitation Section of the Cyber Crimes Center

The U.S. Immigration and Customs Enforcement's (ICE's) **Cyber Crimes Center (C3)** identifies and apprehends Internet child pornographers. Its Child Exploitation Section (CES) "investigates the trans-border dimension of large-scale producers and distributors of images of child abuse, as well as individuals who travel in foreign commerce for the purpose of engaging in sex with minors."

One of the main functions of the C3 is to stop the spread of child pornography over the Internet. CES carries out various operations to combat child pornography. It adopts the latest technology to gain information and apprehend parties engaged in the production and dissemination of child pornography.

CES organizes its investigative activities under a program called Operation Predator. The exploitation of children is a matter of global importance and reach. The CES therefore works closely with law enforcement agencies from around the world. It also conducts secret operations all over the world to identify and apprehend violators.

Under Operation Predator, ICE and the Danish National Police jointly investigated a ring of pedophiles who molested their own children and posted images of this molestation on the Internet. As a result of the investigation, 34 individuals were arrested, and more than 100 children were rescued. The majority of abused children were U.S. citizens.

For more information on C3, see *http://www.ice.gov/partners/investigations/services/ cyberbranch.htm.*

---

ensures that bills for falsely obtained credit cards or bank statements showing unauthorized withdrawals are sent to an address other than the victim's. The victim may not find out that his or her identity has been stolen until the criminal has substantially damaged the victim's assets, credit, and reputation.

 **NOTE**

The U.S. Congress made identity theft a crime in 1998.

## Fraud

**Fraud** is a crime that involves intentional deception for personal gain or to cause other damage to an individual or a company. Three criteria must be met to convict someone who has used a computer to commit fraud. The fraud must be intentional, the person's computer access must be unauthorized, and the victim's loss must have a value of more than $5,000. Similar crimes involving computers include bank fraud, embezzlement, credit card fraud, online auction fraud, counterfeiting, telecommunications fraud, and money laundering.

## Extortion

**Extortion** is an attempt to gain money or something else of value by threatening, coercing, or intimidating a victim. Extortion involving a computer includes threatening to damage a computer or information contained on the computer. Extortion also includes threats to disclose confidential information obtained from a computer. If an extortion attempt is unsuccessful but a computer sustains damage during the attempt, it's still a prosecutable crime.

## Cyberstalking

**Cyberstalking** refers to using the Internet, e-mail, or other electronic communications devices to repeatedly harass or threaten another person. Many states have laws against stalking. Some require that the perpetrator make a credible threat of violence against the victim. Others include threats against the victim's immediate family. Still others require only that the alleged stalker's course of conduct constitute an implied threat.

People should take online stalking seriously because it may be a prelude to physical stalking and violence. Cyberstalking will likely increase as the number of location-based applications and services offered by vendors and social networking companies increases.

## Transmission of Malware

Creating a computer virus is not a crime. However, intentionally transmitting malware that the attacker knows will cause damage is a crime. **Malware** is malicious software designed to infiltrate a computer system without the system owner's or user's consent. Malware includes computer viruses, worms, Trojan horses, spyware, some types of adware, and other malicious and unwanted software.

Unintentional transmission of malware is also a crime. For example, if someone is not authorized to access a computer and accidentally causes damage to that computer, that person can be charged with a computer crime.

## Hacking

**Hacking** is illegal intrusion into a computer system without the permission of the computer owner or user. Hacking is a crime in the United States. The Computer Fraud and Abuse Act states that it applies to anyone who "intentionally accesses a protected computer without authorization, and as a result of such conduct, causes damage." If a hacker's actions affect interstate or foreign commerce, the hacker can be sentenced to one year in jail. If convicted of this crime more than once, the penalty can increase to as much as 10 years.

Laws in countries outside the United States can be more strict. For example, in 2007 and 2008, new cybercrime laws took effect in Germany and England. Lawmakers intended that these laws ban the distribution, use, and even possession of tools considered to be "hacking tools."

## Spamming

**Spam** is unsolicited or undesired electronic messages sent in large quantities to many recipients. Attackers use spamming as an inexpensive way to advertise commercial

### Attacks on Infrastructure

Attacks on critical infrastructure are a huge concern. Military networks tend to be favored targets for hackers. However, imagine that a government is prepared to invest heavily in coordinated strategic attacks on the U.S. military and civilian networks. In the very worst case a sudden, all-out network assault could knock out communications as well as financial, power, transportation, military, and other critical infrastructures. These types of attacks actually go beyond cybercrime, into the realm of cyberwarfare. **Cyberwarfare**, as its name suggests, is the use of computers and the Internet to conduct warfare in cyberspace.

A September 2009 State Department by Andrzej Zwaniecki article says, "A cyber-attack on the electricity grid, which could cut the power supply to one-third of the country for three months, would generate losses close to $800 billion, according to [Scott] Borg [who founded U.S. Cyber Consequences Unit, an independent research group]. But the total expenditures necessary to recover from these losses, including the costs of restoring, restarting, and making up lost production, would be much greater—around $3 trillion, he added."

products or sites. Most people receive dozens of spam e-mail messages each day. Spam causes lost productivity, takes up bandwidth, and can cost victims money if they fall for the fraud.

The CAN-SPAM Act made spamming a crime in 2003. This law sets the rules for commercial e-mail, establishes requirements for commercial messages, and gives recipients the right to have a business stop e-mailing them. It spells out tough penalties for violations.

The CAN-SPAM Act covers all commercial messages. It defines spam as "any electronic mail message the primary purpose of which is the commercial advertisement or promotion of a commercial product or service." This includes e-mail that promotes content on commercial Web sites. Each separate e-mail in violation of the CAN-SPAM Act is subject to penalties of up to $16,000.

**FYI**

According to Symantec, a security software company, about 90 percent of all e-mail in 2009 was spam. On average, 107 billion spam messages are distributed globally each day. In 2009, 85 percent of these spam messages was from botnets. A **botnet** is a collection of software robots that create and send out spam extremely quickly.

Peter Guerra of Black Hat, a digital security company, says that using a botnet can generate nearly $8,000 in profits per week. An attacker can obtain MPack, a software tool that can be used to steal credit card data, for a mere $500.

## Sale and Purchase of Narcotics Over the Internet

Some Web sites sell and ship contraband drugs. These sales are illegal in all cases. In addition, only state-licensed pharmacies located in the United States may sell prescription drugs over the Internet.

## Gambling

Gambling over the Internet is a violation of U.S. law. The Unlawful Internet Gambling Enforcement Act states that no person engaged in the business of betting or wagering may "knowingly accept any money transfers in any way from a person participating in unlawful Internet gambling." This includes credit cards and electronic fund transfers. The law defines "unlawful Internet gambling" as betting, receiving, or transmitting a bet that is illegal under federal, state, or tribal law.

There are many exceptions to the Unlawful Internet Gambling Enforcement Act. The law does not consider free games to be gambling. Fantasy leagues are legal but subject to detailed restrictions. Nevada and other states are allowed to authorize 100 percent intrastate gambling systems. However, Congress requires that state law and regulations block access to minors and persons outside the state.

---

### Recent Trends in Cybercrime

In April 2010, Symantec released its *Internet Security Threat Report* for 2009. The report highlights the following trends:

- **The number of threats targeting enterprises has increased.** Cybercriminals can gain financially by compromising corporate intellectual property. Attackers are targeting attacks on key individuals in companies. To do so, they're taking advantage of the personal information openly available on social networking sites.

- **Attack toolkits are making cybercrime easier all the time.** Attack toolkits have made it easy for even unskilled attackers to compromise computers and steal information. For example, the Zeus toolkit, which costs $700, automates the process of creating malware for stealing personal information.

- **Web-based attacks are becoming increasingly numerous.** Attackers lure unsuspecting users to malicious Web sites. These Web sites then attack the victims' Web browsers and applications used to view video or document files. In particular, the number of Web-based attacks targeted at portable document format (PDF) viewers grew dramatically in 2009.

- **Emerging countries are experiencing malicious activity.** Malicious activity is increasingly common in countries with an emerging broadband infrastructure. Examples are Brazil, India, Poland, Vietnam, and Russia. The report suggests that cybercriminals are launching attacks from the developing world because they are less likely to be prosecuted there.

The Symantec report also notes that malicious code, identity theft, and spam are growing problems.

# Sources of Cybercrime Threats

A **cybercriminal** is an individual who uses a computer or network technology to plan or perpetrate a violation of the law. A person working alone or people working in groups can commit cybercrimes. Even governments may commit cybercrimes. Threat sources include nation-states, cyberterrorists, corporations, activists, criminals, hobbyists, disgruntled employees, business rivals, professional hackers, ex-spouses, soon-to-be-ex-spouses, and others.

## Nation-States

Nations such as China, Brazil, North Korea, and Russia do not have conventional weapons arsenals that match those of the United States. However, such nation-states have proven their capabilities for conducting cyberattacks. The recently published book *Cyberwar: The Next Threat to National Security and What to Do About It* by former U.S. Counterterrorism Chief Richard A. Clarke, along with Robert K. Knake, addresses this topic.

Clarke and Knake say that North Korea selects "elite students at the elementary-school level to be groomed as future hackers." Experts suspect that North Korea was behind the July 2009 cyberattacks that took down the Web servers of the U.S. Treasury, Secret Service, Federal Trade Commission (FTC), and Transportation Department. Many also suspect that North Korea has planted code that allows hackers future access to the networks.

"The United States is currently far more vulnerable to cyberwar than Russia or China," say Clarke and Knake. "The U.S. is more at risk from cyberwar than are minor states like North Korea. We may even be at risk some day from nations or nonstate actors lacking cyberwar capabilities, but who can hire teams of highly capable hackers."

More than a decade ago, an article in the Chinese armed forces newspaper *The Liberation Army Daily* discussed cyberattacks. The article guessed that the first attack objectives would be the networks that connect a country's political, economic, and military installations, as well as its general society.

## Cyberterrorists

Terrorists use cyberspace to assist traditional forms of terrorism, such as suicide bombings. **Cyberterrorists** are attackers who target a country's computers and information, usually through the Internet, to cause physical harm, severely disrupt the country's infrastructure, or create panic. They use Web sites to propagate their messages and to recruit supporters. By crippling a country's economy, cyberterrorists can also potentially weaken the country enough for a military attack to succeed.

> **NOTE**
>
> In late 2009, the Federal Bureau of Investigation (FBI) said it is keeping an eye on al-Qaeda sympathizers who want to develop their hacking skills and appear to want to target the U.S. infrastructure.

### Targets of Cybercrime

Victims of cybercrime range from governments and national infrastructures to organizations, corporations, and individuals. Anyone who has a bank account or medical insurance can be a target for identity thieves. Other potential victims of cybercrime include anyone who is gullible, greedy, desperate, uninformed, or inexperienced—as well as those who are not. Even school-age children can be targets of cybercriminals. Organizations that process and store sensitive data are targets. In fact, most businesses are likely to become victims of some sort of data breach.

The U.S.Department of Veterans Affairs has experienced several well-publicized breaches. The following are a few examples of other recent breaches:

- In January 2009, Heartland Payment Systems announced that it had been the victim of a security breach. The intrusion was called the largest criminal breach of credit card data to date. It affected up to 100 million cards from more than 650 financial service companies.

- In January 2008, GE Money disclosed that it was missing a magnetic tape containing 150,000 Social Security numbers and credit card information from 650,000 retail customers.

- In 2007, TJMaxx reported a data breach of 45 million credit and debit accounts.

- In 2007, the Gap disclosed that information for 800,000 job applicants had been stolen.

## Other Threats

In addition to nation-states and cyberterrorists, several other types of threats exist. The following are some examples:

- **Organized crime**—Organized crime networks may have national or international units. Most often, organized criminals have a financial motive. Their illegal activities include stealing services, stealing individuals' identities, fraudulently transferring funds into their bank accounts, and manipulating stock prices.

- **Activists**—Activists feel strongly about a cause, whether it's environmental concerns, globalization, abortion, human rights, politics, poverty, or religion. Some activist organizations and individuals stage peaceful protests. Others resort to radical and militant actions. Activists have sabotaged Web sites to express their opinions on or opposition to various issues.

- **Corporations**—Corporations sometimes engage in data theft. For example, they might steal a rival's competitive business information, trade secrets, marketing plans, client lists, and more.

- **Individuals**—Individuals who have programming or hacking skills sometimes attack computer systems and networks.

The motives of those who threaten computers and data are considered later in this chapter.

# Means, Motives, and Opportunities of Cybercriminals

In traditional criminal investigations, detectives examine suspects to determine whether they had the means, motive, and opportunity to perpetrate crimes. System forensics specialists look for the same three factors in cybercriminals.

## Means: Tools and Techniques of Cybercriminals

In criminal justice, **means** refers to a suspect's ability to commit a crime. A forensic analyst may need to determine whether a suspect had the knowledge and personal expertise to commit a crime. The analyst also needs to figure out whether the suspect had the necessary tools.

The means for attacking computer systems has changed over the years. The earliest cybercriminals were usually disgruntled, dishonest, or both. As technology spread and evolved, hobbyists with criminal inclinations began to intrude on systems and networks. In the 1980s, programmers began writing malware to attack personal computers. With the widespread use of the Internet, cybercriminals gained access to large numbers of systems throughout the world. They began to commit crimes for many reasons— from boredom and anger to political and financial motives.

Intruders have built automated tools to coordinate large-scale attacks that aim hundreds of hosts at Internet sites. These tools are well documented and freely available on the Internet. Hackers share programs and improve on each other's work.

Because so many powerful tools are readily available, attackers don't need to know how to write computer code to break into computer systems. **Script kiddies** are rather unsophisticated hackers who use this type of point-and-click software rather than program their own software. The upside of script kiddies' low level of computer skills is that they don't always know how to properly use the tools they find. For example, in some break-ins, script kiddies have used sophisticated tools to gain access to an operating system but then typed commands that work only on another operating system.

It's easy for criminals to use the Internet to research and plan crimes. Web sites provide maps and aerial depictions that show details of locations. Criminals can search the Internet and find information of any type. For example, they might look for data on how to "kill with a lead pipe," for pornography, or for tools that will help them carry out attacks. And they may use e-mail accounts to exchange information about planned crimes.

A forensic specialist examines suspect systems to demonstrate and document that a suspect had the means to commit a certain crime. A suspect who searched for "medication overdose" and "murder" or "undetectable bomb," for example, might have left a trail that indicates premeditation. In addition, a suspect's use of certain programs could be used to determine criminal intent. A forensic investigator may find that a suspect's computer files have been encrypted or data is hidden using a steganography program. This could be useful information for investigators and attorneys. A computer that contains recently used password-cracking software could indicate that a suspect had the means to commit a crime that involved access through a hacked account.

> ▶ **NOTE**
> For more information on steganography programs, see Chapter 8.

## Motives of Cybercriminals

Computer crime is not solely a technological issue. It also involves people. A forensic specialist needs to understand **motives**—that is, the reasons a suspect committed a crime. The specialist can then discover, analyze, and reconstruct events leading to the crime.

The motives of cybercriminals are similar to the motives of any other criminals. The following are some examples:

- **Financial gain (greed)**—Financial gain motivates many cybercriminals. Greed is generally behind identity theft, theft of trade secrets, credit card fraud, medical insurance fraud, and extortion. In the United States, many blamed the poor economy and the recession of 2008–2010 for increases in criminal offenses.

- **Revenge (anger, jealousy, resentment)**—Disgruntled and dishonest employees, as well as former employees, saboteurs, and extortionists commit crimes of revenge. Revenge is also often cited as a motive in cyberbullying. For example, the courts convicted Lori Drew, a Missouri mother, in a landmark cyberbullying case. Prosecutors said that Drew wanted to humiliate 13-year-old Megan Meier for saying mean things about Drew's teenage daughter. Megan committed suicide shortly after one of the cyberbullying incidents.

- **Political agenda/information warfare (power)**—Activists may want to force an action that suits their agenda. To do so, they may cause damage to get attention. Nation-states and terrorists may try to weaken a country's economy or digital infrastructure so that the country's defenses are less effective against physical attacks. In December 2009, attackers carried out a sophisticated, coordinated cyber-attack on 34 companies, including Google, Adobe, and Northrup Grumman. Two independent, anonymous sources say that the source of these attacks was China. In another more recent attack, Kenneth Corbin with Internetnews.com reported "a sophisticated network of hackers operating out of China launched cyber attacks against the computer systems of the office of the Dalai Lama, the United Nations,

### Motive Versus Criminal Intent

In criminal law, a *motive* explains why a person acted or refused to act in a certain way. **Criminal intent**, on the other hand, refers to a defendant's mental state in committing a crime. Generally, the prosecution in a criminal case must prove that the defendant intended to commit the illegal act. The prosecution doesn't need to prove the defendant's motive.

Although proof of motive isn't required in a criminal prosecution, a defendant's motive is important in other stages of a criminal case. For example, law enforcement personnel often consider potential motives when investigating perpetrators.

the Indian government, and other nations. Security researchers ... said they recovered a large quantity of sensitive documents in their investigation, including classified materials filched from India's national security agencies and what appeared to be encrypted diplomatic correspondence."

- **Addiction, curiosity, boredom, thrill-seeking, and intellectual gain**—Those who create viruses or worms often seek intellectual challenge. Some hackers who have committed computer intrusions have said that their motive was to test computer security.

- **Recognition**—Some computer criminals are interested in earning a reputation for their skills and becoming famous.

**TABLE 2-1**   Rogers's categories of computer criminals.

| CATEGORY OF CRIMINAL | DESCRIPTION |
| --- | --- |
| Newbies/ toolkits | Also called script kiddies, these criminals have the least amount of technical knowledge and skill. Members of this group use prewritten and compiled scripts and tools to commit computer-related crimes. Motives of this type of computer criminal are typically thrill-seeking and curiosity. |
| Cyberpunks | Cyberpunks are slightly more advanced than newbies. They are novice programmers who have limited experience with computer systems and networks. Cyberpunks commit malicious acts, such as mail bombing, Web page hijacking, and credit card theft. Motives of this type of computer criminal are typically thrill-seeking, financial gain, and recognition. |
| Internals | Internals are disgruntled current or former workers in information technology positions. This type of computer criminal is responsible for the majority of computer crimes and associated financial losses. Motives for insiders include financial gain and revenge. |
| Coders | Coders have advanced technological knowledge and skill. These cybercriminals are responsible for writing the exploit programs that are used by script kiddies and cyberpunks. Coders are typically motivated by financial gain. |
| Old guard | The old guard is hackers who have a relaxed sense of ethics regarding privacy and intellectual property. This type of criminal is usually motivated by a quest for knowledge and information. |
| Professional criminals | Professional criminals are traditionally older and more knowledgeable about computer technology than the other categories. Professional criminals may be former government and intelligence operatives who are motivated by financial gain. |
| Cyberterrorists | Cyberterrorists use computer or network technology to control, dominate, or coerce through the use of terror. Their aim is to further political or social objectives. This type of criminal is most often motivated by a political agenda or power. |

Furthermore, cyber experts classify certain groups of computer users by skill level and motive. Researcher and educator Marc Rogers wrote a paper called *A New Hacker Taxonomy*. In it, Rogers proposed a system for classifying computer criminals. He suggested seven distinct but not mutually exclusive types, as shown in Table 2-1.

## Opportunities for Cybercriminals

Like traditional criminals, cybercriminals need the **opportunity** to commit a crime. That is, they need a chance to attack. Several key factors provide good opportunities for cybercrime. Tom Grubb, an executive at ThreatMetrix, describes five "Big A's," or critical advantages, of cybercrime:

1. **Affordability**—Computers and other devices are becoming increasingly inexpensive and available. Getting online is also becoming increasingly inexpensive and easy. Many libraries, restaurants, and other businesses now offer free Wi-Fi. And many homes leave their wireless networks unprotected and available to anyone driving down the street.

2. **Acceptable risk**—Cybercriminals are at low risk of being caught or prosecuted. Making a solid case against a suspect often requires long hours and great resources. Law enforcement and forensic personnel do not have the resources to keep up with cybercrime. Many cybercriminals escape detection altogether.

3. **Attractiveness**—Businesses, governments, and individuals are relying more and more on computer networks. This creates more opportunities for cybercrime. Many systems connected to the Internet are vulnerable. Technology is constantly evolving, and attackers are quick to find flaws, weaknesses, and vulnerabilities in systems. Also, applying security patches continues to be a challenge for many users.

4. **Availability**—Connecting to the Internet is easy for victims. It is also easy for attackers. In addition, cybercriminals can use automated tools to conduct crimes.

5. **Anonymity**—The inherent anonymity of the Internet is a critical element that enables cybercriminals to freely commit deception that leads to profit. As long as computers and people are vulnerable to hacking, cybercriminals will take advantage of the anonymity the Internet affords them.

The bottom line is that cybercrime offers a large payout for relatively small risk.

## Reporting Cybercrimes

It's wise to plan. Knowing whom to call and when makes the job of a system forensics specialist easier and reduces potential liability.

Cybercrimes in the United States are usually either federal or state offenses. In general, if a state law applies to a crime, a victim should contact the local police department or state police or county sheriff's office. Sometimes, however, state and local authorities

lack the resources to investigate cybercrimes. To involve the
Federal Bureau of Investigation (FBI) and other federal agencies,
a case must be important enough to get their attention. Victims
should report a federal crime to the local offices of federal law
enforcement.

An in-house forensic specialist should make management
aware of the details of an event before reporting it to law
enforcement. An organization's leaders may choose not to report
actual or suspected cybercrimes for many reasons. For example,
personnel may have to take time off to prepare for and appear
at trial. Law enforcement may have to confiscate equipment
as evidence and hold on to it for long periods. In addition, the
company's inside information may be subpoenaed by the defense
attorneys and exposed to the public through the media before
and during the trial.

 **TIP**

Organization leaders need
to know which cybercrime
laws apply to the organization.
For example, industries that
process or store personal
information, such as medical
or financial data, may be
subject to specific reporting
requirements when a data
breach occurs.

## What to Report

Internet-related crime, like any other crime, should be reported to appropriate law
enforcement investigative authorities. The scope of a crime determines whether
a victim should report it at the local, state, federal, or international level. The following
are general guidelines for the types of cybercrimes that should be reported to the
appropriate authorities:

- **Intrusions and attacks that bring down a network**—Unauthorized access to
  a computer network is a crime under many state laws. If there is little or no injury
  or financial loss, law enforcement agencies may only file a report. Computer crimes
  that don't cause much documentable damage are often not investigated in depth.

- **Intrusions or attacks on large corporate networks or those that deal with
  sensitive data**—An organization should report cases in which sensitive data has
  been compromised. Examples of sensitive data are client financial information,
  medical records, customer credit card information, and Social Security numbers.
  If a company has government or defense contracts or deals with other types of
  regulated information, it should also report intrusions. The FBI's Computer Crime
  Squad investigates major network intrusions and network integrity violations.
  An organization should report these types of attacks to both federal and local or state
  authorities. The authorities can work together to sort out the jurisdictional issues.

- **Intrusions or attacks that result in large financial losses**—The amount of financial
  loss due to a cybercrime often determines whether a theft is considered a misdemeanor
  or felony. Felony offenses get more attention from law enforcement agencies.

- **Cases of suspected industrial espionage**—If an intruder goes after a company's
  trade secrets, this is a serious federal offense. The FBI is likely to investigate such
  a situation.

> ### What Not to Report
>
> An organization should not report non-intrusive activities, such as port scans. A port scan can be a step a cybercriminal takes before breaking into a system or network. However, it's usually not a crime.
>
> An organization should also generally not report malware. For example, it shouldn't report spyware, viruses, Trojan horse programs, worms, and so on to the FBI or to local law enforcement. Often the sender of malware is not aware that he or she has sent it. However, if an organization has evidence that a specific person created and released malware with the intent to cause damage, that incident should be reported.

- **Cases involving child pornography**—Downloading child pornography is a violation of law. So is possession of such material. If child pornography is discovered on company computers and is not promptly reported, the network administrator could be held liable in a civil lawsuit. The U.S. Customs and Border Patrol works closely with the National Center for Missing & Exploited Children to combat the proliferation of this disturbing material.

- **E-mailed or other digitally transmitted threats**—All states have laws against threatening and harassing communications. Anyone who receives electronic communications, including physical threats, terrorist threats, bomb threats, and blackmail, should contact local police.

- **Internet fraud**—A victim of phishing or other fraudulent activities perpetrated by e-mail or on the Web should report the incident to the IC3. The FBI operates the IC3 in conjunction with the National White Collar Crime Center.

- **Suspected terrorist activities**—If an organization suspects that its network is being used for communications between terrorists, it should file a report with the local police agency, with the U.S. Department of Homeland Security, or via the FBI's "tips" Web site.

## Where to Report Computer Crimes

In the case of an incident that falls under the jurisdiction of local or state law enforcement, an organization should call the local police department, county sheriff's office, or state police agency. It shouldn't call 9-1-1. The organization should ask for the agency's high-tech crimes unit or, in smaller agencies, the criminal investigation division.

**TABLE 2-2**  Cybercrime reporting and investigating agencies.

| AGENCY | WEB SITE |
| --- | --- |
| Customs and Border Patrol tips line | http://www.cbp.gov/xp/cgov/toolbox/contacts/ |
| FBI local office contact information | http://www.fbi.gov/contact/fo/fo.htm |
| FBI Tips Web site | https://tips.fbi.gov |
| FTC identity theft Web Complaint Assistant | https://www.ftccomplaintassistant.gov |
| IC3 | http://www.ic3.gov |
| National Center for Missing & Exploited Children Cyber Tipline | http://www.cybertipline.com |
| National White Collar Crime Center (NW3C) | http://www.nw3c.org/ |
| Postal Inspection Service child exploitation information | https://postalinspectors.uspis.gov/investigations/MailFraud/fraudschemes/ce/CE.aspx |
| Secret Service Electronic Crimes task forces and working groups | http://www.secretservice.gov/ectf.shtml |

The primary federal law enforcement agencies that investigate domestic crime on the Internet are the FBI, the U.S. Secret Service, U.S. Immigration and Customs Enforcement (ICE), U.S. Postal Inspection Service, and the Bureau of Alcohol, Tobacco, Firearms and Explosives (ATF). Each of these agencies has offices located in various states to which crimes may be reported. Contact information for these local offices is available in local telephone directories and online. In general, federal crime can be reported by calling the local office of an appropriate federal agency and requesting the "duty complaint agent."

Table 2-2 provides Web addresses for a number of cybercrime reporting and investigating agencies.

Each federal law enforcement agency has a headquarters in Washington, DC, with agents who specialize in particular areas. For example, the FBI and the Secret Service headquarters both employ computer intrusion specialists.

Table 2-3 lists some of the federal investigative law enforcement agencies that may be appropriate for reporting certain kinds of crimes. This information and more is available at the U.S. Department of Justice Web site, at *http://www.justice.gov/criminal/cybercrime/reporting.htm*.

> **NOTE**
>
> An organization should report an international crime to a federal agency. The federal agency will determine which international agencies should handle the case.

**TABLE 2-3** Reporting computer crimes to federal agencies.

| TYPE OF CRIME | APPROPRIATE INVESTIGATIVE LAW ENFORCEMENT AGENCIES |
|---|---|
| Hacking | FBI local office<br>U.S. Secret Service<br>IC3 |
| Password trafficking | FBI local office<br>U.S. Secret Service<br>IC3 |
| Child pornography or exploitation | FBI local office<br>U.S. Immigration and Customs Enforcement (if imported)<br>IC3 |
| Child exploitation and Internet fraud matters that involve postal mail | U.S. Postal Inspection Service<br>IC3 |
| Internet fraud and spam | FBI local office<br>U.S. Secret Service (Financial Crimes Division)<br>FTC  Securities and Exchange Commission (if securities fraud or investment-related spam e-mails)<br>IC3 |
| Internet harassment | FBI local office |
| Internet bomb threats | FBI local office<br>ATF local office |
| Trafficking in explosive or incendiary devices or firearms over the Internet | FBI local office<br>ATF local office |
| Copyright piracy | FBI local office<br>U.S. Immigration and Customs Enforcement (ICE)<br>IC3 |
| Trademark counterfeiting | FBI local office<br>ICE<br>IC3 |
| Theft of trade secrets | FBI local office |

## Applicable Laws

Many U.S. federal and state laws address cybercrimes and computer intrusions. A few are listed here:

- Computer Fraud and Abuse Act
- Uniting and Strengthening America by Providing Appropriate Tools Required to Intercept and Obstruct Terrorism Act (U.S.A. PATRIOT Act) of 2001
- Prosecutorial Remedies and Other Tools to End the Exploitation of Children Today Act (PROTECT Act) of 2003
- Homeland Security Act of 2002
- Cyber Security Enhancement Act of 2002
- CAN-SPAM Act of 2003
- Unlawful Internet Gambling Enforcement Act (UIGEA) of 2006

> **NOTE**
> Laws usually lag behind technology development.

The following sections of federal criminal code specifically relate to computer intrusions:

- 18 U.S.C. § 1029: Fraud and Related Activity in Connection with Access Devices
- 18 U.S.C. § 1030: Fraud and Related Activity in Connection with Computers
- 18 U.S.C. § 1362: Communication Lines, Stations, or Systems
- 18 U.S.C. § 2510 et seq.: Wire and Electronic Communications Interception and Interception of Oral Communications
- 18 U.S.C. § 2701 et seq.: Stored Wire and Electronic Communications and Transactional Records Access
- 18 U.S.C. § 2702 et seq.: Disclosures to the National Center for Missing and Exploited Children
- 18 U.S.C. § 3121 et seq.: Recording of Dialing, Routing, Addressing, and Signaling Information
- 50 U.S.C. § 783 (b): Receipt of, or Attempt to Receive, by Foreign Agent or Member of Communist Organization, Classified Information
- 18 U.S.C. § 794 (a): Gathering or Delivering Defense Information to Aid Foreign Government

For more information on laws related to cybercrime, see *http://www.justice.gov/criminal/cybercrime/cclaws.html*.

## The Role of System Forensics in Solving Crimes

Cybercrime is a big and growing problem. In response, the field of system forensics is also growing. Today, a forensic specialist may act as a technical adviser, an evidence collector, and an analyst. A forensic specialist might be involved in any of the following activities:

- **Identifying, collecting, and reviewing evidence**—A forensic specialist must be able to understand and answer questions about a crime. The work of a forensic analyst can be used to help apprehend criminals or to free innocent people from blame. A forensic specialist may be able to show evidence that supports or disproves alibis and witness statements.

- **Forming and testing hypotheses**—A forensic specialist may need to create experiments to determine whether a specific action could have occurred on a certain computer or program. Or an investigator may need to distinguish between actions that were performed by a user or a program. A forensic analyst may need to test an alternative explanation provided by a defendant. For example, people accused of possessing child pornography have claimed that they didn't download the images. Instead, they say, the images were put on their computer by malware or a remote intruder. This defense is so common that it's been named the "Trojan defense."

- **Evaluating evidence to determine the source**—Was a picture taken with a specific digital camera? Was the picture stored on a specific computer? Was a suspect using a specific mobile phone at a certain time? An investigator may need to answer such questions.

- **Working with layers of targets in a cybercrime**—A forensic specialist needs to be able to carefully find clues and follow an evidence trail. Say that a forensic specialist is investigating the case of a system attack in Virginia. In the process of the attack, a hacker breaks into and steals the account of a student at the University of Florida. The hacker then uses that account to hack into the system in Virginia. The hacker, however, is located in Brazil. Although the Virginia system is the intended victim, the student's computer in Florida was exploited and used as a launch pad to mask the intrusion in Virginia, making it harder to trace where the attack originated.

- **Authenticating digital documents**—A forensic investigator may need to determine various facts about digital documents. For example, when was a specific file really created? Was a suicide note created before or after the victim's death? Did a suspect really send a particular e-mail?

- **Attempting to determine intent**—An investigator may be able to determine intent in a number of ways. For example, the investigator may review a suspect's Internet browser history and Google searches. If the computer search history shows that suspect searched for "kill + household accidents" or "poison + spouse," the investigator may be able to show intent in a murder case.

- **Salvaging deleted data from storage media and converting it to a readable form**—Hidden data and traces left by intruders can identify actions of software that was used but may no longer be present on the system. Forensic specialists therefore look for this type of evidence. They also attempt to discover the contents of protected or encrypted files.

- **Documenting findings**—Forensic specialists construct timelines of key findings. They also link analyses to show how significant events or interactions are related. Ideally, an investigator's findings should be repeatable and reliable.

- **Ensuring proper chain of custody and processing of digital evidence**—A forensic specialist needs to be familiar with scientific methods, forensic soundness, and the needs of the justice system.

- **Working with attorneys, management, other investigators and analysts, and law enforcement**—A forensic specialist needs to work with a number of individuals to ensure that proper procedures are followed.

---

### Using System Forensics to Catch a Serial Killer

Catching a cybercriminal often requires both system forensics and traditional investigation techniques, such as interviews and stakeouts. For example, the bind, torture, and kill (BTK) serial killer murdered 10 people in Kansas between 1974 and 1991. Then the BTK killer sent letters describing the details of the murders to police and local television stations. Forensic analysts were able to identify Dennis Rader as the BTK killer after working with a floppy disk he had mailed to a television station.

## CHAPTER SUMMARY

This chapter discusses the role of system forensics in solving crimes. It begins by discussing a number of the many types of cybercrimes. It also describes possible threat sources and likely targets of cybercriminals. This chapter presents an overview of how, why, and when cybercriminals are likely to take actions. In addition, it discusses which cases to report and to which authorities. The chapter concludes by discussing the role of forensic analysts in investigating cybercrimes.

## KEY CONCEPTS AND TERMS

| | | |
|---|---|---|
| Botnet | Distributed denial of service (DDoS) attack | Means |
| Criminal intent | | Motive |
| Cyber Crimes Center (C3) | Extortion | Opportunity |
| Cybercriminal | Fraud | Phishing |
| Cyberstalking | Hacking | Piracy |
| Cyberterrorist | Identity theft | Script kiddy |
| Cyberwarfare | Intellectual property theft | Spam |
| Denial of service (DoS) | Malware | Trade secret |

## CHAPTER 2 ASSESSMENT

**1.** _____ occur when an attacker deprives people of the services they are entitled to access or provide.

**2.** Which of the following are types of intellectual property theft? (Select two.)

A. Piracy

B. Extortion

C. Theft of trade secrets

D. Identity theft

E. Phishing

**3.** Creating a computer virus is a crime.

A. True

B. False

**4.** _____ is unauthorized intrusion into a computer system. The first offense can be punished by a year in jail.

**5.** Which of the following are forms of fraud? (Select two.)

A. Spamming

B. Hacking

C. Phishing

D. Identity theft

E. Malware

**6.** Cybercrimes are committed by individuals, groups, and even countries.

A. True

B. False

**7.** Which of the following is the name for a suspect's ability to commit a crime?

A. Means

B. Motive

C. Opportunity

**8.** The motives of cybercriminals are different from the motives of traditional criminals.

A. True

B. False

**9.** Which of the following is _not_ a factor that makes it easy to conduct cybercrime?

A. It's easy for criminals to use the Internet to research and plan crimes.

B. Many systems connected to the Internet are vulnerable.

C. No one ever finds out because hiding electronic evidence is easy.

D. Numerous cybercrime tools are readily available online, many for free.

**10.** All cybercrimes should be reported to the FBI.

A. True

B. False

**11.** Which of the following should _not_ be reported to a law enforcement agency of some sort?

A. Intrusions or attacks on networks that deal with sensitive data

B. Cases of suspected industrial espionage

C. Cases involving child pornography

D. Port scans, which are often precursors to cyberattacks

**12.** The FBI, the Secret Service, ICE, the U.S. Postal Inspection Service, and the ATF have local offices for reporting _____.

# Challenges of System Forensics

**T**HE FIELD OF SYSTEM FORENSICS is growing and evolving. Forensic tools and methods have improved access to volatile data and remote systems. They have also enhanced analysis of network traffic. Today, more than 50 different software packages assist with system forensics. Examples include Forensic Toolkit (FTK), EnCase, and Paraben's Device Seizure.

In recent years, the world has seen a vast increase in the number of computers, networks, mobile devices, and other embedded systems, such as video games, e-readers, global positioning system (GPS) devices, and digital video recorders. The increasing attacks on those devices have resulted in an increase in the demand for system forensics professionals.

Many types of evidence can be part of an investigation. A few examples are system access information, financial data related to purchases, e-mail and postal addresses, photographs, Web pages retained in temporary storage, and logs recording network connections. This chapter discusses the difficulties related to obtaining digital evidence. It also addresses the dynamic nature of evidence, scope-related challenges, and the need for professionalization.

## Chapter 3 Topics

This chapter covers the following topics and concepts:

- What the difficulties in obtaining forensic digital evidence are
- What role evidence dynamics plays in system forensics
- What the scope-related challenges to system forensics are
- Why there is a need for professionalization

## Difficulties in Obtaining Forensic Digital Evidence

Investigators face four basic difficulties in obtaining forensic digital evidence:

- Deciding what is and what is not evidence
- Gaining access to data
- Understanding the technical considerations related to data collection
- Obtaining obscured data and defeating anti-forensics

The following sections discuss these difficulties.

### What Is Digital Evidence?

**Data** includes raw numbers, pictures, and other "stuff" that may or may not have relevance to a particular event or incident under investigation. **Information** is data that has been processed and assembled so that it is relevant to an investigation. **Evidence** is information that supports a specific finding or determination.

Investigators must carefully show an unbroken chain of custody to demonstrate that evidence has been protected from tampering. The **chain of custody** is continuity of evidence that makes it possible to account for all that has happened to evidence between its original collection and its appearance in court, preferably unaltered. If forensic specialists can't demonstrate that they have maintained the chain of custody, then the court may consider all their conclusions invalid.

 **NOTE**

Evidence may be conclusive and support a single finding—such as an individual's DNA identification. Or evidence may be interpretive and support multiple findings—such as photos placed on a desktop by potentially numerous individuals.

3

Challenges of
System Forensics

Courts deal with four types of evidence:

- **Real**—**Real evidence** is a physical object that someone can touch, hold, or directly observe. Examples of real evidence are a laptop with a suspect's fingerprints on the keyboard, a hard drive, a universal serial bus (USB) drive, and a handwritten note.
- **Documentary**—**Documentary evidence** is data stored as written or printed matter or using information technology. Documentary evidence includes memory-resident data and computer files. Examples are logs, databases, e-mail messages, photographs, and telephone call detail records. Investigators must authenticate documentary evidence.
- **Testimonial**—**Testimonial evidence** is information that forensic specialists use to support or interpret real or documentary evidence. For example, they may employ testimonial evidence to demonstrate that the fingerprints found on a keyboard are those of a specific individual. Or system access controls might show that a particular user stored specific photographs on a desktop.
- **Demonstrative**—**Demonstrative evidence** is information that helps explain other evidence. An example is a chart that explains a technical concept to the judge and jury.

Forensic specialists must often provide testimony to support the conclusions of their analyses. For example, a member of an incident response team might be required to testify that he or she identified the computer program that deleted customer records at a specified date and time. In such a case, the testimony must show how the investigator reached his or her conclusion. The testimony must also show that the specialist protected from tampering the data used in making the determination. That is, the testimony must show that the forensic investigator maintained the chain of custody. It must also show that the testifier based his or her conclusion on a reasonable, although not necessarily absolute, interpretation of the data. Further, the forensic specialist must present his or her testimony in a manner that avoids use of technical jargon and complex technical discussions. Judges, juries, and lawyers aren't all technical experts. Therefore, a forensic specialist should translate technology into understandable descriptions. Pictures often communicate better than just numbers and words, so a forensic specialist may want to create charts and graphs.

---

**FYI**

Most incidents that forensic specialists investigate begin as rather routine investigations. They begin as investigations of system or processing anomalies or routine analysis of system logs. After analysis and evaluation, an investigation may turn into a legal action. For example, forensic analysis may show that what at first appeared to be a system failure was in fact the result of an outsider attack. Thus, all forensic investigations should be conducted using strict rules of evidence and maintain the chain of custody. Taking these measures ensures that the work of a forensic specialist will be admissible in any court proceedings.

## Data Access

Gaining access to digital data is often difficult. A forensic specialist may not be able to gain access to data for a number of reasons. For example, an investigator may face physical constraints, such as the destruction or reformatting of a desktop. Or an investigator may face legal restrictions, such as the owner's refusal to grant access to the data. Another legal restriction might involve data including information that is protected by law. Finally, an investigator may not be able to access data because of technical issues, such as encryption or data being in a nonstandard format.

### Creating a Data Analysis Plan

Data access restrictions may be intentional. An attacker may try to restrict data access to prevent analysis or to prevent the use of the data to support a prosecution. On the other hand, data access restrictions may instead be an unintended consequence of an organization's or individual's normal business practices. Regardless of the cause, forensic specialists should plan their analyses. They can do so by creating a **data analysis plan**, a plan that lists the types of data to be collected and describes the expected source for the data. This plan should also list any anticipated problems as well as recommended strategies to deal with those problems.

Forensic specialists must protect data sources until they have addressed all access restrictions. While planning an investigation, they should keep this in mind. This protection may require legal actions, such as subpoenas. It may also require technical actions, such as mirroring devices to protect the original while analyzing a copy.

Besides identifying the types of data to be collected and their source, a data analysis plan should describe any anticipated problems, along with recommended actions. Table 3-1 lists some of the items that a forensic specialist might include in a data analysis plan.

### Overcoming Search and Seizure Restrictions

Restrictions on search and seizure may apply in many investigations. A forensic investigator should obtain authorization to examine devices and collect data. Data collected without appropriate authorization may not be usable in an investigation.

If the equipment or data owner is not the suspect, an investigator could have the legal right to search the computer through voluntary surrender. **Voluntary surrender** is permission from the owner of a computer or other equipment to search and/or seize equipment as part of an investigation. An investigator would also have a right to voluntary surrender if an employee or a contractor signed a search and seizure consent as a condition of hire.

 **TIP**

Evidence an investigator needs may be located on a business-critical system. In this case, the investigator should arrange to image the drives during off-hours rather than disrupt the business functions. The best evidence is the freshest evidence. However, the need to collect evidence quickly must be balanced with the need to prevent disruption of critical operations.

| DATA TYPE | SOURCE | ANTICIPATED RESTRICTIONS | RECOMMENDED ACTION |
|---|---|---|---|
| Access logs | Corporation server | Corporation requires legal authorization | Obtain subpoena |
| Data transmissions between local and remote sites | Temporary files retained as backup in case of network failure | Insufficient storage to retain for long-term analysis | Mirror to removable media with validation by system administrator to maintain the chain of custody |
| Data contained on desktops sent for destruction | Hard drives from the desktops | Physical damage Erased data Overwritten data | Mirror to stable media Use recovery software Use data reconstruction software |
| Business accounting transactions | Servers located in regional offices that may be in different countries | Legal issues regarding obtaining data from different countries, subject to different laws Subpoenas and search warrants from a U.S. jurisdiction may not be honored in other countries | Obtain voluntary data surrender Provide early notice to legal staff to begin actions to obtain data access Provide specific guidance to obtain data from remote locations and maintain chain of custody |

**TABLE 3-1**   Data analysis plan components.

**NOTE**

A person or company may be unwilling to grant access to digital systems or data. However, this unwillingness may not be a reflection of guilt or innocence. Rather, the person or company might want to protect trade secrets or customer data that also resides on the equipment sought. Thus, forensic specialists should perform analyses based on the data and not based on the restrictions to accessing the data.

An investigator who doesn't have permission to collect evidence can seek one of two court orders:

- **Subpoena**—A **subpoena** is a court order than requires the person or organization that owns the equipment to release it for analysis. Civil actions or court proceedings typically involve subpoenas.

- **Search warrant**—A **search warrant** is a court order that allows law enforcement personnel to collect equipment or data from that equipment. A search warrant may permit collection of the equipment or data with or without advance notice. A forensic specialist should indicate the likelihood that the data could be damaged or lost if the suspect has prior notice. Law enforcement officers typically use search warrants.

## Technical Data Collection Considerations

System forensics specialists must keep in mind three main technical data collection considerations. These are understanding the life span of data, collecting data quickly, and collecting bit-level data.

### Considering the Life Span of Data

In planning data collection efforts, a forensic specialist must be aware that data has a life span. The nature of the data as well as organizational policies and practices determine the data life span. For example, data regarding network traffic and the messages themselves may exist only for the time the transmission is passing through a server. This may be only milliseconds. Information stored in computer memory may have a life span of a millisecond.

As data life spans increase, the life span determinant is typically related to organizational practice. For example, an organization may establish a policy that an e-mail message may be stored within the e-mail system for only 30 days. After 30 days, any message that is not moved to alternate storage is deleted. Log files may be retained for months or years, in accordance with an organization's audit policy. Finance and accounting information may have a multiple-year life span that corresponds with requirements established by state or federal governments.

In planning a data collection effort, forensic specialists must be aware of the life span of the data they are seeking. They must use data collection techniques appropriate to the data life span. For example, data with an extremely short life span may require the use of specialized monitoring tools to collect transmissions in process. (See Chapter 12, "Searching Memory in Real Time with Live System Forensics.")

### Collecting Data Quickly

Once the data collection effort is announced or in process, it is important to collect data as quickly as possible. Data changes easily. It is frequently not possible or practical to determine who made a change or when. In addition, the target of an investigation may try to conceal data, which further obscures changes. Networking systems also increase the potential for unauthorized data changes. The person making a change on a network does not have to be local to the device on which the data is stored.

### Collecting Bit-Level Data

Data is digitally stored as a series of 1s and 0s. This is called *binary representation*. To be useful, data must be converted through hardware and software into text, pictures, screen displays, videos, or other human-readable formats.

Forensic specialists should be able to see data in its useful form as well as in its original format. To do so, they need to collect data at the bit level. The specialists can then analyze the layers of procedures and conversions. By using this process, they can determine whether the data was corrupted. Investigators also look for whether unrelated data was inserted, such as trade secrets buried within other data. Forensic specialists must therefore have tools that allow manipulation and evaluation of bit-level data. Use of bit-level tools also enables an investigator to reconstruct file fragments if data files have been deleted or overwritten.

## Obscured Data and Anti-Forensics

Two more challenges in obtaining digital evidence are obscured data and anti-forensics.

### Obscured Data

Data can be obscured in a number of ways. **Obscured data** may be encrypted, compressed, or in a proprietary format. Sometimes, cybercriminals obscure data to deter forensic examination. More often, companies use data manipulation and storage techniques to protect business-sensitive data. These techniques obscure data. News outlets have reported on many data losses from unintentional and intentional security failures. Therefore, companies and individuals now widely use data protection techniques. Regardless of the reason for obscured data, collecting and analyzing it is difficult.

**TIP**

Before going to the trouble of decrypting data or conducting a live extraction, a forensic specialist should decide whether the encrypted data holds something of significant value.

Data that has been obscured through compression and proprietary formats can sometimes be converted with work and the right tools. Forensic specialists often must do quite a bit of work to decrypt encrypted data. In some cases, however, the investigator cannot decrypt this type of data unless the data owner provides the encryption key and algorithm. When digital evidence has been encrypted and is in use on a live system, an investigator might have to collect evidence through a live extraction process. (Chapter 12, "Searching Memory in Real Time with Live System Forensics," discusses live extraction in more detail.)

### Anti-Forensics

Every investigation is unique. Investigations are not necessarily friendly activities. Forensic specialists may have to conduct them with or without the cooperation of the data provider. And the data provider may or may not be the target of the investigation. Investigations with uncooperative data providers are difficult.

An attacker may use techniques to intentionally conceal his or her identity, location, and behavior. For example, perpetrators may conceal their identity by using networked connections at a library, an Internet café, or another public computer. Or they may use encryption or anonymous services to protect themselves. The actions that perpetrators take to conceal their location, activities, or identity are generally termed **anti-forensics**.

Cybercriminals are becoming better at covering their tracks as their awareness of digital forensics capabilities increases. According to security consultant Scott Berinato, "For every tool forensic investigators have come to rely on to discover and prosecute electronic crimes, criminals have a corresponding tool to baffle the investigation."

Bill Blunden, author of *The Rootkit Arsenal*, describes six types of anti-forensic activities:

- **Data destruction**—Methods for disposing of data vary. They can be as simple as wiping the memory buffers used by a program. Or they can be as complex as repeatedly overwriting a cluster of data with 1s and 0s until all that is left is random bytes of data. Digital evidence can be destroyed easily. For example, starting a computer updates timestamps and modifies files. Attaching a hard disk or USB stick modifies file system timestamps. Powering off a machine destroys volatile memory. Suspects may delete files and folders and defrag their hard drives in an attempt to overwrite evidence.

- **Data hiding**—Suspects often store data where an investigator is unlikely to find it. They may hide data, for example, in reserved disk sectors or as logical partitions within a defined, public partition. Or they may simply change filenames and extensions.

- **Data transformation**—Suspects may process information in a way that disguises its meaning. For example, they may use encryption to scramble a message based on an algorithm. Or they may use steganography to hide a message inside a larger message, often an image file.

- **Data contraception**—Suspects often store data where a forensic specialist can't analyze it. For example, they may prevent data from being written to disk by storing it in memory. To do so, they use memory-resident rootkits.

- **Data fabrication**—Suspects often overwhelm forensic analysts with false positives and false leads. For example, they may alter as many files as possible to make it difficult to use a checksum process to identify changed files.

- **File system alteration**—Suspects often corrupt data structures and files that organize data, such as a Windows NTFS (NT File System) volume.

These anti-forensic methods and how forensic specialists combat them are discussed throughout this book. In particular, see Chapter 8, "Understanding Information-Hiding Techniques," and Chapter 9, "Recovering Data."

## The Role Evidence Dynamics Plays in System Forensics

Edmond Locard worked as a medical examiner during World War I. He identified causes and places of death by looking at stains or dirt left on soldiers' uniforms. Earlier, in 1910, he opened the world's first crime investigation lab. Through his work, he helped found a basic concept of forensic science that became known as **Locard's exchange principle**. Locard's principle is associated with the phrase "with contact between two items, there will be an exchange." Locard's principle states that when two objects come into contact, there is always transference of material from each object onto the other. In other words, every contact leaves a trace. For example, a criminal might leave fingerprints, a hair, a button, or skin cells. At the same time, the criminal might take away hair, dirt, or blood.

Locard believed that it is impossible for a criminal to act without leaving traces of his or her presence. Thus, forensic specialists focus on identifying the traces that perpetrators leave behind about their activities. Locard's principle applies not just to traditional forensics but to system forensics as well. With systems forensics, digital evidence replaces blood, hair, fingerprints, and other physical and biological evidence.

Between the time a forensic specialist collects evidence and the time a court hears and rules on a case, evidence may change in a number of ways and for a number of reasons. As discussed elsewhere in this chapter, evidence changes very easily. Evidence dynamics is anything that changes, moves, obscures, or obliterates evidence, regardless of intent. In other words, evidence dynamics is any force that acts on evidence. For digital forensics, these forces must have a hardware or software component. Three types of forces act on evidence:

- **Human**—Human forces on digital evidence include unintentional or deliberate destruction or concealment of data. For example, a system administrator may inadvertently perform an action that obliterates patterns or adds artifacts to a crime scene. On a shared computer, an uninvolved user could use a computer after a crime and destroy or change evidence. Even forensic investigators may adversely affect evidence. Forensic specialists may cause the loss of volatile data when shutting down a live system. Or they might use other inappropriate data handling practices. For example, they might alter data when they copy a file onto a computer from another network or from removable media. Reconstructing files from a damaged hard disk can also lead to evidence corruption.

- **Natural**—Natural forces include fire, water, weather, dust, electricity, and time. Magnetic and optical media decay over time and eventually become unreadable. Therefore, hard drives, CDs, and DVDs have a data retention life expectancy. Electricity is a natural force that can change evidence. Most people recognize that standard electrical current in a home can cause damage and change evidence. However, many people don't know that an electrostatic discharge (ESD) of only 40 volts can damage equipment. In addition, static electricity can cause data loss.

- **Incidental**—Incidental forces include equipment and software. Operating systems, applications, and forensic software tools such as disk write-blocking software are examples of software that can impact evidence.

Evidence dynamics creates challenges for forensic analysts, making it difficult to prove what actually occurred and to prove that the evidence is reliable. Forensic specialists must establish working environments that eliminate or minimize the impacts of evidence dynamics. The following are some steps they should take:

- Carefully document data received and its source.

- Establish logs and signoffs to demonstrate an unbroken chain of custody.

- Avoid contamination of evidence by placing it on systems where it can be accessed by processes or individuals not involved in the analysis.

**Testing Forensic Tools: The CFReDS**

An investigator should choose forensic tools and utilities with care and be well versed in their reliability. Calibrating digital forensic tools isn't easy. The National Institute of Standards and Technology (NIST) provides the Computer Forensic Reference Data Sets (CFReDS) for testing. (See *http://www.cfreds.nist.gov.*) The four primary applications of CFReDS are testing forensic tools, establishing that lab equipment is functioning properly, testing proficiency in specific skills, and training laboratory staff. Each of these data sets has slightly different requirements. Courts may be more likely to accept evidence collected using tools that have been used in previous trials and that are routinely tested for reliability.

- Wear a grounding wristband and use antistatic protective mats and surfaces, when possible, to prevent ESD.
- Maintain a humidity level of 40 percent to 60 percent to reduce ESD.
- Use static-free storage bags for storing or moving equipment to reduce the potential for ESD damage.
- Use appropriate procedures to ensure that data are purged from all storage devices when no longer needed, with good documentation of the data disposal.
- Destroy data when appropriate by overwriting media with 1s and 0s.
- Test the tools used.

For more information on the steps forensic analysts should take, see Chapter 6, "Controlling a Forensic Investigation," and Chapter 7, "Collecting, Seizing, and Protecting Evidence."

## Scope-Related Challenges to System Forensics

The scope of a forensic effort often presents not just an analytical challenge but a psychological challenge as well. Information systems collect and retain large volumes of data. They store this data in a dizzying array of applications, formats, and hardware components. In completing an analysis, forensic specialists face variations in the following:

- The volume of data to be analyzed
- The complexity of the computer system
- The size and character of the crime scene, which might involve a network that crosses U.S. and foreign jurisdictions
- The size of the caseload and resource limitations

Forensic specialists must be prepared to quickly complete an analysis regardless of these factors. The following sections discuss these factors in more detail.

3

Challenges of
System Forensics

### An Example of Scope-Related Challenges: Times Square, May 2010

Consider the various technologies and systems that law enforcement used to catch the suspect in the May 2010 attempted Times Square bombing. Digital camera systems recorded the actions of Faisal Shahzad, the man who allegedly drove a car bomb into Times Square, as he purchased bomb components. On-scene surveillance photos reportedly showed the suspect setting up the bomb. Investigators traced the vehicle used to deliver the bomb, a 1993 Pathfinder, to its original owner by using hidden vehicle identification numbers. Federal Bureau of Investigation (FBI) agents found that the 1993 Pathfinder had been sold three weeks earlier on Craigslist. Investigators used information from the Craigslist seller to track down the number of the prepaid mobile phone the suspect used. Investigators used call logs to identify the "owner's" calling pattern, callers, and call recipients.

Once the FBI identified Shahzad as a suspect, it added him to the "no fly" list. The Department of Homeland Security U.S. Customs and Border Protection (CBP) then identified Shahzad's presence on a passenger list for a flight to Dubai. Authorities arrested him. Investigators then used financial data, travel histories, and information provided by foreign governments to identify a number of individuals who knowingly or unwittingly helped Shahzad carry out his alleged plan.

The volume of information in the Times Square bombing incident is not unusual. What is unusual is the speed with which investigators were able to collect and analyze the data. In addition, law enforcement used a lot of technology in this case. However, the successful capture resulted from CBP personnel personally calling all airlines to have them immediately check their passenger lists for Shahzad. Thus, the May 2010 Times Square incident showed that forensic investigators need old-fashioned intuition and initiative as well as solid forensic tools that can analyze large volumes of information.

## Large Volumes of Data

Digital forensics is useful in identifying and documenting evidence. It is a disciplined approach that looks at the entire physical media, such as a hard disk drive, for all data representations. A system forensics specialist has access to all the data contained on a device—not just what the end user sees. A forensic analyst examines metadata, such as disk partition structures and file tables. An analyst also examines the often-critical unused areas of the media where data might be hidden. Examining all areas of potential data storage and examining all potential data representations generates extremely large volumes of data. A forensic specialist must analyze, store, and control all this data for the full duration of the investigation and analysis.

The total amount of data that is potentially relevant to a case offers a challenge to forensic analysts. Most hard drives now contain in excess of 1 million file items. It is, in fact, common for a single desktop to have 1 terabyte of data storage. When working with such large volumes of data, a forensic specialist must do the following:

- Ensure that his or her equipment is capable of manipulating large volumes of data quickly
- Provide for duplicate storage so that the original media and its resident data are preserved and protected against tampering and other corruption
- Create backups early and often to avoid losing data
- Document everything that is done in an investigation and maintain the chain of custody

In addition to all these tasks, a forensic specialist must support the forensic budget. Manipulating and controlling large volumes of data is expensive. An investigator should show how budget cost items contribute to the analysis and to maintaining the chain of custody. Resource limitations increase the potential for analysis error and compromise of the analysis. For example, a forensic analyst may need to explain how the addition of data custodians or additional hard drives can multiply costs. (For more information on budgeting for a forensics lab, see Chapter 4, "Forensics Methods and Labs.")

## System Complexity

Modern computer systems can be extremely complex. They use multiple file formats, including Adobe Portable Document Format (PDF) files and Tagged Image File Format (TIFF) image files. They connect to and share data with other systems that may be located anywhere in the world. In addition, the law may protect specific data items. No single forensic software application can deal with all this complexity.

Forensic specialists must use a set of software and hardware tools and supporting manual procedures. Further, a forensic specialist must build a case to support his or her interpretation of the "story" told by the data being analyzed. The specialist therefore must have an understanding of data and technology. The specialist should also be able to show corroboration that meets the traditional legal evidence tests.

The fact that individual pieces of data may have more than one possible interpretation compounds system complexity. To reach a conclusion and turn data into supportable evidence, a forensic specialist must identify and analyze corroborating information. A forensic specialist must use data to create evidence to support a conclusion provided by the data. In building a case for corroborating evidence, a forensic specialist may want to compare the results from using two different tools. By doing so, the specialist could demonstrate that two different analytical tools examining the same set of data reached the same conclusion. Conversely, the tools may reach different conclusions, showing that the data does not support the conclusion. Either case is valuable to a forensic specialist.

**Tracking Individuals' Movements**

Over the next few years, systems that create and store digital records of people's movements through public space will become more common. According to Blumberg and Eckersley in "On Locational Privacy, and How to Avoid Losing It Forever," the following are some examples:

- Electronic tolling devices, such as FastTrak and E-ZPass
- Mobile phones with GPS functionality
- Web applications and phone services that send alerts when friends are nearby
- Searches on a personal digital assistant (PDA) for businesses and services nearby
- Free Wi-Fi with ads for businesses near the network access point being used
- Electronic swipe cards for doors
- Parking meters that can be fed using a mobile phone and that send a text message when the purchased time is running out

These types of location-based systems will provide new information for forensic investigators.

## Distributed Crime Scenes

Digital crime scenes can span the globe. Depending on the type of system connectivity and the in-place controls, a forensic specialist may have to deal with data stored throughout the world. This could involve thousands of devices and network logs. Networks and centralized storage also present challenges because items of interest may not be stored on the target computer.

Because networks are distributed, crime scenes are also distributed. This creates practical as well as jurisdictional problems. (Think about how difficult it is for a U.S. investigator to get evidence out of computers in China.) Criminals take advantage of jurisdictional differences between governments. A criminal may sell fake merchandise from a foreign country to Americans in several states. The criminal may then route his or her Internet access through several other countries before it reaches its final destination. Stopping this type of boundary shifting requires the cooperation of state governments, federal governments, and international agencies in tracking down the criminal and bringing him or her to justice. If all the governments and agencies do not cooperate with one another, the investigation may fail.

## Growing Caseload and Limited Resources

Regardless of the state of the economy, forensic specialists can be assured of two things: Their caseload will grow, and their resources will become more limited.

The forensic analysis workload is growing and will continue to grow for the foreseeable future. Driving this growth is the increasing use of technology in all aspects of modern life, not just in support of business objectives. Perpetrators have found that using technology to commit or support a crime reduces the risk of getting caught. The number of forensic specialists today is too small to analyze every cybercrime. In addition, the "take" from an individual crime generally is too small for law enforcement to pursue every crime.

Organizations and people using technology often do not use proper control measures, which increases the number of potential targets. The number of organizations and individuals who want to prosecute perpetrators is increasing. In part, they want to catch perpetrators who stole from them. In addition, they have a legal and fiduciary duty to protect organizational assets.

 **NOTE**

The tools available to perform forensic analysis are increasing in number, complexity, and cost. The new tools available allow more analyses to be performed in a shorter period. However, forensic specialists need continuing education to learn how to use the tools. They also need to learn how to present their findings to a nontechnical audience.

Forensic specialists can take four basic actions to address the growing workload with constrained resources:

- **Continue learning**—Forensic specialists should learn how to use the new tools. They should also learn best practices and techniques developed by others and incorporate them into their analyses. This will help reduce costs by building on the work of others. It will also maximize the use of technology to reduce the costs associated with the large volumes and complexity of analyses.

- **Formalize procedures**—Establishing strict written procedures for collecting and protecting data will ultimately reduce the costs of analyses. Judges and juries are often more likely to accept a forensic specialist's findings if the specialist can show a clear, documented process that can be independently reviewed and is repeatable.

- **Prepare a business case**—Forensic specialists compete with all other activities in an organization for a share of the funds available. Simply stating that forensic analyses can be improved by using a new tool or a new lab is not sufficient. Forensic analysts must prepare a comprehensive business case that demonstrates the need, provides reliable cost estimates, and shows how the organization will benefit from the resource investment. They should support their position on benefits by discussing past successful case analyses. Benefits derived from the investment should be stated in terms of compliance with law, improved analytical quality, and improved capability to address larger, more complex cases. They should also be stated in terms of reduced cost of performance for equivalent workloads. The business case should clearly show that the return on investment (ROI) can be favorably compared to competing requirements.

- **Prioritize workload**—To take advantage of limited resources, forensic specialists must prioritize their workloads. They should establish a formal process with defined criteria for making choices about which cases to accept, which analyses to perform, and the desired depth of analysis. A formal prioritization structure will allow those seeking forensic support to know how the process works. The information generated through the process—cases accepted, cases declined, and so on—will provide support for a business case for added resources. For example, a forensic specialist may objectively demonstrate that funds provided are used most effectively and that there is a legitimate need for a budget increase.

## The Need for Professionalization

The field of digital forensics is still in the process of maturing. Businesses, institutions, and individuals still view digital forensics as somewhat of a "dark science" where investigators perform analysis in a black box and users accept results without question. Forensic specialists sometimes lose cases because decision makers are not familiar with the capabilities and limitations of forensics and with what constitutes appropriate documentation.

> **NOTE**
>
> The National Academy of Sciences is concerned that there is currently too much variability in and uncertainty about the education, experience, and training of those practicing forensics. Professionalization would resolve this concern.

The field of digital forensics will mature as experts incorporate more rigor into analysis processes. In addition, digital forensics will become an accepted analytical approach as the forensic specialist position becomes a professionalized career. Professionalization involves establishing a body of knowledge that forensic specialists should know and against which training and testing can be directed.

Professionalization will also bring more definition to the field, including guidelines and standards for the following:

- Training and certification of forensic specialists
- How to perform forensic analyses
- Supporting forensic evidence
- Data collection that doesn't disrupt ongoing operations
- Standards for defining digital search warrants and subpoenas
- Standards for protecting digital evidence
- Specific terminology used in describing and documenting forensic activities

A forensic specialist faces many challenges. Among them are lack of a defined career path, lack of standards, and an increasing workload with constrained resources. Resolving these challenges in a new technological discipline can be rewarding. But it requires work. Even as they address the technological challenges associated with performing an analysis, forensic specialists must also begin the process of instituting formal procedures so that the results of their work will be more readily accepted. This means that forensic specialists must not just look at their work as an opportunity to use new tools to perform interesting analyses. They must also recognize the value of maturing their industry.

Forensic specialists can focus their efforts on the following issues to help establish digital forensics as an accepted discipline:

- Training and certification
- Restrictions on search and seizure
- Standards for protecting digital evidence
- Standards for performing digital forensics
- Guidelines for presenting digital evidence
- Requirements for addressing cross-border issues between states and between countries
- Guidelines for analyzing common devices, such as PDAs, GPS devices, mobile phones, laptops, and desktops

## CHAPTER SUMMARY

The field of system forensics faces many challenges. One of the major challenges is the difficulty of obtaining digital evidence. Data access, restrictions on search and seizure, and the ease with which digital evidence can be altered or destroyed play important roles in obtaining accurate and reliable evidence. In addition, evidence dynamics creates challenges for forensic analysts by making it more difficult to prove what actually occurred. Other challenges are related to scope. The amount of data stored on hard drives continues to increase, and this raises the cost of full disk imaging and analysis. Distributed crime scenes, especially those that cross jurisdictions, are also problematic. The great number and variety of devices that can contain digital evidence adds to the broad scope of system forensics. New software and hardware constantly become available, making it impossible for a single forensic analyst to be experienced in all operating systems, hardware platforms, devices, programs, and forensic applications and tools.

The field of system forensics is evolving. Many options for training and education are available. However, there is a need for professionalization and standards. Those involved in its early formative years will be rewarded in performing the work while helping to shape the future characteristics of the discipline.

## KEY CONCEPTS AND TERMS

| | | |
|---|---|---|
| Anti-forensics | Documentary evidence | Real evidence |
| Chain of custody | Evidence | Search warrant |
| Data | Information | Subpoena |
| Data analysis plan | Locard's exchange principle | Testimonial evidence |
| Demonstrative evidence | Obscured data | Voluntary surrender |

**3**

**Challenges of
System Forensics**

## CHAPTER 3 ASSESSMENT

**1.** Which of the following is data that has been processed and assembled so that it is relevant to an investigation?

A. Data
B. Forensic data
C. Information
D. Evidence

**2.** Which types of evidence are used in court? (Select three.)

A. Documentary evidence
B. Forensic evidence
C. Real evidence
D. Testimonial evidence
E  Hearsay

**3.** A forensic specialist may not be able to gain access to data because of physical constraints, legal restrictions, or technical issues.

A. True
B. False

**4.** A _____ should identify the types of data to be collected and describe the expected source for the data. It should also list any anticipated problems as well as recommended strategies to deal with those problems.

**5.** Which of the following is a court order than requires a person or an organization that owns subject equipment to release it for analysis?

A. Voluntary surrender
B. Search warrant
C. Arrest warrant
D. Subpoena
E. Trial

**6.** Which of the following is the name for actions that perpetrators take to conceal their location, activities, or identity?

A. Obscured data
B. Documentary evidence
C. Anti-forensics
D. Evidence dynamics
E. Voluntary surrender

**7.** _____ states that when two objects come into contact, there is always transference of material from each object onto the other. In other words, every contact leaves a trace.

**8.** Evidence dynamics is anything that changes, moves, obscures, or obliterates evidence, regardless of intent.

A. True
B. False

**9.** Perpetrators have found that using technology to commit or support a crime increases the risk of getting caught.

A. True
B. False

**10.** What are some of the challenges that a forensic specialist faces? (Select three.)

A. Lack of tools
B. Increasing workload
C. Constrained resources
D. Lack of professionalization
E. Hearsay

# Forensics Methods and Labs

E VIDENCE CAN MAKE OR BREAK AN INVESTIGATION. For evidence to be forensically sound, it must be collected properly and deemed authentic. This chapter discusses two frameworks for ensuring forensic soundness: the DFRWS framework and an event-based digital forensic investigation framework.

System forensics specialists conduct disk-based analysis investigations, store evidence, and do other work in a computer forensics lab. A lab facility must be physically secure so that evidence is not lost, corrupted, or destroyed. The lab should contain a variety of system forensics hardware and software, including forensic workstations and current and legacy software. In addition, the lab must have defined policies, processes, and procedures. Investigators must follow these policies, processes, and procedures. By doing so, they can ensure the integrity of analysis and results so that they will stand up in court.

## Chapter 4 Topics

This chapter covers the following topics and concepts:

- What forensic soundness is
- What forensic frameworks and processes are
- How to build a business case for creating a forensics lab
- How to set up a forensics lab
- How to use policies, processes, and procedures in maintaining a lab

When you complete this chapter, you will be able to:

- Understand the importance of forensic soundness
- Explain frameworks for forensic soundness, including the DFRWS framework and an event-based digital forensic investigation framework
- Understand how to build a business case for creating a forensics lab
- Understand the factors involved in setting up a forensics lab
- Understand policies, processes, and procedures for maintaining a lab

# Forensic Soundness

System forensics is a discipline that combines elements of law and computer science. It involves collecting and analyzing data from computer systems, networks, wireless communications, and storage devices. A forensic specialist must collect data in such a way that it is admissible as evidence in a court of law. Evidence can make or break an investigation, so it's important that evidence be forensically sound.

The courts currently recognize two main classes of electronic information:

- **Human-generated information**—**Human-generated information** is created by humans. It includes e-mails, text messages, word processing documents, digital photos, and other records that are transmitted or stored electronically.
- **Computer-generated information**—**Computer-generated information** is records that are produced by a computing device. It includes logs, content analysis, packet captures, and reconstructed artifacts. The admissibility of computer-generated records depends on their authenticity.

The investigator should acquire, retain, retrieve, and deliver information in a forensically sound fashion to ensure that it is admissible. **Forensic soundness** occurs when data remains complete and materially unaltered. In other words, the evidence is what a forensic specialist says it is: unchanged since collection. To ensure forensic soundness, forensic examiners must follow a process that is reliable, repeatable, and documented. Various organizations have developed criteria for or explanations of forensic soundness. The U.S. Department of Justice and the International Organization on Computer Evidence are two examples.

Rodney McKemmish proposed the following simplified set of principles for forensic soundness:

- **Minimally handle the original**—A forensic specialist should apply digital forensics processes to original data as little as possible. Instead, an investigator should copy relevant data and examine it.

- **Account for any change**—Changes sometimes occur to evidence during a forensic examination. In such cases, a forensic specialist should note the nature, extent, and reason for the changes.

- **Comply with the rules of evidence**—During an investigation, a forensic specialist should keep in mind the relevant rules of evidence. (See the following sidebar, "Rules of Evidence.")

- **Avoid exceeding one's knowledge**—A forensic specialist should not undertake an examination that is beyond his or her current level of knowledge and skill. It is important to seek help when needed.

Forensic specialists should generally make copies of evidence rather than work with the original evidence. To guarantee forensic soundness, they must collect their evidence using a method that does not alter any data on the drive or device that they are duplicating. Also, the evidence must contain a copy of every bit, byte, and sector of the source drive. The copy should include unallocated empty space and slack space, exactly as the data appears on the source drive or device. Finally, the forensic specialist must document the manner used to obtain the evidence. In other words, the specialist must report on the origin of the evidence as well as its handling by investigators. The specialist should note any hardware or software errors encountered during the forensic examination process and explain their impact. The process used to obtain and analyze evidence should be transparent. This means someone else must be able to independently examine and verify the process. In addition, the process must produce an audit trail.

Accidental human error can easily change or delete electronic data. So can computer processes. The results of the forensic process may become evidence in court. Therefore, it's critical to take measures to ensure the reliability and accuracy of data.

---

### Rules of Evidence

**Rules of evidence** govern whether, when, how, and why proof of a legal case can be placed before a judge or jury. A forensic specialist should have a good understanding of the rules of evidence in the given venue. The rules vary depending on the type of court and the jurisdiction.

The **Federal Rules of Evidence (FRE)** is a code of evidence law. The FRE governs the admission of facts by which parties in the U.S. federal court system may prove their cases. The FRE provides guidelines for the authentication and identification of evidence for admissibility under sections 901, 902, and "Searching and Seizing Computers and Obtaining Electronic Evidence in Criminal Investigations."

For more information on computer records and the Federal Rules of Evidence, see *http://www.justice.gov/criminal/cybercrime/usamarch2001_4.htm*.

**FYI**

In June 2009, a Supreme Court decision in *Melendez-Diaz v. Massachusetts* had an effect on system forensics. This decision extended the Confrontation Clause ("… the accused shall enjoy the right … to be confronted with the witnesses against him") of the Sixth Amendment to include forensic analysts' reports as testimonial evidence. This decision—if it stands—means that for any forensic evidence presented in a case, the investigating analyst might be required to provide in-court testimony about the findings. Or the defense may be allowed to cross-examine the analyst on the findings. This decision increases the need to maintain strong forensic soundness of evidence.

## Forensic Frameworks and Processes

Forensic frameworks and processes come in many models. Further, specialists may take numerous approaches to cyber investigations. The three primary goals of forensics methods are to:

- Acquire evidence without altering or damaging the original.
- Authenticate that recovered evidence is the same as the originally seized data.
- Analyze the data without modifying it.

These three goals apply regardless of the model used.

### The DFRWS Framework

The **Digital Forensics Research Workshop (DFRWS)** is a nonprofit, volunteer organization. Its goal is to enhance the sharing of knowledge and ideas about digital forensics research. DFRWS sponsors annual conferences, technical working groups, and challenges to help drive the direction of research and development. In 2001, the DFRWS developed a framework for digital investigation that is useful today. The **DFRWS framework** is a matrix with six classes:

**NOTE**

For more information on the DFRWS, see *http://www.dfrws.org.*

- Identification
- Preservation
- Collection
- Examination
- Analysis
- Presentation

As shown in Table 4-1, each of these classes has several elements.

### An Event-Based Digital Forensic Investigation Framework

In 2004, Brian Carrier and Eugene Spafford, researchers at the Center for Education and Research in Information Assurance and Security (CERIAS) at Purdue University, proposed

| | | | | | |
|---|---|---|---|---|---|
| **TABLE 4-1** The DFRWS digital investigation framework. | | | | | |
| **IDENTIFICATION** | **PRESERVATION** | **COLLECTION** | **EXAMINATION** | **ANALYSIS** | **PRESENTATION** |
| Even/crime detection | Case management | Preservation | Preservation | Preservation | Documentation |
| Resolve signature | Imaging technologies | Approved methods | Traceability | Traceability | Expert testimony |
| Profile detection | Chain of custody | Approved software | Validation techniques | Statistical | Clarification |
| Anomalous detection | Time synchronization | Approved hardware | Filtering techniques | Protocols | Mission impact statement |
| Complaints | | Legal authority | Pattern matching | Data mining | Recommended countermeasure |
| System monitoring | | Lossless compression | Hidden data discovery | Timeline | Statistical interpretation |
| Audit analysis | | Sampling | Hidden data extraction | Link | |
| | | Data reduction | | Spatial | |
| | | Recovery techniques | | | |

a model that is more intuitive and flexible than the DFRWS framework. This model, an **event-based digital forensic investigation framework**, is shown in Figure 4-1. This model has five phases:

- **Readiness**—There are two readiness phases: the operations readiness phase and the infrastructure readiness phase. The operations readiness phase involves training people and testing investigation tools. The infrastructure readiness phase involves configuring the equipment. This could include adding network monitoring tools and increasing the logging levels.

- **Deployment**—There are two deployment phases: the detection and notification phase and the confirmation and authorization phase. In the detection and notification phase, someone detects an incident and alerts investigators. For example, an intrusion detection system could detect a network intrusion. Or an investigator could use logs or communications of the suspect to detect a contraband incident. In the confirmation and authorization phase, investigators receive authorization to conduct the investigation. In a corporate environment, the incident response team may conduct a brief analysis of a system to confirm that it has been compromised. For a critical system, the response team may need additional permission before it can conduct a full analysis. In a law enforcement environment, an officer may obtain a search warrant at this point.

**FIGURE 4-1**

An event-based digital
forensic investigation
framework.

- **Physical crime scene investigation**—The physical investigation involves examining the physical objects at the crime scene where a digital device exists. Investigators collect physical evidence and try to link a person to the suspect computer activity. This set of phases includes searching for physical evidence and reconstructing physical events. When forensic specialists find physical objects that may have digital evidence in them, they conduct a digital investigation. This phase uses the analysis results from one or more digital crime scene investigations.

- **Digital crime scene investigation**—This set of phases involves examining the digital data for evidence. An investigation occurs for each self-contained digital device. In general, this process involves preserving the system, searching for digital evidence, and reconstructing digital events. The digital crime scene investigation phases are a subset of the physical crime scene investigation phases. The conclusions drawn in the digital investigation are used in the physical investigation.

> **NOTE**
>
> For more information on CERIAS, see *http://www.cerias.purdue.edu.*

- **Presentation**—During the preceding phases, investigators develop and test theories about the events related to the incident. At this point, a forensic specialist presents the results either to a corporation or a court of law.

## Building a Business Case for Creating a Forensics Lab

Most system forensic work occurs in forensics labs. A lab facility must be physically secure so that evidence is not lost, corrupted, or destroyed. Setting up such a lab is expensive and time-consuming.

Organizations try to constantly reduce costs. It's therefore important to plan ahead to ensure that money is available for facilities, tools, supplies, and training for a forensics lab. In addition, setting up a computer forensics lab requires the support of managers and other team members. A **business case** is a reasoned proposal for making a change. A business case can help justify the acquisition of newer and better resources to investigate computer forensics cases.

How to develop a business case depends on the organization in question. For a sole proprietor, creating a business case is fairly simple. If the owner needs money to buy tools, he or she can save money for the purchase or negotiate with a bank for a loan. For a public entity such as a police department, on the other hand, budgets are planned a year or more in advance. Public agency department managers present their budget proposals to upper management. If the supervisors approve the proposal, they then make money available to acquire resources outlined in the budget. Some public organizations might have other funds available to spend immediately for special needs. Managers can divert these funds for emergencies or other unforeseen needs.

Private-sector businesses, especially large corporations, are motivated by the need to make money. A business case should demonstrate how computer forensics investigations can save money and avoid risks that could damage profits. For example, forensic investigations may be able to prevent litigation involving the company. A lawsuit, regardless of who wins, can cost an employer several hundred thousand dollars. A business case should compare the cost of training and conducting forensic investigations with the cost of a lawsuit. A business case should also show how computer forensics investigations can improve profits. Investigations can, for instance, protect intellectual property, trade secrets, and future business plans.

The following are some key elements for creating a computer forensics business case:

- **Justification of the need for a lab**—The business case should justify to the person controlling the budget the reason a lab is necessary. Advertising the lab's services to previous, current, and future customers and clients can justify future budgets for the lab's operation and staff.

- **The lab budget**—As discussed later in this chapter, the budget should include facility costs, hardware costs, and software costs. It's important to be as exact as possible when estimating the costs of these items. Making a mistake could cause delays and possible loss of the opportunity to start or improve the lab.

- **Lab approval and acquisition**—The approval process should include a risk analysis that describes how the lab will minimize the risk of litigation. The business case should also present an educated guess about how many investigations are likely and how long they will take to complete, on average. Acquisition planning involves researching different products to determine which ones are the best and most cost-effective. An organization should contact several vendors and designate engineers to learn more about each product and service. Important considerations include product prices, maintenance costs, and vendor reliability.

- **Implementation**—The next step is to implement facilities and tools. The business case should include a timeline showing expected delivery or installation dates and expected completion dates. The business case should also include a coordination plan for delivery dates and times for materials and tools. The schedule should include inspection of facility construction, equipment, and software tools.

- **Acceptance testing**—Following the implementation scheduling and inspection, an organization should develop an acceptance testing plan for the computer forensics lab to make sure everything works correctly. The acceptance testing should address facility inspection, testing of communications, hardware testing, and installation and use of software tools. The business case must anticipate problems that can cause delays in lab production. It should include contingencies to deal with system or facility failures. For example, the business case should list workarounds for problems, such as the wrong locks being installed on lab doors or electrical power requiring additional filtering.

- **Production**—After taking care of all essential corrections, forensic specialists can begin production in their new computer forensics lab.

## Setting Up a Forensics Lab

> **NOTE**
>
> For more information on ASCLD, see *http://www.ascld.org*. For more information on ASCLD/LAB certification, see *http://www.ascld-lab.org*.

The **American Society of Crime Laboratory Directors (ASCLD)** provides guidelines for managing a forensics lab. It also provides guidelines for acquiring crime lab and forensics lab certification. ASCLD offers voluntary accreditation to public and private crime laboratories in the United States and around the world. It certifies computer forensics labs that analyze digital evidence and other criminal evidence, such as fingerprints and DNA samples. The ASCLD/LAB certification regulates how to organize and manage crime labs.

Achieving ASCLD accreditation is a rigorous process. A lab must meet about 400 criteria to achieve accreditation. Typically, an unaccredited lab needs two to three years to prepare for accreditation. It spends this time developing policies, procedures, document controls, analysis validations, and so on. Then, the lab needs another year to go through the process. The lab manager submits an application. The lead assessor and a team spend one to two months reviewing the application and the policies and procedures, to make sure the lab is ready. The assessment takes about a week. Typically the assessment team generates five to 15 findings that require corrective action. The lab typically requires

> **NOTE**
>
> As of January 2010, in the United States, computer forensics lab certification was not mandated. However, following the quality standards of the ASCLD/LAB program enhances a lab's credibility.

several months to make corrections to the satisfaction of the lead assessor. Once the facility has made all corrections, the lead assessor recommends the lab to the board of directors for accreditation. Finally, the ASCLD/LAB board of directors votes on whether to accredit the lab.

The ASCLD/LAB program includes audits to ensure that forensic specialists are performing lab procedures correctly and consistently for all casework. The society performs these audits in computer forensics labs to maintain the quality and integrity of analysis.

## The Duties of a Lab Manager and Staff

A system forensics **lab manager** performs general management tasks, such as promoting group consensus in decision making, maintaining fiscal responsibility for lab needs, and enforcing ethical standards among staff members. In addition, the lab manager does the following:

- Plans updates for the lab, such as new hardware and software purchases
- Establishes and promotes quality assurance processes for the lab's staff to follow, such as what to do when a case arrives. These processes may include logging evidence, specifying who can enter the lab, and establishing guidelines for filing reports
- Sets production schedules for processing work
- Creates and monitors lab policies for staff and provides a safe and secure workplace for staff and evidence
- Accounts for all activities of the lab's staff. Staff members in a system forensics lab should have sufficient training to perform their tasks. Necessary skill sets include hardware and software knowledge. For example, lab staff members must have knowledge of operating systems and file types, understand how to use forensic tools, be able to clearly document results, and have good deductive reasoning skills. The lab manager and peers should review staff members' work regularly to ensure quality. Staff members are also responsible for continuing technical training to update their investigative and computer skills. It's important to maintain a record of all training completed.

> **NOTE**
>
> Many vendors and organizations hold annual or quarterly training seminars. Some offer certification exams as well. For more information on training, see Chapter 15, "System Forensics Resources."

The ASCLD Web site summarizes the requirements of managing a computer forensics lab. It also discusses handling and preserving evidence, performing laboratory procedures, setting personnel requirements, and encouraging professional development. The site also provides a user license for printed and online manuals of lab management guidelines. ASCLD stresses that each lab should maintain an up-to-date library of resources in its field. For system forensics, these resources include software, hardware, information, and technical journals.

## Planning a Forensics Lab Budget

Budgeting for a forensics lab is similar to budgeting for any other activity. It involves three basic steps:

1. Identify the functions to be performed. Define the activities that must be completed to perform those functions.
2. Estimate the workload.

---

**FYI**

A typical case for an internal corporate investigation involves seizing a hard disk, making forensic copies, evaluating evidence, and filing a report. A forensic analysis of a 500 GB disk can take several days. It often involves running imaging software overnight and on weekends. This means one of the forensic computers in the lab is occupied for days. Based on past experience, the lab manager can estimate how many cases each investigator can handle and when to expect preliminary and final reports for each case.

---

3. Estimate the cost to complete the defined activities for the estimated workload. Divide the costs into two basic categories, fixed and variable. Fixed costs are costs that do not change or that change very slowly as the volume of work changes. They include costs for space, computers, software, and other equipment. Variable costs are costs that are directly related to the volume of work. Examples of variable costs are costs for staff, gloves, disks, ink, and paper.

Depending on the organization, a forensics lab must provide its budget estimate on a monthly, quarterly, annual, or multi-year basis. The budget must comply with the organization's normal budget processes. If it does not, management is sure to deny or reduce it.

Forensics labs must not create their budgets in a vacuum. They must develop them based on prior expenditures and workload histories. Information regarding prior expenditures is available from the organization's accounting and inventory systems. This information serves as a basis for determining what is already available to the lab and what it must acquire to complete the estimated workload.

A forensic specialist should understand the costs associated with a forensics lab. Having this understanding helps the forensic specialist better estimate costs and make good decisions about what cases to accept and which analyses to conduct. The following sections discuss the primary items that affect the budget of a forensics lab.

## Estimating Facility Costs

For a new computer forensics lab, startup costs might consume most of the budget. The first step with a new lab is determining how much floor space is needed. Preserving evidence and stocking enough supplies requires a lot of storage space. A good rule of thumb is to estimate 150 square feet per person. An organization's facility manager can provide an estimate on per-square-foot costs for the area or building.

## Estimating Hardware Needs and Costs

Computers and other hardware are critical to a digital forensics lab. In planning its hardware needs, a lab should consider the following:

> ## Calculating the Facility Costs for a Budget
>
> Answering the following questions can help in determining the facility costs for a budget:
>
> - How many computer forensics examiners does the organization need?
> - How much training will each examiner require per year?
> - Is one lab sufficient, or does the organization need more than one?
> - How many computer forensics examiners will use each lab? Will there be a need to temporarily accommodate other non-examiners to inspect recovered evidence?
> - What are the costs of constructing a secure lab?
> - Is there a suitable room already in the building that the organization can convert into a lab?
> - Are the electrical system and the heating, ventilation, and air-conditioning (HVAC) system in the designated room adequate for a lab? If not, what will be the cost of upgrading these systems?
> - Are there existing telephone lines and network cables in the designated room? If not, how much will installing these additional items cost?
> - Is there an adequate door lock on the door of the designated room?
> - What will the furniture cost?
> - Should the room have an alarm system installed?
> - Are there any other facility costs, such as fees for janitorial services and facility maintenance services?

- **Computers**—Based on the number of cases a lab expects to examine, the lab manager should determine how many computers the lab needs. The hardware equipment a computer forensics lab needs depends on the types of investigations and data the lab will analyze. A lab may need, for example, Windows personal computers (PCs), UNIX workstations, or Linux servers.

- **Storage needs**—The volume of storage used in forensic examinations is increasing as the cost of storage continues to decrease. Therefore, a lab should plan to acquire more storage than initially required.

- **Technological changes**—A lab must keep up with pending technological changes, such as new processors, storage technology, or other devices. For example, forensics labs should be prepared to address cases that include examination of tablet PCs and other newly introduced technologies. In addition, forensic specialists must often evaluate data stored on obsolete systems. Thus, they must be able to examine data stored on both state-of-the-art and legacy systems.

**Calculating Hardware Costs for a Budget**

Answering the following questions will help an organization determine its hardware budget needs:

- What types of investigations and data recovery will examiners perform in the lab?
- How many investigations can the lab expect per month?
- Will there be any time-sensitive investigations that demand rapid analysis of disk data?
- What sizes and how many drives will the lab need to support a typical investigation?
- Will the lab need a high-speed backup system, such as tape backup or digital video disk (DVD) burners?
- What is the predominant type of computer system the lab will investigate?
- What will the lab use to store digital evidence? And for how long?

- **Obsolescence**—A forensics lab's inventory should maintain information about whether hardware items still have a useful life. For example, a computer system might still have a useful life according to accounting procedures. But it may no longer be able to process the expanding volumes of data or new forensic software required to perform analyses. The budget estimate for computers should identify the costs of replacing obsolete equipment as well as the costs associated with repair and maintenance and purchase of new equipment. As a general practice, a lab must replace its computers every one to four years.

## Estimating Software Needs and Costs

Like hardware, software is critical to a digital forensics lab. A lab's software requirements are largely independent of the volume of data processed. Instead, they are based on the functions to be performed. Thus, a lab should develop a profile of the following:

- **Types of cases**—Based on the types of cases expected, the lab can determine the nature of the data—text, database files, graphics, pictures, and so on. It can also determine the activities that will be needed to conduct analyses. For example, if the lab expects cases involving banking transactions, it may need software that can directly examine electronic funds transfers.
- **Licensing**—Software licensing is typically based on the number of users, the number of concurrent users, or the number of systems or processors on which it is installed.
- **Obsolescence**—Like hardware, software also grows obsolete. Software eventually becomes outdated. Its publisher may stop providing support for the software. A lab should consider replacement costs in its software budget.
- **Other costs**—A lab should consider installation, support, and maintenance costs.

**FYI**

In estimating hardware and software costs, a lab might want to consider uniform crime reports. A uniform crime report usually identifies the number of hard disk types and the operating systems used to commit crimes. It also shows the types and frequency of crimes committed. Federal, state, and local authorities generate annual uniform crime reports. For federal reports, see *http://www.fbi.gov/ucr/ucr.htm*. For a summary of crimes, including cybercrimes, see *http://www.ojp.usdoj.gov/bjs/dtd.htm*.

## Considering Miscellaneous Costs

An organization should brainstorm on other items, tools, and supplies to consider purchasing for its lab. For example, it probably needs general office supplies. It may also have specific needs for daily operations, such as errors-and-omission insurance for the lab's operation and staff.

## Determining Physical Requirements for a Computer Forensics Lab

A forensics lab may at first appear to be normal office space. This appearance is deceptive. A lab facility must be physically secure so that evidence isn't lost, corrupted, or destroyed. Lab equipment often requires special power and cooling arrangements. Also, a lab needs humidity controls to minimize the potential for damage by static electricity.

**TIP**

A lab should consider what it needs to maintain a safe and secure environment when determining its physical lab expenses.

### Calculating Software Costs for a Budget

To determine computer software budget needs, a lab should answer questions such as these:

- What types of operating systems will investigators be examining? What operating systems will the lab need to conduct routine examinations?
- How often will the organization need to investigate less popular, uncommon, or older operating systems, such as Mac OS 9.x, OS/2, and CP/M?
- What are the minimum needs for forensic software tools? For example, how many copies of each tool will be necessary? How often will each tool be used in an average week?
- Will there be a need for specialized software, such as QuickBooks or Peachtree?
- Is there a budget to purchase more than one forensic software tool, such as EnCase, FTK, or ProDiscover?
- Which disk-editing tool should the lab select for general data analysis?

4

Forensics Methods and Labs

> **NOTE**
>
> Forensic examiners must be briefed on the lab's security policy. Only examiners and personnel who must know about an investigation should be able to access information about that case.

## Identifying Lab Security Needs

A computer forensics lab should preserve the integrity of evidence and its analytical functions. A number of organizations produce documents that provide guidance in establishing secure facilities, including the National Institute of Standards and Technology (NIST).

The following are some of the physical attributes of a secure forensics lab:

- **True floor-to-ceiling walls**—Drop ceilings and subfloors are acceptable only in a room with true-floor-to-true-ceiling walls.
- **Solid doors that resist penetration**—Tempered-glass doors are acceptable for interior locations.
- **Door access with a locking mechanism**—If possible, each door should also be equipped with a smart card system that records entries and exits. A door should allow egress in the event of a power failure, but entry should require keyed access.
- **Secondary storage for evidence, such as a fire-resistant safe**—This storage should enable evidence to be separated by case.
- **Video monitoring**—The lab should use video to monitor the facility, secured storage, and all entry points.
- **Blast-resistant windows**—Any windows that could provide direct access into the facility must be blast resistant.
- **Visitors' log**—A lab should maintain a paper or electronic sign-in log for all visitors. The log should list each visitor's name, the date and time of arrival and departure, the name of the visitor's employer, the purpose of the visit, and the name of the lab member receiving the visitor. Anyone who is not assigned to the lab should be considered a visitor. This includes cleaning crews, facility maintenance personnel, friends, and family members. All visitors to the lab should be escorted by an assigned authorized staff member. The escort should ensure that the visitors don't accidentally or intentionally tamper with an investigation or evidence.
- **Visitors' badges and alarms**—A lab should use a visible signal, such as visitors' badges, to identify visitors. A lab may also elect to install a visible or audio alarm to let all specialists know that a visitor is in the area.

The level of physical security required depends on the nature of the lab and the type of work the lab does. A regional computer crime lab has high physical security needs because of the impact of lost, corrupted, or otherwise damaged evidence. Physical security needs of a corporation are probably not as high because the impact of lost or compromised data is much lower.

## Conducting High-Risk Investigations

People may be willing to spend significant resources to compromise or stop high-risk investigations, such as those involving national security or murder. These individuals might use physical attacks, such as throwing a bomb. They might use social attacks to compromise an investigator. Or they might use technological attacks, such as planting a Trojan or virus on lab software. High-risk investigations therefore demand increased security.

Protecting against those who have significant resources and incentives to compromise an investigation is extremely difficult. Any security can be broken by unlimited resources and unlimited time. Further, technology improvements tend to help the attacker more than they help prevention. For example, devices for eavesdropping on conversations or computer transmissions are dropping in price while the capabilities are increasing. Detection, on the other hand, is becoming more difficult and expensive. An individual today has the capability to eavesdrop using nanny cams or wireless surveillance systems. A few years ago, such technology was available only to a country's intelligence agencies.

Anyone can go online and find instructions for building a sniffing device that can illegally collect computer emanations. These devices can remotely pick up anything typed on a monitored device that emits electromagnetic radiation (EMR). The EMR from a computer can be picked up as far away as a half mile.

The U.S. Department of Defense shields computers from EMR detection under its **TEMPEST** program. Shielding all computers would be impossible because of the high cost involved. To protect high-risk investigations, however, a lab might also consider implementing TEMPEST protection. TEMPEST certifies equipment that is built with shielding that prevents EMR. In some cases, TEMPEST can be applied to an entire lab. Shielding a lab is an extremely high-cost approach that includes the following measures:

- Lining the walls, ceiling, floor, and doors with specially grounded conductive metal sheets
- Installing filters that prevent power cables from transmitting computer emanations
- Installing special baffles in heating and ventilation ducts to trap emanations
- Installing line filters on telephones lines
- Installing special arrangements for entrances and exits that prevent the facility from being open to the outside at all times

Creating and maintaining a TEMPEST-certified lab is expensive. Such a lab must be inspected and tested regularly. Only large regional computer forensics labs that demand absolute security from eavesdropping should consider complete TEMPEST protection. For smaller facilities, use of TEMPEST-certified equipment is often a more effective approach.

## Using Evidence Storage Containers

Forensic specialists should use **evidence storage containers** to store data and evidence while an investigation is in progress. Storage containers, also known as evidence lockers, must be secure so that no unauthorized person has access. They can be locked using high-quality padlocks, with limited duplicate-key distribution. Or they can be secured with electronic locking systems.

**TIP**

Forensic specialists should inspect evidence storage containers periodically. They should also move evidence for closed cases to a secure offsite facility.

**TIP**

An evidence room must be secure. Therefore, a lab should have at least two controlled exits and no outside windows.

A lab must maintain evidence custody/inventory forms that record the contents of the storage containers. These forms should also indicate when material is removed or entered, when material is transferred, and who authorizes each transfer. A lab should retain these records for at least three years or as required by applicable legal requirements.

Storage containers should be made of a material that resists penetration, such as steel or a modern composite material. The containers should also protect the contents against magnetic fields and against fire and water damage.

In addition to the evidence storage containers, a forensics lab needs an **evidence storage room**. This room provides longer-term storage and storage of items that are too large to fit inside an evidence locker, such as a large server or a disk array. The evidence room should be located close to the lab, but it may or may not be within the lab itself. Security for this room must be equal to or better than the level of security of the lab. That is, evidence should be protected at least as well in the evidence room as it is in the main lab area.

### Overseeing Facility Maintenance

Facility maintenance is critical to maintaining the integrity of investigations. Evidence can easily become contaminated. For example, random flecks of dirt can damage recording media. Or plugging a vacuum cleaner into a power socket for the monitor can destroy a PC. A lab requires proper maintenance at all times to ensure the safety and health of lab personnel. Lab staff should ensure that any damage to the floor, walls, ceilings, or furniture is repaired immediately. Also, cleaning crews should undergo background checks. Their work within highly sensitive areas must be monitored. In addition, a lab should clean its floors and carpets at least once a week to help minimize dust.

A forensics lab should have separate containers for trash disposal. Items unrelated to an investigation should be placed in one of the containers. A second container, or multiple

**TIP**

A lab should maintain a log that documents the destruction of sensitive material.

containers, should be used to destroy items related to investigations, based on destruction technique. For example, one container would be for paper items that will be shredded. Another would be for hard disks and compact disks (CDs) that will be crushed and melted. Yet another would be used for magnetic tapes that will be degaussed. Using separate trash containers maintains the integrity of criminal investigation processes and protects trade secrets and other private information.

### Auditing a Computer Forensics Lab

To make sure a lab is following security policies and practices, it should conduct routine inspections of its facilities. Audits should include the following facility components and practices:

- Inspect the lab's ceiling, floor, roof, and exterior walls at least once a month, looking for anything unusual or new.

- Inspect doors to make sure they close and lock correctly.

- Inspect locks and replace or change them when needed.

- Review visitor logs to see whether they're being used properly and if there are any anomalies.

- Review log sheets for evidence containers to determine when someone has opened and closed them.

- Inspect the evidence storage room and evidence storage containers.

- At the end of each workday, secure any evidence that's not being processed on a forensic workstation.

## Determining the Floor Plan for a Computer Forensics Lab

How to configure the work area for a computer forensics lab depends on a number of factors. It depends on the budget, the amount of available floor space, and the number of computers assigned to each investigator. For a small operation handling two or three cases a month, one forensic workstation may be sufficient to handle the workload. A typical workstation requires approximately the same space as an average desk. A lab that processes multiple, concurrent investigations requires more than one workstation.

A lab must have enough room around each workstation to allow space for discussions and to separate different investigations. For example, a work area for one person, containing three workstations, requires approximately 150 square feet of space. This space allows for two chairs so that the computing investigator can brief another investigator, a paralegal, or an attorney on the case.

An organization can configure a lab in a number of ways. A small lab may consist of two forensic workstations, a research computer, a workbench if space allows, and storage cabinets. A medium-size computer forensics lab, such as a lab in a private business, has more workstations. If possible, cubicles or even separate offices should be part of the layout to reinforce the need-to-know policy. These labs usually have more library space for software and hardware storage. State law enforcement and the Federal Bureau of Investigation (FBI) run most large or regional computer forensics labs. This type of lab has a separate evidence room for digital evidence. One or more custodians might be assigned to manage and control traffic into and out of the evidence room.

**TIP**

In some labs, each computer forensics investigator should have a private office where he or she can manage cases, conduct interviews, and communicate without eavesdropping concerns. Separate offices for supervisors and cubicles for investigators are more practical in other situations.

**NOTE**

Forensic workstations may be connected to an isolated local area network (LAN). Only a few machines should connect to an outside wide area network (WAN) or a metropolitan area network (MAN). Forensic workstations should not directly connect to the Internet.

## Stocking a Forensics Lab

A computer forensics lab must contain a variety of system forensics hardware and software, such as workstations, current and legacy operating systems and other software, and instruments. The following sections look at these components.

### Selecting Forensic Workstations

Many well-designed forensic workstations are available that can handle most computing investigation needs. A forensic workstation should have adequate memory, storage, and ports to deal with the common types of cases that come through the lab. In general, an organization should use less powerful workstations for mundane tasks and multipurpose workstations for higher-end analysis tasks. The following sections provide some guidelines for different settings.

**Selecting workstations for police labs.**   Police departments in major cities have diverse needs for investigation tools because the communities they serve use a wide assortment of computing systems. Not all computer users have the latest technology, so police departments usually need older machines and software to match what's used in their community. For small, local police departments, however, the majority of work involves Windows PCs and Apple Macintosh systems. A small police department's computer forensics lab could be limited to one multipurpose forensic workstation and one or two basic workstations.

Computing systems in a lab should be able to process typical cases in a timely manner. The time it takes to process a case usually depends on the size and type of industries in the region. For example, suppose a lab is located in a region with a large manufacturing firm that employs 70,000 people. Based on crime reports consulted, the lab estimates that 12 percent of those employees might be involved in criminal behavior. The lab therefore estimates that 8,400 employees will commit crimes such as fraud and embezzlement. Such statistics can help estimate how much time is involved in processing these types of cases.

### Using Laptop Forensic Workstations

Recently, important advances in hardware technology have offered increased flexibility in system forensics. It is now possible to use laptops as mobile forensic workstations. Improved data transfer speeds on laptops make it easier to create images of suspect drives.

However, laptops are still limited as forensic workstations. Even with the improved data transfer rates, acquiring data on a laptop with a data compression imaging tool, such as EnCase or SafeBack, creates a bottleneck. The processor, bus, and device speeds determine how quickly a forensic specialist can acquire an image of a hard disk. The faster the central processing unit on any computer, the faster the image is created in a compressed mode.

Until recently, the general rule was at least one law enforcement computer investigator for every 250,000 people in a geographic region. For example, if a community has 1 million people, the regional computer forensics lab should have at least four computer investigators, each with at least one multipurpose forensic workstation and one general-purpose workstation. This rule is quickly changing, however, as the amount of data stored on digital devices increases.

**Selecting workstations for private and corporate labs.**   For a business conducting internal investigations or a commercial business providing system forensics services to private parties, equipment resources are generally easy to determine. Commercial businesses providing system forensics analysis for other companies can tailor their services to specific markets. They can specialize in one or two platforms, such as a Windows PC running a Microsoft operating system. They can also gather a variety of tools to meet a wider market. The type of equipment they need depends on their specialty. For general computer forensics facilities, a multipurpose forensic workstation is sufficient.

Private companies conducting internal investigations can determine what types of forensic workstations they need, based on the types of computers they use. If a company uses only Windows PCs, internal investigators don't need a wide variety of specialized equipment. If a company uses many kinds of computers, the lab needs systems and equipment that support the same types of computers.

## Maintaining Operating Systems and Software Inventories

Operating systems are an essential part of a lab's inventory. A lab should maintain licensed copies of legacy operating systems to handle cases involving those systems. Microsoft operating systems should include Windows 7, Vista, XP, and NT. Macintosh operating systems should include Mac OS X, 9.x, and 8 or older. If an organization uses a UNIX, Linux, or Ubuntu operating system, the lab should maintain current and previous versions of those systems.

Although most high-end system forensics tools can open or display data files created with popular programs, they don't support all programs. A lab's software inventory should include current and older versions of the following programs:

- Microsoft Office
- StarOffice/OpenOffice
- Corel Office Suite
- Database applications
- Programming and development environments, such as Microsoft Visual Studio, Intel assemblers and compilers such as C++, and specialized image viewers, such as ACDSee, ThumbsPlus, XnView, and IrfanView
- If the lab handles a lot of financial investigations, QuickBooks and Peachtree accounting applications

 **NOTE**

Some computer forensics programs enable a forensic specialist to work from a machine running one operating system and examine disk drives running other operating systems. For example, a specialist may be able to use a Windows PC to examine both Windows and Macintosh disk drives.

**4**

Forensics Methods and Labs

If a lab deals with both Windows PCs and Macintosh systems, it should have these programs for both platforms.

Table 4-2 lists some common system forensics software tools that a lab can expect to need.

**TABLE 4-2**    Forensic software tools.

| CATEGORY OF TOOLS | EXAMPLES |
|---|---|
| Chat recovery tools | Chat Examiner |
| Computer activity tracking tools | Visual TimeAnalyser |
| Disk imaging software | SnapBack DatArrest, SafeBack |
| E-mail recovery tools | Email Examiner, Network Email Examiner |
| File deletion software | PDWipe and Darik's Boot and Nuke (DBAN) |
| File integrity checkers | FileMon, File Date Time Extractor (FDTE), Decode–Forensic Data/Time Decoder |
| Forensic work environments | X-Ways Forensics |
| Internet history viewers | Cookie Decoder, Cookie View, Cache View, FavURLView, NetAnalysis |
| Linux/UNIX tools | Ltools, Mtools |
| Multipurpose tools and tool kits | Maresware, LC Technologies Software, WinHEX Specialist Edition, Prodiscover DFT, NTI Tools, Access Data, FTK, EnCase |
| Partition managers | Partimage |
| Password recovery tools | @Stake, Decryption Collection Enterprise, AIM Password Decoder, Microsoft Access Database Password Decoder |
| Slack space and data recovery tools | Ontrack Easy Recovery, Paraben Device Seizure 1.0, Forensic Sorter, Directory Snoop |
| Specialized software for analyzing registries, finding open ports, patching file bytes, simplifying log file analysis, removing plug-ins, examining P2P software, and examining SIM cards and various brands of phones | Registry Analyzer, Regmon, DiamondCS OpenPorts, Port Explorer, Vision, Autoruns, Autostart Viewer, Patchit, PyFlag, Pasco Belkasoft RemovEx, KaZAlyser, Oxygen Phone Manager for Nokia phones, SIM Card Seizure |
| Text search tools | Evidor |

## Stocking Other Items

Forensics labs should stock a wide assortment of cables and spare expansion slot cards. A computer forensics lab should consider stocking the following peripheral devices and other tools:

- An assortment of integrated development environment (IDE) cables and ribbon cables for CDs
- Extra Small Computer System Interface (SCSI), cards, graphics cards, and extra power cords
- A variety of hard drives—as many as possible and in as wide a variety as possible
- 2.5-inch adapters from notebook IDE hard drives to standard IDE/advanced technology attachment (ATA) drives, Serial ATA (SATA) drives, and so on
- Computer hand tools, such as Phillips head and slotted screwdrivers, a socket wrench, and a small flashlight
- Power testing equipment
- Hardware write-blockers, such as PDBlock, Write-blocker, Nowrite, Lockdown, FireWire Drive Dock, IDE Drivelock kit, and SATA Drivelock kit
- Write-protect card readers
- Data sanitization tools, such as WipeMASSter
- High-speed data duplication tools, such as ImageMASSter products

# Policies, Processes, and Procedures for Maintaining a Lab

A number of organizations have created guidelines for lab processes and procedures. An organization should consider available policies and procedures developed by others as a basis for creating policies and procedures specific to its own work environment and organizational objectives. A lab should also establish a process for measuring and enforcing compliance with lab policies and procedures.

## Creating a Disaster Recovery Plan

A computer forensics lab must plan for disasters, such as hard disk crashes, lightning strikes, and power outages. A **disaster recovery plan** helps a lab restore its workstations and file servers to their original condition after a catastrophic failure occurs.

A disaster recovery plan must also specify how to rebuild a forensic workstation after it has been severely contaminated by a virus from a drive it is analyzing. Central to any disaster recovery plan is a system for backing up investigation computers. Tools such as Norton Ghost are useful for restoring files directly.

**TIP**

As a general precaution, it is a good idea to back up a workstation once a week. It is possible to restore programs from the original disks or CDs, but recovering lost data without up-to-date backups is difficult.

A forensics lab should store system backups where they are easily accessible. It should also have at least one copy of backups onsite and a duplicate copy or a previous copy of backups stored in a safe offsite facility. Offsite backups should be rotated on a schedule that varies according to the lab's needs, such as every day, week, or month.

In addition, an organization should record all updates it makes to its workstations by using a process called **configuration management**. Some companies record updates in a configuration management database to maintain compliance with lab policy. Every time someone adds or updates software on a workstation, he or she should enter the change in the database or in a simple notebook to document the changes.

A disaster recovery plan can also address how to restore a workstation that is reconfigured for a specific investigation. For example, if a forensic specialist installs a suite of applications, the workstation might not have enough disk space for normal processing needs, causing problems during reconfigurations or even simple upgrades. The disaster recovery plan should outline how to uninstall software and delete any files the uninstall program hasn't removed in order to restore a system to its original configuration.

> **TIP**
>
> When planning a recovery procedure for RAID servers, a lab should consider whether the amount of downtime it takes to restore backup data is acceptable to the lab operation.

Labs using high-end redundant arrays of inexpensive disks (RAID) servers must consider methods for restoring large data sets. These large servers must have adequate data backup systems available in case of a major failure of more than one drive.

## Planning for Equipment Upgrades

Risk management involves determining how much risk is acceptable for any process or operation, such as replacing equipment. A lab should identify the equipment it depends on and create a schedule for replacing that equipment. The lab should also identify equipment that it can replace when it fails.

Computing components are designed to last 18 to 36 months in normal business operations, and new versions of operating systems and applications that take up more disk space are released frequently. Therefore, systems periodically need more random access memory (RAM), disk space, and processing speed. To keep a lab current with updates in hardware technology, the facility should schedule hardware replacements at least every 18 months and preferably every 12 months.

## CHAPTER SUMMARY

The goal of a forensic investigation is to collect data and find a way to use it as evidence. Evidence must be collected properly and deemed authentic to be forensically sound. This chapter discusses the DFRWS framework and an event-based digital forensic investigation framework, both of which investigators can use to ensure forensic soundness of evidence.

Getting started with forensic investigation involves setting up a lab facility that is physically secure so that evidence is not lost, corrupted, or destroyed. The lab should contain a variety of hardware and software, such as instruments, current and legacy software, and forensic workstations. This chapter details some options for setting up an effective computer forensics laboratory. It provides a foundation for organizing, controlling, and managing a safe, efficient computer forensics laboratory. It also discusses policies, processes, and procedures for maintaining a lab.

## KEY CONCEPTS AND TERMS

American Society of Crime
   Laboratory Directors (ASCLD)
Business case
Computer-generated
   information
Configuration management
DFRWS framework

Digital Forensics Research
   Workshop (DFRWS)
Disaster recovery plan
Event-based digital forensic
   investigation framework
Evidence storage container
Evidence storage room

Federal Rules of Evidence (FRE)
Forensic soundness
Human-generated information
Lab manager
Rules of evidence
TEMPEST

## CHAPTER 4 ASSESSMENT

1. To be _____, data must be complete and materially unaltered.

2. Which of the following governs whether, when, how, and why proof of a legal case can be placed before a judge or jury?

    A. Forensic soundness
    B. Computer-generated evidence
    C. Rules of evidence
    D. Human-generated evidence

3. A framework for digital investigation to ensure forensic soundness must have six phases.

    A. True
    B. False

4. A _____ can help justify the acquisition of newer and better resources to investigate computer forensics cases.

5. Which of the following provides guidelines for managing a forensics lab and acquiring crime and forensics lab certification?

    A. NIST
    B. ASCLD
    C. FRE
    D. DFRWS

6. Only very large computer forensics labs need a lab manager.

    A. True
    B. False

7. Which of the following costs should a computer forensics lab budget include? (Select three.)

    A. Facility costs
    B. Hardware costs
    C. Software costs
    D. Law enforcement costs
    E. Cleaning costs

8. Staff members in a computer forensics lab should have sufficient training to perform their tasks. Necessary skill sets include all *except* which of the following?

    A. Hardware knowledge
    B. Software knowledge
    C. Background as an attorney
    D. Deductive reasoning

9. A forensic workstation should be set up in a secure room in a forensics lab. What are some important features for such a room? (Select three.)

    A. Large room
    B. Floor-to-ceiling walls
    C. Locking doors
    D. Fireproof doors
    E. Secure containers that lock

10. Every organization should strive to make its lab a TEMPEST-qualified lab facility.

    A. True
    B. False

11. Evidence storage containers should store only current evidence. Evidence for closed cases should be moved to a secure offsite facility.

    A. True
    B. False

12. Which of the following logs should a computer forensics lab keep? (Select two.)

    A. Computer use log
    B. Lab visitors' log
    C. Evidence container log
    D. Criminal log

13. A forensics lab work area requires approximately _____ square feet.

14. Which of the following does a forensics lab *not* need to stock?

    A. Workstations
    B. Operating systems
    C. Legal manuals
    D. Hard drives

15. As a general precaution, it is a good idea to back up a workstation once a month.

    A. True
    B. False

# PART TWO

# Technical Overview: System Forensics Tools, Techniques, and Methods

# System Forensics Technologies

A S EXPLAINED IN CHAPTER 1, "System Forensics Fundamentals," system forensics is the art and science of locating, extracting, analyzing, and protecting data from devices and networks. Specialists interpret this data and use it as legal evidence. The field of system forensics has been a mainstay for law enforcement and military agencies since the mid-1980s. It is relatively new to the private sector but is rapidly growing.

This chapter looks at specific types of system forensics technology that specialists in the military, law enforcement, and business use. The analytical techniques are the same for each category. However, the focus of investigations differs, depending on the specifics of the case. Perpetrators have different motives, and their actions have different impacts. Attacks range from trouble-making attempts to theft to attacks that cripple corporations or even governments. Some perpetrators go to great lengths to frustrate a forensic investigation. A forensic investigator must know how to choose and use the most suitable technology for a given case.

## Chapter 5 Topics

This chapter covers the following topics and concepts:

- How the military uses system forensics
- Which technologies law enforcement agencies use
- How businesses use system forensics technologies
- Which system forensics tools are commonly used

### Chapter 5 Goals

When you complete this chapter, you will be able to:

- Understand how the military uses system forensics
- Explain law enforcement system forensics technologies
- Understand the types of system forensics technologies that businesses use
- Describe commonly used system forensics tools

## How the Military Uses System Forensics

The U.S. **Department of Defense (DoD)** coordinates and supervises agencies and functions of the government related to national security and the U.S. armed forces. The DoD uses system forensics to evaluate and examine data related to cyberattacks. The DoD estimates the potential impact of malicious activity. It also assesses the intent and identity of perpetrators.

The **DoD Cyber Crime Center (DC3)** sets standards for digital evidence processing, analysis, and diagnostics. It is involved with DoD investigation that requires computer forensics support to detect, enhance, or recover digital media. DC3 is also involved in criminal law enforcement forensics and counterintelligence. It assists in criminal, counterintelligence, counterterrorism, and fraud investigations. In addition, it supports safety investigations and Inspector General and commander-directed inquiries.

>  **NOTE**
>
> Real-time tracking of potentially malicious activity is especially difficult when a perpetrator has intentionally or maliciously hidden, destroyed, or modified the pertinent information to elude discovery.

DC3 provides computer investigation training. It trains forensic examiners, investigators, system administrators, and others. It also ensures that defense information systems are secure from unauthorized use, criminal and fraudulent activities, and foreign intelligence service exploitation. DC3 partners with government, academic, and private industry computer security officials.

For more information on DC3, see *http://www.dc3.mil.*

## Which Technologies Law Enforcement Agencies Use

Law enforcement agencies use system forensics tools to identify leads and process computer-related evidence. System forensics tools and techniques are important resources in criminal and internal investigations, civil lawsuits, and computer security risk management.

**5**

System Forensics
Technologies

83

Law enforcement forensic specialists use a variety of system forensics technologies. They apply software tools and methods to identify and retrieve passwords, logon information, e-mail messages, accounting information, and other data stored on digital devices or media. They also employ forensic software tools to identify backdated files, tie disks to the computers on which they were created, recover deleted files, and locate data that someone attempted to hide. Like the military, law enforcement agencies have been involved in processing computer evidence for many years.

This section touches on issues related to Windows operating systems and their use in law enforcement system forensics. Many laptop and desktop personal computers (PCs) in corporations and government agencies run the Windows XP, Vista, and 7 operating systems. Those involved in computer investigations and computer security reviews are most likely to encounter these operating systems. The forensic concepts presented here do, however, also apply to non-Windows systems, such as UNIX, Linux, and Mac, although the software and techniques for each differ.

The following sections describe some technologies that are especially important in law enforcement system forensics. Many of these technologies also apply to military and business settings.

## Evidence Preservation

Computer evidence is fragile. A person can easily alter or destroy it. System forensics specialists must know how to use bit stream backup to ensure the preservation of all storage levels that may contain evidence.

## Trojan Horse Programs

A Trojan horse program is an independent program that, when called by an authorized user, performs a useful function. At the same time, it also performs unauthorized functions, often usurping the privileges of the user. Perpetrators may plant these programs and traps with the intention of capturing sensitive data, such as Social Security numbers, passwords, and network logons. Or they may plant them to destroy data and evidence or modify an operating system. A system forensics specialist must know how to identify, use, avoid, and defeat Trojan horse programs.

## Documentation of Methodologies and Findings

Documentation of forensic processing methodologies and findings is critical. Without proper documentation, a forensic specialist has difficulty presenting findings. When security or audit findings become the object of a lawsuit or a criminal investigation, the legal system requires proper documentation. Without documentation, courts are unlikely to accept investigative results. Thus, a system forensics specialist must know the ins and outs of computer evidence processing methodology. This methodology includes strong evidence-processing documentation and good chain of custody procedures.

## Disk Structure

A system forensics specialist should have a good understanding of how computer hard disks and CDs are structured. A specialist should also know how to find data hidden in obscure places on CDs and hard disk drives.

## File Slack Searching

A system forensics specialist should understand techniques and automated tools used to capture and evaluate file slack. A hard disk or CD is segmented into clusters of a particular size. Each cluster can hold only one file. If you write a 1 KB file to a disk that has a cluster size of 4 KB, the last 3 KB of the cluster is wasted. This unused space between the logical end-of-file and the physical end-of-file is known as *file slack* (see Figure 5-1). Most computer users have no idea that they're creating slack space as they use a computer. In addition, data from a file may remain even after you delete it. This residual data in file slack is not necessarily overwritten when you create a new file. File slack is therefore a source of potential security leaks involving passwords, network logons, e-mail, database entries, and word processing documents. A forensic specialist should know how to search file slack, identify what is and is not useful data, document any findings, and eliminate security risks.

## Data-Hiding Techniques

Trade secret information and other sensitive data can easily be hidden using a number of techniques. Data can also be unintentionally left behind. It is possible to hide disks within disks and even to hide entire computer hard disk drive partitions.

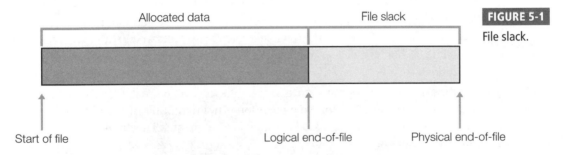

**FIGURE 5-1**

File slack.

Allocated data      File slack

Start of file      Logical end-of-file      Physical end-of-file

### Types of Empty Space

While definitions vary, in general, three types of empty space on a disk or drive are important to forensics:

- **Unused space**—**Unused space** is what's left after a file is deleted. The computer takes the reference to that file out of its index of files, but the data is not erased. Rather, all the data is left behind on the disk. The computer considers this space unused and available for reuse.
- **Unallocated space**—**Unallocated space**, or free space, is the unused portion of the hard drive that is not allocated to any volume.
- **File slack**—**File slack**, or slack space, is the unused space that is created between the end-of-file marker and the end of the hard drive cluster in which the file is stored.

Forensic specialists can often find evidence in file slack and in unallocated file space. These types of computer data are called **ambient computer data**, or residual data. Examples of ambient computer data are document fragments, e-mail fragments, and directory tree snapshots. As much as half of a computer hard disk drive may contain such data. Ambient computer data can be a valuable source of computer evidence. It can potentially provide a large volume of data, and the computer user generally doesn't know that data was created.

A forensic specialist should understand these issues from a detection standpoint, as well as from a security risk standpoint. A forensic specialist should know how to use the software tools discussed later in this chapter to find hidden data. Figure 5-2 shows eight places on hard drives where data can be hidden:

1. **Host protected area (HPA)**—The **host protected area (HPA)** was designed as an area where computer vendors could store data that is protected from user activities and operating system utilities, such as delete and format. To hide data in the HPA, a person would need to write a program to access the HPA and write the data.

2. **Master boot record (MBR)**—The **master boot record (MBR)** requires only a single sector, leaving 62 empty sectors of MBR space for hiding data.

3. **Volume slack**—The volume slack is the space that remains on a hard drive if the partitions do not use all the available space. Say that two partitions are filled with data. When you delete one of them, the data is not actually deleted. Instead, it is hidden.

4. **Partition slack**—File systems store data in blocks, which are made of sectors. If the total number of sectors in a partition is not a multiple of the block size, leftover sectors can't be accessed through typical means. They make a good place to hide data.

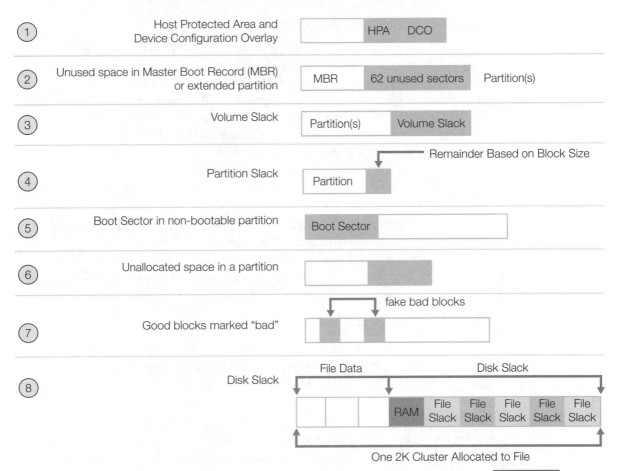

FIGURE 5-2

Data hiding.

5. **Boot sector in a non-bootable partition**—Every partition contains
   a boot sector. In some cases, that partition isn't bootable. The boot sectors
   in non-bootable partitions are available to hide data.

6. **Unallocated space**—An operating system can't access any unallocated space
   in a partition. That space can contain hidden data.

7. **Good blocks marked as bad**—Say that someone manipulates the file system
   metadata to mark unusable blocks as bad. The operating system will no longer
   access these blocks. These blocks can then be used to hide data.

8. **File slack**—As mentioned earlier, file slack is the unused space that is created
   between the end-of-file marker and the end of the hard drive cluster in which
   the file is stored.

## Fuzzy Logic Tools for Identifying Unknown Text

With traditional computer evidence searches, a user should know what he or she is searching for. However, a forensic specialist may not know what is stored on a given computer system. In such cases, the investigator can apply fuzzy logic tools to provide valuable leads about how the subject computer was used. A **fuzzy logic tool** is a tool used to identify unknown strings of text by searching for values between "completely true" and "completely false." A system forensics specialist should be able to use such tools to identify evidence in file slack, unallocated file space, and Windows swap files. Filter_G, discussed later in this chapter, is an example of a fuzzy logic tool.

## Data Encryption

A system forensics specialist should understand the basics of how data is encrypted. A specialist should also be able to illustrate the differences between good encryption and bad encryption. Some software, including Word, Excel, Lotus, PKZIP, and WordPerfect, uses security to provide limited encryption. A specialist should know how to use software to crack this security. Encryption is covered later in this chapter.

## Disk-to-Computer Matching

Computers leave traces of their activity when writing to a hard drive or removable media. A forensic specialist should know how to use specialized techniques and tools to tie a CD to a computer that was used to create or edit files stored on the CD.

## Data Compression

**Compression** is the process of encoding information with fewer bits than the unencoded information would use (see Figure 5-3). Compression programs can be used to hide or disguise sensitive data. A system forensics specialist should understand how compression works.

**FIGURE 5-3**

Data compression.

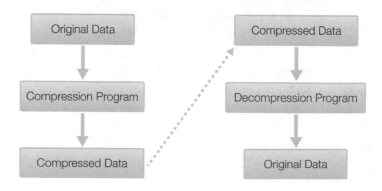

## Recovery of Erased Files

A system forensics specialist should know how to recover previously erased files. A specialist can recover these files by using file recovery software and manual data-recovery techniques.

## Internet Abuse Identification and Detection

A system forensics specialist should understand how to use specialized software to identify how a targeted computer has been used on the Internet. The specialist should know how to examine file slack, unallocated file space, and Windows swap files to find data pertinent to the investigation.

## The Boot Process and Memory-Resident Programs

A user can modify an operating system to change and destroy data. For example, a hacker might use this technique to covertly capture keyboard activity from corporate executives. A system forensics specialist should understand how to examine the boot process and memory-resident programs.

## Flash Memory Media Processing

**Flash memory media** are computer memory chips or cards that retain data without being connected to a power source. They are popular storage devices in digital cameras and other portable electronic gadgets. In recent years, their storage capacities have grown significantly. Because of their ubiquity, these storage devices are commonly part of system forensics examinations. (See the sidebar, "Processing Data Stored in Flash Memory.")

# How Businesses Use System Forensics Technologies

Companies keep their proprietary information and business processes on computers and networks. Therefore, threats to the strategic value of a business almost always involve a computer or network. A simple and virtually undetectable fraud that posts a few cents to a phony account can reap a perpetrator thousands of dollars. A malicious change to an individual's personnel records could cost the innocent person a job and a career. Divulging a company's financial records could damage it on Wall Street, in the marketplace, and with shareholders. Hackers involved in corporate espionage steal trade secrets. Posting libelous information on the Internet about a company or an individual can damage a reputation beyond recovery. Employees of a company might steal from it or use company resources for their own benefit.

Companies turn to system forensics in many situations. For example, they might need system forensics to deal with litigation, such as a wrongful termination suit. They also need system forensics when there is an actual or suspected incident with a serious risk of information being compromised. In addition, they use system forensics when

## Processing Data Stored in Flash Memory

Flash memory cards are used in digital cameras, handheld computers, mobile phones, personal digital assistants (PDAs), and other devices. In dealing with identity theft and fraud, a system forensics specialist may need to process flash memory cards.

A flash memory card is a type of EEPROM chip. (EEPROM stands for *electronically erasable programmable read-only memory.*) Flash memory maintains its data without any external power source. For example, photographs remain on a flash memory card even after the user has removed the card from a digital camera. In contrast, flash random-access memory (RAM) loses its data when it no longer has a power supply. For example, a car radio's presets are erased when a mechanic removes the car's battery.

Computers can write to any flash media they are connected to. Thus, a forensic specialist must protect flash media and the potential evidence it contains against loss or corruption. One precaution a specialist should take is to make mirrored copies of flash drives. Some flash memory media have write-protect tabs or a slider switch that can be moved to prevent writes. However, Windows-based programs often do not read a flash memory storage device that is write-protected. And some forms of flash memory media do not have write-protection. As with all other computer evidence processing, with flash memory, evidence preservation is a priority.

According to Fred Wiechmann, an officer with the Portland Police Bureau, a forensic specialist may need to remove flash media from the device and place it into a compatible reader. He or she may install this reader on the forensic workstation. Or connect it to the workstation using a Universal Serial Bus (USB) or FireWire port on the computer. When evaluating flash memory, a forensic specialist should place the media in the reader and then start the computer in DOS mode. After the computer boots, it will recognize the flash memory media as a standard FAT12 or FAT16 storage device.

The forensic specialist can use an evidence-grade bit stream imaging software program, such as SafeBack, to make a backup image of the data stored on the flash memory media. (For more information on SafeBack, see *http://www.forensics-intl.com/safeback.html.*) The forensic specialist can then process the bit stream backup image as a standard computer storage device. The resulting restored image includes allocated files and deleted files that may contain relevant leads and evidence.

At this point, the forensic specialist can feed the backup image directly into a tool such as ILook (see *http://www.perlustro.com/ustreasury_website/index.html*). Or the specialist can restore the backup image to another drive for evidence processing. The specialist may also use a tool such as GFE Stealth (*http://www.forensics-intl.com/iextract.html*) to automatically extract all deleted and allocated graphics files stored on the original flash memory media.

If the batteries were at some point removed from the suspect device, the date and time on the device will have reverted to the default date and time. However, if the batteries have been left in the device, a forensic specialist can start the device and look at the date and time setting. The specialist can then compare this setting to the date on the files in the backup image to determine when various events occurred.

### Using Forensics to Monitor Employees

A business may call a system forensics specialist if an employee is using the company's computer for personal reasons on the company's time. The employee might be using the Web to access adult Web sites, search auction sites, engage in peer-to-peer file transfers, or swap music and movies using company bandwidth. The legality of such activities is a gray area. Many companies have adopted limited-use policies. Such policies allow employees to use company computers for personal business as long as their activities do not affect their work. Employees must also understand that all activity is monitored and that inappropriate activities will be sanctioned and may result in dismissal and prosecution. An employee suspected of engaging in inappropriate activities might try to delete information in the hope that no one will find the files or other evidence.

A company may hire a forensic specialist to gather various types of information from an employee's computer. A specialist can recover deleted files, track network activity, and create reports that summarize the employee's activities. This can give the company legal, binding evidence against an employee.

they face a potential loss of competitive capability or potential damage to reputation and brand. Some companies regularly use forensic investigations to check employee computers. In theory, employees are less tempted to stray when they know their company is watching them. In addition, companies check for Trojans and other malware.

Disgruntled insiders may launch attacks from within a protected network. In recent years, malicious-minded individuals have assaulted numerous e-commerce Web sites with denial of service (DoS) attacks. Attackers have committed other malevolent acts against corporations and governments, including spreading viruses, wiretapping, and committing financial fraud. Cybercrime costs the United States billions of dollars in unrealized profits and exposes organizations to significant risk.

System forensics specialists must be familiar with a number of basic techniques and tools for investigating computer-related crimes. They should be able to trace the source of an e-mail message, acquire digital evidence, and crack passwords. In addition, they may need to monitor computers remotely, track online activity, find and recover hidden and deleted data, and locate stolen computers.

The following sections discuss a number of system forensics technologies used to investigate business systems.

**Forensic Services**

Forensic experts must understand and be able to perform services such as the following:

- Recovery of lost passwords and files
- Location and retrieval of deleted and hidden files
- File and e-mail decryption
- E-mail supervision and authentication
- Tracing of threatening e-mail messages to their sources
- Identification of Internet activity
- Computer usage policy and supervision
- Remote PC and network monitoring
- Tracking and location of stolen electronic files
- Traps for cybercriminals that involve **honeypots**—a system or data that is attractive to hackers
- Location and identity of unauthorized software users
- Theft recovery software for laptops and PCs
- Creation of investigative and security software
- Protection from hackers and viruses

> **TIP**
>
> The legal restrictions regarding collection of data apply whether an investigator physically takes control of a computer or gains remote access. Thus, an investigator must have a search warrant, subpoena, or authorization by the system owner before collecting data remotely.

## Remote Monitoring of Target Computers

Forensic tools can remotely monitor activities of target computers. System forensics specialists can use tools to remotely seize and secure digital evidence before physically entering suspect premises. These tools include F-Response (*http://www.f-response.com*) and various key- and screen-logging tools.

## Trackable Electronic Documents

Intrusion detection tools allow the user to create trackable electronic documents. These tools identify unauthorized intruders who access, download, and view tagged documents. The tools also allow security personnel to trace the chain of custody of all who possess stolen electronic documents.

## Theft Recovery Software for Laptops and PCs

Most stolen computers are never recovered. Laptop theft costs U.S. businesses billions of dollars each year. Consider the real costs to replace a stolen computer:

- The price of replacing the hardware
- The price of replacing the software
- The cost of re-creating data—if re-creating the data is even possible

- The cost of lost production time or instruction time
- The loss of customer goodwill due to lost faxes, delayed correspondence or billing, and problems answering questions and accessing data
- The cost of reporting and investigating the theft, including the time required to file police reports and insurance claims
- The cost of increased insurance
- If personally identifying information or financial data is lost, huge fines and mandatory audits for up to 20 years, as well as litigation costs
- The cost of processing and ordering replacements, cutting checks, and so on
- If law enforcement catches the thief, then the cost of time involved in prosecution

**NOTE**

In some cases, a company can't re-create data. The theft of a laptop containing sensitive data could be devastating for a small business. The data a device holds can be worth many times the cost of replacing the hardware and software.

To prevent such losses, a business can install software to track and locate a lost or stolen PC or laptop anywhere in the world. One option is PC PhoneHome (*http://www .pcphonehome.com*). PC PhoneHome sends a stealth e-mail to a designated e-mail address once a day or every time the user connects to the Internet and is assigned an IP address different from the previous IP address. If the computer is lost or stolen, the user reports the loss to the police and uses the PC PhoneHome Recovery Center to monitor the designated e-mail address. When the stolen computer accesses the Internet by any method, the lost or stolen computer sends a stealth e-mail message that gives its location.

## Handling Evidence

Preserving computer evidence requires planning and training in incident discovery procedures. The following sections describe tasks related to handling evidence and measures to take when gathering evidence.

**FYI**

System administrators sometimes think they are helping a forensic examiner when they are actually destroying evidence. Managers should minimize disturbance of the computer, peripherals, and area surrounding a machine under investigation. In addition, consider the following advice:

- If a computer is turned on, leave it on, and if it is turned off, leave it off.
- Never run programs on a subject computer. For example, running Windows to examine files destroys evidence in the swap file.
- Never let a suspect help open or turn on a machine.
- Never let a technically inexperienced individual examine computers or devices. Evidence that these people collect is almost always inadmissible in court.

**5**

System Forensics
Technologies

### Evidence-Handling Tasks

A system forensics specialist has three basic tasks related to handling evidence:

- **Find evidence**—Gathering computer evidence goes beyond normal data recovery. Finding and isolating evidence to prove or disprove allegations can be difficult. Investigators may need to investigate thousands of active files and fragments of deleted files to find just one that makes a case. System forensics has therefore been described as looking for one needle in a mountain of needles. Examiners often work in secure laboratories, where they check for viruses in suspect machines and isolate data to avoid contamination. (For more information on system forensics labs, see Chapter 4, "Forensics Methods and Labs.")

- **Preserve evidence**—Preserving computer evidence is important because data can be destroyed easily. The 1s and 0s that make up data can be hidden and vanish instantly with the push of a button. As a result, forensic examiners should assume that every computer has been rigged to destroy evidence. They must proceed with care in handling computers and storage media.

- **Prepare evidence**—Evidence must be able to withstand judicial scrutiny. Therefore, preparing evidence requires patience and thorough documentation. Failing to document where evidence comes from and ensure that it has not been changed can ruin a case. Judges have dismissed cases because of such failures.

### Evidence-Gathering Measures

Forensic specialists should take the following measures when gathering evidence:

- **Avoid changing the evidence**—Forensic specialists should photograph equipment in place before removing it. They should label wires and sockets so computers and peripherals can be reassembled exactly in a laboratory. They should transport computers, peripherals, and media carefully to avoid heat damage or jostling. They should avoid touching original computer hard disks and CDs. They should make exact bit-by-bit copies and store the copies on a medium that cannot be altered, such as a CD-ROM.

- **Determine when evidence was created**—Timelines of computer usage and file accesses can be valuable sources of computer evidence. The times and dates when files were created, last accessed, or modified can make or break a case. Forensic specialists should not trust a computer's internal clock or activity logs. The internal clock might be wrong, a suspect might have tampered with logs, or the mere act of turning on the computer might change a log irrevocably. Before logs disappear, an investigator should capture the time a document was created, the last time it was opened, and the last time it was changed. The investigator can then calibrate or recalibrate evidence, based on a time standard, and work around log tampering.

- **Trust only physical evidence**—The physical level of magnetic materials is where the 1s and 0s of data are recorded. In system forensics, only this physical level is real. A forensic specialist should consider everything else untrustworthy. For example, a suspect might have corrupted all the software operating systems, applications, and communications on a computer. Or software itself might erase evidence while it operates.

- **Search throughout a device**—Forensic specialists must search at the bit level. That is, they should search at the level of 1s and 0s across a wide range of areas inside a computer. This includes e-mail and temporary files in the operating system and in databases. Specialists should also search swap files that hold data temporarily, logical file structures, and slack and free space on the hard drive. They must also search software settings and script files that perform preset activities. In addition, they must investigate Web browser data caches, bookmarks and history, and session logs that record patterns of usage. Forensic specialists can then correlate evidence to activities and sources.

- **Determine the contents of encrypted files**—Investigators often should not attempt to decode encrypted files. Rather, they should look for evidence in a computer that tells them what is in the encrypted file. Frequently, this evidence has been erased, but unencrypted traces remain to make a case. For data concealed within other files or buried inside the 1s and 0s of a picture, an investigator can tell if the data is there even though it is inaccessible. The investigator can compare nearly identical files to identify minute differences.

- **Present the evidence well**—Forensic examiners must present computer evidence in a logical, compelling, and persuasive manner. A jury must be able to understand the evidence. In addition, the evidence should be solid enough that a defense counsel cannot rebut it. Therefore, a forensic specialist must create a step-by-step reconstruction of actions, with documented dates and times. In addition, the specialist must prepare charts and graphs that explain what was done and how as well as exhibits. All these charts, graphs, and other exhibits must be able to withstand scrutiny. The specialist's testimony must explain simply and clearly what a suspect did or did not do.

## Encryption Methods and Vulnerabilities

Encryption is the process of making data unreadable to anyone except those who have the correct key. The use of encryption provides a unique challenge for a forensic specialist. Decryption is the process of making encrypted material readable again. Decryption provides a potentially greater obstacle than data recovery. Encryption, whether built into an application or provided by a separate software package, comes in different types and strengths.

**FYI**

Case presentation requires experience, which a forensic specialist can gain only through experience. An experienced examiner knows the questions that opposing attorneys will ask and the ways to provide answers that withstand challenge. A skilled litigator can defeat an inexperienced examiner for failing to collect evidence properly and failing to show that evidence supports allegations. Not long ago, attorneys knew little about computers and how they operated. However, attorneys are increasingly skilled at challenging examiners' methods.

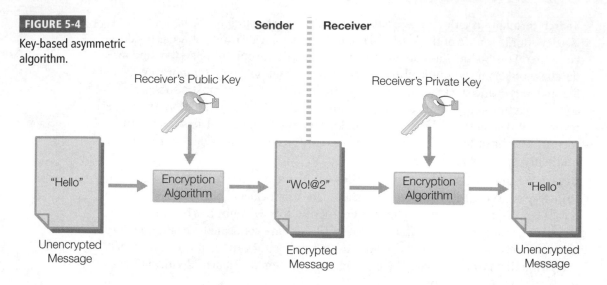

**FIGURE 5-4**

Key-based asymmetric algorithm.

## How Encryption Works

The objective of encryption is to protect information by scrambling the data into an unrecognizable form. An encryption process consists of two basic components:

- An algorithm that provides specific computer instructions about how information is to be scrambled
- A key that provides direction to the algorithm about the specific order in which the algorithm is to execute

The same algorithm and key used to encrypt information must be used to decrypt the information. As shown in Figure 5-4, some encryption processes provide for two keys. One of the keys performs the customary encryption and decryption functions. The other is a public key that can decrypt the information but cannot encrypt information.

According to Jamie Morris in "Forensics on the Windows Platform, Part Two," even when facing tough encryption, a forensic specialist may still be able to decrypt data by widening the scope of the investigation to include intelligence sources beyond the suspect computer. For example, **public-key cryptography** can be used to create highly secure, encrypted data. Decrypting data encrypted in this fashion requires a public key and a private key. The investigator might find the private key on the suspect's machine or backed up to removable media. Similarly, the investigator might find the public key recorded somewhere on the computer in case it is forgotten or written down and kept in a nearby location.

A number of different encryption algorithms are used in information technology systems. Algorithms differ in their strength. Some are more able than others to resist attempts to bypass or breach the encryption. The U.S. National Institute of Standards and Technology (NIST) is a measurement standards laboratory in the U.S. Department of Commerce. According to its Web site, NIST's mission is "to promote U.S. innovation and industrial competitiveness by advancing measurement science, standards, and technology in ways that enhance economic security and improve our quality of life." NIST certifies the integrity and robustness of encryption algorithms. All federal systems must use NIST-certified encryption algorithms. Many other organizations also choose to use these algorithms.

For more information on NIST, see *http://www.nist.gov.*

It is very unlikely that information that has been encrypted using a NIST-certified algorithm can be decrypted without the decryption key. Thus, when hackers and forensic specialists encounter an encrypted file, they first try to determine what encryption algorithm has most likely been used. If a NIST-certified algorithm was used, the hacker or forensic specialist focuses on determining the encryption key.

Some of the most commonly used applications provide encryption protected by passwords. These products—such as word processing and spreadsheet software— use algorithms that are not NIST certified. Investigators who have the right tools and the time to use them can defeat the passwords used in these products. It is possible to compromise these products by using widely available software.

Phil Zimmerman invented **Pretty Good Privacy (PGP)**, a widely used encryption program, more than a decade ago. Of the 1.8 billion people using the Internet today, about 113 million use PGP to encrypt e-mail. Another 400 million use other forms of encryption. PGP is also used for whole-disk or file-level encryption. PGP uses two keys and a NIST-certified algorithm. It makes encrypted data practically impossible to decipher without the appropriate key.

Encryption is now one of the most common controls for protecting information both when stored and in transit. For example, the Internet uses encrypted protocols— HTTPS and TLS—to secure financial transactions over the Web.

## Problems with Encryption

Encryption has two basic problems:

- **Key management**—Encryption users must retain the encryption key. Without the key, the scrambled information usually can't be decrypted. To avoid losing the key, encryption users often "hide" the encryption key on a note in their wallet or desk. Anyone who has physical access to the user's wallet or desk can copy the key and use it to decrypt the information. Just as users often create weak passwords that they can easily remember, they often create weak encryption keys that are easy to remember. Unfortunately, others who know something about these users can often guess the keys. Further, hackers have developed sniffers—software that captures keystrokes as they are entered and transmits those keystrokes to a hacker. A hacker who has physical access to a computer can generally install a sniffer to collect encryption keys and passwords. Once the sniffer collects and transmits this information to the hacker, the hacker has access to the user's encrypted information. The hacker could even change the encryption key and deny the user access to his or her own information.

- **Key distribution**—Encryption is often used to protect information that is shared among multiple users. Everyone who is to share the information must have the decryption key. However, distributing the key to these individuals means multiple machines can decrypt messages. This creates a vulnerability.

These two problems with encryption don't help just hackers. Forensic specialists can also take advantage of them. For example, a forensic specialist who has the appropriate legal authorization could plant a sniffer and covertly collect any needed passwords. In addition, the forensic specialist could retrieve a key from any of the individuals sharing encrypted information.

## Security and Wireless Technologies

Your PDA contains a lot of personal information. The more you use your PDA, the greater the chance that a thief could extract data that accurately reflects and tells a story about you. Recognizing the potential vulnerabilities of PDAs, government and major commercial organizations generally require that all PDAs use encrypted storage and transmissions. Protecting PDA data from thieves and attackers, however, also poses obstacles for forensic specialists.

Most forensic acquisitions focus on performing a bit-by-bit copy of the original media. They then compare the unique cryptographic signatures of the original and the copy to ensure that they match. This process is well established in traditional hard drive-based computer forensics. Hard drives can be removed, and many computers can start in special read-only forensic environments. However, the process for mobile forensic devices is quite challenging. With mobile devices such as smartphones, the primary memory is typically not removable. In addition, mobile devices have limited operating systems and cannot boot into a forensic environment. To perform forensics on mobile devices, forensic specialists make both logical and bit-by-bit copies. They read data from removed memory cards as well as subscriber identity module (SIM) cards.

The following sections look, in particular, at forensics for Apple iPhones and BlackBerry smartphones.

 **NOTE**

The top three tools for forensics on wireless devices are Cellebrite's UFED, Paraben's Device Seizure, and the Zdziarski technique. These tools are discussed later in this chapter.

 **TIP**

Anyone performing forensic analysis on an iPhone should download the iPhone software development kit (SDK). The SDK is free to download after registration.

### Forensics on iPhones

Apple introduced the iPhone in 2007. Since then, the iPhone has become the most commonly used smartphone. Therefore, the iPhone can be expected to play a role in many system forensics cases. The active iPhone hacking community has yielded research and tools that support forensic investigations.

According to Andrew Hoog and Kyle Gaffaney in their *iPhone Forensics* white paper, an investigator can use several approaches to acquire and analyze information from iPhones. As with any other forensic investigation, with iPhone forensics, it's important not to modify the source information in any manner. If it is impossible to eliminate all modifications, an investigator must detail the changes and the reasons they were necessary.

Investigators use the following techniques in iPhone forensics:

- **Acquire data directly from the iPhone**—An iPhone's data is automatically updated as necessary to ensure that information on the iPhone and on a particular computer is the same. When possible, an investigator should recover files from a suspect iPhone rather than from the computer with which the iPhone was synchronized. A forensic analyst must understand how the iPhone was acquired and whether the iPhone is modified in any way. For example, iPhones are often "unlocked" to permit their use on multiple networks.

- **Acquire a backup or logical copy of the iPhone file system, using Apple's protocol**—The investigator should read files from the suspect iPhone using Apple's synchronization protocol. By querying the databases directly, an investigator can generally recover more information, such as deleted text messages and e-mail messages.

- **Make a physical bit-by-bit copy**—An investigator should create a physical, bit-by-bit, copy of the file system. This process is similar to the approach taken in PC forensic investigations. Using this approach, an investigator can recover a great deal of data, including deleted files. However, the process is complicated and requires that the investigator modify the system partition of the iPhone.

> **NOTE**
>
> One key consideration for an iPhone forensic tool is how it handles an iPhone that has a pass code set. Different products have different strategies for this situation, each with benefits and drawbacks.

### Forensics on BlackBerry Smartphones

As with other devices, on a BlackBerry, deletion doesn't totally remove data from the device. However, the BlackBerry's always-on, wireless push technology adds a unique dimension to forensic examination. Changing and updating data does not require desktop synchronization.

Michael W. Burnette, in *Forensic Examination of a RIM (BlackBerry) Wireless Device*, detailed several data-collection techniques. To collect evidence from a BlackBerry, a forensic specialist's examination includes the following processes:

- **Gathering logs**—Unlike with a PC, with a smartphone, an investigator begins by accessing logs on the original unit. The investigator doesn't access the logs via the standard user interface. Rather, the investigator reviews them using hidden control functions. After examining the logs, the specialist applies the programmer's SDK.

- **Imaging and profiling**—A system forensics specialist often must create a bit-by-bit backup image. An investigator does this by using an SDK utility that dumps the contents of the flash RAM into a file. The investigator can then easily examine this file by using a hex editor. The program loader is used to perform most of the inspection and to take the image. Each time the program loader is run, it causes a reset. A reset can cause a file system cleanup. Therefore, in inspecting a BlackBerry, a forensic specialist risks changing the file system and spoiling the data.

---

**FYI**

BlackBerry service providers offer an important service to those who lose their devices. They can immediately remotely delete all data on the device when a device user notifies the service provider of the loss. This is handy for BlackBerry users who don't want their information to fall into the wrong hands. It's also handy for perpetrators who don't want forensic investigators to access their information. Therefore, an investigator who obtains a suspect BlackBerry should quickly notify the BlackBerry service provider that the device is subject to subpoena, search warrant, or court order. In this case, the service provider must not delete the information on the device.

---

- **Evidence review**—Two options are available for information review using the hex dump. The investigator can manually review the hex file using a hex editor. Or the investigator can load the hex file into the BlackBerry SDK simulator for review. The hex editor provides access to the entire file system, including deleted or dirty records. By using the SDK, a forensic specialist can decode the dates on records.

To simplify programming, the BlackBerry file system is abstracted to appear as a database to most available application programming interfaces (APIs). This abstraction hides a complicated system of file management. Under the hood of the BlackBerry is standard flash RAM used to store all nonvolatile data.

Data can be hidden on a BlackBerry in several different ways, including using hidden databases and partition gaps. Custom-written databases with no icon in the **graphical user interface (GUI)** are capable of providing hidden data transport. A hacker could write a program that utilizes a database accessible only through device synchronization. The average user or uninformed investigator doesn't know about this hidden database. However, it is possible to install a database reader to see all databases on the unit. An investigator can thus thwart a hacker in such a case.

## Firewall Forensics

Many companies and individuals use firewalls to protect system resources from attack. A **firewall** is a set of hardware and software components that intercept and check network traffic for potential threats. Figure 5-5 shows an example of a firewall. Networks almost always use firewalls to protect against attacks that originate outside the network. With increasing frequency, organizations are using firewalls to protect against attacks that originate *within* the network.

All the traffic going through a firewall is part of a connection. A **connection** consists of two Internet Protocol (IP) addresses that are communicating with each other and two port numbers that identify the protocol or service. The destination port number of the first packet often indicates the type of service being connected. When a firewall blocks a connection, it saves the destination port number to its log file. This section describes the meanings of some of these port numbers and explains how to avoid some of the pitfalls.

Port numbers are divided into three ranges:

- **Well-known ports**—The well-known ports are those from 0 through 1023. Usually, traffic on one of these ports clearly indicates the protocol for that service. For example, port 80 almost always indicates Hypertext Transfer Protocol (HTTP) traffic.

- **Registered ports**—The registered ports are those from 1024 through 49151. They are loosely bound to services, which means that although numerous services are "bound" to these ports, these ports are also used for many other purposes that have nothing to do with the official servers.

- **Dynamic ports**—The dynamic, or private, ports are those from 49152 through 65535. In theory, no service should be assigned to these ports. In reality, machines start assigning dynamic ports at 1024. However, there are exceptions. For example, Sun starts its Remote Procedure Call ports at 32768.

Attempts on the same set of ports from widely varying sources all over the Internet are usually due to "decoy" scans. One of the attempts is the attacker; the others are not attackers. A system forensics specialist can use protocol analysis to track down who the attacker is. For example, the specialist can ping each of the systems and match up the time to live (TTL) fields in those responses with the connection attempts. The TTLs should match. If they don't, then they are being spoofed. Newer versions of scanners now randomize the attacker's own TTL, making it harder to identify the attacker.

A system forensics specialist can also attempt to go back further in the logs, looking for all the decoy addresses of people from the same subnets. The specialist is likely to see that the attacker has actually connected recently, while the decoyed addresses haven't.

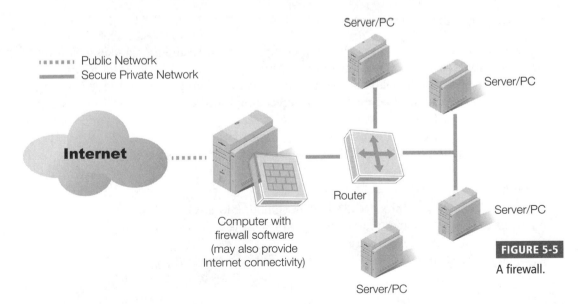

**FIGURE 5-5**

A firewall.

## Commonly Used System Forensics Tools

The following sections look at a few system forensics tools used especially in military and law enforcement but also in business. For a more complete list of forensic software and hardware products, see Chapter 15, "System Forensics Resources."

### EnCase

EnCase from Guidance Software is a well-known forensic tool. This commercial software package has the ability to make bit-level images and then mount them for analysis. EnCase preview mode allows a forensic investigator to use a null modem cable or Ethernet connection to view data on the subject machine without changing anything. Guidance Software states that it is impossible to make any alterations to the evidence during this process. Many law enforcement groups around the world use EnCase.

For information on EnCase, see *http://www.guidancesoftware.com*.

### Forensic Toolkit (FTK)

FTK from AccessData takes a snapshot of an entire disk drive and then makes a bit-level copy for analysis. FTK has many features and is easy to use. FTK is a good all-in-one forensic tool. It includes features such as registry viewing, in-depth easy-to-read logging, easy-to-use standalone disk imaging, and direct e-mail and zip file analysis. FTK is a great forensic analysis tool for those who are just starting to learn about forensics or do not have the time to invest in many different expensive tools.

For information on FTK, see *http://www.accessdata.com/forensictoolkit.html*.

### Helix

Helix is a customized Linux live CD used for computer forensics and computer security response. The collection of tools included with Helix is a virtual toolbox to analyze a computer system. The software is free.

For information on Helix, see *http://www.e-fense.com/products.php*

## AnaDisk Disk Analysis Tool

AnaDisk from NTI turns a PC into a sophisticated disk analysis tool. The software was originally created to meet the needs of the U.S. Treasury Department in 1991. AnaDisk scans for anomalies that identify odd formats, extra tracks, and extra sectors. It can be used to uncover sophisticated data-hiding techniques.

AnaDisk supports all DOS formats and many non-DOS formats, such as Apple Macintosh and UNIX TAR. If a disk will fit in a PC CD drive, it is likely that AnaDisk can be used to analyze it.

For information on AnaDisk, see *http://www.forensics-intl.com/anadisk.html.*

## CopyQM Plus Disk Duplication Software

CopyQM Plus from NTI essentially turns a PC into a disk duplicator. In a single pass, it formats, copies, and verifies a disk. This capability is useful for system forensics specialists who need to preconfigure CDs for specific uses and duplicate them.

In addition, CopyQM Plus can create self-extracting executable programs that can be used to duplicate specific disks. CopyQM is an ideal tool for use in security reviews because once a CopyQM disk-creation program has been created, anyone can use it to make preconfigured security risk assessment disks. When the resulting program is run, the disk image of the original disk is restored on multiple disks automatically. The disk images can also be password-protected when the disk images are converted to self-extracting programs. This is helpful when security is a concern, such as when disks are shared over the Internet. CopyQM Plus is particularly helpful in creating computer incident response toolkit disks.

CopyQM Plus supports all DOS formats and many non-DOS formats, such as Apple Macintosh and UNIX TAR. It copies files, file slack, and unallocated storage space. However, it does not copy all areas of copy-protected disks—extra sectors added to one or more tracks on a CD; AnaDisk software should be used for this purpose.

For information on CopyQM Plus, see *http://www.forensics-intl.com/copyqm.html.*

## TextSearch Plus

TextSearch Plus was specifically designed and enhanced for speed and accuracy in security reviews. TextSearch Plus is government tested and specifically designed for security reviews in classified environments. It is currently used by hundreds of law enforcement computer crime units, several government military and intelligence agencies, and numerous Fortune 500 corporations.

TextSearch Plus is used to quickly search hard disk drives and other media for keywords or specific patterns of text. It operates at either a logical or physical level. It can quickly search huge hard disk drives. TextSearch Plus is primarily used to find occurrences of words or strings of text in data stored in files, file slack, and unallocated file space. It can identify data leakage of classified information on nonclassified computer systems. It can also be used in internal audits to identify violations of corporate policy.

TextSearch Plus can be used on Windows XP, Vista, and 7. Tests indicate that this tool finds more text strings than any other forensic search tool. It is sold as a standalone tool and is also included in several of the NTI tool suites. As a standalone tool, it is ideal for security risk assessments.

For information on TextSearch Plus, see *http://www.forensics-intl.com/txtsrchp.html*.

## Filter_G Intelligent Forensic Filter

The Filter_G forensic filter utility from NTI is used to quickly make sense of nonsense. Forensic specialists can use it to analyze ambient data sources, such as Windows swap files, file slack, and data associated with erased files. Filter_G is a unique fuzzy logic filter. It can quickly identify patterns of English language grammar in ambient data sources and identify English language communications in erased file space. It is used as a data sampling tool in law enforcement, military, and corporate investigations.

Filter_G is DOS based for speed. It can be operated in batch mode with other forensic tools and processes.

For information on Filter_G, see *http://www.forensics-intl.com/filter_g.html*.

## UFED

Cellebrite's UFED is a standalone device capable of acquiring data from mobile devices. It can store the information it acquires on a USB drive, flash memory card, or PC. The UFED package ships with about 70 cables for connecting to most mobile devices available today. It uses a number of connection protocols, including serial, USB, infrared, and Bluetooth. A forensic investigator can use UFED in a lab or in the field.

UFED has a built-in SIM card reader and cloner. An investigator can create a clone of the original SIM card. When the clone is inserted into the mobile device, the device functions normally.

The UFED Report Manager has an intuitive interface. It allows an investigator to print a report or to export data into Excel, Outlook, Outlook Express, or comma-separated values (CSV) files. The UFED device can process phones with any language enabled.

Cellebrite UFED is simple to use and easy to update. It performs data acquisitions quickly and is portable. The firmware is updated often to support new phones and functionality.

For information on Cellebrite's UFED, see *http://www.cellebrite.com/=UFED-Standard -Kit.html*.

## Device Seizure

> **NOTE**
>
> Paraben's SIM Card Seizure allows an analyst to read or clone a SIM card. This product does not ship with DS but can be purchased separately.

Paraben's Device Seizure (DS) is a forensic software tool for use with mobile devices. It can acquire data from more than 2,200 devices, including phones, PDAs, and global positioning system (GPS) devices. DS runs on Microsoft Windows. It is designed to support the full acquisition and investigation process. DS provides the ability to recover deleted files and other important information.

A forensic specialist can use DS to acquire data, view data in several formats, and bookmark important data. The tool also allows an investigator to export data and run various reports. The acquisition and reporting processes are fast and thorough. The user interface for subsequent analysis is also quite mature and provides more features than most other tools.

Paraben offers certification for handheld forensics. Paraben Certified Mobile Examiners (PCMEs) attend three levels of training covering multiple tools, theory, and practical application. To learn more, see *http://www.paraben-training.com/pcme.html.*

For information on Paraben's DS, see *http://www.paraben.com/catalog/product _info.php?cPath=25&products_id=405.*

## The Zdziarski Technique

Jonathan Zdziarski is a research scientist for McAfee, Inc. In addition, he is well known in the iPhone community as a significant contributor to research on the iPhone and iPod Touch. Zdziarski has authored many utilities and devised many methods to open the iPhone's platform to the open source community.

Zdziarski has created a forensic technique for iPhones. His method provides a way to make a bit-by-bit copy of the original media. By analyzing the image this method provides, an examiner can discover a wealth of information that other tools can't provide. In addition, an investigator can use the Zdziarski technique along with standard hard drive-based forensic analysis tools and approaches.

Zdziarski's method requires modifying a read-only system partition to make the bit-by-bit copy. This partition remains isolated from the partition containing user data. The technique therefore modifies the system partition only and preserves the user partition. Zdziarski's process is more reliable and complete than other approaches. It provides access to the raw disk images and allows the examiner to bypass any security added on the iPhone, such as a user pass code.

**Jailbreaking** is a hacking process by which the iPhone firmware is overwritten to install third-party applications or unlock the device. The jailbreaking process modifies the user data partition and is therefore forensically unsound. Zdziarski's procedure, on the other hand, operates only on the read-only system partition. Unlike jailbreaking, it does not install additional software or modify the user data partition.

> **FYI**
>
> Zdziarski maintains a forensics guide for the iPhone at *http://www.iphoneinsecurity.com.* According to this site, "Site access is freely available to full time, active duty law enforcement or military personnel tasked with mobile forensic imaging as part of their duties. To [qualify] as a law enforcement agency, the agency must have arrest and search/seizure powers."

## CHAPTER SUMMARY

Law enforcement and military agencies have used system forensics since the mid-1980s. System forensics is relatively new to the private sector, but it's a quickly growing field. Investigators use system forensics tools and methodologies to identify and document computer evidence associated with a variety of computer abuses and activities.

This chapter discusses specific system forensics technologies that are used by computer specialists in the military, law enforcement, and business. It also describes some of the forensic tools that are most commonly used in these three sectors.

## KEY CONCEPTS AND TERMS

Ambient computer data
Black-box system forensics
    software tools
Compression
Connection
Department of Defense (DoD)
DoD Cyber Crime Center (DC3)

File slack
Firewall
Flash memory media
Fuzzy logic tool
Graphical user interface (GUI)
Honeypot
Host protected area (HPA)

Jailbreaking
Master boot record (MBR)
Pretty Good Privacy (PGP)
Public-key cryptography
Unallocated space
Unused space

## CHAPTER 5 ASSESSMENT

**1.** The _____ is the department of the U.S. federal government that coordinates and supervises agencies and functions of the government related to national security and the U.S. armed forces.

**2.** What is the name of the organization that is involved with DoD investigations that require computer forensics support to detect, enhance, or recover digital media?

  A. U.S. Army
  B. U.S. law enforcement
  C. DoD Digital Media Center (DDMC)
  D. DoD Cyber Crime Center (DC3)

**3.** Law enforcement agencies do not have to be as careful as corporations about preserving evidence.

  A. True
  B. False

**4.** It is almost impossible to use forensic technologies to find evidence on flash memory media.

  A. True
  B. False

5. Which of the following is the process of encoding information using fewer bits than the unencoded information would use?

A. Compression
B. Encryption
C. Decryption
D. Jailbreaking

6. A _____ is a tool used to identify unknown strings of text by searching for values between "completely true" and "completely false."

7. Which of the following is the name for the process of making data unreadable to anyone except those who have the correct key?

A. Compression
B. Encryption
C. Decryption
D. Jailbreaking

8. Port numbers are divided into three ranges. Which of the following is not one of the ranges?

A. Well-known ports
B. Open ports
C. Registered ports
D. Dynamic ports

9. Which of the following is a good forensic analysis tool for those who are just starting to learn about forensics or do not have the time to invest in many different expensive tools?

A. EnCase
B. FTK
C. AnaDisk
D. TextSearch Plus
E. Filter_G

10. _____ is a commercial software package that has the ability to make bit-level images and then mount them for analysis.

11. Which of the following commonly used system forensics tools is utilized primarily to scan for anomalies that identify odd formats, extra tracks, and extra sectors?

A. EnCase
B. FTK
C. AnaDisk
D. CopyQM Plus
E. Filter_G

12. Which of the following commonly used system forensics tools can quickly search hard disk drives, zip disks, and CDs for keywords or specific patterns of text?

A. AnaDisk
B. CopyQM Plus
C. TextSearch Plus
D. Filter_G

13. Which of the following commonly used system forensics tools is a fuzzy logic tool employed for data sampling?

A. AnaDisk
B. CopyQM Plus
C. TextSearch Plus
D. Filter_G

14. Which of the following forensic tools is a stand-alone device capable of acquiring data from mobile devices?

A. UFED
B. Device Seizure
C. The Zdziarski technique
D. EnCase

15. Unlike jailbreaking, which of the following does not install any additional software or modify the user data partition in any way?

A. UFED
B. Device Seizure
C. The Zdziarski technique
D. EnCase

# Controlling a Forensic Investigation

A COMPUTER FORENSICS CRIME SCENE INVESTIGATION should begin with a plan to approach and secure the crime scene. As a forensic specialist, you must identify and collect evidence or potential evidence, and you must process and analyze the evidence so that it has value in court. Forensic specialists must carefully document crime scene activity and all activity related to evidence.

Computer evidence frequently faces challenges in court. Most challenges are related to the evidence's authenticity. The courts want to know whether the data was altered. They also question whether the program that generated the output was reliable. Other challenges in court can involve the forensic analyst. Attorneys sometimes challenge the expertise, methods, or integrity of computer forensics experts who testify.

Whether an investigation is of a corporate, civil, or criminal nature, the approach and processes are similar. Documentation and professionalism are essential in conducting an investigation that will hold up in court. This chapter deals with controlling a computer forensics investigation. It also provides a discussion of the legal aspects of acquiring evidence.

## Chapter 6 Topics

This chapter covers the following topics and concepts:

- How to preserve a digital crime scene
- What to consider when collecting evidence in a forensic investigation
- What the differences between physical analysis and logical analysis are
- What the legal aspects of acquiring evidence are

## Chapter 6 Goals

When you complete this chapter, you will be able to:

- Preserve a digital crime scene
- Correctly collect evidence in a forensic investigation
- Describe the difference between physical analysis and logical analysis
- Legally acquire evidence

# Preserving a Digital Crime Scene

As a system forensics investigator, you may be the first responder to a scene. You must be concerned about destructive processes and devices that the computer's owner may have planted. You must also know how to deal with evidence preservation and collection on mobile devices and monstrous hard drives.

> **NOTE**
>
> Multiple types of computing devices, bigger hard drives, and increased use of encryption make the job of a digital forensics examiner tougher than ever.

In addition, think about the computer's operating system and applications. You can easily find evidence in typical storage areas, such as spreadsheets, databases, and word processing files. Unfortunately, potential evidence can also reside in file slack, erased files, and the swap file (you'll read more about swap files later in this chapter). This evidence is usually in the form of data fragments. Simply booting the computer or running Microsoft Windows can overwrite it. When Windows starts, it generally creates new files and opens existing ones. These processes can cause erased files to be overwritten and can alter or destroy data previously stored in the swap file. Furthermore, Windows XP, Vista, and 7 have a habit of updating directory entries for files as a normal operating process. File dates are important from an evidence standpoint.

Be careful about running any programs on a subject computer. Criminals can easily modify a computer's operating system to destroy evidence when standard operating system commands are executed. For example, a perpetrator could modify the operating system in such a way that the execution of the DIR command destroys simulated evidence. Or a crafty high-tech criminal could alter standard program names and familiar Windows program icons and tie them to destructive processes.

Even trusted word processing programs, such as Microsoft Word and WordPerfect, can create problems for a forensic investigator. When word-processing files are opened and viewed, the word-processing program creates temporary files. These files overwrite the temporary files that existed previously, and potential evidence stored in those files can be lost forever.

**Forensic Investigation Tips**

Keep in mind the following tips to safely conduct an investigation:

- Never work directly on a suspect computer. Instead, always work from a backup, a duplicate, a copy, or an image of the suspect hard drive. A perpetrator may have rigged the startup sequence to destroy data, content, or files.
- Don't trust the perpetrator if he or she reveals the password. And don't trust anything found on slips of paper near the machine because they could be booby traps.
- Be ready to spend a lot of time doing forensic duplication and know when there is too much information to duplicate. When dealing with servers and redundant array of inexpensive disks (RAID) devices, making a bit stream backup may be impossible. In such cases, create a logical backup that contains system and application logs.

Computer evidence processing is fraught with potential problems. Any loss of crucial evidence or exculpatory material falls on the shoulders of the computer investigator. You can eliminate many of the problems by using tried and proven processing procedures.

Preservation of evidence is the primary element of all criminal investigations, and computer evidence is certainly no exception. You must first secure the subject computer.

**Imaging**

Simply copying all the potentially useful files from a system may not be sufficient for a complete investigation. For example, a hacker could delete all file system-level clues, leaving you unable to fully piece together the incident.

**Imaging** is the process of creating a complete sector-by-sector copy of a disk drive. You must frequently perform imaging as a part of data collection. Often you must make a complete copy of a disk drive and then do low-level analysis at a later time.

In most cases, an operating system doesn't overwrite the contents of sectors upon deletion. Instead, the operating system simply unlinks the sectors from the file system table. The operating system leaves the sectors untouched until it needs them. With a complete image of a disk drive, you can search the hard drive for unallocated sectors that contain useful information. Analyzing a disk image therefore allows you to probe deeper into the system's state and perform a more thorough investigation.

In most cases, image all disk drives. The cost of imaging is not great, but today's huge hard drives can make it a time-intensive process. A number of hardware and software tools are available for imaging. See Chapters 5, "System Forensics Technologies," and 15, "System Forensics Resources," for more information on these tools.

You must then make a complete **bit stream backup** of all computer data before reviewing or processing it. As stated previously, evidence can reside at multiple levels, such as allocated files, file slack, and erased files. It is not enough to do a standard backup of a hard disk drive. Doing so would eliminate the backup of file slack and erased file space. Without backing up evidence in these unique areas, you could damage or destroy evidence.

Bit stream backups are much more thorough than standard backups. They involve the copying of every bit of data on a storage device. The importance of bit stream backups cannot be stressed enough. After you make a backup, you should also create an additional copy of this backup. Then, you should perform any processing on one of the backup copies. As previously recommended, preserve the original evidence at all costs. After all, it is the best evidence.

## Considerations in Collecting Evidence

An investigator must attempt to avoid permanently losing data. Therefore carefully secure the physical evidence. Then you can collect volatile and temporary data. **Volatile data** is memory that is highly sensitive to system usage, such as registers, memory, and cache. Such data is lost whenever a system is used. It should be collected first to minimize corruption or loss. The following are examples of volatile data:

- **Central processing unit (CPU) cache and register contents**—This data has no forensic value.
- **Random access memory (RAM) memory dump**—This data is important to get, but accessing it changes the contents.
- **State of network connections**—This data is important and easy to get from tables in kernel memory.
- **State of running processes**—This data is important and is in kernel memory.

After collecting volatile data, you collect **temporary data**—data that an operating system creates and overwrites without the computer user taking a direct action to save this data. The likelihood of corrupting temporary data is less than that of volatile data. But temporary data is just that—temporary—and you must collect it before it is lost. Only after collecting volatile and temporary data should you begin to collect persistent data.

---

**FYI**

The two goals of data collection are maximizing the usefulness of the evidence and minimizing the cost of collecting it. These goals are not mutually exclusive; in fact, they overlap quite frequently. Increasing the usefulness of evidence typically involves collecting corroborating evidence, which increases the data collection cost. You must base the balance between evidence cost and usefulness on an investigation's overall goals.

The following sections look at these important principles of computer forensics evidence handling and collection.

## Securing the Physical Evidence

When seizing computer equipment, before turning off a suspect computer, take the following measures to secure the physical evidence:

- Photograph the system setup, wiring, and area.
- Tag and bag all cables, cords, and peripheral devices.
- Write-protect all storage media.
- When transporting, make sure to be grounded and place everything in antistatic bags.
- Avoid exposing the items to any heat above 75 degrees and avoid letting any magnetic fields, such as police radios, come near the equipment. Gentle handling is important.
- Record the names of individuals who occupy or have access to the area.

## Volatile Data: Two Schools of Thought

> **TIP**
>
> If an attack is in progress, don't shut down the computer right away.

Volatile data consists of running processes on a live computer. A computer's system state changes constantly, even if no applications are running. For example, power cycles, timed backups, and logon processes are always running in the background. If a computer is hooked up to a network, more processes are running. Some types of Internet attacks require that the computer be left on for long periods of time.

**TABLE 6-1**   Live analysis school of thought recommendations.

| DESCRIPTION | PROGRAM | RESULT |
|---|---|---|
| Establish a new shell | `cmd.exe (Windows)` | `bash (UNIX)` |
| Record system date/time | `date, time` | `W` |
| Determine logon | `loggedon` | `W` |
| Record open sockets | `netstat` | `netstat -anp` |
| List socket processes | `fport` | `lsof` |
| List running processes | `pslist` | `ps` |
| List systems connected | `nbtstat` | `netstat` |
| Record system time | `date, time` | `W` |
| Record steps taken | `doskey` | `script, vi, history` |

**TABLE 6-2** Safe shutdown school of thought recommendations.

| OPERATING SYSTEM | PROCEDURE |
|---|---|
| MS-DOS | 1. Photograph the screen.<br>2. Pull the power cord from the computer. In a laptop, also remove the battery. |
| UNIX | 1. Photograph the screen.<br>2. Right-click and choose Console.<br>3. If the root user prompt (#) is not present, change the user by typing su –<br>4. If the password is available, use it and type sync;sync;halt<br>5. If there is no password, pull the power cord from the computer and in a laptop, also remove the battery. |
| Mac | 1. Photograph the screen.<br>2. Click Special.<br>3. Click Shutdown.<br>4. Pull the power cord from the computer. In a laptop, also remove the battery. |
| Windows | 1. Photograph the screen.<br>2. Determine whether the self-destruct program is running.<br>3. Pull the power cord from the computer. In a laptop, also remove the battery. |

There are two schools of thought on how to handle volatile data in forensic investigations: the live analysis school and the safe shutdown school.

The **live analysis school of thought**, as its name suggests, recommends leaving a suspect computer turned on and working on it immediately after securing it. This school recommends attaching a Small Computer System Interface (SCSI) device or using an open network connection to get results for the commands shown in Table 6-1.

The **safe shutdown school of thought** believes that a suspect computer should be carefully shut down immediately after the computer is secured. This school recommends the shutdown procedures shown in Table 6-2.

## Determining How Much to Duplicate

Large hard drives are becoming less expensive and more popular. Therefore, a forensic investigator must recognize the trade-off between spending resources and duplicating everything. An investigator must consider the suspect's intelligence and how high profile or harmful the incident is. In addition, the investigator should decide whether a low-impact search of the hard drive might suffice instead of a high-impact search that looks for file slack and the like. For example, a sample of evidence might suffice with minor offenders. On the other hand, the jurisdiction, judge, or the other side may demand a printout of everything. If a business or institution is going to handle a case administratively instead of criminally, printing all this evidence is unnecessary.

### Balancing Speed and Thoroughness

According to Joseph Sremack, a forensic analyst should perform an investigation quickly to return the affected system to its regular job. The presumption is that quicker data collection results in a quicker investigation. However, this call for speed can result in the collection of insufficient evidence, which is the worst-case scenario for an investigation. If evidence is insufficient, you must once again perform the time-consuming process of data collection. Even worse, the needed data may be volatile and may have been lost during the first attempt at data collection.

The primary goal of most investigations is thoroughness. The main purpose of an investigation is to arrive at a complete understanding of the causes and effects of an incident. Carefully perform the data collection so as not to overlook data that could potentially be useful—even if the data does not directly relate to any of the clues collected from the preparation phase.

The standard method to ensure that you have collected every piece of potentially useful data is to gather all volatile data, logs, and other system-specific information that may not be gatherable at a later time. Collecting this information allows you to begin the investigation without the possibility of losing potentially useful information.

### Approaches to Duplicating Data

The following are some of the possible approaches to take in duplicating a suspect computer:

- Remove the hard drive and attach it to a forensic workstation.
- Attach a hard drive to the specimen computer and use it as an imaging system.
- Use another computer in the office area as an imaging system.
- Use a crossover cable or an Ethernet connector to send the contents to another network computer or the hooked-up forensic workstation.

The best approach depends on the resources available and whether your equipment is compatible with the specimen's network system.

## Making a Bit Stream Backup

As mentioned earlier in this chapter, make a bit stream backup of all computer data. Then review and process the backup rather than the original disk drive or other media. To create a bit stream backup, you can use programs such as EnCase, SafeBack, Code Blue, Norton Ghost, and the UNIX dd (data dumper) utility.

> ### Automating Data Collection
>
> Toolkits automate the data collection process by using scripts and data collection software wherever possible. Automation provides the advantages of faster collection and error-free execution of the procedure. Scripts reduce the amount of typing required and therefore also reduce the possibility of user typing-errors. Scripts also eliminate the delays associated with typing numerous commands.
>
> A computer forensics specialist uses a sector-copying tool, such as dd or EnCase, to send an image to either an attached investigation hard drive or to a forensic workstation system through a network connection. The process cost is determined by the speed of the hard drive or the speed of the network connection.

A bit stream backup is a recording of every bit of data that signals a storage device. It is the electronic version of the radio frequency (RF) stream that a radio receiver picks up. A bit stream backup copies not only working files that a conventional backup utility finds but also hidden, erased, fragmented, corrupted, temporary, and special attribute files. These files are not easily hidden on floppies, but a hard drive is full of them. A temporary file, in particular, contains data from a document that someone worked on but never saved to disk.

SafeBack and EnCase are two widely used tools for making bit stream backups:

- **SafeBack**— The world's first cybercop, Chuck Guzis, created SafeBack. This tool duplicates anything attached to the controllers on a computer motherboard. It can even handle removable devices, if the appropriate drivers are installed. Built-in utilities can scan ports for other devices. Put the Remote.exe imaging program on a boot compact disk (CD) to boot the specimen computer and use a crossover parallel cable to connect to the forensic workstation. You can then use the Backup, Restore, Verify (checksum), and Copy commands. SafeBack makes its own audit file. To save space, it saves everything it images in a compressed format on the forensic workstation. The process takes anywhere from a few minutes to many hours. For more information on SafeBack, see *http://www.forensics-intl.com/safeback.html.*

- **EnCase**—EnCase technically produces accurate duplicate files. EnCase uses a Windows interface and focuses on hard drive contents. You add the specimen hard drive to a forensic workstation as hard disk drive 1 or 2. EnCase, a Windows Explorer-like program, does the rest, with Preview, Save, and Output functions. It displays graphics files in thumbnail format. You can even do string searches for text in Preview mode. Imaged files can be compressed or not, but anything saved is in a proprietary, read-only format, so it is tamper-proof. You can control the size of the evidence files, so that they write to CD-ROM for presentation in court, along with any comments and password protection added. For more information on EnCase, see *http://www.guidancesoftware.com.*

After making a backup copy, validate that it is an exact mirror copy. Programs such as CrCheck.exe and CRC32 are available to do this. But large storage devices require a mathematical algorithm, such as the "fingerprint checker" Message Digest 5 (MD5), to estimate the probabilities of match and error. All these programs use a checksum or hashing algorithm that holds up in court as verifying an accurate and reliable copy.

The more numerous the files, the more you must make mathematical computations. And the more read errors you get, the more you need a program that uses conventional-style placeholders. Probability theory plays a vital part in the admissibility of most modern forms of evidence, such as DNA, forensic psychology, social science, and computer forensics.

## Booting a Computer

In computer forensics, booting a computer requires special care. A **boot process** is one that starts an operating system when the user turns on a computer system. Never boot from an evidence drive; instead boot from a DOS startup CD. In addition, get in the habit of bypassing the operating system and going straight to the basic input/output system (BIOS)—by holding down Shift, Ctrl+F1, or Delete, depending on the chipset. Whenever you run Windows, it changes the swap file, bookmarks, histories, and cache. These areas, particularly the swap file, hold valuable data remnants, such as passwords, graphics, and sometimes whole documents. Whenever a BIOS runs, the boot block on the hard drive may change, including file-access timestamps, partition information, registry or configuration files, and essential log files.

Record information that appears on opening screens. These screens should display autoexec devices, config.sys programs, directories, and file allocation table (FAT) and data storage areas. At some point, also document the results of running a program such as SCANDISKor CHKDISK. Document errors and, if appropriate, correct or repair them. The specialist must document any such corrective actions.

To make a system CD, insert a blank CD. Then, at the C:\ prompt, type `format a:\ /s` to write the system files, and only the system files, to the CD. Table 6-3 lists the system files.

## Examining Evidence

After booting up a suspect system, do the following:

- **Verify the time and data stamp**—Verify the time and data stamp stored in the CMOS chip of the specimen computer. This information helps determine the times and dates of other computer files. Many clock settings that record the file date are inaccurate, but the CMOS stamp helps with estimation and might make the all-important connection with ownership and the start of operation. Computers don't commit computer crimes; people do. You must pay attention to dates, times, and alibis.
- **Visually inspect the hard drives**—Visually inspect and document the make, model, and size of all hard drives. The manufacturing specifications tell what the capabilities are and might even provide the best diagnostic utilities for use with a hard drive that is difficult to read.

**TABLE 6-3** System files.

| FILE | DESCRIPTION |
|------|-------------|
| COMMAND.COM | COMMAND.COM stands for *command interpreter*. It allows a forensic specialist to use DOS commands as if he or she had a mini-version of DOS to work with. |
| AUTOEXEC.BAT | This file, which is edited with EDIT.COM, is a **batch file**—a text file that contains a series of commands intended to be executed by the command interpreter. This file handles drivers for all the devices hooked up to the controllers and ports. A CD-ROM device will not run unless the file MSCDEX is present and referenced in the AUTOEXEC.BAT file. |
| CONFIG.SYS | This is another batch file. It starts up terminate-and-stay-resident programs (TSRs), which are the little icons that show up in the lower-right corner of a monitor when a machine is on. They are the visible processes running in the background, eating up memory and consuming system resources. |
| IO.SYS | This is a code file first processed by the computer. It initializes the system, loads MSDOS.SYS, if present, or the command interpreter, and tests and resets the hardware by looking for and installing device drivers. |
| DRVSPACE.BIN | This is a driver file for the compression software DriveSpace. A similar program is DoubleSpace. These programs are used to set up virtual memory space if the user is low on RAM. They operate by setting up part of the hard drive as a compressed file storage area. You generally don't want DriveSpace and similar programs to run because they change the time and date stamps. You may, therefore, need to use a hex editor to go into IO.SYS and change any references to the word *space* to equivalent nonsense symbols. For even greater safety, you can use an interrupt blocker such as PDBLOCK to disable any possibility of writing to the hard drive. |

- **Scan for viruses**—Before running any type of diagnostic program or software, ensure that you have not inadvertently introduced any computer virus into the specimen computer. Therefore, document all forensic software as being regularly and recently scanned by a virus utility—and preferably two of them. You can virus-scan the specimen computer and any CDs and, if appropriate, remove any viruses found. Take into account that viruses can hide in compressed files.

- **List and catalog files**—List and catalog all files with their dates and times of creation, update, and last access. Investigative leads come out of cross-referencing these dates and times with other files on the same computer or files on a different computer.

- **Document forensic tools**—Document the forensic tools you have used, along with their purchase. You must also register software with the publisher, and document any upgrade or update history.

## Physical Analysis and Logical Analysis

This chapter has so far discussed general preparations involved in the initial seizing, duplication, and finding of digital evidence. There's much more to learn, especially about examining data to find **incriminating evidence**—evidence that shows, or tends to show, a person's involvement in an act, or evidence that can establish guilt. One of the three techniques of forensic analysis has been covered already—live analysis, which is the recording of any ongoing network processes. The remaining two techniques are physical analysis and logical analysis, which both deal with hard drive structures and file formats.

   **Physical analysis** is offline analysis conducted on an evidence disk or forensic duplicate after booting from a CD or another system. **Logical analysis** involves using the native operating system, on the evidence disk or a forensic duplicate, to peruse the data. Put another way, physical analysis is looking for things that may have been overlooked, or are invisible, to the user. Logical analysis is looking for things that are visible, known about, and possibly controlled by the user. There is some overlap, as Figure 6-1 indicates.

### Physical Analysis

Two of the easiest things to extract during physical analysis are a list of all Web site URLs and a list of all e-mail addresses on the computer. The user may have attempted to delete these, but you can reconstruct them from various places on the hard drive.

**FIGURE 6-1**

Physical and logical analysis.

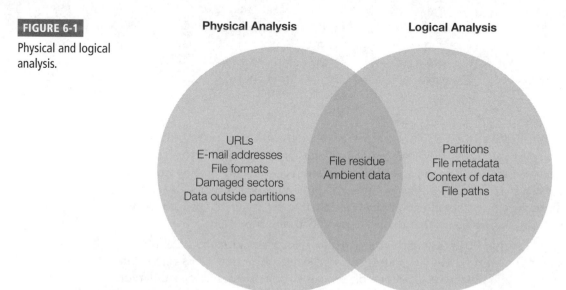

Physical Analysis

Logical Analysis

URLs
E-mail addresses
File formats
Damaged sectors
Data outside partitions

File residue
Ambient data

Partitions
File metadata
Context of data
File paths

Next, you should index the different kinds of file formats. The file format you start with depends on the type of case. For example, you might want to start with graphics file formats or document formats in a pornography or forgery case. There are lots of other file formats: multimedia, archive, binary, database, font, game, and Internet related. Computers generally save things in file formats beyond the user's control. For example, all graphics files have header information attached. Collectors of pornography usually don't go to the trouble of removing this header information, so it's an easy matter of finding, say, one graphics' header at the beginning of a JPEG file and doing a string search for all other graphics of that type. (This chapter discusses examination of sectors and partitions in the section "Logical Analysis.")

The following sections describe some of the places that an investigator must physically analyze.

> **NOTE**
>
> *File residue* is a broad term for a number of types of data, such as ambient data, file slack, free space, and shadow data. The term *ambient data* describes data stored in nontraditional computer storage areas and formats. Computer experts often use it to describe data stored in the swap file, unallocated (free) space, or file slack.

## The Swap File

A swap file is the most important type of ambient data. Windows uses a swap file on each system as a "scratch pad" to write data when additional random access memory (RAM) is needed. A swap file is a virtual memory extension of RAM.

Most computer users are unaware of the existence of swap files. The size of these files can range from 40MB to more than 400MB. Swap files contain remnants of word processing, e-mail, Internet browsing activity, database entries, and almost any other work that has occurred during past Windows sessions. Swap files can be temporary or permanent, depending on the version of Windows installed and the settings selected by the computer user. Permanent swap files are of the greatest forensic value because they hold larger amounts of information for longer periods of time. However, temporary, or dynamic, swap files are more common. These files shrink and expand as necessary. When a dynamic swap file reduces its size close to zero, it sometimes releases the file's content to unallocated space, which you can also forensically examine.

> **NOTE**
>
> In Windows NT and Windows Server 2003, *swap files* are called *page files.*

## Unallocated (Free) Space

*Unallocated space,* or free space, is the area of a hard drive that has never been allocated for file storage, or the leftover area that the computer regards as unallocated after file deletion. It's where the hard disk often sends fragments of files when someone deletes or removes files.

The only way to clean unallocated space is with cleansing devices known as *sweepers* or *scrubbers.* However, few commercial products scrub free space to Department of Defense (DoD) standards. The fragments of old files in free space can be anywhere on the disk, even on a different partition, but they tend to fall next to partition headers, file allocation tables (FAT), and the last sectors of a cluster. FAT, clusters, and sectors are defined as follows:

- A **file allocation table (FAT)** stores associations between files and the clusters assigned to them.
- **Clusters** are fixed-length blocks of data—one to 128 sectors—in which DOS- and Windows-based computers store files. Clusters are made up of blocks of sectors.
- **Sectors** are the smallest unit of storage on a computer. They are composed of bits and are generally a power of two bytes in size. A "regular" disk sector is 512 bytes.

Unallocated space often contains intact files, remnants of files and subdirectories, and temporary files that were transparently created and deleted by computer applications or the operating system. Furthermore, unallocated space contains information resulting from trying to save something to a CD that is too large for it, recently sending something to a printer, trying to repartition or reformat a hard drive, or having a system crash while working on a file.

### File Slack

File slack is the empty space attached to every file. All DOS and Windows programs store files in fixed-length blocks called *clusters.* Rarely do file sizes exactly match the size of these clusters perfectly. The extra space from the end of the file to the end of the cluster is called *file slack.*

Cluster sizes vary in length, depending on the operating system and the size of the logical partition. Larger cluster sizes have more forensic value. With normal 512-byte sectors, if there is not enough data in the file to fill the last sector in the cluster, DOS or Windows makes up the difference by padding the remaining space with data from the memory buffers. This means that the file slack is filled with RAM slack that potentially contains information from previous work sessions. If the computer has been left on for several days, the file slack areas contain a tremendous amount of information. RAM slack technically refers to the last sector of a file. If the operating system needs additional sectors to round out the block size for the last cluster, then it creates a different type of slack. Drive slack, unlike RAM slack, which comes from memory, is padded with what was stored on the storage device, not just from previous work sessions.

Swap files, unallocated space, and file slack contain mostly binary information, which is tedious to look at. File slack, in particular, is random in nature, and you might find a logon name or password or might find just fragments of messages and documents. Analysis can be time-consuming. On large hard disk drives, file slack can involve gigabytes of data. File slack also can be found on CDs and other storage media.

---

**FYI**

Computer applications that use fuzzy logic or artificial intelligence to analyze file slack are available. EnCase has some capabilities for this use, too, but other programs are commonly used. Some examples are NTA Stealth (see *http://www.forensics-intl.com/nta.html*), Forensic Toolkit (see *http://www.digitalintelligence.com/software/accessdata/forensictoolkit3/*), and SilentRunner (see *http://www.accessdata.com/silentrunner.html*).

## Shadow Data

**Shadow data** is fringe data that remains on the physical track of storage media after deletion, sweeping, or scrubbing. Regardless of the storage medium—CD, hard disk, tape, and so on—a mechanical device called a *head* is used to write the data. The data is stored electronically in magnetic patterns of 1s and 0s. These patterns are in the form of sectors, which are written consecutively in concentric rings called *tracks.* However, head alignment is just a little bit different each time an attempt is made to erase data, and data remnants sometimes bleed over the tracks. Recovering shadow data is not an easy task. You need specialized equipment to retrieve it. There is no guarantee that one scrubbing will have completely eliminated shadow data. Therefore, government agencies require multiple scrubs or burning for media that have held sensitive or classified data.

## Logical Analysis

You must examine the logical file and directory structure to reconstruct what the user was doing with his or her computer. Rarely does an investigator run across a signed confession in the My Documents folder. Most perpetrators are smarter than that.

They use various tactics to hide what they've been doing. For example, perpetrators often use unusual file paths. In addition, many try to thwart investigators by using encryption such as Pretty Good Privacy (PGP). They may also use steganography to hide data in graphics or other files. Or they may use metadata to combine different file formats into one format. You can also expect to find lots of deleted, professionally scrubbed, data.

An investigator hopes to trace the uses that a suspect computer has been set up for. Certain types of criminals optimize their system for different uses. For example, a programmer optimizes for speed, a pornographer for storage, and a stalker for messaging. You must go about logical analysis methodically. Divide the data on the hard drive into layers and try to find evidentiary information at each layer. Look for peculiarities on each layer and then choose the right extraction tool. Table 6-4 shows the location of evidence at each layer.

| TABLE 6-4 Logical analysis layers of evidence. | | |
|---|---|---|
| **APPLICATION STORAGE** | **WINDOWS FILES** | **UNIX FILES** |
| **Physical** | Absolute sectors | Absolute sectors |
| **Data Classification** | Partition | Partitions |
| **Blocking Format** | Clusters | Blocks |
| **Storage Space Allocation** | FAT | Inode and data bitmaps |
| **Information Classification** | Directories and folders | Directories |

Proceed through the logical analysis layers of evidence as follows:

- **Physical layer**—Starting at the Physical layer, look for how the hard drive is set up to read and write in blocks and sectors. Intel chips allow the user to adjust the cylinder/head/sector (C/H/S) settings through the BIOS. Anything different from the standard default 512-byte absolute sector size means that the machine is set up to buffer large amounts of data to and from the hard drive. Certain types of hackers do this.

- **Data Classification layer**—At the Data Classification layer, look at the partition tables. Using partition is a way of splitting up the hard drive into separate areas, usually for different operating systems. Windows assigns separate drive letters and tables to FAT and NTFS (NT File System) partitions. UNIX, on the other hand, uses hybrid tables that represent all partitions. This is because UNIX is more flexible and integrates with other operating systems. Evidence could easily be hidden in the UNIX tables.

- **Blocking Format layer**—The Blocking Format layer contains customizations that only the system administrator in UNIX and administrator in Windows can make. More sophisticated users may optimize their block sizes for the size of their disk or partition. They do so because the machine doesn't have to search thousands of allocation units each time a file is written or updated. Other users want to have lots of allocation units per block. These people have lots of wasted space and slack to examine.

- **Storage Space Allocation layer**—The Storage Space Allocation layer is the FAT system, where the allocation tables are located. Each partition has at last two FATS, located at the starting sector of each partition. Sometimes you can find hundreds of allocation tables spread throughout the drive, especially in UNIX. Computer systems automatically run validity checks on these tables all the time, but many of them are corrupted. You can rebuild these tables to their original state by using simple recovery tools. In this way, you may be able to re-create what the computer looked like in the past.

- **Information Classification and Application Storage layers**—The Information Classification and Application Storage layers contain both active and deleted files. Every file system has a method for chaining together lists of files. Sometimes, the more unlinked the file, the more important it is. File date and timestamps are the most valuable pieces of information in reconstructing who accessed what, when, and where.

## Legal Aspects of Acquiring Evidence

In the case of federal investigations, after a court has issued a search warrant, specially trained analysts typically perform forensic analysis at government laboratories. Weeks or months may pass before system forensics investigators have collected all the evidence.

In most cases, investigators seize the computer and associated hardware, and then they look through the computer files at a police station or a laboratory. State and local investigations may vary from this approach. They're likely to involve less seizure of equipment and instead involve a copy-and-scan approach. These investigations generally involve analysis at the police station. In civil cases, the litigants typically hire private companies to perform forensic analysis.

> **TIP**
>
> Some states require that forensic professionals be licensed as private investigators. These requirements vary by state. As more states move toward requiring licensing for forensic investigators, it's a good idea to keep informed of your state's requirements.

## The Fourth Amendment

An important consideration in computer forensics is the **Fourth Amendment to the U.S. Constitution**. This amendment guards against unreasonable searches and seizures. The amendment specifically requires that search and arrest warrants be judicially sanctioned and supported by probable cause. A number of issues in system forensics raise questions about Fourth Amendment rules:

- **In computer seizure, when exactly does the search occur?** The Fourth Amendment was set up to address physically entering a home. With digital forensics, computers are not exactly "entered" or physically "observed." Nothing is physically moved inside them, and they basically contain 1s and 0s. The notion of seizure is tied to the concepts of physicality and invasiveness. Digital information becomes physical when it can be readily observed by ordinary human perception.

- **Who actually owns a suspect computer and the data it contains?** Computers in the home typically involve a complex status of ownership and possession. A home computer may very well be the "family" computer, with several users. An employer typically owns work data and equipment and has authority to search corporate data systems.

- **If forensic investigators work with images and do their analysis in labs, how does the Fourth Amendment apply?** A computer forensics analyst usually works from a bit stream copy of the hard drive. So it's not the actual computer that the analyst is searching but a copy of the actual. In addition, the search may occur on government property, not private property. Under current Fourth Amendment interpretation, copying something does not constitute seizing it.

- **Does a user's attempt to delete things constitute an attempt at privacy or an attempt at cover-up?** When is a forensic expert allowed to attempt recovery of "deleted" files? Hidden files, files with renamed extensions, and encrypted files generally trigger extra law enforcement effort.

▶ **NOTE**

Individuals may lose their right to privacy when they transfer data to a third party. The right to privacy does not extend to searches that are conducted by private parties who are not acting for the government. For example, if a person takes a computer to a repair shop and the technician notices child pornography on the computer, the repair shop must notify the authorities.

- **Where does one computer search end and another begin?** Due to the vast amount of information computers hold, it is increasingly difficult to determine this. Law enforcement analysts cannot go on a "fishing expedition." For example, if they are looking for evidence of drug sales but find an image of child pornography, they can't abandon the original search and begin looking for more evidence of child pornography. Plain view doctrine, on the other hand, allows police to follow up on things when the incriminating nature of the evidence discovered is immediately apparent.

## Processing and Logging Evidence

For evidence to be admissible in court, you should follow at least one of these three criminal evidence rules:

- **Authentication**—Authentication means showing a true copy of the original.
- **The best evidence rule**—Best evidence means presenting the original.
- **Exceptions to the hearsay rule**—Allowable exceptions involve a confession or business or official records.

Authentication appears to be the most commonly used of these rules. However, experts disagree about which is the most essential, or most correct, element of this in practice. Some say it's documentation of what has been done. Others say preservation—or integrity of the original. Still others say authenticity—that is, the evidence is what the investigator says it is. Good arguments could be made for the centrality of each, or all, as the standard in computer forensics law. The following sections provide further discussion.

### Documentation

If your documentation is poor, it will look as if your processing procedures were poor. Without a good written record, your testimony in court will look ridiculous.

### Practical Considerations in Forensic Data Collection

The following are some fundamental requirements of forensic data collection:

- Forensic data collection should be complete and non-software specific, thus avoiding software traps and hidden partitioning.
- In operation, forensic data collection should be as quick and as simple as possible to avoid error or delay.
- Anyone should be able to use a forensic data collection system with the minimum amount of training.
- Necessary costs and resources should be kept to a minimum.

Problems in the documentation area arise when an investigator tries to take shortcuts or doesn't have adequate time, equipment, and resources. In general, the condition of all evidence must be documented. For example, it has to be photographed, weighed, and sketched. Then a laboratory worker should figure out which tests are appropriate, decide on which part of the evidence to examine first, dissect or copy the part to be tested, and prepare the testing ground. In addition, the worker must document each of these steps. Only then does any testing begin—and that's heavily documented with bench notes, which are subject to discovery and review by experts from the other side.

## Preservation

Collecting and transporting evidence gives rise to numerous possibilities for error in the form of destruction, mishandling, and contamination. Problems in the preservation area have implications for the integrity of law enforcement and crime labs. The basic chain of custody, for example, involves at least three initial potential sources of error:

- Evidence has to be discovered.
- It has to be collected.
- It has to be packaged, labeled, and transported to the lab.

When evidence gets to the lab, it has to be logged in. For each piece of evidence, someone must assign an identification number, place it in storage, and keep it from intermingling with other evidence. All workplaces must be clean and contamination free. Some workplaces are required to meet the standards of professional accrediting organizations. Written policies must be in place. The quality assurance policy, for example, must act as a check on quality control.

## Authenticity

If your authenticity is poor, then you, your agency, and the prosecutor will look like inexperienced rookies. Computer evidence, like computer simulations, hasn't fared well under the more rigorous standards of admissibility for scientific evidence. Case law varies by jurisdiction. The following are some of the relevant scientific evidence standards:

- **Relevancy test (Federal Rules of Evidence 401, 402, 403)**—The relevancy test is embodied in the Federal Rules of Evidence and some state rules of evidence. These rules liberally allow anything that materially assists the trier of fact to be deemed relevant by the trier of law.

- **Frye standard (*Frye v. U.S., 1923*)**—For the results of a scientific technique to be admissible, the technique must be sufficiently established to have gained general acceptance in its particular field. This is referred to as a *general acceptance test.*

- **Coppolino standard (*Coppolino v. State, 1968*)**—Even if the profession as a whole isn't familiar with a new test or new science on a particular problem, the court allows it if an adequate foundation can be laid.

- **Marx standard (*People v. Marx, 1975*)**—The court is satisfied if it does not have to sacrifice its common sense in understanding and evaluating the scientific expertise put before it. This is a *common sense* or *no scientific jargon test.*

> **FYI**
>
> You must be able to demonstrate that the evidence is what you say it is, came from where you say it did, and has not been modified in any way since it was obtained. How you go about this depends on the circumstances and the computer systems involved. It's futile to talk about any one correct way to do it, or any perfect printout. There's no "silver bullet" standardized checklist, and there's no "magic" software to produce the perfect printout.

- **Daubert standard (*Daubert v. Merrell Dow, 1993*)**—This rigorous test requires special pretrial hearings for scientific evidence and special discovery procedures. The rules on validity, reliability, benchmarking, algorithms, and error rates are laid out beforehand.

The federal courts were the first to recognize that files on computers are similar to and dissimilar to files kept on paper. In recent years, the best evidence rule has also seen the growth of a standard known as *representational accuracy,* which means it's not necessary to present all the originals. Therefore, a modern clause in the Federal Rules of Evidence (FRE 1001-3) states, "If data are stored by computer or similar device, any printout or other output readable by sight, shown to reflect the data accurately, is an original." This exception to the best evidence rule has found a mostly welcome reception in state courts.

Many argue that it's more appropriate to consider digital evidence as demonstrative rather than documentary. The history of computers in the courtroom ties in with demonstrative standards, and computer forensics, after all, is about reconstructing the crime, or criminalistics. Computer forensics specialists and technicians work from a copy, duplicate, mirror, replica, or exemplar of the original evidence. Digital evidence is easily lost; there's nothing else in criminal justice more easily damaged, corrupted, or erased.

## The Computer Evidence Collection Process

Perhaps one of the most crucial points of a case lies hidden in a computer. The digital evidence collection process allows you to not only locate that key evidence but also maintain the integrity and reliability of that evidence. Timing during this digital evidence collection process is of the essence. Any delay or continuous use of the suspect computer may overwrite data before a forensic specialist can analyze it, resulting in destruction of critical evidence.

The following are some helpful tips for preserving data for future computer forensics examination:

- Do not turn on or attempt to examine the suspect computer. Doing so could result in destruction of evidence.
- Identify all devices that may contain evidence, including the following:
  - Workstation computers
  - Offsite computers, such as laptops, home computers, senders and recipients of e-mail, and personal digital assistants (PDAs)

- Removable storage devices, such as external hard drives, flash drives, and CDs
- Network storage devices, such as servers, tapes, storage area networks (SANs), and network-attached storage (NAS)

- Quarantine all in-house computers, following these protocols:
  - Do not permit anyone to use the computers.
  - Secure all removable media.
  - Turn off the computers.
  - Disconnect the computers from the network.
  - Consider the need for court orders to preserve and secure the digital evidence on third-party computers and storage media.
- Forensically image all suspect media.

## Computer Forensics Policies

Protecting an organization from outside threats is clearly important. Protecting an organization from internal threats is also important. Corporations and government agencies now provide Internet access to their employees. Providing this access opens a Pandora's box. Workers can easily spend countless hours online every day, entertaining themselves at their employer's expense. In addition, employee use of Internet pornography can create a hostile workplace environment and potentially expose an organization to civil liability.

According to the 2008 Computer Crime and Security Survey conducted by the Computer Security Institute and the Federal Bureau of Investigation (FBI), 72 percent of the respondents reported unauthorized access to information by persons inside the organization, compared with just 47 percent who reported intrusions by outsiders. More than 27 percent reported theft of proprietary information, and 85 percent reported theft of laptop computers. Ninety-seven percent reported virus contamination, and a staggering 99 percent reported systems abuse—pornography, pirated software, inappropriate e-mail usage, and so on—by insiders. According to SexTracker, an organization that tracks the online pornography trade, 87 percent of online pornography viewing occurs during the 9-to-5 workday.

Detailed policies on the use of computers within an organization are an ever-increasing necessity. Regulations are increasing.

A computer forensics policy manual should address all manner of computer-related policy needs. The content should be based on the corporation's experience in employment-related investigations, computer crime investigations, civil litigation, and criminal prosecutions.

 **NOTE**

Countless organizations use comprehensive and effective computer forensics policies. These organizations include banks, insurance companies, law firms, local governments, retailers, technology firms, educational institutions, charitable organizations, manufacturers, and distributors.

Approximately half of the manual should consist of detailed discussions on each of the policy topic areas. The other half should be sample policies that can be readily customized by parts of an organization. The discussions should include topics such as why policies are needed, potential liability, employee productivity considerations, and civil litigation. The manual should discuss in detail safeguarding critical and confidential information. The policies should directly address the problems that would typically occur in an organization of this size and type.

## CHAPTER SUMMARY

Computer forensics is a field that demands precision. Every investigation is critical, so a computer forensics specialist must be precise and control every investigation. A computer forensics crime scene investigation starts with a plan to approach and secure the crime scene. You must be able to document crime scene activity, engage in discovery and identification of evidence or potential evidence, collect and retrieve such material, and process or analyze it as evidence. You must understand how to control a computer forensics investigation and understand the legal aspects of acquiring evidence.

## KEY CONCEPTS AND TERMS

| | | |
|---|---|---|
| Batch file | Imaging | Sector |
| Bit stream backup | Incriminating evidence | Shadow data |
| Boot process | Live analysis school of thought | Temporary data |
| Cluster | Logical analysis | Volatile data |
| File allocation table (FAT) | Physical analysis | |
| Fourth Amendment to the U.S. Constitution | Safe shutdown school of thought | |

## CHAPTER 6 ASSESSMENT

1. What type of data is lost whenever a system is used and should therefore be collected first to minimize corruption or loss?

   A. Bit stream data
   B. Forensic data
   C. Temporary data
   D. Volatile data

2. The _____, as its name suggests, recommends leaving a suspect computer turned on and working on it immediately after securing it.

3. Why is it important to create a bit stream copy of a disk drive or another type of storage media?

   A. A bit stream copy can be created very quickly.
   B. A bit stream copy exactly replicates all sectors on the storage device, including all files and ambient data storage areas.
   C. The Department of Defense requires bit stream copies in all investigations.
   D. It's not. Standard file backups and network server backups are sufficient in most cases.

4. You should always work on the suspect hard drive rather than a backup, a duplicate, a copy, or an image.

   A. True
   B. False

5. In a forensic investigation, speed is more important than thoroughness.

   A. True
   B. False

6. Which of the following is a batch file that handles drivers for all the devices hooked up to the controllers and ports?

   A. AUTOEXEC.BAT
   B. COMMAND.COM
   C. CONFIG.SYS
   D. DRVSPACE.BI

7. Which techniques of forensic analysis are discussed in this chapter? (Select three.)

   A. Live analysis
   B. Volatile analysis
   C. Physical analysis
   D. Logical analysis

8. Which of the following does Windows use on a system as a "scratch pad" to write data when additional RAM is needed?

   A. Batch file
   B. Swap file
   C. File residue
   D. Unallocated space

9. Which of the following is the smallest unit of storage on a computer?

   A. File allocation table (FAT)
   B. Cluster
   C. Sector
   D. File

10. _____ is the area of a hard drive that has never been allocated for file storage, or the leftover area that the computer regards as unallocated after file deletion.

11. One of the first questions that can be asked in computer seizure law is when exactly the search occurs. The _____ Amendment to the U.S. Constitution deals with search and seizure.

12. Which of the following is *not* a best practice in preserving data for future computer forensics examination?

    A. Immediately turn on and attempt to examine the suspect computer.
    B. Identify all devices that may contain evidence.
    C. Quarantine all in-house computers.
    D. Forensically image all suspect media.

# Collecting, Seizing, and Protecting Evidence

O RGANIZATIONS ARE BATTLING ATTACKERS with increasingly sophisticated skills. System forensics is crucial to determining how an attack succeeded and developing controls to prevent future strikes. However, companies often make mistakes that prevent successful forensic investigations. They may fail to incorporate security controls to prevent attacks. They may also fail to collect appropriate data to support a forensic examination. Businesses should have their environments forensically ready.

Collecting data as evidence is difficult in any situation. This is why forensic examiners document the process and maintain a chain of custody throughout their investigations. Collecting electronic evidence involves special complexities. Electronic evidence has none of the permanence of conventional evidence. It can't be touched or seen, and it is difficult to assemble into a coherent argument. This chapter discusses some of these difficulties and what a system forensics expert can do to overcome them. The first part of this chapter focuses on the basics of evidence collection, including why it's important to collect evidence, obstacles to data collection, and types of evidence. It then examines issues related to seizing and protecting evidence.

## Chapter 7 Topics

This chapter covers the following topics and concepts:

- How to collect forensic evidence
- What steps are required to seize forensic evidence
- How to protect forensic evidence

## Chapter 7 Goals

When you complete this chapter, you will be able to:

- Explain the basics of collecting forensic evidence
- Describe the steps in seizing forensic evidence
- Explain how to protect forensic evidence

# Collecting Forensic Evidence

Collecting electronic evidence can be expensive. Data collection processes are strict and exhaustive. Systems affected may be unavailable for regular use for extended time frames. Data is useful only after analysis. In light of the costs and business interruption caused by a forensic investigation, why should one ever be conducted? Organizations have three reasons:

- Determine what has been stolen or damaged and assess the damage to the organization.
- Determine how the event occurred and develop controls to prevent a recurrence.
- Determine who is responsible and has legal culpability. An organization needs evidentiary support for criminal prosecution and civil damage recovery.

It's important for an organization to learn from a breach. Without knowledge of what happened, it is impossible to prevent repeated breaches using the same techniques. The cost of data collection may be high, but the cost of repeatedly recovering from compromises is much higher—in terms of money, business disruption, and corporate image.

The two key stakeholders after an attack are the attacker and the victim. The attacker is responsible for the damage done. However, the only way to bring that person to justice and to seek recompense is with adequate evidence to prove the person's actions. The victim must collect information regarding the damages caused and restore normal operations as much as possible. Information provided by the victim is also used to assess the

---

**FYI**

Use this chapter as a guide only. No single answer can steer you through all investigations. No two investigations are the same. Seek further information from technical and legal experts for your specific circumstances. This chapter does not provide legal advice. Different regions have different legislation. If in doubt, consult a lawyer.

### Steps in Collecting and Analyzing Evidence

Collecting and analyzing evidence involves a general four-step procedure:

1. **Identify the evidence**—Distinguish between evidence and unnecessary data. Evidence is information directly related to the incident. Unnecessary data, on the other hand, is any data that has no relation to the incident. Know what the data is or represents, where it is located, and how it is stored. Then you can work out the best way to retrieve and store the data and determine whether it is useful as evidence.

2. **Preserve the evidence**—Preserve the evidence as close to its original state as possible. Document and justify any changes made during this phase.

3. **Analyze the evidence**—Analyze stored evidence to extract the relevant information and re-create the chain of events. Also, have in-depth knowledge of what you are looking for and how to get it. Those who are analyzing the evidence must be fully qualified to do so.

4. **Present the evidence**—Communicating the meaning of evidence is vitally important. The manner of presentation is crucial. To be most effective when presenting evidence, be clear enough that a layperson can understand your argument. Your case should remain technically correct, credible, and validated by other sources where possible.

---

severity of the sanctions—damage recovery, fines, length of incarceration—that should be applied against the attacker. Under some legal theories, victims also have a community responsibility to provide information that may prevent future attacks perpetrated by the same individual or group or using the same techniques. Victims might also have a legal obligation to perform an analysis of evidence collected—for instance, if the attack affected customer health or financial records.

## Obstacles to Data Collection

Electronic crime is difficult to investigate and prosecute. Build your case on data that remains on storage media after an attack.

Computer transactions are fast, including transactions with criminal intent. They can be conducted from anywhere, through anywhere, and to anywhere. They can be in clear text, encoded, encrypted, or anonymized. Unlike handwriting or signatures, computer transactions have no intrinsic identifying features. Perpetrators can modify or destroy any paper trail or computer records. Also, auditing programs intended to monitor transaction accuracy may automatically destroy data remnants left by computer transactions.

You can often restore the details of transactions through analysis. Even so, tying a transaction to an attacker is difficult. Attaching identifying information such as personal identification numbers does not automatically prove who was responsible for a transaction. Such information shows that whoever did it either knew or could get past those identifiers. Systems must be designed with protected methods for recording responsibility for transactions. Forensic examinations must document that those access controls were in place and functional at the time the system recorded the data.

## Types of Forensic Evidence

Legal proceedings recognize three types of evidence:

- **Real evidence**—Real evidence is any evidence that speaks for itself, without relying on anything else. This may be a visitors' log, the physical presence of a server or desktop, or the date of a letter validated by a third party, such as the U.S. Postal Service.

- **Testimonial evidence**—Testimonial evidence is any evidence supplied by a witness. This type of evidence is subject to the perceived reliability of the witness. If the witness is considered reliable, testimonial evidence can be almost as powerful as real evidence. Documents from a word processing program written by a witness may be considered testimonial—as long as the author is willing to state that he or she wrote it.

- **Hearsay**—Hearsay is any evidence presented by a person who was not a direct witness. An example of hearsay is documents from a word processing program written by someone without direct knowledge of the incident under investigation. Hearsay is generally inadmissible in court, so avoid using it.

In your role as forensic investigator, take these three categories of evidence into consideration to ensure that the data you collect is useful.

## The Rules of Evidence

Follow these five rules when collecting electronic evidence:

- **Admissibility**—The evidence must be able to be used in court. Failure to comply with this rule is equivalent to not collecting the evidence in the first place. However, the cost of collection has already been spent.

- **Authenticity**—To make a case, show that the evidence relates to the incident.

- **Completeness**—Evidence must show more than one perspective of the incident. A forensic specialist is also an independent evaluator. He or she collects evidence that can prove the attacker's actions as well as evidence that can prove a person's innocence. For example, if an investigator can show that an attacker was logged on at the time of the incident, he or she also must show who else was logged on and why those people likely didn't do it. The phrase for this is **exculpatory evidence**— that is, evidence that clears or tends to clear someone of guilt—and it is an important part of proving a case.

- **Reliability**—The evidence collected must be reliable. Don't let evidence collection and analysis procedures cast doubt on the authenticity and veracity of your evidence.

- **Believability**—The evidence presented should be clearly understandable and believable by a jury. A binary dump of process memory, for example, might not make sense to a jury. Similarly, if the jury sees a formatted, human-understandable version of the same information, you must be able to show its relationship to the original binary.

## Do's and Don'ts of Data Collection

Use the preceding five rules to derive some basic do's and don'ts of data collection:

- **Minimize handling and corruption of original data**—Create a master copy of the original data and then don't touch the original itself but always secondary copies. Any changes made to the originals will affect the outcomes of analysis later done to copies. Also, don't run any programs that modify the access times of all files. In addition, remove any external avenues for change and, in general, analyze the evidence after collecting it.

- **Account for any changes and keep detailed logs of actions**—Sometimes evidence alteration is unavoidable. For example, in photo enhancement, the software changes the original bit patterns in the picture. In these cases, it is absolutely essential that you document the nature, extent, and reasons for the changes. Remember to account for any changes—not only data alteration but also physical alteration of the originals, such as the removal of hardware components. In addition, collect supporting research that backs use of a particular data enhancement technique in case the analytical results require proof.

- **Comply with the five rules of evidence**—Following the five rules is essential to guaranteeing successful evidence collection.

- **Do not exceed current knowledge**—If you find that you are out of your depth, either learn more before continuing or find someone who knows the territory. It is important to establish ongoing relationships with subject matter experts. No one person is an expert in everything. Soldiering on without the needed knowledge damages an investigation and compromises any results.

- **Follow local security policy**—Failure to comply with a company's security policy could create problems both for you and for the evidence you gather.

- **Capture an image of the system that is as accurate as possible**—Capturing an accurate image of the system minimizes the handling or corruption of original data. Differences between the original system and the master copy count as changes to the data. Always account for any differences.

- **Be prepared to testify**—If you are the forensic specialist on your team who collects the evidence, the court will need you to appear to validate the material collected. If you are unable to testify for any reason—illness, other duties, etc.—any document created related to the data collection process must stand on its own. Otherwise, the evidence becomes hearsay, which is inadmissible.

- **Ensure that actions are repeatable**—No one is going to believe an investigator whose actions can't be repeated and provide the same results each time. Don't base your plan of action on trial and error.

- **Proceed from volatile to persistent evidence**—Some electronic evidence is more volatile than other evidence. Therefore, collect the most volatile evidence first. See the section "Volatile Data: Two Schools of Thought" in Chapter 6, "Controlling a Forensic Investigation," for information on whether to shut down a suspect system before collecting evidence.

- **Work fast but thoroughly**—The faster you work, the less likely the data is to change. Volatile evidence may vanish entirely if you don't collect it in time. Although the evidence you collect must be accurate data, don't rush. If a crime involves multiple systems, a team of investigators can work on them in parallel. They should work on each single system methodically. Automation of certain tasks makes collection proceed even faster.

- **Don't run any programs on the affected system**—An attacker may have left trojaned programs and libraries on a suspect system. Running programs on the system might inadvertently trigger something that could change or destroy evidence. With this danger in mind, remember to use programs from read-only media, such as CD-ROMs, that are statically linked.

### Creating an Order of Volatility

Much of the evidence on a system does not last very long. Some evidence resides in storage that requires a consistent power supply. Other evidence may sit in media locations that are continuously changing. As described in Chapter 6, "Controlling a Forensic Investigation," proceed from collecting the most volatile evidence to the least volatile. To determine what evidence to collect first, draw up an **order of volatility**—a list of evidence sources ordered by their relative volatility. The following is an example of an order of volatility:

1. Registers and cache
2. Routing tables
3. Arp cache
4. Process table
5. Kernel statistics and modules
6. Main memory
7. Temporary file systems
8. Secondary memory
9. Router configuration
10. Network topology

> **NOTE**
>
> Today's digital forensics involves more than just laptops and desktops. Look at network and communication data, which makes logging essential. Proving an incident has occurred is impossible with just a hand-sketched network diagram and some Web access logs. You will also need logs from firewalls, routers, and intrusion detection systems.

## Logging and Monitoring

A system should be running a system logging function. Keep these logs secure and back them up periodically. Effective system logs are time stamped, showing when each activity occurred. So, digitally sign and encrypt any logs collected to protect them from contamination.

You should copy and remove a log from the machine on which it was created. If logs are kept locally on a compromised machine, an attacker could possibly alter or delete them. Storing logs on a remote device can reduce this risk. However, it is still possible for an attacker to add decoy or junk entries to the logs prior to the date on which you copied them.

Regular auditing and accounting of a system is useful for detecting intruders. The forensic expert can draw on audit results as evidence. You can use messages and logs from programs to show what damage an attacker did. Audits and log reviews can verify the timing of when various events occurred.

Monitoring network traffic can be useful for many reasons. For example, it can help gather statistics to provide a usage profile, identify irregular activity and possibly stop an intrusion in process, and trace where an attacker is coming from and what he or she is doing. Monitoring logs as they are created can provide important information and help identify suspiciously missing information.

You can compile information gathered while monitoring network traffic into statistics to define normal behavior for a system. Then use these statistics to get early warning of an attacker's actions. In addition, monitoring the actions of users can provide early warning: Unusual activity or the sudden appearance of unknown users should trigger closer inspection.

## Methods of Data Collection: Freezing the Scene and Honeypotting

Investigators work with two basic methods of data collection: freezing the scene and honeypotting. The two aren't mutually exclusive. It is possible to collect frozen information after or during any honeypotting.

**FYI**

No matter the type of monitoring done, be very careful not to inadvertently break any laws. In general, an investigator should limit monitoring to traffic or user information and leave the content unmonitored unless a situation necessitates it. A system should also display a disclaimer when users log on, stating what monitoring is performed. An organization should work out the content of this disclaimer with the help of a lawyer.

**Freezing the scene** involves taking a snapshot of the system in its compromised state. The organization must notify the necessary authorities—the police and the organization's incident response and legal teams. However, the organization should avoid letting the media find out about the incident yet, if possible.

As a forensic specialist, your job is to collect whatever data is available and put it on removable nonvolatile media in a standard format. The programs and utilities you use to gather the data should also be collected onto the same media as the data. Create a cryptographic message digest for all the data you pull together, and then compare the digests to the originals for verification.

**Honeypotting** is the process of creating a replica system and luring an attacker into it to monitor his or her activities. A related method, **sandboxing**, involves limiting what an attacker can do while still on the compromised system, so you can monitor the attacker without much further damage. The placement of misleading information and the attacker's response to it is a good method for determining the attacker's motives. Either remove or encrypt any data on the system related to the attacker's detection and actions. Otherwise, the attacker can cover his or her tracks by destroying this data.

---

### The Law Enforcement Dilemma

The laws surrounding the collection and preservation of evidence are complex. The local law enforcement department may not have a system forensics expert on staff. However, it will know the basic rules of evidence collection and should have contacts within the law enforcement community who are experts in system forensics.

Deciding when to call law enforcement after a breach can be difficult. It usually involves weighing a lot of factors, such as whether criminal activity is suspected, the extent of damages, and the risk of public disclosure. Many organizations have defined procedures for involving law enforcement officials that require first notifying a member of senior management, such as general counsel, the vice president of operations, or the chief information officer.

Law enforcement can have great resources for tracking down culprits. However, an organization essentially gives up control of an investigation when it calls for official help. Plus, there's a risk that corporate confidential information or trade secrets could be revealed in a court case.

Before calling law enforcement, an organization should have a good idea of what happened and what losses it has sustained, including estimates of downtime, personnel, and lost business. An organization or individual can report computer and Internet crimes to federal law enforcement (see *http://www.justice.gov/criminal/cybercrime/reporting.htm#cc*). Federal agencies determine what crimes to pursue based on the level of damages and other potential impacts. An organization may need to decide whether to file a criminal action, a civil action, or both, depending on the nature and severity of the incident.

Honeypotting and sandboxing are extremely resource intensive, so they may be infeasible. They also involve legal issues such as entrapment. As in any other questionable situation, an organization should obtain legal advice before beginning honeypotting and sandboxing operations.

## The Steps in Seizing Forensic Evidence

In case of intrusion—either from outside or inside the company—an organization should have a response plan and a team ready to take charge. This team should involve information technology (IT), management, legal, and human resources representatives. Those on the frontlines, typically the IT staff, must know who to call and the first course of action. As discussed in Chapter 13, "Incident and Intrusion Response," a clearly documented plan is essential for an investigation team to be successful in collecting admissible evidence. The team should design the plan with the assistance of legal counsel and law enforcement agencies to ensure compliance with all applicable local, state, and federal laws. After developing a plan of attack and identifying the evidence that the team should collect, investigators can begin the process of capturing the data, also referred to as *seizing evidence*.

The following sections provide a general guideline for steps involved in processing computer evidence. These steps present only one of many approaches that investigators use to process computer evidence.

### Shutting Down the Computer

Depending on the computer operating system, shutting down the computer usually involves pulling the plug or shutting down a network computer by using the necessary commands. You may wish to take pictures of the screen image. However, keep in mind that destructive processes may be operating in the background. These can be in memory or available through a connected modem. Depending on the operating system involved, a password-protected screen saver may also kick in at any moment. This can complicate the computer's shutdown. Generally, time is of the essence, and you should shut down the computer system as quickly as possible.

---

**FYI**

It's a good idea to configure a test network in a lab environment and invite members of the IT staff to attempt to circumvent the security measures installed in the lab network. The organization should treat the intrusion as an actual incident and follow its incident handling and evidence collection procedures. The team should review the results and evaluate whether evidence collected would be admissible, based on the procedures followed and the analysis results.

**Shutting Down Versus Monitoring the Intruder**

When an organization has detected a compromise of its systems, it has two options: Pull the system off the network and begin collecting evidence or leave it online and attempt to monitor the intruder. Both options have pros and cons. Which one you choose depends on the situation.

Monitoring may accidentally alert the intruder that you are watching him or her. The intruder might then wipe his or her tracks, destroying evidence. This approach also leaves your organization open to possible liability issues if the attacker launches further attacks at other systems from the organization's own network system.

However, if you disconnect the system from the network, you may obtain insufficient evidence. The attacker may also have left a **dead man's switch** to destroy evidence when the system detects that it's offline.

## Documenting the Hardware Configuration of the System

Move the subject computer system to a secure location where you can maintain a proper chain of custody and begin processing evidence. Before dismantling the computer, it is important to take pictures of the computer from all angles to document the system hardware components and how they are connected. Labeling each wire is also important, so that you can easily reconnect each one when the system configuration is restored to its original condition.

## Transporting the Computer System to a Secure Location

Seized computers are often stored in less-than-secure locations. Both law enforcement agencies and corporations sometimes fail to properly transport and store suspect systems. It is imperative that you treat a subject computer as evidence and store it out of reach of curious computer users.

Sometimes, individuals operate seized computers without knowing that they are destroying potential evidence and the chain of custody. A seized computer left unattended can easily be compromised. Someone could plant evidence or destroy crucial evidence. Lack of a proper chain of custody can make a savvy defense attorney's day. Without a proper chain of custody, you can't ensure that evidence was not planted on the computer after the seizure.

> **TIP**
>
> Don't leave a suspect computer unattended unless it is locked up in a secure location.

## Mathematically Authenticating Data on All Storage Devices

You should be able to prove that you didn't alter any of the evidence after taking possession of a suspect computer. Such proof helps rebut allegations that the investigator changed or altered the original evidence.

Since 1989, law enforcement and military agencies have used a 32-bit mathematical process to support device authentication. Mathematically, a 32-bit validation is accurate to approximately 1 in 4.3 billion. However, given the speed of today's computers and the vast amount of storage capacity on today's computer hard disk drives, this level of accuracy is no longer accurate enough. A 32-bit cyclical redundancy check (CRC) can be compromised. Some forensic tools can mathematically authenticate data with a high level of accuracy. You can use these programs to authenticate data at both a physical level and a logical level. New Technologies, Inc. (NTI), offers two such programs: CrcMD5 and DiskSig Pro. (For more information on these tools, see *http://www.forensics-intl.com*.)

## Making a List of Key Search Words

Modern hard drives are voluminous. It is impossible for a computer specialist to manually view and evaluate every file on a computer hard drive. Therefore, you need state-of-the-art automated forensic text search tools to help find the relevant evidence. One such tool is NTI's TextSearch NT, which is certified for use by the U.S. Department of Defense. Intelligent filtering tools can also be helpful in crafting lists of keywords for use in computer evidence processing. Some examples are NTI's NTA Stealth, Filter_N, FNames, Filter_G, GExtract, and GetHTML. (For more information on these tools, see *http://www.forensics-intl.com*.)

 **TIP**

It's important for an investigator to determine where the evidence he or she is looking for is stored. Using a checklist helps collect evidence and also helps double-check that the data being sought is there.

Usually some information is known about the allegations, the computer user, and any alleged associates. Gather information from individuals familiar with the case to help compile a list of relevant keywords. Then apply these keywords in a search of all computer hard drives and CDs using automated software. Keeping the list as short as possible is important, and the list should avoid common words or words that make up part of other words.

The following sections discuss three areas to search for keywords: the Windows swap file, file slack, and unallocated space.

### Evaluating the Windows Swap File

The Windows swap file is a potentially valuable source of evidence and leads. With Windows Server 2003, Vista, Server 2008, and 7, the swap file may be set to be dynamically created as the computer is operated. This is the default setting, and when the computer is turned off, the swap file is erased. However, all is not lost because the swap file's contents can easily be captured and evaluated.

In the past, investigators carried out the tedious task of evaluating the swap file with hex editors. Evaluating just one swap file took days. With the use of automated tools, this process now takes only a few minutes. NTA Stealth, Filter_N, FNames, Filter_G, GExtract and GetHTML are examples of intelligent filters that automatically identify patterns of English language text, phone numbers, Social Security numbers, credit card numbers, Internet e-mail addresses, Internet Web addresses, and names of people. They are all available from NTI (see *http://www.forensics-intl.com*).

## Evaluating File Slack

Most people who use computers are unaware of a data storage area called file slack. However, it is a source of significant security leakage. File slack contains raw memory dumps that occur during a work session as files are closed. The data dumped from memory ends up being stored at the end of allocated files, beyond the reach or view of the normal computer user. File slack can provide a wealth of information and investigative leads. Like the Windows swap file, this source of ambient data can provide relevant keywords and leads for your forensic research.

On a well-used hard disk drive, file slack may occupy several gigabytes of storage space. Evaluate file slack for relevant keywords to supplement the keywords identified in the previous steps. You should add these new keywords to your original list of keywords for use later.

> **NOTE**
>
> File slack is typically a good source of Internet leads. According to NTI, tests suggest that file slack provides approximately 80 times more Internet leads than the Windows swap file. Therefore, cases involving possible Internet uses or abuses shouldn't overlook this source of potential leads.

Specialized forensic tools are required to view and evaluate file slack. You can analyze file slack with computer applications that use fuzzy logic or artificial intelligence. Examples are NTA Stealth (see *http://www.forensics-intl.com/nta.html*), Forensic Toolkit (see *http://www.digitalintelligence.com/software/accessdata/forensictoolkit3/*), and SilentRunner (see *http://www.accessdata.com/silentrunner.html*).

## Evaluating Unallocated Space

On a well-used hard disk drive, gigabytes of storage space may contain data associated with previously erased files. This space is known as *free space,* or *unallocated space.* Unallocated space is typically a good source of data that was previously associated with word processing temporary files and other temporary files created by various computer applications.

Evaluate unallocated space for relevant keywords to supplement the keywords identified in the previous steps. Such keywords should be added to your list of keywords for use in the next processing step.

Because of the nature of data contained in unallocated space and its volume, system forensics investigations need specialized and automated forensic tools for evaluation. Ontrack's EasyRecovery DataRecovery (see *http://www.ontrackdatarecovery.com/ file-recovery-software/*) and Evidor from X-Ways Software Technology AG (see *http:// www.x-ways.net/evidor/*) do this. So does NTI's utility GetFree (see *http://www.forensics -intl.com/getfree.html*).

## Searching Files, File Slack, and Unallocated Space for Keywords

Use the list of relevant keywords identified in the previous step to search all pertinent computer hard disk drives and removable media. Several forensic text search utilities are available in the marketplace. For example, NTI's TextSearch NT and TextSearch Plus are state-of-the-art tools that federal government intelligence agencies have validated as security review tools (see *http://www.forensics-intl.com*).

**TIP**

Text search utilities can also be used effectively in security reviews of computer storage media.

It is important to review the output of the text search utility. It is equally critical to document relevant findings. When you have identified relevant evidence, note the fact and then completely review the identified data for additional keywords. You should then add these new words to the original list of keywords and conduct a new search using the text search utility.

## Documenting Filenames, Dates, and Times

From an evidence standpoint, filenames, creation dates, and last modified dates and times can be relevant. Therefore, it is important to catalog all allocated and "erased" files. Sort the files based on the filename, file size, file content, creation date, and last modified date and time. Such sorted information can provide a timeline of computer usage. The output should be in the form of a word processing-compatible file to help document computer evidence issues tied to specific files.

## Identifying File, Program, and Storage Anomalies

Encrypted, compressed, and graphics files store data in binary format. As a result, text search programs can't identify text data stored in these file formats. These files require manual evaluation, which may involve a lot of work, especially with encrypted files. Depending on the type of file, view and evaluate the content as potential evidence.

Reviewing the partitioning on seized hard disk drives is also important. Evaluate hidden partitions for evidence and document their existence.

With Windows operating systems, you should also evaluate the files contained in the Recycle Bin. The Recycle Bin is the repository of files selected for deletion by the computer user. The fact that they have been selected for deletion may have some relevance from an evidentiary standpoint. If you find relevant files, thoroughly document the issues involved.

---

### Handling Artifacts

When compromising a system, the attacker almost always leaves something behind—such as code fragments, trojaned programs, running processes, or sniffer log files. This left-behind information is an **artifact**. It is important for you to collect artifacts. However, never attempt to analyze an artifact on the compromised system. Artifacts are capable of anything, and it's important to restrict their effects.

Artifacts may be difficult to find. For example, trojaned programs may be identical in all obvious ways to the originals in terms of file size, Media Access Control (MAC) times, and so on. Use of cryptographic checksums may be necessary, so you may need to know the original file's checksum. When performing regular file integrity assessments, this shouldn't be a problem. Analysis of artifacts can be useful in finding other systems the attacker—or his or her tools—has broken into.

## Evaluating Program Functionality

Depending on the application software involved, you may need to run programs to learn their purpose. Destructive processes tied to relevant evidence can prove willfulness on the attacker's part. Such destructive processes can be tied to hot keys or the execution of common commands linked to the operating system or applications.

## Documenting Findings

When you identify issues and discover evidence, document these findings. In addition, document all the software used in a forensic evaluation of evidence, including the version numbers of the programs you use.

When appropriate, your documentation should indicate licensure to use the forensic software involved. Screen captures of the operating software also help to verify the version of the software and how you used it to find and/or process the evidence.

> **NOTE**
>
> Have a legal copy of any forensic software you use. Smart defense lawyers usually question software licensing, and software pirates do not stand up well under the rigors of a trial. Software piracy is a criminal violation of federal copyright laws.

## Retaining Copies of Software Used

As part of the documentation process, include a copy of any software used for an investigation with the output of the forensic tool involved. Normally, this is done on an archive CD or an external storage device such as an external hard drive. This documentation methodology eliminates confusion about which version of the software was used to create the output. Often it is necessary to duplicate forensic-processing results during or before trial. Duplication of results can be difficult or impossible to achieve if the software has been upgraded and the original version used was not retained. Most commercial software is upgraded routinely, but it may take years for a case to go to trial. Retention of archival copies of programs should be included in software license agreements.

> **NOTE**
>
> It isn't reasonable to expect all nations to know about and abide by the laws and rules of other countries. However, countries need a means for exchanging evidence. Components of the U.S. Department of Justice and the Department of State can help coordinate evidence sharing between countries.

# Protecting Evidence: Controlling Contamination

An investigation goal is to collect and preserve evidence that will be admissible in a court of law. Forensic specialists must protect forensic data from contamination. They must be able to demonstrate that evidence has been successfully protected from corruption or loss.

With this in mind, never use originals in forensic examination. Instead, use verified duplicates. This ensures that the original data remains protected and enables you to run tests that might corrupt data. Run any tests on a clean, isolated host machine. You could create problems by allowing an attacker's programs to access a network.

---

**FYI**

Without proper training, even a world-class computer scientist can do the wrong things. Computer science has areas of specialty. No one individual can be an expert in all areas. System forensics investigators are often informed that a computer-knowledgeable internal auditor or systems administrator has attempted to process a computer for evidence. In some cases, valuable evidence is lost or the evidence is tainted such that it loses its evidentiary value.

According to many forensic experts, it's best if organizations train their staff to take a hands-off approach to evidence collection. If they suspect that a forensic investigation may be required on a device, the rule is to not touch it but to wait for a computer specialist who has been trained in computer evidence processing procedures.

---

A big part of forensics is carefully documenting how evidence is handled so you can present it in court. As discussed in Chapter 1, "System Forensics Fundamentals," a good way of ensuring that data remains uncorrupted is to maintain a chain of custody. This is a detailed list of what actions were performed with subject systems and data after they were seized. Without a chain of custody, lawyers can allege that evidence was tampered with and prevent successful prosecution. The chain of custody involves the following measures:

- Keeping evidence within an investigator's possession or control at all times
- Documenting the collection of evidence
- Documenting the movement of evidence between investigators
- Securing evidence appropriately so it can't be tampered with or corrupted

> **NOTE**
>
> After you have successfully collected data, analyze it to extract the evidence needed to document and describe what actually happened. Again, documentation of analysis is crucial. You must be able to show that you can consistently obtain your results from the procedures performed and that others can independently repeat these procedures with the same results.

It is important to document all data characteristics, such as who found the data; when, where, and how it was transported; who had access to it; where it is stored; and what was done with it. Sometimes a case ends up with more documentation than collected data, but this can be necessary to prove a case.

## Creating a Timeline

To reconstruct the events that led to corruption of a system, create a timeline. This can be particularly difficult when it comes to computers. Clock drift, delayed reporting, and different time zones can create confusion. Never change the clock on a suspect system. Instead, record any clock drift and the time zone in use.

Log files usually use timestamps to indicate when an entry was added. Timestamps must be synchronized to make sense within an event timeline. For example, timestamps on remote systems should be synchronized to the time of the subject computer. You should also use timestamps. After all, you are not just reconstructing events but making a chain of events that you can account for.

## Forensic Analysis of Backups

When analyzing backups, it is best to use a dedicated host. This examination host should be secure and clean, with a fresh, hardened installation of the operating system. Also, isolate the host from any network so that it can't be tampered with and so problems aren't accidentally sent out to other machines. Once the dedicated host system is available, you can begin analyzing the backups.

> **NOTE**
>
> Forensic investigators typically make copies of a compromised system or other evidence and perform analysis on the copies. Courts also accept evidence that is produced in the normal course of business. For example, if a firewall administrator routinely examines logs on a daily basis and sees evidence of a hack, those logs can be considered a normal business record.

## Reconstructing an Attack

After collecting data, an organization can attempt to reconstruct the chain of events leading to and following a break-in. As an investigator, correlate all the evidence gathered. When reconstructing the attack, include all the evidence you find, no matter how small. It is possible to miss important connections or interactions if evidence is left out.

### CHAPTER SUMMARY

Companies spend millions of dollars each year to ensure that their networks and data are properly protected against intrusion. Companies use a defense-in-depth approach because they know that attackers—given enough time and money—can bypass or subvert any single control. Layering controls substantially improves security by increasing an attack's cost and complexity. When unauthorized access occurs, the last line of defense is legal action against the intruder. If system forensics investigators do not properly collect and maintain evidence of an intrusion, it is inadmissible in a court of law. It is important to remember one of the basic rules of the U.S. legal system: If there is no evidence of a crime, there is no crime in the eyes of the law. Therefore, investigators must take utmost care in collecting, seizing, and protecting digital evidence.

Collecting electronic evidence is not a trivial matter. Investigators have many complexities to consider, and must always be able to justify their actions. An investigator needs the right tools and knowledge of how the process works to properly gather and document the evidence required.

### KEY CONCEPTS AND TERMS

| | |
|---|---|
| Artifacts | Hearsay |
| Dead man's switch | Honeypotting |
| Exculpatory evidence | Order of volatility |
| Freezing the scene | Sandboxing |

## CHAPTER 7 ASSESSMENT

**1.** No two investigations are the same.

   A. True
   B. False

**2.** Which of the following is *not* a step in the process of collecting and analyzing evidence?

   A. Identifying the evidence
   B. Preserving the evidence
   C. Creating the evidence
   D. Analyzing the evidence
   E. Presenting the evidence

**3.** Which of the following is the best type of evidence to support a case?

   A. Testimonial evidence
   B. Real evidence
   C. Hearsay
   D. Rules of evidence

**4.** Admissibility, authenticity, completeness, reliability, and believability are called the
   _____.

**5.** Never store system logs on a remote server.

   A. True
   B. False

**6.** When is the best time to notify law enforcement when dealing with a breach?

   A. Immediately after the breach is suspected
   B. After evidence collection has begun
   C. After the attacker is identified
   D. It depends on the circumstances of the case.

**7.** Which of the following is a data collection process that involves creating a replica system and luring an attacker into it for further monitoring?

   A. Collecting artifacts
   B. Honeypotting
   C. Freezing the scene
   D. Sandboxing

**8.** Which of the following are important factors in maintaining the chain of custody? (Select three.)

   A. Keeping evidence within an investigator's possession or control at all times
   B. Locking the evidence in an airtight chamber
   C. Documenting the collection and movement of evidence
   D. Securing the evidence appropriately so it can't be tampered with
   E. Videotaping all data collection

**9.** To search a hard drive for forensic evidence, an investigator should prepare a list of keywords to search for. What are the three main areas of a system that should be searched for these keywords? (Select three.)

   A. C: drive
   B. Swap file
   C. Recycle Bin
   D. File slack
   E. Unallocated space

**10.** Forensic investigators should never use originals. Instead, they should use verified duplicates.

   A. True
   B. False

**11.** The _____ is a detailed list of what was done with original copies and systems after they were seized.

**12.** An investigator should set the clock on a suspect system to the GMT time zone.

   A. True
   B. False

# Understanding
# Information-Hiding Techniques

**M**OST USERS ARE UNAWARE THAT COMPUTERS CONTAIN large volumes of hidden data. In some cases, normal system use hides this data. In other cases, people deliberately conceal it using various techniques. As discussed in earlier chapters, hidden data includes fragments of deleted e-mail messages, backup copies of word processing files, deleted directory structures, and files reflecting a computer user's Internet browsing history. A careful examination of hidden data may tell a compelling story about document destruction or theft of intellectual property.

You can use a number of techniques to locate and retrieve hidden information. One method is to scan and evaluate alternate data streams. Another is to use rootkits. Finally, you can use steganalysis to find data hidden through steganography. This chapter looks at each of these techniques, as well as the history of data hiding.

## Chapter 8 Topics

This chapter covers the following topics and concepts:

- How data hiding began
- How alternate data streams (ADS) hide data
- How rootkits hide data
- What steganography is, how it works, and what tools are available
- How to defeat steganography by using steganalysis and other methods

## Chapter 8 Goals

When you complete this chapter, you will be able to:

- Describe the history of data hiding
- Describe how ADS hide data
- Describe how rootkits hide data
- Explain concepts related to steganography
- Describe how to defeat steganography

# History of Data Hiding

Data hiding has been used for centuries. Before the invention of the computer, people hid data using physical techniques. With the advent of electronic, stored-program computers, people began hiding data using digital approaches.

In the late 1970s, it was possible to hide data on 5¼-inch double-sided, double-density floppy disks. Microsoft's Disk Operating System (DOS) recognized only the first 80 tracks of a disk. Therefore, data could be hidden above track 80. This became one of the most common data hiding techniques in the early microcomputer era. Individuals and companies used this technique to protect copyrighted software. However, its effectiveness was short-lived because application programs could access the tracks beyond track 80. They did so by bypassing the operating system function calls and accessing disk controllers directly. To defeat this form of copy protection, individuals learned how to **pirate** software. More sophisticated approaches to data hiding have since been developed.

Just as it's possible to hide data on a floppy disk, it's possible to hide data on a network. Attackers can use a **covert channel** to pass information between computers on a network. The covert channel slips information through a firewall and past an intrusion detection system. It uses ports that most firewalls permit through. In addition, the covert channel conceals data in a packet header but appears to be an innocuous packet carrying ordinary information. Two popular covert channel techniques are protocol bending and packet crafting.

**Protocol bending** is a covert channel technique that embeds data in packet headers. It uses a network protocol for some unintended purpose. Typically, it involves embedding data in Transmission Control Protocol/Internet Protocol (TCP/IP) packets in unexpected places. This is very similar to hiding data in higher-level DOS tracks. In addition, someone who wants to hide data can "bend" Internet Control Message Protocol (ICMP) to establish a covert channel between network endpoints. It's possible to use the ICMP options field in an ICMP packet to convey application-layer covert data. ICMP packets are not expected to carry application-layer data, so most firewalls and intrusion detection systems don't inspect these packets.

Loki is one of the most widely known ICMP covert channel tools. In the absence of exhaustive packet analysis, Loki traffic looks like any other routine ICMP request-reply pattern for pings, source quenching, and so on. In fact, however, these ICMP packets transmit covert data. Another popular protocol bender is Reverse WWW Shell, which uses a form of protocol bending called *shell shoveling* over Hypertext Transfer Protocol (HTTP).

ICMP packets contain very short messages. No legitimate reason exists for large ICMP packets. If an ICMP packet is larger than 1,024 bytes, it may mean that a hacker is using the ICMP as a channel for transmitting covert messages (see Figure 8-1). The presence of large ICMP packets might indicate a compromised machine or some other kind of suspicious activity.

**Packet crafting** is a technique for embedding data in packet headers. Covert_TCP is a packet crafter that uses active channeling, generating its own packet train to create the channel. NUSHU is a passive channeler that piggybacks on packets transmitted to the TCP/IP stack by other applications.

**FIGURE 8-1**

A large ICMP packet that might carry a covert message.

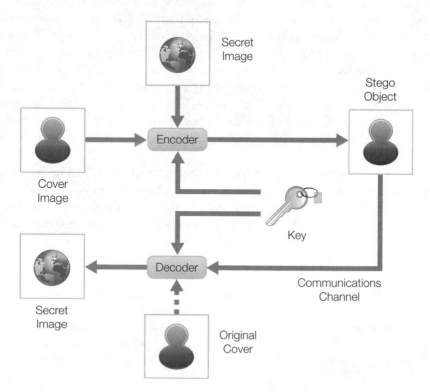

## Alternate Data Streams (ADS)

A data stream is a sequence of bytes. One or more streams make up a file. A stream is created when a file is created. The stream stores the file's contents. Extra streams within a file can also be created. These are called **alternate data streams (ADS)**. Developers invented multi-stream files to allow a file to store metadata about the file itself outside the normal file system structures.

In a computer file, **metadata** provides information about a file. This information includes the means of creation, the purpose of the data, the time and date of creation, the creator or author of data, where the data was created, and what standards were used. Metadata is a technical description of a data element. It is not the data itself. Metadata is important in forensic investigations. For example, metadata may describe data that is relevant to a case. Or if data does not correspond to its metadata, there may be hidden data.

A *fork* is metadata associated with a file system object, such as a data element. A fork's size is arbitrary. In some cases, a fork may be even larger than the file's data. A data element may have one or more forks. In Microsoft's NTFS (NT File System), forks are known as ADS.

In Windows 2000, Microsoft began using ADS in NTFS to store information such as author or title file attributes and image thumbnails. ADS can store anything, so they are good hiding places. With Windows XP, Service Pack 2, Microsoft introduced the Attachment Execution Service, which stores details on the origin of downloaded files in ADS. Microsoft did this to help protect users from downloaded files that may present a risk. By using Attachment Execution Service, a user can automatically include or exclude files from specific origins.

> **▶ NOTE**
>
> Microsoft makes no guarantee that it will support ADS in any newer Windows file systems. The metadata it contains, however, will carry forward in some form. Thus, forensic specialists must review operating system characteristics to determine how metadata is created and maintained and what data that metadata provides.

With ADS, each stream is unique, and multiple streams may be associated with a single file or directory. Streams can store any type of information that a normal file in an NTFS volume can store. Other file systems, such as File Allocation Table (FAT), the Windows predecessor to NTFS, allow access to only one unnamed stream of data that it perceives as the file's actual contents.

If a file or directory with alternate stream data moves to a non-NTFS volume, the stream data and other non-supported attributes become unrecoverable. Windows operating systems currently support ADS only on NTFS volumes. They do not provide a means for disabling ADS, which is a plus for forensic examinations.

### Risks Associated with ADS

ADS are not inherently a security risk. However, the lack of native Windows support for locating, editing, and removing them presents opportunities for potential abuse. How a system's virus scanner and other security mechanisms deal with streams, if at all, plays a large part in mitigating potential risks associated with using NTFS volumes.

Ultimately, the benefits of NTFS volumes far outweigh the potential risks of ADS, as long as system administrators are aware of streams and have the proper security tools to handle them.

## Using ADS to Hide Data

 **NOTE**

Attaching an ADS to a critical file or directory has a high probability of triggering a security mechanism.

Attackers have many methods to hide data in ADS. For example, kernel space filter drivers such as kdl use ADS by attaching their log files to system files or directories. Extensions such as StrmExt.dll do not show the existence of a stream used by kdl while active. However, other tools, such as ADSspy, LADS, and Streams, do reveal the stream. kdl holds a lock to ensure that external tools cannot delete or alter the stream until the lock is released. kdl is set up by default to use Registry keys for configuration. Therefore, changing the log file to be stored as an ADS is trivial.

The System File Checker (sfc.exe) verifies versions of protected system files. However, it ignores any ADS associated with those files. Any user who has the appropriate permissions can attach stream data to protected system files, and sfc.exe can't detect it.

The following are a few other methods attackers may use to avoid detection of hidden data:

- Using stream names such as encrypted, archive, or other common Windows terms
- Creating streams that have no extension identifier
- Creating streams attached to obscure system files for data dumps, log files, and so on—for example, packager.exe and sqlsodbc.chm
- Storing encrypted data in single streams or across multiple streams
- Storing binary data across multiple streams to be reassembled and executed at the time of use to avoid detection
- Storing device drivers as streams

## Destructive and Other Uses for ADS

Train system administrators to identify, prevent, and repair the results of destructive behavior. Attackers make dangerous use of ADS. The following are a few harmful ADS techniques:

- Flooding a guaranteed available critical file such as ntoskrnl.exe with useless stream data to use all available disk space
- Attaching Trojans, worms, viruses, spyware, and other malware as streams
- Embedding trade secrets in streamed files

In addition to having destructive uses, ADS also have constructive uses. Don't overlook ADS as viable solutions for new feature support. The following are some capabilities you might add through ADS:

- Encryption information
- Backup and maintenance information on files and directories
- Extended information about file activity
- Message Digest 5 (MD5) data

## Executing Code from ADS

Computer criminals sometimes modify ADS to embed executable malware. These files execute with the `start` command from the command shell. ADS that contain executable code do not run simply because you access the default stream. You must call ADS code directly. For example, to execute a binary data stream from a file, use the following command:

```
start ./ADSFile.txt:notepad.exe
```

To execute a binary data stream from a directory, use this command:

```
start %systemroot%:notepad.exe
```

Next, use `regedit` to add the executable stream to the Windows startup process by executing from the Registry, as follows:

1. Choose Start, Run and enter `regedit`.
2. Navigate to the key
   `HKEY_LOCAL_MACHINE\Software\Microsoft\Windows\CurrentVersion\Run`.
3. Create a REG_SZ string value.
4. Right-click on the new entry and select Modify.
5. In the Value Data box, enter (*PATH TO FILE*)`\ADSFile.txt:notepad.exe`.

By using `wscript` to run scripts from streams, you can execute `wsh` from a stream by using the following command:

```
wscript ADSFile.txt:wsh.vbs
```

The next command forces execution of a script from a stream with an incorrect extension:

```
wscript //E:vbs ADSFile.txt:wsh.bob
```

The `//E:`*engine* switch explicitly defines which engine to use when executing the script.

# Rootkits

A rootkit is also good for data hiding. A **rootkit** is a software application that attackers typically use to hide their presence or cover their tracks. A rootkit does not itself actually hide data. Instead, it subverts the tools an investigator might use to find the data. A rootkit is a program or a combination of several programs designed to hide or obscure the fact that a system has been compromised.

Rootkits originated as applications for taking control of a failing or unresponsive system. In recent years, attackers have begun using rootkits for malicious purposes. Intruders employ them to conceal malware and gain undetected access to systems. Rootkits exist for a variety of operating systems, including Microsoft Windows, Linux, Mac OS, and Solaris.

The manner in which an attacker installs a rootkit varies, depending on the operating system. Rootkits often modify parts of the operating system or install themselves as drivers or kernel modules. An attacker may use a rootkit to replace or corrupt system executables. The rootkit then hides installed processes and files. The software hidden by rootkit allows the attacker to establish the Internet footprint of the targeted organization. **Footprinting** is the process of collecting data about a specific network environment, usually for the purpose of finding ways to attack the target. Once the computer criminal has established the Internet footprint, he or she enumerates live hosts and identifies active network services with a tool, such as Nmap.

Rootkits sometimes install a backdoor in a system. A **backdoor** provides a difficult-to-detect way to bypass normal authentication, gain remote access to a computer, obtain access to plain text, and so on. To install a backdoor, a rootkit may replace the logon mechanism with an executable that accepts a secret logon combination. The backdoor allows an attacker to access the system, regardless of changes to system accounts or other access control techniques.

A **kernel module rootkit** is a type of rootkit that installs itself into the application programming interface (API). The rootkit then intercepts system calls that programs send to request low-level functions. Because of its position in the stack, the rootkit has the ability to act as a man-in-the-middle, deciding what information and programs the user does and does not see. For example, someone may perform a directory listing and see all files except those prohibited by the rootkit. Well-written rootkits also control what the user sees in the Registry and the process list.

# Steganography Concepts and Tools

The term *steganography* comes from the Greek for "concealed writing." In computer science, **steganography** is the science of hiding secret data within nonsecret data. It is based on the fact that data files can be slightly altered without losing their original functionality and without being detected by the human senses. The following are some important terms related to steganography:

- The hiding data is called the **carrier file**, or *cover file*. Today, multimedia files, such as pictures or sound, are the most common carrier messages, but attackers use other types of carrier files as well.
- Data that is to be kept a secret is called the **embedded file**, or *embedded message*.
- The process of hiding is called **embedding**, or *running the steganography algorithm*.
- The embedding process results in the **stego message**.
- The recovering of the embedded message is called **extraction**.

Steganography's covert nature appeals to criminals. Therefore, a forensic investigator is likely to encounter steganography during a digital investigation. By searching for hints of steganography, an investigator might be able to collect otherwise undiscovered evidence from various digital media. Fortunately, an investigator can use automatic routine procedures to do this.

## Types of Steganography

**Simple steganography**—also called *pure steganography*—is based on keeping the method for embedding a secret. However, with simple steganography, it is unwise to rely only on the secrecy of the steganography algorithm. Forensic specialists know about many of these techniques and test for them.

With **public key steganography (PKS)**, the sender and receiver share a secret key called the **stego key**. Only someone who possesses the stego key can detect the presence of an embedded message. Without the stego key, an adversary can't even see that there is an embedded message. PKS works like this (see also Figure 8-2):

1. The recipient's public key encrypts the covert message. This creates a pseudo-random bit string.
2. The stego key decides which bits to use to possibly alter the carrier file.
3. The steganography algorithm embeds the message.
4. The owner of the correct stego key extracts the message.

**FIGURE 8-2**

Public key steganography.

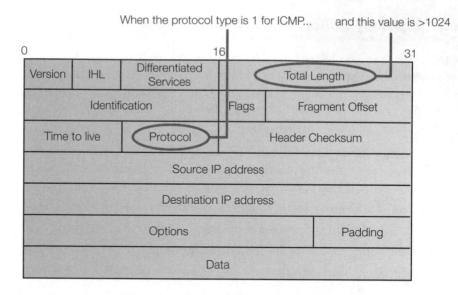

## Steganography Algorithms

According to Andreas Furuseth in *Digital Forensics: Methods and Tools for Retrieval and Analysis of Security Credentials and Hidden Data*, there is a variety of steganography algorithms. An **algorithm** is a step-by-step procedure that a computer follows to solve a problem. As shown in Table 8-1, each one uses different locations in digital data to hide secret messages. Simple embedding methods do not alter the carrier file's perceptive properties, but you can easily detect them. Slightly more sophisticated steganography software does the embedding in the least significant bit.

### Steganography Versus Cryptography

Steganography is about hiding information. Don't mistake it for cryptography. With cryptography, the individuals involved know that a secret message exists, but they don't know its content. Cryptography obscures a message to prevent disclosure. Steganography, on the other hand, completely hides information. Whereas text data run through a cryptographic algorithm might look like E0F7E3AC, data hidden using steganography is invisible.

You can use steganography and cryptography concurrently. Together, they provide additional secrecy because the cryptographic functions make steganalysis more difficult.

From a forensic point of view, knowing that communication takes place can be essential. Steganography keeps traffic flow confidential. It conceals the source and destination, message length, or frequency of communication. Discovering the presence of hidden communication is important to an investigation. Once you reveal the presence of steganography, you defeat its purpose—even if you don't manage to extract or decipher the message content.

| **TABLE 8-1** Steganographic embedding methods. | |
|---|---|
| **METHOD** | **DESCRIPTION** |
| **Simple Embedding** | |
| Data appending | Data appending is a simple form of steganography. This method relies on the algorithm's secrecy. It embeds the message by adding it to the end of the carrier file. This works, for instance, for some image file formats, such as Joint Photographic Experts Group (JPEG) and bitmap (BMP), because the file header contains a field indicating the total amount of data or data after the "end of image" marker. Because most image viewers ignore the additional data, a stego message remains hidden. |
| Addition of comments | Many file formats allow for optional comments. Various source codes allow comments to aid the understanding of the code, and the interpreters ignore the comments. For example, Hypertext Markup Language (HTML) files have a comment tag that browsers ignore. You can easily view these comments in most browsers, however, by selecting an option to view the HTML source code. Therefore, such comments can serve as hiding places for information. |
| Use of file headers | Various data structures have header information, and some fields in the header are not mandatory or have values that are insignificant. Attackers can use such fields to communicate covertly. TCP/IP packets, for example, have unused space in the packet headers. |
| **Least Significant Bit Embedding** | |
| Use of the least significant bit | Intruders can embed data in the least significant bit of an image, such as GIF and BMP, because browsers often think of this bit as random noise. Attackers can do the actual embedding in several ways, from sequential changes to random walks with a pseudorandom generator. |
| **Frequency Domain Embedding** | |
| Frequency embedding | A common type of embedding targets frequency. Attackers use this type of embedding with JPEG compression and the MPEG Layer 3 (MP3) encoding of Waveform Audio File Format (WAV) files. |
| **Preservation of the Original Statistical Properties** | |
| Statistics-aware embedding | Embedding methods alter the carrier file's statistical properties. For example, with least significant bit embedding in images, the frequency of colors changes. Statistics-aware embedding uses a model of the carrier file to preserve these characteristics. |
| Pseudorandom embedding | Some steganography software falls into the category of secret key steganography. This software uses a pseudorandom generator to select locations for the actual embedding. |

**8**

**Information-Hiding Techniques**

> ### Steganography Versus Digital Watermarking
>
> **Digital watermarking** is a technique for adding copyright notices or other verification messages to digital audio, video, or image signals and documents. Digital watermarking is closely connected to steganography, but the two are somewhat different from one another. With steganography, the carrier's value or importance is insignificant. The only purpose of the stego message is to communicate the embedded message. With watermarking, the carrier is the important signal, and the embedded message is present to give some information about the carrier. Consider the watermark a carrier attribute.

Frequency domain methods are quite robust against perceptive inspection. However, the embedding introduces statistical changes to the carrier, resulting in stego messages with different statistical properties that cover messages. To prevent statistical attacks, the next generation of steganography algorithms preserves the carrier's original statistical properties. Some steganography software even does spatial and frequency domain embedding by utilizing pseudorandom techniques.

## Steganography Software

Many tools hide information, including many types of steganography software. Most often, the information is hiding in some form of multimedia, such as an image, an audio file, or a video file. Many people have legitimate needs for these tools, such as those in government, military, law enforcement, and the academic community. However, criminals and terrorists also use steganography.

The following sections describe several steganography software tools.

### EzStego

EzStego is an open source tool that uses least significant bit embedding in Graphics Interchange Format (GIF) images. GIF supports bitmap images and gets wide exposure on the Internet. It operates on the red-green-blue (RGB) color model, where each color is a combination of those primary colors. GIF uses eight bits per pixel, and each image can reference a palette of up to 256 distinct colors. A GIF image is a grid, with each cell—or pixel—pointing to the palette's appropriate position. Therefore, when rendering the picture, the color for each pixel is looked up in the palette. EzStego embeds data in GIF images by altering the colors of pixels.

EzStego adds a message to a pixel's least significant bit of a pixel, following these steps:

1. Create a copy of the palette and rearrange it so that colors close to each other in the RGB color model are close in the palette.

2. If there is an extra bit in the message, do the following:
   - Find the index, $i$, of this pixel's RGB color in the sorted palette.
   - Replace the least significant bit of $i$ with a bit from the message, creating $i^*$.
   - Find the RGB color that $i^*$ points to in the sorted palette.

The changes to the carrier file won't be apparent. The palette stays the same as the original, and the EzStego tool adds no other strange artifacts to the stego file with the embedding. Recovering the hidden message from the carrier involves finding the index of the pixel's color in the sorted palette.

One method to detect messages embedded with EzStego is to run all files through EzStego with the -unsteg option and check the result. Is the embedded message plaintext readable? The header information can indicate encryption. If the encrypted message has been stripped of header information, the extracted message is a pseudorandom bit string. These bits do not seem different from a bit stream you've extracted from a carrier image.

## MandelSteg

The MandelSteg tool is freeware. It differs from other steganography tools in that it does not use an existing carrier. Instead, it creates its own stego images, based on a mathematical concept called *Mandelbrot fractals*. MandelSteg creates a Mandelbrot image and stores the hidden message in the specified bit of the image pixels. The tool GIFExtract pulls the message from the stego image.

MandelSteg is, from the forensic viewpoint, not a good alternative for hiding messages. The use of a Mandelbrot fractal image is unusual. Therefore, if you inspect seized data and detect the presence of Mandelbrot fractal images, it's safe to suspect the use of steganography.

An adversary can extract a MandelSteg message by running GIFExtract. A brute-force attack is possible because the different command-line options provide only 164 possibilities. If the embedded message is not encrypted or if known encryption headers are identified, you can detect the presence of steganography and defeat the tool. When the message is encrypted and stripped of headers, it appears pseudorandom and cannot be differentiated from other extracted messages.

## Spam Mimic

Spam Mimic is a freeware steganography tool that uses spam as stego media. Spam Mimic works similarly to MandelSteg in that it does not need an existing carrier. The output from Spam Mimic is real text that looks like spam. The idea behind Spam Mimic is that spammers send junk mail all the time, so users who receive these messages don't suspect steganography.

Spam Mimic is simple steganography. You can run the algorithm in reverse and use the freely available tool to get the embedded message.

One challenge with Spam Mimic is that it is always inbound. Perhaps William is monitoring traffic coming to and from Alice. Inbound spam should not raise suspicion, but spam originating from Alice probably would. Spam Mimic is freely available, so William considers applying the algorithm for decoding and encoding. A forensic investigation monitoring traffic to and from a suspect can detect traffic going to the Spam Mimic home page, alert the investigator, and defeat the steganography.

## Snow

Snow—which stands for *steganographic nature of whitespace*—is simple open source steganography software. It appends whitespace to lines in American Standard Code for Information Interchange (ASCII) text files, where the embedded message is encoded as space and tab characters. This whitespace at the ends of lines does not change the file's appearance in normal text viewers. Therefore, the resulting stego message is not visibly different from the original carrier. But Snow sometimes appends new lines to the carrier file, which clearly alters the stego message's visual characteristics.

Snow is not very sophisticated, and it leaves clear indicators of its presence that a diligent investigator can easily find. The trailing spaces are not normal and are a give-away. You can detect Snow with a visual inspection of text files or by using a detection algorithm that automates this process.

## OutGuess

OutGuess is an open source tool that serves as a framework for information hiding, regardless of the carrier data type. But an attacker has to create a handler for each type, and OutGuess typically uses JPEG images. Using OutGuess efficiently on several images requires the computer criminal to create a small script.

You cannot visually detect OutGuess. The academic community created this open source tool. This same community has also attacked and broken OutGuess. Stegdetect can detect OutGuess 0.13b. It does this by using a statistical technique. OutGuess 0.2 outsmarts Stegdetect by preserving the statistics from the carrier image.

An investigator who knows the correct key can easily extract a message embedded with OutGuess. However, without the key, message extraction is more problematic.

## appendX

appendX is a simple open source steganography tool. Its embedding method is to append data to the end of the carrier file. The carrier file is generally an image file such as a Portable Network Graphics (PNG), JPEG, or GIF.

The appendX tool supports Pretty Good Privacy (PGP) header stripping. When an attacker encrypts a message with PGP, the PGP package adds a header that clearly identifies the hidden data as ciphertext. But the tool appendX strips this header, so the appended data looks like noise.

appendX adds hidden data to the end of the carrier. Following the embedded message, appendX pads the embedded message, from the left, until it has appended 10 characters. This can help you identify the software an attacker has used.

The appendX tool is classified as weak because you can relatively easily detect the presence of embedded data. After you have identified appendX, you can easily extract the additional data in the file.

### Invisible Secrets

Invisible Secrets is a commercial product from Neobyte Solutions (see *http://www .neobytesolutions.com*). This software security package provides encryption, safe deletion, and steganography. The steganography part of the package can hide information inside JPEG, BMP, PNG, HTML, and Waveform Audio File Format (WAV) data files. It uses least significant bit embedding, comment insertion, and whitespace appending. The software is easy to use, is well documented, and integrates into the Windows shell and Start menu by default. Invisible Secrets' embedding techniques are not more sophisticated than freely available steganography tools. However, this software is more user friendly.

Invisible Secrets is not difficult to detect because the methods used to embed a message are well known. An interesting feature of Invisible Secrets is the possibility of creating bogus stego messages. Doing so could increase the difficulty of detecting a specific hidden message. However, more stego messages would increase the possibility of detecting the use of steganography. Therefore, such a move would defeat the covert channel. This is especially true when using simple steganography software, which is fragile to algorithm exposure.

## Defeating Steganography

System forensics investigators are experts at finding information from a digital crime scene. While searching for digital evidence, an investigator might find hints of steganography or, for some other reason, suspect its use. An absolute indication of the use of steganography is the discovery of steganography software. This software could be on the suspect's disk drive or hidden on a memory stick, compact disk (CD), or other removable media.

Search automatically for known steganography software. To do this, maintain a database of cryptographic hash values for known components of such software. The National Institute of Standards and Technology (NIST) keeps up a list of digital signatures of software applications—including steganography software—called the National Software Reference Library (NSRL). For more information, see *http://www.nsrl.nist.gov*.

### Detecting the Use of Steganography Software

The following sections discuss some of the ways a forensic investigator can find evidence of the use of steganography.

### Traces of Steganography Software

If you aren't able to find any steganography software during an investigation, you might discover traces of its use in various locations. The Windows Registry, a recently used file list, the Web browser history, or tools used for software extraction may show signs of steganography. For example, the list of recently used files in WinZip or WinRAR can present evidence of a recent extraction of EzStego.zip or some other software file.

### Location of Pairs of Carrier/Stego Files

As discussed earlier in this chapter, steganography software often creates stego messages based on an original carrier file. A pair of files that have different hash values but the same perceptual properties—that is, two images that look similar but have slightly different least significant bit planes—is a potential carrier/stego file pair. Even if the carrier file were deleted, you could in some cases undelete it by using forensic tools.

Some forms of steganography hide information within an image by using mathematic algorithms. These math procedures replace unused or little-used bits within an image with bits representing the data an attacker aims to conceal. The algorithms change only a few of the many bits that comprise an image and do not damage the image's appearance. Thus, the image looks the same even though it now contains covert data. Use software to analyze images and detect the small variations imposed by the attacker's steganographic program. Then extract the hidden data for analysis. To help analyze images, collect characteristics of images such as child pornography images and use those characteristics to aid in the automatic detection of steganography. Also, it is possible to apply the same principle to other media types used for steganography.

### Keyword Search and Activity Monitoring

In addition to having a database of hash signatures for steganography software, compile a dictionary of key terms, as discussed in Chapter 7, "Collecting, Seizing, and Protecting Evidence." You can perform searches on seized data to try to locate the listed terms. The search for keywords is done not only with steganography. The contents of the dictionary decide the target.

The rate of false positives depends on the words used. Good candidates are software names such as *OutGuess* and words such as *carrier* and *cover*. To create part of the database of keywords, use strings to extract words from steganography software binaries.

In addition to keyword searches, history logs in a suspect's Web browser might show visits to steganography Web sites. Have your system forensics team keep a list of such Web sites to compare against browser histories.

### Suspect's Computer Knowledge

Most steganography software is fairly easy to use, and a suspect need not have a lot of computer knowledge to use it. However, if a suspect has advanced computer skills, you might speculate on the suspect's use of homemade steganography tools or algorithms. Examine any unknown software you encounter during an investigation to discover its functionality.

### Unlikely Files

Some steganography software uses or creates uncommon file types. The MandelSteg tool described earlier in this chapter uses no existing carrier but creates a Mandelbrot image based on the message it will embed with hidden data. These images clearly stand out among vacation and other typical images contained on a PC. Consider what use a suspect might have of such images. A similar example is inconsistencies between religion, interests, and so on, and file types. Consider the speculation of al-Qaeda hiding information in pornographic images. Such images are against the Muslim religion. So consider findings of this kind unlikely and suspicious.

### Location of Steganography Keys

Some steganography software uses steganography keys—called stego keys—to seed a pseudorandom number generator when it's used to select locations for bit manipulations. These tactics attack weak passwords in a brute-force manner. Software is available to support such attacks on steganography.

During the physical crime scene investigation phases, forensic specialists collect handwritten notes or markings. You should determine whether any of these are passwords or other key information. In addition, try to guess passwords with dictionary attacks and other brute-force methods, such as cryptanalysis and steganalysis.

Steganography software sometimes encrypts a message prior to embedding it. Analysis of steganography involves separating the embedded message from the stego message. After extracting a hidden encrypted message, attack this ciphertext by using cryptanalysis techniques or other forensic techniques.

Encryption schemes add a header to an encrypted message. This header could contain data, such as an encryption algorithm. In addition, this plaintext can aid steganalysis by simply sending out an amount of random-looking data. You can also use it to identify a successful brute-force attack on a secret key steganography system. For instance, Stegdetect relies on detecting known headers in the extracted message to signal success. Sometimes, however, an embedded encrypted message has been stripped of headers. The extracted message is a random-looking bit string, which makes it difficult to assess whether it is valid ciphertext you need to treat further or just noise.

### Strengths and Weaknesses of Today's Detection Methods

The methods described so far for detecting steganography software let you know that an attacker has embedded malicious code, but they don't help you decipher what data has been hidden or what works as evidence. Skilled investigators must put the pieces together into a cohesive description of the event.

Some of the techniques just described are minor expansions of already existing forensic procedures. Adding steganography keywords to the dictionary for the keyword search is one such example. Adaptation of methods requires little work and little expense, yet it can be very effective. Some of the tools used for detecting steganography or extracting data are quite expensive and, with large data volumes, can be quite time-consuming. One option is to automate these tasks.

**8**

Information-Hiding
Techniques

## Steganalysis

**Steganalysis** is the process of detecting messages hidden with steganography. In other words, steganalysis is about separating cover messages from stego messages. It tries to defeat a steganography algorithm by looking for weaknesses. Steganalysis often involves the use of statistical properties to look for abnormalities in files, such as strange palettes in GIF images or other known signatures in stego messages.

According to Andreas Furuseth, a system forensics specialist must have a good grasp of steganalysis and its use when attacking steganography. However, system forensics encompasses more methods in addition to just steganalysis to attack steganography. For example, items from the physical scene can provide security credentials in the form of written passwords. Well-known forensic methods include searching for keys, passwords, and known keywords and recovering deleted data. Locating such artifacts helps an investigator defeat steganography.

Steganalysis is limited to the detection of an embedded message, not message extraction. Steganalysis detects stego messages among cover messages. The detection of a hidden message can identify the embedding method. After identifying a tool or method, you might be able to extract the message.

Most steganalysis algorithms and tools target specific steganography software. Such tools rely on specific signatures left in the stego message. The embedding of a message can give a specific statistical property, which is another way to detect stego messages.

The following sections discuss some of the common steganalysis methods.

### File Signatures

Some steganography software adds specific signatures to stego messages. For example, the string "CDN" is always present when using a tool called Hiderman. Use these file signatures to spot stego messages.

### File Anomalies

Some simple steganography software embeds messages by appending data to the end of the carrier file. appendX and Invisible Secrets, discussed earlier in this chapter, are examples of this type of steganography software. When software, such as image viewers, reads these files, the amount of data read depends on the file length defined in the file header. Therefore, the appended data is not read, and the changes to the carrier are not perceptible.

When using Invisible Secrets and least significant bit embedding in BMP images, all the bits it hasn't used for embedding are set to 0 or to 1. You can detect such file anomalies when examining steganography software via steganalysis.

### Visual Attacks

It is possible to remove all parts of an image covering a hidden message and visually determine whether it contains a potential message. Visual attacks succeed only when the cover image has clearly structured contents. Image textures typically withstand this type of attack.

---

### Creating Better Tools

The tools available for steganography today are usable but not completely secure. The academic community is working toward achieving secret key steganography that adheres to **Kerckhoffs' principle**. That is, it will be secure even if everything about the software except the key is public knowledge.

Steganography algorithms often create artifacts in the stego message, such as signatures or altered statistics. The academic community has created sophisticated steganography algorithms, such as OutGuess, discussed earlier in this chapter. The same community also attacks these algorithms, creating an evolving cycle of better and better steganography software.

State-of-the-art steganalysis is limited to attacking known steganography algorithms. Therefore, in the case of unknown steganography software, security through obscurity might be successful. **Security through obscurity** is a principle that attempts to provide security through the use of secrecy of design, implementation, and so on. A system that relies on security through obscurity may have security vulnerabilities, but its owners or designers believe that the flaws are not known, and that attackers are unlikely to find them. However, attackers will eventually break security by obscurity algorithms. In addition, investigators can defeat even secure steganography with the retrieval of security credentials at a crime scene.

---

## Extracting Hidden Information

After you detect hidden information, you can extract the embedded message. In some situations, this means running the identified steganography software. With simple steganography, this is relatively easy. In the presence of a stego key, you need that key to succeed. In this case, perform a brute-force or dictionary attack on the system.

Even though not all users of steganography encrypt their message, it's wise to expect encryption. Stripping headers from encrypted files results in an embedded message being indistinguishable from noise. PGP Stealth is a tool that strips all headers from a PGP encrypted message. The complexity of a brute-force search is then much greater. For each stego key, try all encryption keys. Only a successful cryptanalysis of the embedded message will show whether the currently tried stego keys are correct.

You can disable hidden information in several ways. A drastic step is to disallow all communication—that is, intercept the communicated image. When this is not possible or wanted, change the assumed stego message by giving it a different file format, performing image processing such as blurring or cropping, or adding noise to the least significant bit of a GIF image. You will probably lose the original embedded message because of these changes. However, note the existence of watermarks, which are quite robust and can withstand multiple changes. There is a trade-off between robustness and the amount of hidden information. Adding error correction to the message reduces the amount of information the message can carry.

## Steganalysis Software

Certain tools, called **steganalysis software**, can detect the presence of steganography. Some of the tools are open source, whereas others are quite expensive. This section describes steganalysis software to use for dictionary attacks against steganography software.

### StegSpy

StegSpy v2.1 is freely available steganalysis software to spot Hiderman, JPHideandSeek, Masker, JPegX, and Invisible Secrets. It has a graphical interface that allows you to manually select one file at a time to examine.

StegSpy does signature-based steganalysis. It looks for particular strings to detect steganography software used for message embedding. For example, it looks for the string CDN, which is always present with Hiderman. Also, after discovering a known signature, StegSpy locates the embedded data position by detecting the end of the image, based on header information.

Because StegSpy can examine only one file at a time and because it examines signatures but not file anomalies, this tool's forensic value is low. However, the knowledge it contains—the signatures—is quite useful.

### Stegdetect

Stegdetect is open source steganalysis software developed by the academic community. It unearths the presence of messages embedded with JSteg, JPHide, Invisible Secrets, OutGuess 01.3b, F5, appendX, and Camouflage. Newer theoretical steganalysis algorithms have been suggested, but no publicly known steganalysis software supports those algorithms at this time.

Stegdetect can find any JPEG-based steganography system. It can classify new images as stego images or carrier images.

### Stegbreak

Stegbreak is open source software developed by the same author who developed Stegdetect. This is not software that detects the presence of steganography. Rather, it is for message extraction and attempted dictionary attacks against JSteg-Shell, JPHide, and OutGuess.

A forensic investigation can dig up password clues. Add these clues, such as name, birthday, pet's name, and so on, to the dictionary that Stegbreak uses. Stegbreak's success is closely related to the quality of the password and the dictionary. The rules to permute words in the dictionary also determine Stegbreak's success.

Stegbreak tries to verify that the extracted bit string is an embedded message and not just noise. It does this by identifying file headers in the extracted bit string.

## Stego Suite

WetStone Technologies (see *http://www.wetstonetech.com*) offers Stego Suite. This commercial package consists of the detection tools Stego Hunter, Stego Watch, and Stego Analyst, and a password cracker called Stego Break. WetStone also offers training in using these tools. These tools can scan audio files, JPG, BMP, GIF, PNG, and more to identify more than 500 known steganography programs.

## StegAlyzer

The Steganography Analysis and Research Center (see *http://www.sarc-wv.com/products.aspx*) sells three steganalysis products:

- StegAlyzerAS searches file systems for traces of known steganography software.
- StegAlyzerSS includes the functionality to detect known stego file signatures.
- StegAlyzerRTS detects steganography artifacts and signatures in real-time over a network.

These tools are expensive but are available on a free 30-day trial basis. Freely available tools such as The Sleuth Kit and Autopsy Browser support the detection of file hash signatures and known stego file signatures. However, the StegAlyzer products have a large database of software and stego file signatures.

### CHAPTER SUMMARY

It isn't a question of whether an attacker has hidden covert data on the hard drives of unsuspecting users but what data, for what purposes, and where. Well-funded hackers, criminals, and terrorists hide data, and forensic investigators and law enforcement try to catch up with the latest tactics.

You'll be flushing out a number of data-hiding techniques, such as ADS, rootkits, and steganography, in your future investigations. To detect their embedded messages, it's important to be aware of attackers' methods. In turn, many methods and programs are available to help you defeat steganography, including steganalysis.

## KEY CONCEPTS AND TERMS

Algorithm

Alternate data streams (ADS)

Backdoor

Carrier file

Covert channel

Digital watermarking

Embedded file

Embedding

Extraction

Footprinting

Kerckhoffs' principle

Kernel module rootkit

Metadata

Packet crafting

Pirate

Protocol bending

Public key steganography (PKS)

Rootkit

Security through obscurity

Simple steganography

Steganalysis

Steganalysis software

Steganography

Stego key

Stego message

## CHAPTER 8 ASSESSMENT

**1.** Packet crafting and protocol bending are two _____ techniques.

**2.** _____ can be modified to embed executable malware.

**3.** The benefits of NTFS volumes far outweigh the potential risks of ADS, as long as system administrators are aware of streams and have the security tools to handle them.

A. True

B. False

**4.** A _____ is software that prevents users from seeing all items or directories on a computer.

**5.** Steganography is the science of extracting secret data from nonsecret data.

A. True

B. False

**6.** Which of the following do attackers use to hide secret data in steganography?

A. Metadata

B. Embedded file

C. Carrier file

D. Stego message

**7.** Which of the following is another name for running a steganography algorithm?

A. Embedding

B. Digital watermarking

C. Extraction

D. Packet crafting

**8.** With PKS, the sender and receiver share a secret key called the stego key. Only a possessor of the stego key can detect the presence of an embedded message.

A. True

B. False

**9.** Steganography is another name for cryptography.

A. True

B. False

**10.** Which of the following is *not* a steganographic embedding method?

A. Simple embedding

B. Least significant bit embedding

C. Frequency domain embedding

D. Digital watermarking

E. Preservation of the original statistical properties

**11.** Which of the following are examples of steganography software? (Select three.)

A. StegAlyzerAS
B. MandelSteg
C. EzStego
D. Stegdetect
E. Snow
F. Stegbreak

**12.** The only way to defeat steganography is to use steganalysis.

A. True
B. False

**13.** Which of the following is *not* true of steganalysis?

A. It involves separating cover messages from stego messages.
B. It hides secret data within nonsecret data.
C. It is the process of detecting messages hidden using steganography.
D. It often involves the use of statistical properties to look for abnormalities in files.

**14.** _____ is the name for separating an embedded message from a stego message.

**15.** Which of the following are examples of steganalysis software? (Select three.)

A. StegAlyzerAS
B. MandelSteg
C. EzStego
D. Stegdetect
E. Snow
F. Stegbreak

# Recovering Data

C OMPUTER SYSTEMS CRASH, CORRUPTING FILES. Software fails, corrupting files. Workers accidentally delete files. Malware, disgruntled employees, and outside attackers intentionally corrupt or delete files. Regardless of the cause, system and data owners turn to individuals who have skills and experience to recover lost data.

In many instances, an organization won't be able to find lost data using the limited software tools available to most users. It can't even salvage data using the general recovery tools available to system administrators. In such cases, the business may need to call in a system forensics expert to apply special tools and techniques to recover and restore files. For example, a forensic expert may be able to recover file fragments and assemble or integrate them into a useful recovered file.

Data recovery involves finding lost data and assembling it into useful data files. Data recovery is of potential interest to anyone who has lost data for any reason—whether through intentional or unintentional action. Forensic analysis involves finding data that others have thrown away or left behind—burglary tools, data files, correspondence, and other evidence. This chapter focuses on recovering data from backups.

## Chapter 9 Topics

This chapter covers the following topics and concepts:

- What data recovery is and how it's used
- How disks are structured and how to recover data after physical and logical damage
- What data backup is and how to use it in data recovery
- What some of the challenges are in data recovery today

## What Is Data Recovery?

Properly managed information systems have in place data backup and recovery procedures. These procedures typically provide for timely recovery of lost data and files. The time frame between backup snapshots is generally 24 hours. Therefore, recovery procedures ensure that no more than one day's worth of data is lost. Recovery of data from backup files is the first and most cost-effective data recovery technique. However, with regard to system forensics, **data recovery** is the process of salvaging data from damaged, failed, corrupted, or inaccessible primary storage media when it cannot be accessed normally.

As a part of your data recovery duties, you will evaluate and extract data from intentionally or unintentionally deleted, hidden, or corrupted files or damaged media. You then return the data to an intact format. A data recovery technique may return data to its original format and data structure, or it may return the data to a standardized format. Using forensic techniques, it is possible to retrieve deleted files and data. It is also possible to find forgotten passwords. And it is feasible to recover data from physically damaged devices.

The need for individuals skilled in data recovery has grown in importance with the use of technology. Loss or corruption of data in today's environment can result in significant financial loss. Such a loss could cause an organization's failure or leave it exposed to significant liability. Data recovery experts can mitigate financial loss and legal liability by recovering lost or corrupted data and re-establishing normal operations.

 **NOTE**

Data persistence is remarkable. Computer systems make copies of data as part of routine processes. It is difficult to entirely remove all data from a system. Without special action, there will always be a prior version or remnants of a data file remaining to be recovered through forensic techniques.

**9**

Recovering Data

When someone realizes that critical data has been lost or corrupted, the first reaction is usually panic. Management typically gives directions to "do whatever it takes" to recover the lost data. Resist the temptation to take immediate, visible action to show that you are doing just anything to recover the data. As with a forensic investigation, carefully plan your data recovery effort.

Take the following steps to recover data:

**TIP**

You should be able to complete these steps in less than an hour or two. If planning a recovery takes longer than this, you have almost certainly stopped planning and are beginning the recovery—but without a clear understanding of what activities will have the greatest likelihood of success.

1. Determine what data has been lost and in what time frame. You can satisfy many requests for emergency data recovery by restoring the lost data from backup files.

2. Determine whether the system on which the data was lost has been used recently or is still in use. If the data loss occurred within the past 24 hours, it may be relatively easy to restore. Whether the loss was recent or occurred some time ago, stop system use until forensic actions are complete.

3. Estimate the cost and time frame needed to restore the lost data. In-depth data recovery can be quite expensive. It may be less expensive to reconstruct the data than to use extraordinary data recovery techniques.

4. Prepare a data recovery plan that lists the work steps you will perform and their order of performance.

## Disk Structure and Recovery Techniques

**NOTE**

The loss of volatile data usually causes much disruption. For example, a four-hour data loss for an airline reservation system could result in millions of dollars in lost reservations and legal liability. Thus, in cases where data volatility is high, organizations should make frequent backups. They should also use forensic techniques to identify and resolve corrupted data on an ongoing basis.

System forensics experts must often recover data from storage media. They often work with hard disk drives, solid state memory, storage tapes, compact disks (CDs), digital video disks (DVDs), redundant array of independent disks (RAID) servers, and other electronics.

The two main types of storage device damage are physical damage and logical damage. The following sections discuss the considerations in recovering from each type of damage.

### Recovering Data After Physical Damage

A wide variety of failures cause **physical damage** to storage media. CDs can have their metallic substrate or dye layer scratched. Hard disks can suffer any of several mechanical failures, such as head crashes and failed motors. Tapes can simply break. Physical damage always causes some data loss, and in many cases, the file system's logical structures sustain damage as well. This results in logical damage that must be dealt with before any files can be salvaged from the failed media. (See the section "Recovering Data After Logical Damage," later in this chapter.)

## Data Recovery Examples

If there is any data anywhere on a disk or tape, you can recover it with the right set of skills. The following are some interesting disk recovery examples:

- A dog chewed CDs containing data related to an important presentation. The damage to the disk cases was severe, with large tooth marks evident on the disks' surface. Eventually, a specialist imaged the disks, with only 15 percent sector damage, and rebuilt the File Allocation Tables (FATs). The specialist successfully recovered and restored all the files.

- A well-known credit card company experienced the failure of a system containing the last few hours' transactions. There was no backup. Using a database of drive components and technical knowledge, a specialist worked to correct the faults on the drives so he could take images. When the specialist finished, he had imaged all 18 drives, with a total sector loss of just 7 bad sectors. The total good sectors imaged that night was just under 88 million! The customer's valuable data was safe.

- Having flown numerous times on business without a problem, a businessman was surprised to find that his laptop wouldn't boot. The laptop had traveled in the cargo hold of a plane, so it had probably not only been thrown around by the baggage handlers but also bounced its way down the carousel. Luckily, the airport's x-ray equipment hadn't damaged the laptop. Hardware specialists opened the head disk assembly and found some speckle damage, confirming that it had bounced around. Following a successful headstack swap, a specialist imaged the drive. She found 112 bad sectors, of which she was finally able to read only 86.

End users can't repair most physical damage. Generally, they don't have the hardware or technical expertise required to make physical repairs. Further, end users' attempts to repair physical damage often increase the damage.

Normally you shouldn't attempt to repair physical media. You may try a number of techniques to recover data from damaged media. However, only organizations with specialized equipment and facilities, such as clean rooms, should attempt repair or enhanced data recovery. A **clean room** is an environment that has a controlled level of contamination, such as dust, microbes, and other particles.

## Physical Damage Recovery Techniques

A hard disk—also called a *hard drive* or *hard disk drive*—is a nonvolatile storage device that magnetically encodes digital data. A hard disk has one or more rotating rigid platters on a motor-driven spindle within a metal case. Recovering data from a hard drive should start with the assumption that, unless the case is visibly damaged, the drive itself is still operable. Today's hard disks are built to be rugged enough to protect against damage.

Thus, when presented with a "failed hard drive," use the following techniques to evaluate the drive and retrieve needed data:

1. Remove the drive from the system on which it is installed and connect it to a *test system*—a compatible system that is functional. Make the connection without installing the drive but only connecting the data and power cables.

2. Boot the test system from its own internal drive. Listen to the failed drive to determine whether the internal disks are spinning. If the disks are spinning, it generally means the disk has not experienced a catastrophic failure. Therefore, you can likely recover the data.

3. Determine whether the failed drive is recognized and can be installed as an additional disk on the test system. If the drive installs, copy all directories and files to a hard drive on the test system. If a drive fails on one system but installs on another, the drive may be usable. The drive may have failed because of a power supply failure, corruption of the operating system, virus infection, or some other event. If you can operate the drive, run a virus check on the recovered data and test for directory and file integrity.

4. If the hard drive is not spinning or the test system does not recognize it, perform limited repair. You may be able to get the hard drive to start and be recognized by the test system. If you can repair the drive, use specialized software to image all data bits from the failed drive to a recovery drive. Use the extracted raw image to reconstruct usable data. Try open source tools such as DCFLdd to recover all data except for data in physically damaged sectors.

5. If necessary, send the device to data recovery specialists for extraordinary recovery techniques.

Management may determine that the data is "lost," and there will be no increased loss if you attempt local repair and fail. If such activity won't void any disk drive warranties, try the following:

- Remove the printed circuit board and replace it with a matching circuit board from a known healthy drive.
- Change the read/write head assembly with matching parts from a known healthy drive.
- Remove the hard disk platters from the original drive and install them into a known healthy drive.

## Recovering Data After Logical Damage

**Logical damage** to a file system is more common than physical damage. Logical damage may prevent the host operating system from mounting or using the file system. Power outages can cause logical damage, preventing file system structures from completely writing to the storage medium. Even turning off a machine while it is booting or shutting down can lead to logical damage. Errors in hardware controllers—especially RAID controllers—and drivers and system crashes can have the same effect.

Logical damage can cause a variety of problems, such as system crashes or actual data loss. It can result in intermittent failures. It can also trigger other strange behavior, such as infinitely recursing directories and drives reporting negative free space remaining.

Some programs can correct the inconsistencies that result from logical damage. Most operating systems provide a basic repair tool for their native file systems. Microsoft Windows has chkdsk, for example, Linux comes with the fsck utility, and Mac OS X provides Disk Utility. A number of companies have developed products to resolve logical file system errors, such as The Sleuth Kit (see *http://www.sleuthkit.org*). Third-party products may be able to recover data even when the operating system's repair utility doesn't recognize the disk. TestDisk is one example (see *http://www.cgsecurity.org/wiki/TestDisk*). It can recover lost partitions and reconstruct corrupted partition tables.

 **NOTE**

People often mistake logical damage for physical damage. For instance, when a hard drive's read/write head clicks, end users tend to think it signals internal physical damage. This is not always the case. A failure of firmware on the drive or its controller may cause the clicking. Restoring the firmware can make the data accessible.

## Preventing Logical Damage

Journaling file systems, such as NTFS (NT File System) 5.0 and ext3, help to reduce the incidence of logical damage. In the event of system failure, you can roll these file systems back to a consistent or stable state. The data most likely to be lost will be in the drive's cache at the time of the system failure.

Using a consistency checker should be a routine part of system maintenance. A consistency checker protects against file system software bugs and storage hardware design incompatibilities. For example, a disk controller may report that file system structures have been saved to disk, but the data is actually still in the write cache. If the computer loses power while this data is in the cache, the file system may be left in an inconsistent or unstable state. To avoid this problem, use hardware that does not report the data as written until it actually is written. Another solution is to use disk controllers with battery backups. When the power is restored after an outage, the pending data is written to disk. For greater protection, use a system battery backup to provide power long enough to shut down the system safely.

## Logical Damage Recovery Techniques

Two techniques are common for recovering data after logical damage: consistency checking and zero-knowledge analysis. Use these techniques to either repair or work around most logical damage. However, applying data recovery software doesn't guarantee that no data loss will occur. For example, when two files claim to share the same allocation unit, one of the files is almost certain to lose data.

**Consistency checking.** **Consistency checking** involves scanning a disk's logical structure and ensuring that it is consistent with its specification. For instance, in most file systems, a directory must have at least two entries: a dot (.) entry that points to itself and a dot-dot (..) entry that points to its parent. A file system repair program reads each directory to ensure that these entries exist and point to the correct directories. If they do not, the program displays an error message, and you can correct the problem. Both `chkdsk` and `fsck` work in this fashion. However, consistency checking has two major problems:

- A consistency check can fail if the file system is highly damaged. In this case, the repair program may crash, or it may believe the drive has an invalid file system.
- The `chkdsk` utility might automatically delete data files if the files are out of place or unexplainable. The utility does this to ensure that the operating system can run properly. However, the deleted files may be important and irreplaceable user files. The same type of problem occurs with system restore disks that restore the operating system by removing the previous installation. Avoid this problem by installing the operating system on a separate partition from the user data.

**Zero-knowledge analysis.**    Zero-knowledge analysis is the second technique for file system repair. With **zero-knowledge analysis**, you make few assumptions about the state of the file system. You rebuild the file system from scratch, using knowledge of an undamaged file system structure. In this process, scan the drive of the affected computer, noting all file system structures and possible file boundaries. Then match the results to the specifications of a working file system.

Zero-knowledge analysis is usually much slower than consistency checking. You can use it, however, to recover data even when the logical structures are almost completely destroyed. This technique generally does not repair the damaged file system but allows you to extract the data to another storage device. Some third-party programs include zero-knowledge analysis features.

## Data Backup and Recovery

Information drives today's world. It is one of the most highly valued assets of any business striving to compete in the global economy. Companies that provide reliable and rapid access to their information are now the fastest-growing organizations in the world. To remain competitive and succeed, they must protect their most valuable asset—information.

### Boot Media

It's often impossible to perform data recovery and forensic operations on a running system. Forensic specialists commonly use a specialized boot disk with a minimal operating system and a set of repair tools. Floppy disks were the boot disk of choice in the past. Today, developers include recovery tools on the same media as the operating system installer. For example, repair tools are now frequently included on higher-capacity flash drives, such as 4 gigabytes (GB) or more. These flash drives contain programs and data, including their own encryption and virus protection software.

Specialized hardware and software companies manufacture products for backup and recovery of business-critical data. A **backup** is a copy of data that can be used to restore data if it is lost or corrupted. Hardware manufacturers offer automated tape libraries that can manage millions of megabytes of backed-up information and eliminate the manual work once required to make backups. Software companies offer solutions to back up and recover dozens of disparate systems from a single console. Companies offer backup as a service, using the Internet to maintain backups of thousands of geographically dispersed systems.

## Obstacles to Data Backup

Despite all the hardware and software available today to make backups, a good deal of data in client/server networks is still not backed up on a regular basis. The following common obstacles often prevent organizations from regularly backing up all their data:

- **Backup window**—The **backup window** is the period of time when an organization can run backups. Businesses generally time their backup window for non-production periods, when network bandwidth and the central processing unit (CPU) utilization are low. However, many now conduct operations seven days a week, 24 hours a day—effectively eliminating the traditional backup window.

- **Network bandwidth**—Many companies now have more data to protect than they can transport across existing local area networks (LANs) and wide area networks (WANs). If a network cannot handle the impact of transporting hundreds of gigabytes of data over a short period of time, the organization's centralized backup strategy is not viable.

- **System throughput**—Three input/output (I/O) bottlenecks are common in traditional backup schemes: the ability of the system being backed up to push data to the backup server, the ability of the backup server to accept data from multiple systems simultaneously, and the available throughput of the tape devices onto which the data is moved. Any or all of these bottlenecks can render a centralized backup solution unworkable.

- **Lack of resources**—Many companies fail to make appropriate investments in data protection until it is too late. Often, information technology (IT) managers choose not to allocate funding for centralized data protection because of competing demands resulting from emerging issues, such as e-commerce, Internet/intranet applications, and other new technologies.

> **▷ NOTE**
>
> A number of companies provide specialized expertise in design and deployment of integrated storage solutions. These solutions focus on providing secure backup solutions using techniques such as agent-based storage, where a software agent makes backups throughout the day.

## Key Elements of Data Backup

Successful data backup and recovery involves four key elements: the backup device, the network, the backup window, and the backup storage devices. These components are highly dependent on one another, and the overall system can operate only as well as its weakest link. To help define how data backup is changing to overcome the obstacles described in the previous section, the following sections look at each element of a backup and recovery design and review the improvements being made.

### The Backup Device

The backup device can be either a backup server or a software agent. A **backup server** is responsible for managing the policies, schedules, media catalogs, and indexes associated with the systems it is configured to back up. The systems being backed up are called *clients.* Traditionally, all managed data in an enterprise that was being backed up had to be processed through the backup server. All data that needed to be restored had to be accessed through the backup server as well. This meant that the overall performance of a backup or recovery was directly related to the ability of the backup server to handle the I/O load created by the backup process.

In the past, the only way to overcome a backup server bottleneck was to invest in larger, more powerful backup servers and divide the backup network into smaller, independent groups. Fortunately, developers of backup software have created methods to work around these bottlenecks. One workaround is to create tape servers that allow administrators to divide the backup tasks across multiple systems, while maintaining scheduling and administrative processes on a primary, or backup, server. This approach often involves attaching multiple tape servers to a shared tape library, which reduces the overall cost of the system. A second workaround is to direct backup files to hard drives through mirrored approaches, where data continually duplicates on geographically dispersed systems.

A newly offered approach requires installation of a software agent on all systems that need backing up. This approach involves making backups continually throughout the day and transmitting them to a backup facility as long as the system is connected to the network.

### The Network Data Path

Centralization of a data-management process, such as backup and recovery, calls for a robust and available network data path. The movement and management of hundreds or thousands of megabytes of data can strain even the best-designed networks. Unfortunately, many companies are already struggling with simply managing the existing data traffic created by applications such as e-commerce, the Internet, e-mail, and multi-media document management. Although technologies such as Gigabit Ethernet can provide relief, they are rarely enough to accommodate management of large amounts of data movement.

If not enough bandwidth is in place to move the data, you have some options. Once again, the developers of backup software have created a remedy. An enterprise-class backup solution can distribute backup services directly to the data source while at the same time centralizing the administration of these resources. For example, if a business must back up an 800 GB database server nightly, it can attach a tape backup device directly to that server. This effectively eliminates the need to move the 800 GB database across the network to a centralized backup server. This approach, called a *LAN-less backup*, relies on remote tape server capability.

A second option is to install a network path dedicated to the management and movement of data. This data path can be Small Computer System Interface (SCSI), Ethernet, Asynchronous Transfer Mode (ATM), Fiber Distributed Data Interface (FDDI), or Fibre Channel. Creating a dedicated data path is the beginning of a **storage area network (SAN)**—an architecture in which a network separate from the traditional LAN connects all storage and servers in such a way that they appear to be locally attached to the operating system. SANs are quickly dominating the backup landscape, and applications such as serverless and LAN-less backup will continue to push this emerging technology forward.

A third option is to structure the backup process such that you create a backup baseline weekly or monthly, depending on data volatility. Each night, perform a differential backup or an incremental backup. (For more information on these types of backups, see the next section, "The Backup Window.")

Each of these options seeks to smooth backup maintenance by minimizing the volume of data that needs moving and by maximizing the use of available network capacity.

>  **NOTE**
>
> SAN-based backup offers benefits such as higher availability, increased flexibility, improved reliability, lower cost, manageability, improved performance, and increased scalability. Remember, however, that effective backup provides for offsite storage and encryption of data while in or en route to the offsite location.

## The Backup Window

A **backup window** defines how much time is available to perform backups. In its early days, the backup window typically ran when interaction with staff was minimal. This was usually after 6:00 p.m. and before 6:00 a.m., when organizations performed testing or processed jobs that required no user interaction. As system operations have expanded geographically and in hours worked, the normal operational requirement has become 24/7, and the backup window has shrunk. Mainframes and larger servers have compensated for this decreased backup window. They use technology such as faster equipment to expand the capability to create backups. They also use continual backups—that is, backups made throughout the day. These techniques have expanded the backup window.

Some organizations have taken the continual backup technique further by installing a client on each system. The client monitors all files on the system and automatically encrypts and transmits changed files to a backup facility. This approach both expands the backup window and optimizes use of network resources by making many small transmissions throughout the day as opposed to one large transmission during a constrained timeframe.

In the past, inadequate backup windows forced companies to add additional backup servers and to divide the backup groups into smaller and smaller clusters of systems. However, the backup software community developed methods to overcome this time obstacle:

- **Incremental backups**—An **incremental backup** transfers only the data that has changed since the last backup. On average, no more than 9 percent of data in a file server changes daily. This means an incremental backup may only require 9 percent of the time it takes to back up the entire file system. Even then, a full backup has to be made regularly, or restoration of the data will take too long.

- **Differential backup**—In a **differential backup**, only files that have changed since the last full backup are backed up to the backup facility. This approach reduces the nightly backup volume and allows a weekly backup baseline of all files on weekends. Use it where the resource requirements of production work are comparatively low.

- **Block-level incremental backups**—**Block-level incremental backups** provide similar benefits as incremental backups but with even more efficiency. Rather than backing up entire files that have been modified since the last backup, only the blocks that have changed since the last backup are marked for backup. This approach can greatly reduce the amount of incremental data requiring daily backup. However this benefit comes at a price: Often, the file system of the client must be from the same vendor as the backup software.

- **Image backups**—**Image backups** are quickly gaining favor among storage administrators. This type of backup creates copies or snapshots of a file system at a particular point in time. It is possible to make image backups much more quickly than incremental backups. Incremental backups enable barebones recovery of a server without loading the operating systems, applications, and the like. Image backups also provide specific point-in-time backups with the option of running one every hour rather than once a day.

- **Data archiving**—Removing infrequently accessed data from a disk drive can reduce the size of a scheduled backup substantially. By moving static, infrequently accessed data to tape, backup applications can focus on backing up and recovering only the most current and critical data. By archiving static data, an organization maintains easy access to the information without adding to its daily data backup requirements. This method provides the additional benefit of freeing up existing disk space without adding capacity.

## Backup Storage Devices

In many cases, the single most expensive item in a backup project is the backup storage device itself. Therefore, it is important that the device provide adequate capacity and performance to accommodate existing and planned data. Determining the nature of the backup device—tape, magnetic disk, optical disk, and so on—and its capability depends on a number of variables, including the following:

- The volume of devices to be backed up
- The number of backup copies to be retained
- The amount of time backups need to be retained

- The backup approach—full, incremental, differential, or a combination
- The backup window available
- The backup device and capacity—online backup or offline backup and physical location

For example, the size of automated tape libraries depends on two variables: the number of tape drives and the number of tape slots. Tape libraries are available with a few to hundreds of thousands of slots and can support anywhere from one to hundreds of tape drives.

As a forensic investigator, know the number of tapes for each system, when those tapes are rotated, how long they are kept, and when they are destroyed. An organization should provide a complete inventory of the backup tapes for current backups and for the relevant time under investigation. The list should contain as much of the following information as possible:

- Tape identifier or label information
- Tape format
- Backup date and time
- Names of backed-up servers and systems
- The tape's current location—for example, in the backup device, the tape room, or offsite storage
- Schedule of rotation or destruction

> **TIP**
>
> When designing a centralized data backup, an organization should take particular care in selecting the backup storage device. It should provide the required throughput, support the needed backup volume, and be scalable to meet long-term storage needs.

### Recommended Backup Features

In today's global economy, applications such as e-mail, relational databases, and e-commerce systems must be accessible and online 24 hours a day. Organizations can't shut them down to perform administrative tasks such as backups. The following are some important features to look for in a backup system:

- **Data interleaving**—To back up multiple systems concurrently, a backup application must be able to write data from multiple clients to tape in an interleaved manner. Otherwise, the clients must be backed up sequentially, which takes much longer.

- **Remote backup**—A backup application should have a method to back up systems across a network. Many remote systems are exposed to unrecoverable data loss. Businesses often do not back up offsite locations because of the cost of deploying hardware and software remotely and the lack of administrative support in remote locations. Laptop computers are especially vulnerable to data loss.

- **Global monitoring**—Companies are deploying applications that they can manage and monitor from any location in the enterprise. They should also be able to access and administer their backup applications from multiple locations. A robust backup application should support reporting and administration of any backup system, regardless of location.

- **Performance**—An enterprise backup application should benchmark backup data rates exceeding 1 terabyte (TB) per hour. These benchmarks show that backup performance is limited to the hardware and network and not to the application itself.

## The Role of Backups in Data Recovery

The first step in a successful data recovery is the backup of data. An effective data recovery approach requires a backup process that is quick, performs timely backups, and requires minimal interaction with the user community. That is, backups should be automatic and consistent.

The following are some of the many factors that affect backups:

- **Decreasing storage costs**—The cost per megabyte of primary storage has fallen dramatically over the past several years. It continues to drop as disk drive technologies advance. This has a huge impact on backups. As users become accustomed to having immediate access to more and more information online, the time required to restore data from secondary media is often unacceptable.

- **The need to have systems online continuously**—24/7 operations are now the norm in many of today's businesses. The volume of data they keep online and available is very large and constantly increasing. The primary data repository requires higher and higher levels of fault tolerance. Because systems must be continuously online, it is often impractical to take files offline to perform backups.

- **Increasing backup retention requirements**—Operational and legal requirements have increased the need to maintain backup copies for longer time periods to support litigation, historical analysis, and auditability.

- **The changing role of backups**—Backups are no longer just for restoring data. Operationally, mirrored data does not guard against data corruption and user error. The role of backups is now taking on the responsibility for recovering user errors and ensuring that *good* data has been saved and can quickly be restored.

Storage vendors and backup vendors offer a number of network backup solutions. To effectively accomplish backup in today's environment, they generally bundle software with hardware components to provide a total backup solution. A typical backup management system consists of a server with a front-end interface to the network and a SAN repository with tape or other offline storage capability.

The decreasing cost of online storage has made mirroring a viable backup option. With **mirroring**, a business can keep at least two copies of data online at all times. The advantage of mirroring is that data does not have to be restored, so the backup is immediately available. Further, with today's communications capability, an organization can geographically disperse the mirrored devices and increase system survivability.

Today's backup and data availability solutions have several drawbacks:

- **Network backup creates network performance problems**—Using a production network to carry backup data as well as for normal user data access can overburden network resources. Minimize this problem by installing a separate network exclusively for backups. However, even dedicated backup networks may become performance bottlenecks.

- **Offline backup affects data accessibility**—To minimize the time that the host is offline for data backup requires high-speed, continuous parallel backup of the raw image of the data. Even if you make such backups, you still face the problem of the time needed to restore the information. In addition, data restoration should occur at the file level so that you bring back the most critical information into operation first.

- **Live backups allow data access during the backup process but affect performance**—Many database vendors offer live backup features. The downside to a live backup is that it puts a tremendous burden on the host.

- **Mirroring doesn't protect against user error and replication of *bad* data**—Fully replicated online data sounds great. However, it costs twice as much per megabyte as a single copy of online data. Synchronizing, breaking, and resynchronizing mirrors is not a trivial process. These activities influence data access speeds. Also, duplicating data after a user has deleted a critical file is problematic. So is making a mirrored copy of a file that has been corrupted by a host process. Mirroring has a place in data backup and recovery, but it cannot solve the problem by itself.

Backups need to occur at extremely high speeds, and the host processor should be independent of the underlying file structures supporting the data. Recovery must be available at the file level. Eliminate the time that systems are offline for backup. In addition, for data that an organization always needs handy, highly fault-tolerant primary storage is not enough, nor is a time-consuming backup and restoration. Mirroring—using remote hot recovery sites—does the job of immediate resumption of data access. Mirroring, however, still requires backup of critical data to protect against data errors and user errors.

 **NOTE**

Backup and mirroring are complementary, not competing, technologies.

## Data Recovery Today

*Availability* used to mean that an application would be available during the week, from 9 to 5, regardless of whether customers needed anything. Batch processing took over the evenings and nights, and most people didn't care because they were at home asleep or out having fun.

But the world has changed. It's now common for companies to offer extended service hours in which a customer can call for help with a bill, an inquiry, or a complaint. Even if a live human being isn't available, many enterprise applications are Web enabled so that customers can access their accounts in the middle of the night while sitting at home in their pajamas.

Increased availability is good. However, the complex systems that have evolved over the past decades must be monitored, managed, controlled, and optimized. Backups must now take place while an application is running and application changes take place on the fly.

## Handling Failures

System outages occur. If an outage isn't mitigated or quickly resolved, it can cost a company thousands of dollars in revenue and resources. Hardware failures were once more common than they are today. And disk storage is more reliable than it's ever been. However, increasing risks of software failures and power fluctuations have offset these performance improvements.

System failures have a number of causes, including the following:

- **Programming errors**—An application programmer, a system programmer, or an operations person can make a simple mistake in logic, timing, or even typing. Such a simple mistake can have serious or catastrophic results, including a system crash and data corruption. Programming or other errors that reach production are typically found because of their impact on operations. For example, they may crash a system or corrupt data. Detection of software errors could thus be delayed for minutes, hours, days, or longer when a system crashes or performs inconsistently or when a customer calls with a problem.

 **NOTE**

Businesses today simply can't tolerate availability problems, no matter the source. Systems must remain available to make money and serve customers. Downtime is much too expensive to tolerate. An organization should balance its data management budget against the cost of downtime.

- **Natural and other disasters**—Snowstorms, floods, earthquakes, and fires often strike with limited or no warning. Flooding doesn't always occur when it's raining. A flood can result from a broken water main, a broken dam, or a quickly melting snowfall. Meteorologists know the weather conditions that spawn tornadoes, but they still can't forecast when or where they will strike. Hurricanes announce their presence, but the associated wind and water effects remain unpredictable. Earthquake forecasting is in its infancy, but at least engineers know how to build structures to minimize their impact. All these problems and more can cause system failures.

Recognize and plan for outages and failures to reduce their frequency and impact.

## Critical Thinking and Creative Problem Solving

Today's businesses need skilled system forensics experts who can make better decisions, spur creativity, and implement practical solutions. Critical thinking and critical problem solving are separate modes of thought that help forensic specialists make better decisions:

- **Critical thinking**—This involves breaking down a complex problem or decision into smaller, more manageable components. This process helps to make the forensic solution more evident and the problem easier to solve.

- **Creative problem solving**—These skills allow a forensic specialist to think "outside the box" to come up with inventive solutions. In today's competitive environment, these out-of-the-box forensic solutions ensure that individuals and organizations remain future-focused in a changing marketplace.

>  **NOTE**
>
> After you recover data, you may face an enormous amount of data. Develop a strategy for extracting the relevant files. Software such as EnCase Forensic (see *http://www .guidancesoftware.com*) can help you filter for file type and date, duplicates, and keywords. In setting a strategy, consider data amount, costs, and possibly deadlines.

Each of these modes of thinking uses a separate part of the brain. One analyzes existing facts, figures, and other data. The other focuses on intuitive, holistic, and feeling-based solutions. These correspond to the brain's left and right sides. Use both types of thinking to arrive at the best forensic solutions to problems and in making the best forensic decisions.

## Preparing for Recovery

One of the most critical data management tasks is recovering data in the event of a problem. For this reason, organizations around the world spend many hours each week preparing their environments for the possibility of having to recover. These preparations include backing up data, accumulating changes, and keeping track of all the needed resources.

Preparing for recovery involves evaluating procedures, making sure all resources are available in usable condition, automating processes as much as possible, and ensuring the efficiency of recovery. The following sections take a look at each of these factors.

### Evaluating Procedures

Often the procedures that organizations use to prepare for recovery were designed many years ago. Although a recovery strategy may have been adequate when it was designed, it may be dangerously obsolete, given today's requirements for increased availability. What if a required resource is damaged or missing? Finding out at recovery time that some critical resource is missing can be disastrous.

For example, an organization that makes weekly image copies on the weekend and performs system changes at midweek will not have adequate backup if the volatility of its data requires daily backup for adequate coverage. An important step in preparing for recovery is evaluating the procedures currently in place for recovery and updating them where needed. At a minimum, the organization should review and evaluate recovery strategies at least annually.

### Ensuring That Resources Are Available

Many organizations use image copies of various groups of databases, as well as change accumulations, all staggered throughout the week. In a complex environment, how is it possible to make sure that every database is being backed up? Is the organization making image copies—either batch or online—as frequently as planned? Are change accumulations taken as often as needed? What if media errors occur? Identifying these types of conditions is critical to ensuring a successful recovery.

To plan for problem recovery, make a list of required resources, their location, or how you might acquire them. This list will be invaluable when implementing a recovery action.

### Automating Recovery

Having people with the required expertise available to perform recoveries is a major consideration, particularly in disaster situations. However, if a business plans and automates its recovery processes so that less-experienced personnel can aid in or manage them, the organization can maximize use of its resources and reduce the risk to its operations.

Automation takes some of the human error factor and thought requirement out of the recovery equation, and it makes the complexity of the environment less of a concern. Creating an automated and easy-to-use system requires the right tools and some planning for the inevitable. However, compared with the possible loss of the entire business, it is worth the investment. With proper planning and automation, recovery is possible, reliance on specific personnel is reduced, and the human-error factor is nearly eliminated.

### Making Recovery Efficient

Planning for efficient recovery is critical. Multithreading tasks shorten the recovery process. Recovering multiple databases with one pass through the log data saves time. Making image copies, rebuilding indexes, and validating pointers concurrently with the recovery process further reduces downtime. Where downtime is costly, time saved is money in the bank. Any measures an organization can take to perform recovery and related tasks more quickly and efficiently allows the business to resume more quickly and saves money.

## CHAPTER SUMMARY

Computer system crashes, software failures, and file deletions all happen frequently. Natural disasters, programming errors, and malicious attacks are just some of the many potential causes of data loss. Regardless of the cause, a data loss can potentially rob you of your most current data. This is where data recovery steps in.

Data recovery involves finding lost data and assembling it into useful data files. Often, recovery specialists handle data recovery. However, sometimes forensic specialists must also be involved in finding data that others have thrown away or left behind. This chapter discusses data recovery as it relates to system forensics.

## KEY CONCEPTS AND TERMS

| | | |
|---|---|---|
| Backup | Consistency checking | Logical damage |
| Backup server | Data recovery | Mirroring |
| Backup window | Differential backup | Physical damage |
| Block-level incremental backup | Image backup | Storage area network (SAN) |
| Clean room | Incremental backup | Zero-knowledge analysis |

## CHAPTER 9 ASSESSMENT

**1.** Data recovery is the process of salvaging data from damaged, failed, corrupted, or inaccessible primary storage media when it cannot be accessed normally.

A. True
B. False

**2.** A _____ is a nonvolatile storage device that magnetically encodes digital data.

**3.** Physical damage always causes at least some data loss, but it does not affect the logical structures of the file system.

A. True
B. False

**4.** What are the two main techniques used to recover data after logical damage? (Select two.)

A. Putting a hard drive in the freezer
B. Repairing the damage in a clean room
C. Consistency checking
D. Zero-knowledge analysis

**5.** Which of the following is a data recovery technique that involves scanning the logical structure of the disk and checking to make sure that it is consistent with its specification?

A. Consistency checking
B. Zero-knowledge analysis
C. Mirroring
D. Backup

**6.** Which of the following is a file system repair technique in which a recovery specialist assumes very little about the state of the file system to be analyzed, uses any hints that any undamaged file system structures might provide, and rebuilds the file system from scratch?

A. Consistency checking
B. Zero-knowledge analysis
C. Mirroring
D. Backup

**7.** Common obstacles that prevent organizations from regularly backing up all their data include the backup window, network bandwidth, system throughput, and lack of resources.

A. True
B. False

**8.** Which of the following is not one of the key elements of data backup?

A. Backup server
B. Network
C. Backup window
D. Mirroring
E. Backup storage devices

**9.** Which of the following is a backup that creates copies or snapshots of a file system at a particular point in time.

A. Image backup
B. Incremental backup
C. Mirroring
D. Block-level incremental backups

**10.** Which of the following is a backup that transfers only the data that has changed since the last backup.

A. Image backup
B. Incremental backup
C. Mirroring
D. Block-level incremental backup

**11.** _____ is physical replication of all data, with two copies of the data kept online at all times.

**12.** The main problem with mirroring is that it doesn't protect against user error and replication of bad data.

A. True
B. False

# Investigating and Scrutinizing E-mail

E-MAIL IS THE ELECTRONIC EQUIVALENT of a letter or a memo. Computers and servers retain these electronic messages in digital format. An e-mail may include attachments or enclosures. And organizations and individuals use e-mail for communicating sensitive, protected, or confidential information. E-mail is also a very common method for distributing intellectual property, such as client lists or copyrighted material. You may send one with desktop and laptop computers and other portable devices, such as mobile phones and personal digital assistants (PDAs).

E-mail creates a security vulnerability. It is a virtual door that leads directly into a network and indirectly into every desktop. In its natural form, e-mail is as secure as a postcard: Anyone can easily see its contents as it passes through the networks. Hackers can use e-mail to sneak into a network. Staff can use it to send secrets out of a company. Attackers can also use e-mail as a portal for data destruction.

Investigating, recovering, and analyzing e-mail is one of the most common system forensics activities. E-mail is a starting point or key element in forensic investigations. A forensic investigator can examine e-mail and identify what messages have been sent, when, and to whom. An investigator can also use information contained in e-mail to show a pattern of behavior. An e-mail investigation may involve corporate e-mail or Web-based mail, such as Gmail or Hotmail. The evidence from an e-mail investigation can be enough to show that other systems, possibly in a third party's control, may need investigating. In addition, an investigation may lead you to research a piece of received e-mail as a way of tracking down its source or author. This chapter discusses some of the issues related to investigating and scrutinizing e-mail.

## Chapter 10 Topics

This chapter covers the following topics and concepts:

- How mail servers and e-mail clients are involved in sending and receiving e-mail messages
- How to understand the information contained in an e-mail header
- How to use e-mail tracing in a forensic investigation
- What legal considerations are involved in investigating e-mail

## Chapter 10 Goals

When you complete this chapter, you will be able to:

- Describe the roles of mail servers and e-mail clients in sending and receiving e-mail messages
- Understand what information is contained in e-mail headers
- Understand how e-mail tracing contributes to a forensic investigation
- Understand the legal considerations involved in investigating e-mail

# The Roles of Mail Servers and E-mail Clients

 **NOTE**

Microsoft Exchange Server and Sendmail are examples of mail servers.

Different types of devices and methods generate e-mails. Most commonly, a user composes a message on his or her computer and then sends it to his or her mail server. At this point, the user's computer is finished with the job, but the mail server still has to deliver the message. A **mail server** is like an electronic post office: It sends and receives electronic mail. Most of the time, the mail server is separate from the computer where the mail was composed, as shown in Figure 10-1.

**FIGURE 10-1**

Generating e-mail.

Sender      E-mail Message      Mail Server

**FIGURE 10-2**

Delivering e-mail.

The sender's mail server forwards the message through the organization's network or the Internet to the recipient's mail server (see Figure 10-2). The message then resides on that second mail server and is available to the recipient. The software program used to compose and read e-mail messages is the **e-mail client**.

Depending on how the recipient's e-mail client is configured, copies of the message may exist in a number of places. The recipient's computer, another electronic device such as a smartphone or a PDA, and the mail server or its backups may all hold copies of the message. In addition, the sender's computer may still hold a copy of the message in the Sent box or trash folder. And the sender's mail server or its backups may also have a copy. In addition, any of the servers that relays the message from the sender to the recipient may retain a copy of the e-mail message. The number of relay "hops" may be only one if the sender and recipient are on the same network. Transmitting a message to a remotely located recipient might require many hops.

> **NOTE**
>
> Some of the most commonly used e-mail clients are Microsoft Outlook, Yahoo! Mail, Hotmail, Windows Live Mail, Apple Mail, Gmail, and AOL.

> **TIP**
>
> Regardless of the type of e-mail client used, a message can be stored in multiple locations. Consider obtaining a message from as many sources as possible.

A forensic investigation of e-mail might reveal information such as the following:

- E-mail messages related to the investigation
- E-mail addresses related to the investigation
- Sender and recipient information
- Content of the communications
- Internet Protocol (IP) addresses
- Date and time information
- User information
- Attachments
- Passwords
- Application logs that show evidence of spoofing

The following sections describe how an investigator can find such information.

## Understanding E-mail Headers

You can use various methods to create and send an e-mail message. An e-mail message's appearance depends on the device or software program you use. However, a message typically has several common parts:

- **Header**—The **e-mail header** contains addressing information and the route that an e-mail takes from sender to receiver.
- **Body**—The **e-mail body** contains the communication's content.
- **Attachments**—**E-mail attachments** may be any type of file, such as pictures, documents, sound, and video.

Make sure that any e-mail you offer as evidence includes the message, any attachments, and the full e-mail header.

**TIP**

**Internet Protocol (IP)** is the protocol that networks use to communicate data to other networks. IP is the primary protocol in the Internet layer of the Internet Protocol suite. Its job is to deliver data packets from the source host to the destination host, based on their IP addresses.

**NOTE**

Every machine identified in the e-mail header could have accessed, retained a copy of, or altered the e-mail message.

The header keeps a record of the message's journey as it travels through the communications network. As the message is routed through one or more mail servers, each server adds its own information to the message header. Each device in a network has a numeric label called an **Internet Protocol (IP) address** that identifies the device and provides a location address. The IP address is the virtual equivalent of a street address for a computer on a network. A forensic investigator may be able to identify IP addresses from a message header and use this information to determine who sent the message.

Most e-mail programs normally display only a small portion of the e-mail header along with a message. This usually is information that the sender puts in the message, as shown in Figure 10-3. You can view and examine the full header record by using tools available in the e-mail client.

An e-mail investigation begins with a review of an e-mail message followed by a detailed examination of the message header information. The e-mail message shown in Figure 10-3 shows the limited header display generally provided. Look at the header in more detail to find additional information associated with the e-mail message. The message header provides an audit trail of every machine through which the e-mail has passed.

**FYI**

In June 2010, Paraben Corporation released updates to Paraben's E-mail Examiner 6.0 and Paraben's Network E-mail Examiner 3.1. According to the company, the updates include feature enhancements to both tools, including the Batch Processing Wizard. The new wizard allows an investigator to view and automatically export e-mail archives into a variety of mail formats, including Microsoft Outlook. For more information, see *http://www.paraben.com*.

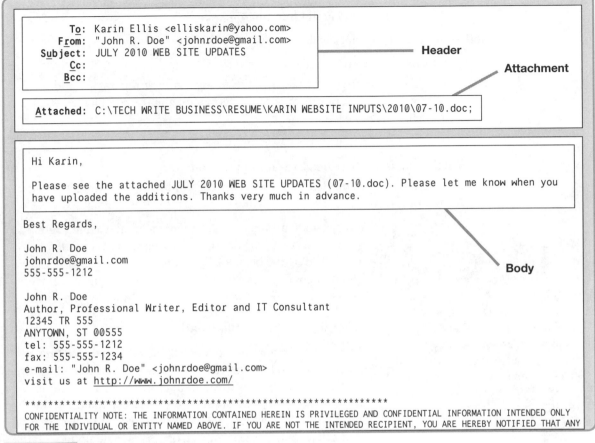

**FIGURE 10-3**

Components of an e-mail message.

## Viewing an E-mail Header

How you look at the entire header depends on the e-mail client. For example, follow these steps to view the header information in Microsoft Outlook 2007:

1. Open the message whose header you want to examine.

2. On the Message tab, click the arrow to the right of Options. A new dialog appears, with the header in the bottom section.

To see the header information in Windows Live Mail, follow these steps:

1. Open the message whose header you want to examine.

2. Select File, Properties.

3. In the dialog that appears, select the Details tab. The window in this tab shows the complete header information.

4. To see the entire message, including the complete header, click Message Source. A dialog appears, showing this information.

As another example, these steps will let you view the header information in Gmail:

1. Open the message whose header you want to examine.
2. In the message's top-right corner, click the downward-pointing arrow and select Show Original. A new browser tab opens, showing the complete message, including the entire header.

To see the header information in Yahoo! Mail, use these steps:

1. Open the message whose header you want to examine.
2. Select Actions, View Full Header. A dialog appears, showing the complete header information.

> **NOTE**
>
> Copies of a message on the sender's system don't show a message's routing path. The routing path is available only on the recipient system. Further, a typical e-mail client provides no assurance that the recipient has received and read an e-mail message. In some cases, a sender requests a message receipt. However, the recipient can choose not to provide a receipt.

> **NOTE**
>
> E-mail clients allow senders to defer and manually initiate or schedule the time they send an e-mail. Also, some servers send e-mails at a certain prescheduled time. Either of these situations could allow an individual to be at another location at the time an e-mail message is actually sent. Therefore, the times shown in the header may not be able to verify the sender or receiver location at any point in time.

Every e-mail message has a header, no matter what client and Internet service provider (ISP) an organization or individual uses. Finding the header information generally requires a few simple steps that are easy to figure out by poking around in the client.

## Interpreting an E-mail Header

Reconstruct an e-mail's journey by reading the e-mail header from bottom to top. The "From:" line shows the e-mail's source. As the message passes through mail servers, each mail server adds its information above the previous information in the header in a "Received:" line. The "Received:" lines list every point the e-mail passed through on its journey, along with the date and time.

One of the most important pieces of information for you to obtain from the detailed header is the originating IP address. In the example shown in Figure 10-4, for example, the originating IP address is 165.247.94.223.

The information in an e-mail header does not always tell a simple story. For example, anything up to the topmost "Received:" line in a message header can be faked, or spoofed. (Spoofing is discussed later in this chapter.) If a message header contains inconsistent information, the e-mail message may have been spoofed.

Times shown in e-mail headers do not always appear to be consistent. Different servers in different parts of the world and in different time zones may have added timestamps. In addition, clocks built into computer systems may not always be accurate. Scrutinize timestamps in headers, look for apparent inconsistencies, and identify clues that validate the message authenticity.

**FIGURE 10-4**

An e-mail header.

```
X-Message-Info: JGTYoYF78jEv6iDU7aTDV/xX2xdjzKcH
Received: from web11603.mail.yahoo.com ([216.136.172.55]) by mc4-
f4 with Microsoft SMTPSVC(5.0.2195.5600);
            Mon, 5 Jul 2010 18:53:07 -0700
Message-ID: 20100709015303.27404.qmail@web11603.mail.yahoo.com
Received: from [165.247.94.223] by web11603.mail.yahoo.com via
HTTP; Mon, 05 Jul 2010 18:53:03 PDT          ──── Originating IP address
Date: Mon, 5 Jul 2010 18:53:03 -0700 (PDT)
From: John Sender <sendersname2010@yahoo.com>
Subject: The Plan!
To: RecipientName_1@hotmail.com
MIME-Version: 1.0
Content-Type: multipart/mixed; boundary="0-2041413029-
1063072383=:26811"
Return-Path: sendersname2010@yahoo.com
X-OriginalArrivalTime: 05 Jul 2010 01:53:07.0873 (UTC)
FILETIME=[1DBDB910:01C37675]

--0-2041413029-1063072383=:26811
Content-Type: multipart/alternative; boundary="0-871459572-
1063072383=:26811"

--0-871459572-1063072383=:26811
Content-Type: text/plain; charset=us-ascii

Received the package. Meet me at the boat dock.
See attached map and account numbers
```

# E-mail Tracing

**E-mail tracing** involves examining e-mail header information to look for clues about where a message has been. This will be one of your more frequent responsibilities as a forensic investigator. You will often use audits or paper trails of e-mail traffic as evidence in court.

After a suspect comes to the authorities' attention, your organization may ask you to monitor that person's traffic. For example, administrators might order security checks on an employee who appears to be disgruntled or who has access to sensitive information. This employee's e-mail logs and network usage may, for example, show him or her sending innocent family photos to a Hotmail account but no traffic coming back from that Hotmail account. These seemingly innocent photos might carry a stego message, and so provide evidence of the employee's part in corporate espionage. As discussed in Chapter 8, "Understanding Information-Hiding Techniques," steganography is a process in which someone buries the 1s and 0s of digital text or images inside the pixels of ordinary-looking photographs. Your job may be to determine whether the employee possesses a steganography program.

Forensic e-mail tracing is similar to traditional gumshoe detective work. It involves looking at each point through which an e-mail passed. Work step-by-step back to the originating computer and, eventually, the perpetrator.

> **Avoiding E-mail Tracing via Shared Accounts**
>
> One technique computer criminals use to counter e-mail examination is to sign up for a Web mail account and type a draft e-mail message but not send it. Other individuals sharing the Web mail account can log on and read the draft e-mail. Because no one ever sent the message, it isn't susceptible to packet sniffing by law enforcement. In addition, if the message doesn't list recipients, and it hasn't been sent, its header doesn't contain helpful information. Look for shared accounts to find these types of information-sharing arrangements.

An e-mail message may travel through machines outside a company's network. In these cases, try sleuthing tools such as Whois (available at many sites, such as *http://www.whois.com*) or BetterWhois (*http://www.betterwhois.com*) to do further tracking. These services search databases that record online users and their IP addresses. For example, running a Whois search on a domain name such as XYZ.com will identify the name and address of the domain name's holder, administrative and technical points of contact, and the domain name servers responsible for the domain. In some cases, you may need a more sophisticated tracing tool such as Webtracer (*http://www.webtracer.com*).

If an address isn't fake, determine who used the machine at the time the suspect message was sent. For example, say that an attacker used a school or library computer to send a bomb threat through a commercial e-mail account. In this case, the logon times in the school's or library's sign-on logs might be helpful.

## Faking E-mail

Sophisticated suspects may fake their e-mail messages. Some of them use e-mail programs that strip the message header from the message before delivering it to the recipient. Or they may bury the message header within the e-mail program. In other cases, the "From:" line in a message header is fake. Offenders may "steal" someone else's e-mail account or set up a temporary, bogus account. The following sections look at some common methods of faking e-mails: spoofing, anonymous remailing, using mail relays, spamming, stealing, and using bogus accounts.

### Spoofing

**Spoofing** involves making an e-mail message appear to come from someone or someplace other than the real sender or location (see Figure 10-5). The e-mail sender uses a software tool that is readily available on the Internet to cut out his or her IP address and replace it with someone else's address. However, the first machine to receive the spoofed message records the machine's real IP address. Thus, the header contains both the faked ID and the real IP address.

## Anonymous Remailing

**Anonymous remailing** is another attempt to throw tracing or tracking off the trail. A suspect who uses anonymous remailing sends an e-mail message to an anonymizer. An **anonymizer** is an e-mail server that strips identifying information from an e-mail message before forwarding it with the mailing computer's IP address.

To find out who sent remailed e-mail, try to look at any logs maintained by these remailer or anonymizer companies. However, these services frequently do not maintain logs. In addition, you can closely analyze the message for embedded information that might give clues to the user or system that sent the message.

## Using Mail Relays

Using mail relays involves hiding an e-mail's origin and having someone else's mail server send the message. Local networks typically use **mail relays**—servers that transmit e-mail messages among local users. A college campus, for example, might use a mail relay to transmit all the student and faculty e-mail. In e-mail aliasing, multiple e-mail addresses are used to send mail to a single account. A mail relay forwards all these messages to the specified single e-mail address. A properly configured mail server processes mail only from within its system and doesn't relay mail from IP addresses originating from outside its network. But if the mail server is not configured properly, it becomes vulnerable to a wide variety of remote access programs.

> **NOTE**
>
> Internet access is available in many public locations, such as libraries, schools, airports, hotels, and Internet cafes. If an attacker sends an e-mail message from such a location, determining the actual sender may be difficult.

**FIGURE 10-5**

A spoofed e-mail.

```
X-Original-To: jvacca@frognet.net
Delivered-To: jvacca@frognet.net
X-Yahoo-Newman-Property: ymail-3
X-Yahoo-Newman-Id: 693514.52142.bm@omp508.mail.sp1.yahoo.com
DomainKey-Signature: a=rsa-sha1; q=dns; c=nofws;
   s=s1024; d=yahoo.com;
   h=X-YMail-OSG:Received:Date:From:Subject:To:MIME-Version:Content-Type:Content-Transfer-Encoding:Message-ID;

b=cwCl+MYAUFgzd8yq7xdZmadvFqP7vOKlfb0nZwGXBj5yd06OxhlwyKPD1kwOGg+etdt/8Xq9oRC1fKu/ktWfosk+5+N/3g34nl5i8OU/FH+U62Vc1ns3A/SDYqHpD3t

X-YMail-OSG: Fjhp1TsVM1kWbVg.vP4TlQA1NAZNdE0p0IEpSQrdBblllgoBr6784Ql8A3JSvnEWfkYz6580via0f5wrmBvepJoc1lnz3IUNIDZL
Date: Thu, 24 Jan 2008 19:47:24 -0800 (PST)
From: Web Frognet <web_protectfrognet@yahoo.com>
Subject: Protection Notice.
To: info@frognet.com
```

**FrogNet**

PLEASE PROTECT YOUR FROGNET.NET ACCOUNT FROM BEING CLOSED

Greetings to you,

This is to formally notify you that we are presently working on the Frognet web, and this can close your webmail account with Frognet completely.

To avoid this, please send your Surname and Password to Frognet customer care email address: web_protectfrognet@yahoo.com Please do this,so your Frognet account can be protected from being close.

### A Sample Fake E-mail Message

The header is from a faked e-mail message:

*From A@b.c.d Sat Nov 11 13:16 EST 2009*

*Received: from wavenet.com (wavenet.com [198.147.118.131]) by ddi.digital.net (8.6.11/8.6.9) with ESMTP id NAA04656 for <gandalf@ddi.digital.net>; Sat, 11 Nov 2008 13:16:03 -0500*

*Received: from ddi.digital.net (ddi.digital.net [198.69.104.2]) by wavenet.com (8.6.12/8.6.9) with SMTP id KAA27279 for gandalf@ddi.digital.net; Sat, 11 Nov 2009 10:27:52 -0800*

*Received: from wavenet.com (wavenet.com [198.147.118.131]) by ddi.digital.net (8.6.11/8.6.9) with ESMTP id OAA18017 for <gandalf@ddi.digital.net>; Tue, 24 Oct 2009 14:09:46 -0400*

*Received: from inetlis.wavenet.com (port16.wavenet.com [198.147.118.209]) by wavenet.com (8.6.12/8.6.9) with SMTP id LAA02685 for <gandalf@ddi.digital.net>; Tue, 24 Oct 2009 11:21:12 -0700*

The message's faked parts are the sections that say "from wavenet.com." It looks as if the message originated from inetlis.wavenet.com when in reality it came from ddi.digital.net. If you read the headers from the bottom to the top, you can see what sites the message has gone through. The date and time tell you something is wrong. Running a tool such as Whois on the IP addresses verifies that 198.147.118.131 is wavenet.com, but this IP address doesn't jive with the name of the IP address of the e-mail faker (A@b.c.d). Port16.wavenet.com is 198.147.118.209, wavenet.com is 198.147.118.131, and ddi.digital.net is 198.69.104.2.

### Spamming

**Spamming** occurs when a perpetrator sends an e-mail message to a large number of recipients, usually routed through an unsuspecting company's mail server. The e-mailer uses that mail server as a relay point, and the server's owner may never be aware that the e-mail sender has been there. The sender then disappears before anyone gets suspicious. This is not only a theft of services but potentially a denial of services as well, if the volume of e-mail sent through the server causes it to crash.

The problem of spam offers no easy solutions. The following are some methods to reduce spam:

- **Keyword filters**—On the server end, an administrator can try using keyword filters. The keyword approach must be creative enough to keep up with all the ways a spammer can spell "VI@Gra," for example.

- **IP database block lists**—Attempting to blacklist, or block, spam by specific IP addresses may not work as well as blocking a whole IP address block. A spammer can spoof an address but can't hide the IP domain he or she is using for a relay.

The drawback of this method is that it blocks innocent relay points and mail servers even though they don't know they're being used to send spam.

- **Whitelists**—A server administrator can try whitelists, which allow e-mail only from known and trusted senders. However, this is a drastic solution that defies the purpose of e-mail in the first place.

- **Graylists**—Graylisting is a method of protecting users from spam e-mails by temporarily rejecting senders the server system does not recognize. When an e-mailer gets a message saying a message didn't go through but the system is "trying again in about 24 hours," multiple e-mail servers are communicating with one another to require messages to be re-sent or re-transmitted later. Because spam originates from places that don't usually recognize a request to re-send or re-transmit later, this method eliminates much spam.

Congress has been trying to crack down on spam. However, the problem will probably not go away, no matter how much legislation Capitol Hill passes. Until changes are made in e-mail and related protocols, spam will likely always be around. Also, one person's spam may be another person's business advertising.

## Stealing

*Stealing* can be broadly defined as unauthorized use of someone else's password and e-mail account. One common way in which stealing occurs is shoulder-surfing—watching over someone's shoulder as he or she enters a password and ID. Another method is **sniffing** a network—watching all the network traffic and intercepting user IDs and passwords.

---

### E-mail Protocols

A protocol is a set of rules for determining the format and transmission of data. The following are some of the protocols related to e-mail:

- **Internet Message Access Protocol (IMAP)**—**Internet Message Access Protocol (IMAP)** allows an e-mail client to access e-mail on a remote mail server.

- **Post Office Protocol (POP)**—Local e-mail clients use **Post Office Protocol (POP)** to retrieve e-mail from a remote server.

- **Simple Mail Transfer Protocol (SMTP)**—Mail servers use **Simple Mail Transfer Protocol (SMTP)** to send and receive mail messages. E-mail clients use SMTP to send messages to a mail server for relaying.

- **Hypertext Transfer Protocol (HTTP)**—**Hypertext Transfer Protocol (HTTP)** is involved in requesting and transmitting files over the Internet or another network.

- **Transmission Control Protocol/Internet Protocol (TCP/IP)**—Together, **Transmission Control Protocol (TCP)** and **Internet Protocol (IP)** send messages between computers over the Internet. IP handles data delivery. TCP keeps track of the individual units of data, called packets, in a message.

### Using Bogus Accounts

Bogus free e-mail accounts are quite common among both valid users and spammers. Anybody can give a false identity and address when opening a Hotmail account, for example. It is difficult to catch someone who has done this because the e-mail company doesn't know who opened the false account. Like disposable mobile phones, these accounts are quickly used and discarded. Pornographers often use bogus accounts.

## E-mail Tracing in Forensic Investigations

E-mail tracing in forensic investigations relies on computer logs. An **e-mail log** is a record of each e-mail message that passes through a computer in a network. For evidence purposes, you may need to prove that a certain e-mail originating address traveled through a machine. Do this by verifying the message ID on a log of e-mail transactions, together with the date and time the address was recorded. This is not always easy to do. Legal limits and jurisdictional issues create tough challenges.

Many ISPs do not log e-mail. Some keep only partial data, such as information on logons and File Transfer Protocol (FTP) transfers. ISPs vary in their willingness to assist with forensic investigations. Some readily produce computer logs to help. Others refuse to give up logs without a court order or subpoena. They are legitimately concerned about violating users' privacy rights.

**NOTE**

Foreign jurisdictions are notoriously uncooperative in forensic investigations, even when an investigation has the backing of the U.S. State Department.

**NOTE**

If a message is Web based and stored by a service provider such as Yahoo! or Hotmail, time is of the essence. Many of these companies have a policy of purging information after a certain period of time. In most cases, you must send a preservation letter to the provider to prevent purging of data.

If an official public law enforcement officer notifies an ISP that a certain user is being investigated, the ISP is obligated by law to preserve any information it would have normally logged or collected. This gives investigators time to seek the legal authority to seize the relevant information. The law doesn't require ISPs to escalate their monitoring activities in this situation, however. If they were not keeping a log to begin with, they are under no obligation to start doing so.

In a forensic investigation, use e-mail tracing to determine the physical location of the device a perpetrator used to send e-mail. If possible, confiscate the device and make exact copies of its hard drive. As discussed in other chapters, to avoid tainting the original evidence, analyze an image copy of the device or media rather than the original. In your analysis, look for file fragments or portions of any e-mails that contain specific references to the offending message. For example, if the suspect were using Hotmail, you could check the browser's Internet cache, which shows where the user has been online. The cache contains copies of any e-mails created, sent, or received via Hotmail. Even if the attacker has emptied the cache, you can undelete and recover this information by using forensic software. Examples of this software include Network E-mail Examiner and E-mail Examiner (*http://www .paraben.com*), F-Response (*http://www.f-response.com*), and EnCase Enterprise (*http://www.guidancesoftware.com*).

Several worrisome trends suggest that e-mail tracing will become more difficult in the future:

- Organizations routinely require encryption of all e-mail messages.
- Products currently available automatically strip e-mail headers, encrypt the message, and then destroy the message after a period of time.
- Thorough e-mail deletion utilities are commonly available.

Smart programmers are always looking for ways to get around the audit trail, and investigators always seem to be playing catch-up when tracing e-mail. Nevertheless, e-mail tracing will likely remain an essential part of computer forensics.

## An E-mail Tracing Example

This section provides an example of e-mail tracing. The example is from the "Tracing Email" Web page at *USUS.org*. The following e-mail header is part of a faked e-mail. As described earlier in this chapter, perpetrators have a number of ways to fake e-mail messages. The following example is a rather unsophisticated spoofed e-mail:

Received: from SpoolDir by IFKW-2 (Mercury 1.31);

13 May 09 15:51:47 GMT +01

Return-path: <kuno@seltsam.com>

Received: from bang.jmk.su.se by ifkw-2.ifkw.uni-muenchen.de (Mercury 1.31) with ESMTP;

13 May 09 15:51:44 GMT +01

Received: from [130.237.155.60] (Lilla_Red_10 [130.237.155.60]) by bang.jmk.su.se (8.7.6/8.6.6) with ESMTP id PAA17265 for <luege-ti@ifkw.uni-muenchen.de>; Wed, 13 May 2009 15:49:09 +0200 (MET DST)

X-Sender: o-pabjen@130.237.155.254

Message-Id: <v03020902b17f551e91dd@[130.237.155.60]>

Mime-Version: 1.0

Content-Type: text/plain; charset="us-ascii"

Date: Wed, 13 May 2009 15:49:06 +0200

To: luege-ti@ifkw.uni-muenchen.de

From: Kuno Seltsam <kuno@seltsam.com>

Subject: Important Information

X-PMFLAGS: 34078848 0

The following lines show who claims to have sent the mail, to whom it was sent, and when:

Date: Wed, 13 May 2009 15:49:06 +0200

To: luege-ti@ifkw.uni-muenchen.de

From: Kuno Seltsam <kuno@seltsam.com>

Subject: Important Information

The next line is a number that the receiver's e-mail program adds to the mail to keep track of it on the local hard drive:

X-PMFLAGS: 34078848 0

The next lines indicate that the message contains plaintext with no accented or other fancy characters:

Mime-Version: 1.0 Content-Type: text/plain;

charset="us-ascii"

If you think that the message didn't really come from someone at seltsam.com, use the following line to figure out where the message really came from. The next line contains the Message-Id, which is a tracking number that the originating host assigned to the message:

Message-Id: <v03020902b17f551e91dd@[130.237.155.60]>

The Message-Id is unique for each message, and it contains the IP address of the originating host. You can use a number of sites and programs to translate IP addresses into domain names. For example, if you apply TJPing (*http://www.topjimmy.net/tjs/*) with the IP address in this Message-Id, you get the following information:

Starting lookup on 130.237.155.60 - May 14, 2009

22:01:25

Official Name: L-Red-10.jmk.su.se

IP address: 130.237.155.60

This result shows the originating computer from which the perpetrator sent the message, not the mail server. Because this address is at a university, it's not very helpful because many students share computers on a campus. However, if this were a company computer, it would be useful because employees tend to have their own computers. You can fairly easily use this information to determine what company is involved at this point. You just eliminate the first set of digits from the "Official Name:" line (L-Red-10.), add www, and type the URL into a browser. In this case, you see that www.jmk.su.se is the journalism department of the University of Stockholm. If you have tracked down this much information from the header, you could call the university's system administrator and ask who uses node 60.

The following line tells you who was logged on to the mail server when the message was sent:

X-Sender: o-pabjen@130.237.155.254

Not all e-mail programs add this line. But if you see this line, you know the name of the user who sent the mail—in this case, o-pabjen. The IP address shown here is the address of the mail server used. If you check with TJPing, you learn that it's called bang.jmk.su.se. Now you could actually reply to the message by sending mail to o-pabjen@130.237.155.254 or o-pabjen@bang.jmk.su.se.

Here's the rest of the header:

Received: from [130.237.155.60] (Lilla_Red_10 [130.237.155.60]) by bang.jmk.su.se (8.7.6/8.6.6) with ESMTP id PAA17265 for <luege-ti@ifkw.uni-muenchen.de>; Wed, 13 May 2009 15:49:09 +0200 (MET DST)

These lines name the computer from which the mail server received the message. They also tell when the message was sent and that the recipient was supposed to be luege-ti@ifkw.uni-muenchen.de.

Similarly, the next lines tell you what mail server—ifkw-2.ifkw.uni-muenchen.de— sent the message to the recipient's mail server:

Received: from bang.jmk.su.se by ifkw-2.ifkw.uni-muenchen.de (Mercury 1.31) with ESMTP; 13 May 09 15:51:44 GMT +01

You know that this must be the recipient's mail server because it is the last server that received anything. It follows this fake return path:

Return-path: <kuno@seltsam.com>

The mail server generates the following internal message about where and how it distributed the message within its system:

Received: from SpoolDir by IFKW-2 (Mercury 1.31); 13 May 09 15:51:47 GMT +01

You know that SpoolDir cannot be the recipient's mail server because it lacks an Internet address.

## Legal Considerations in Investigating E-mail

In all investigations involving computer evidence, you must follow specific legal requirements and reliable forensic procedures. Otherwise, the evidence you obtain may not be admissible. The following sections discuss some of the legal considerations in investigating e-mail. Chapter 14, "Trends and Future Directions," provides more information on legal considerations in system forensics.

>  **NOTE**
>
> In addition to these sources for legal information, state laws often apply to e-mail investigations.

## The Fourth Amendment to the U.S. Constitution

If an e-mail message resides on a sender's or recipient's computer or other device, the Fourth Amendment to the U.S. Constitution and state requirements govern the seizure and collection of the message. Determine whether the person on whose computer the evidence resides has a reasonable expectation of privacy on that computer. The Fourth Amendment requires a search warrant or one of the recognized exceptions to the search warrant requirements, such as consent from the device owner. Chapter 6, "Controlling a Forensic Investigation," discussed the Fourth Amendment in more detail.

## The Electronic Communications Privacy Act

If an ISP or any other communications network stores an e-mail, retrieval of that evidence must be analyzed under the **Electronic Communications Privacy Act (ECPA)**. The ECPA creates statutory restrictions on government access to such evidence from ISPs or other electronic communications service providers.

The ECPA requires different legal processes to obtain specific types of information:

- **Basic subscriber information**—This information includes name, address, billing information including a credit card number, telephone toll billing records, subscriber's telephone number, type of service, and length of service. An investigator can obtain this type of information with a subpoena, court order, or search warrant.

- **Transactional information**—This information includes Web sites visited, e-mail addresses of others with whom the subscriber exchanged e-mail, and buddy lists. An investigator can obtain this type of information with a court order or search warrant.

- **Content information**—An investigator who has a search warrant can obtain content information from retrieved e-mail messages and also acquire unretrieved stored e-mails.

- **Real-time access**—To intercept traffic as it is sent or received, get a wiretap order.

## CHAPTER SUMMARY

E-mail has quickly become one of the most common formats for communication. However, it is a security vulnerability because attackers can use it for a variety of nefarious purposes. Information obtained from an e-mail message can provide valuable evidence.

To probe an e-mail crime, you need a basic understanding of how e-mail works, as well as the roles mail servers and e-mail clients play in sending and receiving e-mail messages. In addition, know how to read the information contained in an e-mail header. In your investigations, you will often execute e-mail tracing to research and scrutinize e-mail. Always keep federal and state legal considerations in mind when investigating e-mail.

## KEY CONCEPTS AND TERMS

Anonymizer

Anonymous remailing

Electronic Communications
    Privacy Act (ECPA)

E-mail attachment

E-mail body

E-mail client

E-mail header

E-mail log

E-mail tracing

Hypertext Transfer Protocol
    (HTTP)

Internet Message Access
    Protocol (IMAP)

Internet Protocol (IP)

Internet Protocol (IP) address

Mail relay

Mail server

Post Office Protocol (POP)

Simple Mail Transfer Protocol
    (SMTP)

Sniffing

Spamming

Spoofing

Transmission Control Protocol/
    Internet Protocol (TCP/IP)

**10**

Investigating and
Scrutinizing E-mail

## CHAPTER 10 ASSESSMENT

**1.** The _____ is like an electronic post office: It sends and receives electronic mail.

**2.** A software program used to compose and read e-mail messages is referred to as _____.

**3.** A forensic investigator can find copies of e-mail messages in a number of places. Which of the following are some of them? (Select three.)

A. The recipient's computer
B. The sender's computer
C. The Whois database
D. The e-mail header
E. The sender's mail server

**4.** Microsoft Outlook, Windows Mail, Gmail, Yahoo! Mail, Hotmail, and AOL are examples of mail servers.

A. True
B. False

**5.** What is the name of the numeric label that identifies each device on a network and provides a location address?

A. E-mail header
B. Mail server
C. IP address
D. Sniffer

**6.** As an e-mail message is routed through one or more mail servers, each server adds its own information to the message header.

A. True
B. False

**7.** It is possible to reconstruct the journey of an e-mail message by reading the e-mail header from top to bottom.

A. True
B. False

**8.** The _____ lines list every point an e-mail passed through on its journey, along with the date and time.

**9.** Which of the following are common methods of faking e-mails? (Select three.)

A. Spoofing
B. Routing
C. Anonymous remailing
D. Spamming
E. Adding an attachment

**10.** Which of the following is the name for making an e-mail message appear to come from someone or someplace other than the real sender or location?

A. Spoofing
B. Routing
C. Anonymous remailing
D. Spamming
E. Adding an attachment

**11.** Keyword filters, IP database block lists, whitelists, and graylists are examples of methods used to prevent or reduce _____.

**12.** Which of the following is not a legal consideration in investigating e-mail?

A. ECPA
B. Fourth Amendment
C. Fifth Amendment
D. State laws

# Performing Network Analysis

**N**ETWORK FORENSICS, AS YOU FIRST READ back in Chapter 1, deals with evidence that moves across one or more computer networks. It involves capturing, recording, and analyzing network events. Businesses are marketing advanced networking technologies, such as network-attached storage devices, firewalls, and Gigabit Ethernet, to home users today. Therefore, nearly any computer seized will have been used in a network environment of some type.

Network forensics can involve a variety of digital evidence, including information from router, NetFlow, and firewall logs. Forensics can also involve evidence from the logs of Internet service providers (ISPs), intrusion detection systems, and captured network traffic. This chapter presents the basics of network forensics, including tools and techniques for investigating specific types of attacks.

## Chapter 11 Topics

This chapter covers the following topics and concepts:

- What networks are and how they are used
- What network-related attacks you may encounter
- How to investigate network traffic
- How to investigate router attacks

## Chapter 11 Goals

When you complete this chapter, you will be able to:

- Understand basic network types, configurations, and protocols
- Understand a variety of network-related attacks
- Recognize the significance of log files as evidence
- Understand the array of sniffers and other tools for investigating network traffic
- Investigate a router attack

## Network Basics

A **network** is a collection of computers and devices joined by connection media. In a typical enterprise network environment, network components work together to make information and resources available to many users. From their workstations, users access resources that are connected to an organization's networks. Table 11-1 lists three basic network types and their characteristics.

As a forensic investigator, you'll work with two categories of networks:

- **Peer-to-peer (P2P) network**—In a **peer-to-peer (P2P) network**, each user manages his or her own resources and configures who may access those computer resources and how. On a P2P network, each computer is configured individually.

- **Server-based network**—In a **server-based network**, a central server manages which users have access to which resources through a database called a *directory*. This is the best option when an organization has 10 or more network users. The central server runs a network operating system (NOS).

Networks can be set up using a number of **topologies**—that is, designs that specify the devices, locations, and cable installation as well as how data is transferred in the network. The most common physical network topologies are the star and hybrid star. In a star topology, all computers and network devices, such as printers and firewalls, connect to a central hub or switch. This topology allows central management but can also fail easily. Advances in communications and switching technology have blurred the lines in network designs.

**TABLE 11-1** Network types.

| NETWORK TYPE | SIZE | DESCRIPTION |
|---|---|---|
| Local area network (LAN) | A LAN covers a small physical area, such as an office or a building. | Local area networks (LANs) are common in homes and businesses and make it easy to share resources, such as printers and shared disks. |
| Metropolitan area network (MAN) | A MAN connects two or more LANs but does not span an area larger than a city or town. | Metropolitan area networks (MANs) connect multiple buildings or groups of buildings spread around an area larger than a few city blocks. |
| Wide area network (WAN) | A WAN connects multiple LANs and can span very large areas, including multiple countries. | Wide area networks (WANs) provide network connections among computers, devices, and other networks that communicate across great distances. For example, the Internet is a WAN. |

> ### Other Types of Networks
>
> You may see a few more terms used to describe networks. These terms aren't in widespread use, but they describe specific types of networks:
>
> - **Personal area network (PAN)**—A **personal area network (PAN)** consists of one or more workstations and its network devices, such as printers, personal digital assistants (PDAs), network disk systems, and scanners. A PAN refers to the networked devices one person would likely use and normally does not span an area larger than an office or cubicle.
>
> - **Campus area network (CAN)**—A **campus area network (CAN)** is larger than a LAN but generally smaller than a MAN. CANs connect LANs across multiple buildings that are all in fairly close proximity to one another.
>
> - **Global area network (GAN)**—A **global area network (GAN)** is a newer term for a super-WAN. A GAN is a collection of interconnected LANs, CANs, MANs, and even WANs that spans an extremely large area.

The interconnection of networks, including the Internet, can make it difficult to distinguish individual network types. Even so, learn all about the different types of networks. Documenting a network involves creating a diagram of the network's physical layout. This is vital to show where you have collected evidence. Figure 11-1 shows a basic network diagram.

Use a tool, such as Microsoft Visio, to draw a network diagram. Visio offers templates that include network design symbols. Download these templates at no charge from the Visio downloads page, *http://visio.mvps.org/3rdparty.htm.* In addition, automatic network discovery tools make the network documentation easier. Examples of such tools include LANsurveyor (see *http://www.solarwinds.com/products/lansurveyor/*), NetCure (see *http://www.rocketsoftware.com/products/netcure*), and WhatsUp Gold (see *http://www.whatsupgold.com*). You can also use radio-frequency detectors, such as AirWave 7 (see *http://www.airwave.com/products/*), to identify and document wireless networks.

## Wireless Networks

Wireless networks are almost everywhere today—including homes, offices, hotels, airports, and coffee shops. Some cities even provide wireless network access to citizens in their areas. Wireless connections allow devices to connect to a network without having to physically connect to a cable. This makes it easy to connect computers and devices when running cables is either difficult or not practical.

Many wireless LANs are either not secured or are not well secured. Attackers may compromise a server to allow public access to stolen software, music, movies, or pornography. The following are the most important forensic concerns with wireless networks:

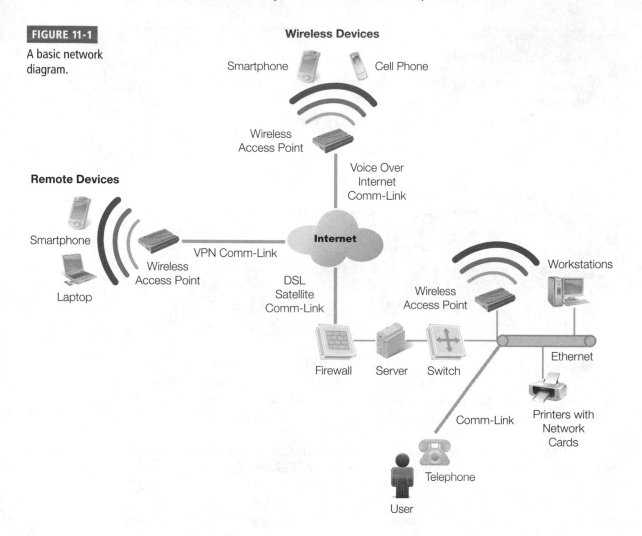

**FIGURE 11-1**

A basic network diagram.

- Did a perpetrator use a wireless network entry point for a direct network attack or theft of data?

- Did an attacker use a third-party wireless network, such as a hotel hotspot, to conceal his or her identity?

In addition to evidence that moves across wireless networking devices, you may find evidence in wireless storage devices. These devices include wireless digital and video cameras, wireless printers with storage capacity, wireless network-attached storage (NAS) devices, PDAs and smartphones, wireless digital video recorders (DVRs), and wireless game consoles.

## Common Network Protocols

To investigate activity that involves networks, become familiar with a number of protocols. Protocols allow applications to exchange information with other applications on other computers. To communicate, computers must use the same protocol. For example, most Web browser applications communicate with a Web server application by using Hypertext Transfer Protocol (HTTP). Web browsers can use other protocols, but HTTP is the most common protocol for regular Web pages.

HTTP is based on a request/response standard. A client requests a resource, such as text, an image, or a multimedia file from the server. The server responds with a status line and additional information. HTTP is important to understand because Web browsing can be used for any online communication. Whenever someone accesses a resource on a Web server over the Internet, the server records an entry in an access log. That entry shows which computer was used to access what files and the HTTP return status code. Most server access files use or resemble the Common Log Format (CLF). This format includes the remote host, user ID, date, time, request, status code, and number of bytes returned. An extended CLF format also includes the referring uniform resource locator (URL) and the browser version.

A common networking protocol is Transmission Control Protocol/Internet Protocol (TCP/IP), which you read about in Chapter 10. TCP/IP is a combination of two separate protocols that work together in so many environments that they are often referenced as a single protocol. Table 11-2 lists some of the most common network communication protocols.

The Institute of Electrical and Electronic Engineers (IEEE) defines many computing and communications standards. For example, the IEEE **802.11 standards** define communications protocols for **wireless local area networks (WLANs)**. A WLAN is a LAN that links devices wirelessly. IEEE 802.11 currently uses four main protocols: 802.11a, 802.11b, 802.11g, and 802.11n. The technical details are beyond the scope of this chapter, but it is important to know the basic differences between different wireless protocols.

**Bluetooth** is a popular wireless protocol for connecting devices over short distances. The most popular use of Bluetooth is to create PANs of devices that communicate with a computer or device. Headsets, mouse devices, and printers are some examples of devices that commonly support the Bluetooth protocol. Unless you protect all the wireless connections in a Bluetooth-enabled computer, the computer can be vulnerable to several types of wireless attacks.

## Types of Network-Related Attacks

Attackers can target networks in a number of ways. They sometimes aim attacks at specific parts of a network, such as routers. They also attack specific Web sites, server applications, or entire networks. The following sections describe some common network-related attacks that you may have to deal with.

**TABLE 11-2** Common network communication protocols.

| PROTOCOL | DESCRIPTION |
|---|---|
| Telnet | Used for connecting terminals to servers. Sends text to and from the server. Telnet is useful for remote administration using command-line utilities. |
| Secure Shell (SSH) | Similar to Telnet, except this protocol encrypts messages. Useful for secure remote system administration using command-line utilities. |
| Hypertext Transfer Protocol (HTTP) | Used for most Web browser/Web server communication. |
| Hypertext Transfer Protocol Secure (HTTPS) | Secure HTTP. Useful for exchanging confidential information between Web browsers and Web servers. |
| Secure Socket Layer/Transport Layer Security (SSL/TLS) | SSL is the predecessor of TLS. Both protocols provide encryption for application layer protocols, such as HTTPS. |
| Transmission Control Protocol/Internet Protocol (TCP/IP) | The most common protocol pair for Internet communication. |
| Dynamic Host Configuration Protocol (DHCP) | Used to assign Internet Protocol (IP) addresses to computers. |
| User Datagram Protocol (UDP) | Another common protocol used in place of IP when persistent connections are not necessary or desirable. |
| Internet Protocol Security (IPSec) | A protocol suite used to secure IP communication by encrypting each IP packet. |
| Point-to-Point Protocol (PPP) | Used to establish a direct connection between nodes. |
| Point-to-Point Tunneling Protocol (PPTP) | One of three common protocols used for virtual private networks (VPNs). |
| Layer 2 Tunneling Protocol (L2TP) | Another common protocol used for VPNs. |
| Secure Socket Tunneling Protocol (SSTP) | A VPN protocol that uses SSL/TLS to encrypt HTTP traffic in a tunnel. |
| Wired Equivalent Privacy (WEP) | An older protocol for securing wireless network traffic. |
| Wi-Fi Protected Access (WPA) | A more secure protocol than WEP, with stronger encryption for wireless network traffic. |
| Kerberos | Used to authenticate network nodes to one another over a network that is not secure. |

## Types of Router Attacks

Routers can be vulnerable to several types of attacks, including:

- **DoS attacks**—In a DoS attack, the attacker uses one of three approaches. The attacker can damage the router's ability to operate, overflow the router with too many open connections at the same time, or use up the bandwidth of the router's network. In a DoS attack, the attacker usually floods the network with malicious packets, preventing legitimate network traffic from passing. The following section discusses specific types of DoS attacks.

- **Packet mistreating attacks**—A packet mistreating attack occurs when a compromised router mishandles packets. This type of attack results in congestion in a part of the network.

- **Router table poisoning**—Router table poisoning is one of the most common and effective attacks. To carry out this type of attack, an attacker alters the routing data update packets that the routing protocols need. This results in incorrect entries in the routing table. This, in turn, can result in artificial congestion, can overwhelm the router, and can allow an attacker access to data in the compromised network.

## DoS Attacks

A perpetrator launches a DoS attack to make a computer resource unavailable to its users by flooding the network or by disrupting the connections. A DoS attack can target a specific Web site, a server application, or an entire network. A distributed DoS attack is a DoS attack in which a large number of compromised systems attack a single target.

The following are symptoms of a DoS attack:

- Unusual slowdown of network services
- Unavailability of a specific Web site
- Dramatic increase in the volume of spam

Attackers use a number of specific types of DoS attacks. The following are some of the most common examples:

- **Ping of death attack**—In a ping of death attack, an attacker sends an Internet Control Message Protocol (ICMP) echo packet of a larger size than the IP protocol can accept. At one time, this form of attack caused many operating systems to lock or crash, until vendors released patches to deal with the ping attacks. Some firewalls block ICMP ping messages.

- **Teardrop attack**—In a teardrop attack, the attacker sends fragments of packets with bad values in them which cause the target system to crash when it tries to reassemble the fragments. Like the ping of death attack, the teardrop attack has been around long enough for vendors to have released patches to avoid it.

- **SYN flood attacks**—In a SYN flood attack, the attacker sends unlimited SYN packets to the host system. The SYN packets, which are requests, arrive so quickly that the system doesn't have time to handle them properly.

- **Land attacks**—In a land attack, the attacker sends a fake TCP SYN packet with the same source and destination IP addresses and ports as the target computer. Basically, the computer is tricked into thinking it is sending messages to itself because the packets coming in from the outside are using the computer's own IP address.

- **Smurf attacks**—A smurf attack generates a large number of ICMP echo requests from a single request, acting like an amplifier. This causes a traffic jam in the target network. Worse still, if the routing device on the target network accepts the requests, hosts on that network will reply to each echo, increasing the traffic jam.

- **Fraggle attacks**—A fraggle attack is similar to a smurf attack, except that it uses spoofed UDP packets instead of ICMP echo replies. Fraggle attacks can often bypass a firewall.

Techniques for detecting DoS attacks include activity profiling, sequential change point detection, and wavelet-based signal analysis. Detecting DoS attacks can be challenging. For example, it can be difficult to detect and distinguish malicious packet traffic from legitimate packet traffic. In addition, false positives, missed detections, and detection delays cause problems.

## Web Attacks

Web sites and Web applications are increasing in number and complexity. Many business applications are now delivered over the Web using HTTP. Many types of attacks target Web sites and Web applications. The following are some of the best-known attacks:

- **Cross-site scripting attacks**—These attacks occur when a Web page collects data from a user and displays that input on the page without validating the input. The attackers insert malicious code—such as JavaScript, VBScript, ActiveX, HTML, or flash code—into the Web page. The Web page then executes the malicious script on the user's machine and collects information about the user, steals the session cookies. and takes over the user's account, or executes malicious code, such as a virus, on the end user's computer.

- **SQL injection attacks**—These attacks occur when structured query language (SQL) code—not created by the developer—passes into an application. A SQL injection attack targets the database that supports a Web application. In this type of attack, user-provided data in the form of a dynamic SQL statement is placed in the SQL query. Unless the input is validated for correct format or checked for embedded escape strings, the malicious code modifies user input to execute arbitrary SQL commands. To locate a SQL attack, review intrusion detection system (IDS) log files, database server logs, and Web server log files.

- **Code injection attacks**—A code injection attack is similar to a SQL injection attack. In this attack, instead of passing SQL commands as user input, the attacker sends other types of malicious input, such as shell commands or Hypertext Preprocessor (PHP) scripts. The server receives and executes the request, often allowing the attacker to access Web sites or databases normally restricted to authorized users. Perpetrators often use this sort of attack to access databases that contain personal information, such as credit card numbers and passwords.

  An IDS, which you'll read more about in the next section, detects code injection attacks. The IDS looks for a series of executable instructions in the network traffic. It then executes the instructions in a matched, monitored environment. If the instructions use system resources, the IDS sends an alert indicating that the incoming packet contains malicious data.

- **Buffer overflow attacks**—Buffer overflow attacks are among the most common attacks on the Web. In this type of attack, a buffer, which is a temporary data storage area, is overloaded with more data than the buffer can handle. One of the reasons that this type of attack is so common is that it's easy to write beyond the bounds of data objects in languages such as C and C++. When a buffer overflows, it transfers the data to any adjacent buffers, which can corrupt the data in those buffers. This can damage a system's files. The extra data may include malicious code. Excess requests to a server may result in a server compromise and allow an attacker to run commands directly on the server.

- **Cookie poisoning**—Cookie poisoning is the process of tampering with the value of cookies. Web applications use cookies to store information, such as user ID, passwords, account numbers, items ordered online, and prices. Cookie poisoning results in an attacker gaining unauthorized access to a user's sensitive personal information.

  Use software packages to detect poisoned cookies. Intrusion prevention products trace the set cookie commands issued by the Web server. For each set command, the software stores the cookie name, value, IP address, and session identifier. The product then intercepts every HTTP request sent to the server and compares the cookie information with the stored cookies. If a cookie's content has changed, the software determines that an attack has occurred.

## Investigating Network Traffic

Many different types of evidence exist on networks. For example, evidence can exist in clients, servers, network devices, and network traffic. You can often determine the source, nature, and time of an attack by analyzing a compromised system's log files. Once you've identified that an attack has occurred or is occurring, inspect the firewall and IDS logs to determine whether the attack is from a compromised computer on your network or from outside your network. You can also use sniffers and other tools to examine network traffic.

## Using Log Files as Evidence

An end-to-end investigation looks at an entire attack. It looks at how an attack starts, at the intermediate devices, and at the result of the attack. Evidence may reside on each device in the path from the attacking system to the victim. Routers, VPNs, and other devices produce logs. Network security devices, such as firewalls and **intrusion detection systems (IDS)**, also generate logs. An IDS is software that automates the process of monitoring events occurring in a computer system or network and analyzing them for signs of possible incidents and attempting to stop detected possible incidents.

A device's **log files** contain the primary records of a person's activities on a system or network. For example, authentication logs show accounts related to a particular event and the authenticated user's IP address. They contain date and timestamps as well as the username and IP address of the request. Application logs record the time, date, and application identifier. When someone uses an application, it produces a text file on the desktop system containing the application identifier, the date and time the user started the application, and how long that person used the application.

Operating systems log certain events, such as the use of devices, errors, and reboots. You can analyze operating system logs to identify patterns of activity and unusual events. Network device logs, such as firewall and router logs, provide information about the activities that take place on the network. You can also use them to support logs provided by other systems.

> **▶ TIP**
>
> Because user accounts can be shared or hacked, you can't prove that the account owner is the person responsible for an attack. You can, however, say that the server authenticated a specific user account at a specific time. You can also attribute specific events to an individual account.

Examine log files to discover attacks. For example, a firewall log may show access attempts that the firewall blocked. These attempts may indicate an attack. Log files can show how an attacker entered a network. They can also help find the source of illicit activities. For example, log files from servers and Windows security event logs on domain controllers can attribute activities to a specific user account. This may lead you to the person responsible.

IDS record events that match known attack signatures, such as buffer overflows or malicious code execution. Configure an IDS to capture all the network traffic associated with a specific event. In this way, you can discover what commands an attacker ran and what files he or she accessed. You can also determine what files the criminal uploaded, such as malicious code.

You bump into a few problems when using log files, however. One is that logs change rapidly, and getting permission to collect evidence from some sources, such as ISPs, takes time. In addition, volatile evidence is easily lost. Another is that hackers can easily alter logs to include false information.

You can use log files in court if the files meet certain requirements: The logs must be created reasonably contemporaneously with the event. The log files must not be tampered with, and the logs must be kept as a regular business practice. This means that logs instituted after an incident has begun do not qualify as a customary business practice.

This is one of the reasons security professionals recommend routinely logging events in an organization. For example, an organization can configure an IDS to capture network traffic whenever a specific condition occurs, such as whenever an alert goes out.

Logs can be admissible in court under the business records exception of the hearsay rules. The Federal Rules of Evidence provide a general definition of hearsay as a "statement, other than one made by the declarant while testifying at the trial or hearing, offered in evidence to prove the truth of the matter asserted." The business records exception says that the courts consider business records, created during the ordinary course of business, reliable. An organization can use these records if it lays the proper foundation when introducing the records as evidence. Depending on the jurisdiction, either the records custodian or someone with knowledge of the records must lay a foundation for the records.

This person must be able to testify about the system used, where the logging software came from, how and when records are created, and so on. Any record of failures of the hardware or software platform used to create the logs will call the evidence into question.

## Firewall Forensics

As mentioned in Chapter 5, all the traffic going through a firewall is part of a connection. A connection consists of two Internet Protocol (IP) addresses that are communicating with each other and two port numbers that identify the protocol or service. To review, the three ranges for port numbers are:

- **Well-known ports**—The well-known ports are those from 0 through 1023.
- **Registered ports**—The registered ports are those from 1024 through 49151.
- **Dynamic ports**—The dynamic, or private, ports are those from 49152 through 65535.

Attempts on the same set of ports from many different Internet sources are usually due to "decoy" scans. In a decoy scan strategy, an attacker spoofs scans that originate from a large number of decoy machines and adds his or her IP address somewhere in the mix. Using protocol analysis may help you determine who the attacker is. For example, you can ping each of the systems and match up the time to live (TTL) fields in those responses with the connection attempts. The TTLs should match; if they don't, they are being spoofed by an attacker. One drawback is that scanners may randomize the attacker's own TTL, making it difficult to pinpoint the source.

Analyze the firewall logs in depth to look for decoy addresses originating from the same subnets. You will likely see that the attacker has connected recently, whereas the decoyed addresses have not.

## Tools for Identifying Attackers

This sidebar outlines a process that helps identify a host that has attacked a system. It is not intended to be a tutorial for how to use each tool on its own. Many sources of information cover each of these tools in more detail. A useful site is *http://network-tools.com*.

Find a Web proxy or gateway Web site for conducting any type of intelligence collection operation against an attacking host. In this way, you do not run the risk of antagonizing or scaring off potential intruders who might be watching the connection logs from their victimized host.

When trying to identify an attacker, use the following tools and processes, in the order presented here:

- **dig -x /nslookup**—First, reverse the offending IP address. The `dig -x ip` command performs a reverse lookup on an IP address from its domain name server. The `-x` option ensures that you receive all records possible about your host from the Domain Name System (DNS) table. This might include name servers, e-mail servers, and the host's resolved name. The `nslookup ip` command also performs a reverse lookup of the host IP address, but it only returns the resolved name.

- **whois**—Next, perform a `whois` lookup on the IP address to see whom the offending IP address is registered to. This can be somewhat tricky. Use the resolved name previously mentioned to try to determine what country or region the IP address might be based in and then be sure to use the proper `whois` gateway for that region of the world. The main gateways are ARIN (the American registry), APNIC (the Asia-Pacific registry), and RIPE (the European registry). There are dozens of others, but most addresses should be registered in one of the previously mentioned online centralized databases. If your `whois` data does not match your resolved name, such as the resolved name *http://www.cnn.com*, and ARIN indicates that the registered owner is the CNN network (a match), you may have to do some more digging. The `whois` databases can contain outdated information. You might want to research the IP address with the appropriate country-specific `whois` database to determine the correct registered owner. You can find a good collection of country-specific `whois` databases at *http://www.allwhois.com*. For more information on conducting detailed `whois` queries, check out *http://www.sans.org*.

- **ping**—Next, use `ping ip` to determine whether a user from the attacking IP address is currently online. Note that ping uses Internet Control Message Protocol (ICMP), but many administrators block ICMP traffic; therefore, the results from this tool are not conclusive evidence either way.

- **traceroute**—Next, use `traceroute ip` to determine possible paths from your proxy site to the target system. `traceroute` may help you in two ways. If the IP address does not resolve possible paths from your proxy site to the target system, there may be a clue about its parentage. Look at the resolved host just before your target. This host's name may be the upstream provider for the attacking host and thus a point of contact; it may have the same domain as your attacking host, although that is not always true. Also, using `traceroute` might give you an important clue as to the physical location of the attacking box. Carefully look at the path that the packets traveled. Does it tell you the city? If you can determine what city the attack came from, you have just narrowed down considerably the possible pool of attacker candidates.

- `finger`—Next, use the `finger root@ip` command to determine who is currently logged onto the system that attacked you. This command rarely works because most administrators wisely turn off this service. However, it does not hurt to try. Keep in mind that many systems that are compromised and used as lily pads to attack other hosts are poorly configured. (That is why they were compromised in the first place!) They may also have the `finger` service running. If it is running, finger `root@ip` sees the last time `root` was logged on and, more importantly, where `root` was logged on. You might be surprised to see `root` logged on from a third system in another country. Keep following the trail as long as your commands are not refused. You should be able to trace back hackers through several countries using this simple, often-overlooked technique. Look for strange logon names and for users logged onto the system remotely. This may indicate from where the host was compromised, and it is the next clue about where to focus your research.

- **Anonymous surfing**—Surfing anonymously to the domain from which the attacking IP address is hosted is the next step in the threat identification process. You will know this domain name by looking at the resolved name of the host and the `whois` data. One technique that is useful is to use a search engine with the specialized advanced search option `+host:domain name and hack*`. This query will return the Web links of possible hackers who operate from the domain name you queried. You can substitute warez or MP3, for example, to focus on terms of interest specific to warez or MP3 dealers. The number of Web pages returned by the query, as well as the details on those pages, indicate the level of threat to assess to a certain domain. For example, if you were investigating a host registered to demon.co.uk—known as the Demon Internet—you would type `+host:demon.co.uk and hack*` in the search engine query box. You might be surprised to see a return of some 70,000-plus hacking-related pages hosted on this domain. The Demon Internet seems to harbor many hackers and, as a domain, represents a viable threat to any organization. As a standard practice, you might want to block certain domains at your firewall, if you are not already blocking `ALL:ALL`. Another possibility to widen the search is to use `+link:domain name` at a search engine. This will show every Web page that has a link to the domain in question listed on its Web page. In other words, the ever-popular "here is the list of my hacker friends and their c001 hacker sites" pages will appear via this search. You will also want to keep in mind the target of the attack. What were the hackers going after? Can you tell? Conduct searches for the resources targeted and combine these terms with Boolean operators such as `and espionage`. Check newswires or other competitive intelligence sources to determine, if possible, who might be going after your company's resources. A good site to use to conduct your searches anonymously is *http://www.anonymizer.com*.

*continued*

**Tools for Identifying Attackers,** *continued*

- **Usenet**—The last step in the process of threat identification is to conduct a Usenet traffic search on your domain. Sites such as *http://groups.google.com* are excellent for this. Search on the attacking IP address in quotes to see if other people are reporting activity from this IP address in security newsgroups. Search on the domain name or hacker aliases that you might have collected from your anonymous surfing or from the returns of your finger queries. You can expand the headers of the postings by clicking on View Original Posting. This may show you the actual server that posted the message, even if the hacker attempted to spoof the mailing address in the visible header. This method can reveal the true location of your hacker. Clicking on Author Profile can also give you valuable information. Look at the newsgroups that your hacker posts to and look at the number and sophistication of those postings. Pay attention to off-subject postings. A hacker will often let down his or her guard when talking about a favorite band or hobby, for example. You can also search sites such as *http://www.icq.com* if you have a hacker alias from a defaced Web page or your Web search narrowed by the domain +hacker criteria previously noted.

After you have completed this process and gathered information from these tools, you should be able to make an educated guess about the threat level from the domain you are analyzing. Hopefully you were able to collect information about the numbers and sophistication levels of the hackers who operate from the attacking domain, possible candidates for the attack, and what others may be seeing from that domain.

Also, excellent sites to check for archived postings of recently seen attacks are *http://www.sans.org* and *http://www.securityfocus.com*. Were thousands of hacker pages hosted on the domain that you were investigating? And did you find thousands of postings concerning hacking on Usenet? Did you run a search on your organization's name plus hack*? Were there postings from other administrators, detailing attacks from this domain? Were the attacks they mentioned similar to yours or different?

Now you might be able to determine whether that file transfer protocol (FTP) probe, for example, was just a random probe that targeted several other companies as well as yours or targeted your company specifically. Could you tell from the logs that the attacker was attempting to find a vulnerable FTP server to set up a warez or MP3 site perhaps? Being able to make an educated guess about the motivation of your hacker is important. Knowing whether your company has been singled out for an attack as opposed to being just randomly selected will change the level of concern you have when assessing the threat. Use the process described here to narrow down possible candidates or characterize the threat level from responsible domains. And, as a byproduct, it will provide you with all the necessary names, phone numbers, and points of contact that may be useful when it comes time to notify the pertinent parties involved.

## Using Sniffers and Other Traffic Analysis Tools

A sniffer is computer software or hardware that can intercept and log traffic passing over a digital network. You use sniffers to collect digital evidence. Configure them to work in specific environments. Commonly applied sniffers include Tcpdump (see *http://www .tcpdump.org/tcpdump_man.html*) for various UNIX platforms and WinDump (see *http:// www.winpcap.org/windump/*), which is a version of Tcpdump for Windows. These programs extract network packets and perform a statistical analysis on the dumped information. Use them to measure response time, the percentage of packets lost, and TCP/UDP connection startup and end.

The following are some other popular tools for network analysis:

- NetIntercept (see *http://www.sandstorm.net/products/netintercept/*)
- Wireshark (see *http://www.wireshark.org*)
- CommView (see *http://www.tamos.com/products/commview/*)
- Softperfect Network Protocol Analyzer (see *http://www.softperfect.com*)
- HTTP Sniffer (see *http://www.effetech.com/sniffer/*)
- ngrep (see *http://sourceforge.net/projects/ngrep/*)
- OmniPeek (see *http://www.wildpackets.com*)

Some software tools for investigating network traffic include:

- NetWitness (*http://www.netwitness.com*)
- NetResident (*http://www.tamos.com/products/netresident/*)
- InfiniStream (*http://www.netscout.com/products/infinistream.asp*)
- Snort (*http://www.snort.org*)

When collecting evidence on a network, it's vital to document what you've collected. Specifically, note in detail who collected the evidence, when it was collected, where it was collected, and how it was collected. Then analyze the evidence to construct a clearer picture of all activities that have occurred. If possible, organize the evidence by time and function.

## Investigating Router Attacks

Using network forensics, you can determine the type of attack over a network. You can also in some cases trace the path back to the attacker. A **router** is a hardware or software device that forwards data packets across a network to a destination network. The desti-nation network could be multiple networks away. A router may contain read-only memory with power-on self-test code, flash memory containing the router's operating system, nonvolatile random-access memory (RAM) containing configuration information, volatile RAM containing the routing tables, and log information.

> **NOTE**
>
> The basic functions of a router are to:
> • Forward packets
> • Share routing information
> • Filter packets
> • Perform network address translation
> • Encrypt or decrypt packets when used with VPNs

A router is located where two networks meet. A router connects to at least two networks. A router can connect any type of networks, as long as they use the same protocols. Routers are more intelligent than switches. They actually inspect the address portion of the packets on a network.

Basically, a router checks the destination address on a packet, determines the best path for the packet to reach its destination, and passes the packet either to its destination network or across another network to the next router on the path. Router software chooses the best path and next location based on information about the state of the networks the router is connected to. Routers use headers and forwarding tables to make decisions about where to send packets. Routers use protocols, such as ICMP, to communicate the best route between hosts.

Routers operate in the first three levels of the OSI seven-layer protocol stack. The **Open Systems Interconnection (OSI) reference mode**l is a tool for understanding communications systems. As shown in Figure 11-2, the OSI reference model divides networking into seven layers. Each layer contains similar functions that provide services to the layer above it and receive services from the layer below it.

A routing table determines the final destination of the data packets sent through the router. Among other information, router tables contain:

- An address prefix, which is the packet's final address
- A next-hop address, which is the address of the next router the packet will be delivered to on its route
- A value for choosing between several routes with similar prefixes
- The route duration
- The route type

**FIGURE 11-2**

The OSI reference model.

**OSI Reference Model**

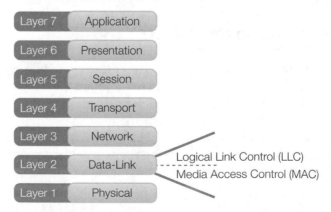

> **FYI**
>
> A computer connected to a LAN has two addresses. The first is the Media Access Control (MAC) address. The MAC address uniquely identifies each node in a network and is stored on the computer's network interface card (NIC). The second address is the IP address, which applications use. A router contains an Address Resolution Protocol (ARP) cache. The ARP cache is a table that stores mappings between IP addresses and Ethernet MAC addresses.

Routers are vital to the Internet and are the backbone of any network infrastructure. This makes routers preferred targets for those who want to break into a specific network. If an attacker can control the router, the attacker can transmit any kind of traffic to any network the router is connected to. The attacker can also discover vulnerabilities in the network and open the network to several types of attacks. An attacker can monitor and record logs on traffic into and out of routers to discover which routers handle the most traffic.

The attacker can interrupt communication by dropping or misrouting packets as they pass through the router. A denial of service (DoS) attack will occur if the attacker disables the router. An attacker can often disable neighboring routers and networks and stop communications among several networks. If an attacker can compromise a router, he or she can avoid firewalls and IDS.

> ▶ **NOTE**
>
> As discussed earlier in this chapter, routers can be vulnerable to several types of attacks, including DoS attacks, packet mistreating attacks, and router table poisoning.

## Collecting Router Evidence

When you investigate a router, have the system online to determine what kind of traffic is going through the router. To analyze an attack, you must recover live data. Be extremely cautious in investigating routers because you can lose valuable evidence if you mishandle the router. For example, never restart or reboot a router as part of incident response. Routers can contain important evidence in volatile memory. You can lose this evidence if you disconnect the router from the network or if you shut down or reboot the router.

Record all the steps that you take while investigating a router. For example, record when you log onto the router and record the actual and router time of each step you take. You can show the current time by using the `show clock detail` command, as follows, in the router console:

```
>(router name)#show clock detail
```

Access a router through the router console and not through the network. Configuration commands may change the state of the router. Therefore, use only `show` commands and not configuration commands.

For most router investigations, follow these steps:

1. Link to the console port and document the system time by using the following command:

   >(*router name*)#show clock detail

2. Examine the logs to see who has gained access to the router:

   >(*router name*)#show users

3. Examine the router's uptime, which is the time since the previous bootup:

   >(*router name*)#show version

4. Save the running router configuration:

   >(*router name*)#show running-config

5. Save the startup router configuration:

   >(*router name*)#show startup-config

6. Examine the routing table to detect vulnerable and static routes that are modified by the router through Routing Information Protocol (RIP) spoofing:

   >(*router name*)#ip route

   This reveals the IP address to which the attack was directed and exactly how the attack was carried out.

7. Verify the interface configuration:

   >(*router name*)#show ip interface

8. Inspect the ARP cache:

   >(*router name*)#show ip arp

By following these steps, you can gather information about where users on the network have been and when. You can also find out who or what has been trying to get into the network.

## Router Logs

Check logs to see who logged into a router during a specific time period. Other types of logging are also useful. Common router log files contain the following information:

- System time
- Total time for message delivery, or duration
- Client IP address
- Actual size of the data transferred to the client
- Requested URLs
- Server name
- Server IP address
- Server port
- Request method (for example, get)

- Client's uniform resource identifier (URI) query
- Bytes sent by the server
- Bytes received by the server
- Client's protocol version
- Host header name
- HTTP status code
- Cookie contents

Many routers and switches have a logging feature called NetFlow services. NetFlow logs provide information about network traffic and activities. NetFlow logs don't capture network content. Therefore, these logs allow you to monitor without the privacy issues associated with full packet capture and analysis. NetFlow logs from internal and bordering routers provide information such as the start and end times for data flow, source and destination IP addresses, port numbers, and the number of packets.

In an investigation, you can use NetFlow logs to show the source of an attack, the protocols used, the ports accessed, and the amount of data transferred. When you have identified the source of an attack, search the NetFlow logs for other compromised devices and computers on the network.

A free set of utilities for collecting and analyzing NetFlow logs is called the flow-tools package. Download this free, open source package from *http://www.splintered.net/sw/flow-tools/*. Other tools available for processing NetFlow data include SiLK, at *http://tools.netsa.cert.org/silk/*, and the Orion NetFlow Traffic Analyzer, at *http://www.solarwinds.com/products/orion/nta*.

 **TIP**

While router logs are useful, some evidence exists only inside data packets. To review the contents of packets, you can capture network traffic by using a sniffer, as discussed earlier in this chapter.

## CHAPTER SUMMARY

Collecting network data is one of a forensic investigator's greatest challenges. Because of the amount of network data, it can be difficult or even impossible to record all the data moving through a network. As a system forensics analyst, you must be able to use a variety of tools to sort through large amounts of data to extract what is most useful. To investigate computer networks, learn all you can about network architecture, network devices and protocols, and various logs. Documenting in detail the steps you take in gathering and analyzing the evidence is essential.

## KEY CONCEPTS AND TERMS

802.11 standards
Bluetooth
Campus area network (CAN)
Global area network (GAN)
Intrusion detection system (IDS)
Local area network (LAN)
Log file

Metropolitan area network (MAN)
Network
Open Systems Interconnection (OSI) reference model
Peer-to-peer (P2P) network
Personal area network (PAN)

Router
Server-based network
Topology
Wide area network (WAN)
Wireless local area networks (WLANs)

## CHAPTER 11 ASSESSMENT

1. A _____ is a collection of computers and devices joined by connection media.

2. Which of the following is a network that covers a small physical area, such as an office or a building?

   A. PAN
   B. LAN
   C. MAN
   D. WAN

3. The Internet is an example of which of the following types of networks?

   A. PAN
   B. LAN
   C. MAN
   D. WAN

4. In a P2P network, each user manages his or her own resources and configures who may access the user's computer resources and how. On a P2P network, each computer is configured individually.

   A. True
   B. False

5. Which of the following is the most common protocol for regular Web pages?

   A. TCP/IP
   B. IP
   C. HTTP
   D. DHCP
   E. IPSec

6. Software that automates the process of monitoring the events occurring in a computer system or network and analyzing them for signs of possible incidents and attempting to stop detected possible incidents is known as _____.

7. Which of the following is *not* an example of a network-related attack?

   A. Buffer overflow attack
   B. Firewall attack
   C. Cookie poisoning
   D. DDoS attacks
   E. Fraggle attack

8. Log files provide good forensic information, but they can't be used in court.

   A. True
   B. False

9. Which of the following are wireless technologies? (Select two.)

   A. TCP/IP
   B. Bluetooth
   C. DDoS attacks
   D. 802.11b
   E. Firewalls

10. Port numbers are divided into three ranges. Which of the following is *not* one of the ranges?

    A. Well-known ports
    B. Open ports
    C. Registered ports
    D. Dynamic ports

11. A _____ is a hardware or software device that forwards data packets across a network to a destination network.

12. The _____ divides networking into seven layers that provide services to and receive services from the layers directly above and below.

# Searching Memory in Real Time with Live System Forensics

**N**ETWORKS HAVE BECOME INCREASINGLY DISTRIBUTED yet remain interconnected. The number and types of threats to computer systems have grown. Meanwhile, the number of forensic tools to prevent unauthorized access and thwart illegal activity has also grown.

Computers store more information today than in the past. The price of storage media has decreased while the capacity has increased. Many people carry flash drives, smartphones, and iPods that contain gigabytes of information. Forensic specialists must sift through a wealth of devices and data as they search for evidence.

As threats have grown and changed, so have the tools for conducting forensic investigations. At one time, forensic inspectors were limited to conducting research only after an unauthorized or illegal activity had taken place. They are now more likely to capture evidence in **real time**—both on disk and in a computer's memory. In the past, many forensic examiners shut down a system before going to work on it. Many examinations now focus on malware exploitation. Examiners must often collect data from the memory of a running machine that would be lost if the machine were to lose power. Engineers have developed tools to capture data from live, up-and-running systems.

The preceding chapters discuss data collection using an offline approach, such as removing a suspect hard drive and making a write-protected image of the contents. Forensic investigators can also collect information in real time—that is, the actual time during which a process takes place. For example, they can collect data from random access memory (RAM). This chapter discusses live system forensics, which involves uncovering illicit activity and recovering lost data by searching memory in real time.

### Chapter 12 Topics

This chapter covers the following topics and concepts:

- How live system forensics helps solve some of the problems facing traditional forensic tools
- Why live system forensics improves on dead system analysis
- How consistency issues relate to live system forensics
- Which tools to use for analyzing computer memory

### Chapter 12 Goals

When you complete this chapter, you will be able to:

- Explain how live system forensics helps solve some of the problems facing traditional forensic tools
- Explain how live system forensics improves on dead system analysis
- Describe consistency issues related to live system forensics
- Describe some of the tools available for analyzing computer memory
- Explain how live analysis and volatile memory analysis work and when each is most desirable

## The Need for Live System Forensics

Forensic investigators can take advantage of a wide variety of system forensics tools. Some are open source and some are commercial tools. These tools let you safely make copies of digital evidence and perform routine investigations. Many existing tools provide intuitive user interfaces. In addition, forensic tools prevent you from having to deal with details, such as physical disk organization, or the specific structure of complicated file types, such as the Windows Registry.

Unfortunately, the current generation of system forensics tools falls short in several ways. These tools can't handle the recent massive increases in storage capacity. Storage capacity and bandwidth available to consumers are growing extremely rapidly. At the same time, unit prices are dropping dramatically. In addition, consumers want to have everything online—including music collections, movies, and photographs. These trends are resulting in even consumer-grade computers and portable devices having huge amounts of storage. From a forensics perspective, this translates into rapid growth in the number and size of potential investigative targets. To deal with all these targets, you'll need to scale up both your machine and human resources.

> ### Computer Forensics Tool Testing (CFTT)
>
> More than 150 open source and commercial forensic tools are available. Choosing tools that will yield accurate and valid results is a crucial part of building a forensic strategy. To improve tools, the National Institute of Standards and Technology (NIST) established the **Computer Forensics Tool Testing (CFTT)** project. CFTT focuses on developing standards to ensure reliable results during forensic investigations. The project seeks to help forensic tool providers improve their products. It also keeps the justice system informed about forensic best practices. And it makes information regarding successful forensic techniques available to federal agencies and other organizations. For more information, see *http://www.cftt.nist.gov.*

The traditional investigation methodology was to use a single workstation to examine a single evidence source, such as a hard drive. However, this approach doesn't work with storage capacities of hundreds of gigabytes or terabytes. In some cases, you can speed up traditional investigative steps, such as keyword searches or image thumbnail generation, to meet the challenge of huge data sets. Even so, the forensic world needs much more sophisticated investigative techniques. For example, manually poring over a set of thousands or tens of thousands of thumbnails to discover target images may be difficult but possible. But what will an investigator do when faced with hundreds of thousands— or even millions—of images? The next generation of digital forensics tools must employ high-performance computing and sophisticated data analysis techniques.

An interesting trend in next-generation digital forensics is live system forensics— analysis of machines that may remain in operation as you examine them. You first read about live system forensics in Chapter 1. The idea is appealing particularly for investigation of mission-critical machines. These machines would suffer from the substantial downtime required to do typical **dead system analysis** by first shutting down the machines. Also, some data exists only in RAM.

## Live System Forensics Versus Dead System Analysis

 **TIP**

Whether using traditional or live system forensics, avoid contaminating or corrupting evidence. If you contaminate a crime scene, you probably can't use the evidence gathered.

A prominent argument among system forensics specialists is whether to conduct analysis on a dead system or a live system. Regardless of the mode you use, keep in mind the three A's:

- *Acquire* evidence without altering or damaging the original.
- *Authenticate* that the recovered evidence is the same as the originally seized data.
- *Analyze* the data without modifying it.

## Problems with Dead System Forensics

Unplugging a machine before acquiring an image of the hard drive has several serious drawbacks:

- It leads to data corruption and system downtime. It therefore causes revenue loss.

- The development of new criminal techniques leaves law enforcement techniques outdated. You can't always use dead digital forensics to gather sufficient evidence to lead to a conviction.

- In an attempt to defeat dead system analysis, criminals have resorted to the widespread use of cryptography. While you can create a complete bit-for-bit hard drive image of a suspect system, you can't access its data if the perpetrator has encrypted the system. You'll need the drive's unique password to decrypt it. Investigators often have trouble cracking the password or getting the suspect's cooperation.

- The need for acquiring network-related data, such as currently available ports, has grown dramatically. When a computer powers down, it loses volatile information. Therefore, use live system forensics analysis techniques on volatile data.

- Traditional forensic rules require you to gather and examine every piece of available data for evidence. As mentioned earlier in this chapter, modern computers consist of gigabytes, and even terabytes, of data. It is increasingly difficult to use modern tools to locate vital evidence within the massive volumes of data. Log files also tend to increase in size and dimension, complicating a forensic investigation even further.

 **NOTE**

Criminals aren't the only ones who use whole-disk encryption. It's now a default feature of government and corporate system configurations.

### A Small Window of Opportunity in Dead Forensics

From a forensics perspective, the primary difference between a live device and a dead device is the presence of volatile data. Computers and other devices maintain data in RAM to support their operation. This volatile data can be valuable when collecting evidence. Once you remove power from a computer or other device, you lose any data stored in RAM. Contrary to popular belief, the data doesn't go away immediately. In fact, the contents stored in modern RAM chips decay over the course of several seconds after you remove power. The longer RAM has no power to refresh its values, the less reliable it is. Although you could technically capture the state of a computer's RAM after turning the power off, the small time frame makes it too brief to be useful.

## Live Forensic Acquisition

Although dead forensic acquisition techniques can produce a substantial amount of information, they can't recover everything. Much potential evidence is lost when you remove the power. To avoid losing any valuable evidence when you turn off a device, forensic techniques have expanded to include evidence acquisition from a live system. Instead of just capturing an image of a persistent storage device, live forensic acquisition captures an image of a running system. A properly acquired live image includes volatile memory images and images of selected persistent storage devices, such as disk drives and universal serial bus (USB) devices. Live forensic acquisition images have the advantage of capturing state information of a running system instead of only producing historical information of a dead system.

Using live forensic acquisition techniques has advantages. It also involves some barriers. For example, the process of proving a live image that's forensically sound and unaltered is more complex than with dead system images. Running systems write to memory many times each second. Each program routinely accesses different areas of memory in its normal operation. The overall procedures in live forensics are similar to dead system image acquisition. However, additional controls are necessary to ensure that all images acquired from a live system are forensically sound.

Live forensic acquisition methods are very similar to the methods commonly used on dead systems. In both cases, you collect, examine, analyze, and report on evidence. Whether you take evidence from a live or dead system, provide proof that you've protected the evidence's integrity. You'll also have to prove that you've taken proactive steps to ensure that the evidence didn't change during the acquisition process.

### Isolating a Suspect System

One of the most important steps in handling security incidents of any type is to contain the effects. Forensic investigations are often part of the response process. Containing damage often means isolating one or more computers and related data. In other words, disconnect the computer from networks or other computers. This step satisfies the isolation requirement of any forensic investigation. Isolating computers or devices is important for two main reasons:

- By isolating suspect computers and devices, you can contain the effects of the incident you're investigating. A failure to isolate suspect computers or devices can result in the incident affecting other parts of your information technology (IT) infrastructure.

- The technique of isolating suspect computers and devices includes stopping them from carrying out further operations. This action helps to maintain the state of the suspect systems, which helps in collecting evidence. System images are far more useful when they contain fresh evidence that provides proof of suspected actions.

One of the first steps when acquiring data in an investigation is to determine whether you will use live or dead forensic acquisition techniques. If the computer or device has already been turned off, the best choice is to use dead forensic acquisition techniques. In this case, follow the procedures covered in Chapter 7, "Collecting, Seizing, and Protecting Evidence." Any data that was in volatile memory was lost when power was removed. Dead forensic acquisition techniques provide evidence from only the remaining persistent data.

If the computer or device hasn't been turned off since the decision was made to acquire evidence, you have the option of using live forensic acquisition techniques to collect evidence. Using live forensic techniques can provide more information about the state of the suspect computer or device than similar dead acquisition procedures. If you choose to acquire evidence using a live acquisition process, follow these steps:

1. Choose between a local or remote connection to acquire evidence. Local connections generally provide a higher transfer rate and make it harder for others to intercept the transfer. Any time interception of evidence collection is a possibility, so is tampering with the evidence. If local connections are possible, choose them rather than remote network connections.

2. Plan acquisition tasks based on whether the process will be overt or covert. Obviously, covert acquisition should not alert any user that you are collecting evidence.

3. Acquire all evidence through a write blocker. The courts will require you to demonstrate that you maintained the state of the evidence and didn't modify it in any way. Using a write blocker can provide the assurance that the acquisition process didn't taint the evidence. Depending on the methods you use to acquire evidence, you can employ either hardware or software write blockers.

Even if you have chosen to pursue a live forensic investigation, you have no guarantees that you will get more valuable evidence than you'd get by using dead forensic acquisition techniques. A live system in which a user is logged on may allow you to acquire additional evidence. However, you'll be limited by the access restrictions of the logged-in user. A user account that has administrative or superuser privileges will allow you to access more resources and carry out more tasks than a user account with lesser privileges. However, many user accounts lack this additional level of capability. For instance, many organizations limit what files standard users can access and don't allow them to install new software. You'll have an easier time acquiring evidence when using a user account with elevated privileges.

Another common situation you may encounter during a live forensic investigation is the use of virtual environments. A **virtual machine** is a software program that appears to be a physical computer and executes programs as if it were a physical computer. You commonly use a virtual machine when you need to run an operating system on another computer. For example, you can run one or more Linux virtual machines on a computer running a Microsoft Windows operating system. Virtual machines are popular in organizations that want to save IT costs by running several virtual machines on a single physical computer. Two of the most popular software packages that implement virtual machines are VMware and VirtualBox.

### Write Blockers

A **write blocker** is a device or a software program that supports read operations but not write operations. This program's restrictions offer assurance to the courts that you didn't modify evidence as you collected it. The write blocker sits between the evidence device and the program collecting the evidence. It allows the acquisition programs to read from the device at full speed but denies any attempt to write back to the device.  Even though many programs routinely write to disks and other data devices during operation, the write blocker ensures that nothing is written to a protected data device during data acquisition. Write blockers make it possible to collect evidence while maintaining its original state.

Use either hardware write blocker devices or write blocker software. A *hardware write blocker* is a physical device that provides two connections. The computer running data acquisition software connects to one side of the write blocker and the evidence device connects to the other. The write blocker physically prevents any write operations from passing through the device. A *software write blocker* replaces the device driver software the operating system uses to access one or more evidence devices. The replacement device driver blocks any write operations in the driver software. In either case, write blockers provide assurance that you have written nothing to a device that contains evidence.

If the computer or device that contains evidence has a physical switch that disables writing, use this handy option instead of using a software write blocker. Physical write blockers are generally easier to support in court than software write blockers.

---

Whether the suspect computer is a physical machine or virtual machine, you follow basically the same methods. However, if you find that your suspect computer is a virtual machine, you must follow a few additional steps. Because a virtual machine runs as a program on a physical machine, conduct forensic acquisition on the physical computer as well. Many physical computers that host virtual machines tend to host multiple virtual machines. Part of your evidence collection activities should include collecting images of all virtual machines on the same physical computer as the suspect computer. Other virtual machines may contain evidence related to the suspect computer as well.

Today's virtual machine software does a good job of emulating physical computers. It can be difficult to determine whether an environment is operating in the virtual or physical space. You may not immediately know whether a suspect computer is a virtual or physical computer. You can look for a number of clues to determine whether you're examining a virtual machine. Check in system files for notes or vendor identification strings. Common virtual machine software installs easily recognizable device drivers, network interfaces, virtual machine BIOS, and specific helper tools. Look for the existence of any of these telltale indications that you're examining a virtual environment. Another common technique is to use **hardware fingerprinting** to detect hardware that's always present in a virtual machine. For example, if you're examining a Mac environment but hardware fingerprinting shows that Microsoft Corporation made your motherboard, you can be sure you're looking at a virtual machine. You can also find software that detects the presence of virtual machines. These tools can be handy but may affect the soundness of the evidence you collect. Always investigate tools you plan to use to ensure that they protect the integrity of your evidence. The following are examples of tools that can help detect virtual machines:

- ScoopyNG (see *http://www.trapkit.de/research/vmm/scoopyng/index.html*)
- DetectVM (see *http://ctxadmtools.musumeci.com.ar*)
- Virt-what (see *http://people.redhat.com/~rjones/virt-what/*)
- Imvirt (see *http://sourceforge.net/projects/imvirt/*)

## Benefits and Limitations of Live Acquisition

Live acquisition gives you the ability to collect volatile data that can contain valuable information, such as network and system configuration settings. This volatile data can provide evidence to help prove accusations or claims in court. Examples of volatile data include a list of current network connections and currently running programs. This information would not be available from dead forensic acquisition.

The process of collecting useful volatile data limits your actions more than when you're conducting dead forensic acquisition activities. Live forensic acquisition yields the most valuable data when you collect that data before it changes. As a computer continues to run, it changes more and more of its volatile memory. The sooner you collect evidence, the more pertinent it will be to your investigation. Because volatile memory changes continually, the passing of time decreases how much useful information you can expect to collect. Also, just the presence of another program you're using to collect volatile data may change existing volatile data. It's important that you prioritize what data you need for your investigation and collect it as soon as possible. Focus on the most volatile data first and then collect data that is less sensitive to the passage of time. In other words, collect the data you most need and that is most likely to change in the near term. You can collect data that is not as likely to change later.

Although live acquisition can provide much more useful information than dead forensic acquisition, it poses unique challenges. The richness of today's software provides many options for users to customize their own environments. A forensic specialist must possess a wide breadth of knowledge of common computer hardware, operating systems, and software. Users have many different ways to configure each computer component, and knowing how these components operate is crucial to successfully collecting solid information. For example, one question is whether to terminate a program. Many Web browsers make it easy to delete history and temporary files upon exit from the program. In these cases, you may not want to terminate the program before collecting evidence. Other programs may automatically save data periodically and overwrite previous evidence you may need. In such a case, collect evidence before the program overwrites it. It is also helpful to understand the general reasons users may choose some configuration options. If you find that a user has configured a Web browser to automatically delete all history, you may be investigating someone who has something to hide. While this is not always the case, it may be productive to look for other signs that someone is hiding or cleansing evidence.

Evidence that you can use in court must be in pristine condition. It must be in the same state it was in when you collected it. Any action that changes evidence will likely make the evidence inadmissible and useless in court. Evidence that was changed in the process of acquisition or analysis is forensically unsound. Live forensic acquisition poses more dangers to the soundness of evidence than dead forensic acquisition. Any action, such as examining the central processing unit (CPU) registers, can actually cause the CPU registers, RAM, or even hard drive contents to change values. Any change that is a result of acquisition activities violates the soundness of the evidence. Because today's operating systems use virtual memory, a portion of any program is likely to be swapped, or paged, out to the disk drive at some point during its lifetime. Even the use of write blockers will not protect your disk drive from modifications due to swapping and paging. This common operating system behavior can ruin evidence. It is important that you understand how the live forensic acquisition process works and how to protect evidence from accidental changes.

> **NOTE**
>
> Because computers update volatile memory constantly, it is difficult to acquire a true snapshot of memory. The memory changes during the acquisition activity, and the evidence collected represents a span of time. Write blockers generally don't protect volatile memory from write operations, and the changing nature of memory makes it difficult, if not impossible, to create checksums to validate the data's integrity.

Another issue that is a common problem with live analysis is slurred images. A **slurred image** is similar to a photograph of a moving object. A slurred image, in the context of live forensic acquisition, is the result of acquiring a file as it is being updated. Even a small file modification can cause a problem because the operating system reads the metadata section of the hard disk before accessing any file. If a file or metadata folder in the file system changes after the operating system has read the metadata but before it acquires the data, the metadata and data sectors may not totally agree.

Anytime you use live forensic acquisition, recognize that external influences may affect your investigation. Part of your collection process should be to ensure the authenticity and reliability of evidence, especially when acquiring evidence remotely using a network connection. Advances in technology have made anti-forensic devices and software available to a determined person. Suspects can use a number of tools to interfere with or even totally invalidate your evidence collection efforts. One of the simplest methods they use is to monitor a computer for forensic activity and then destroy all evidence before you can collect it. Other programs make it easy to clean up evidence before being detected or just hide it from prying eyes. The following are some programs that remove or hide evidence of activity:

- Evidence Eliminator (see *http://www.evidence-eliminator.com*)
- Track Eraser Pro (see *http://www.acesoft.net*)
- TrueCrypt (see *http://www.truecrypt.org*)
- Invisible Secrets (see *http://www.invisiblesecrets.com*)
- CryptoMite (see *http://www.baxbex.com*)

# Live System Forensics Consistency Issues

As discussed in earlier chapters, volatile data is vital to digital investigation. In traditional computer forensics, where you carry out an investigation on a dead system such as a hard disk, data integrity is the first and foremost issue for the validity of digital evidence. In the context of live system forensics, you acquire volatile data from a running system. Due to the ever-changing nature of volatile data, it is impossible to verify this data's integrity. In addition, data consistency is an especially critical problem with data collected on a live system. This section presents a UNIX-based model to describe data inconsistencies related to live system data collection.

Traditional computer forensics focuses on examining permanent nonvolatile data. This permanent data exists in a specific location and in a file system-defined format. This data is static and persistent. Therefore, you can verify its integrity in the course of legal proceedings from the point of acquisition to its appearance in court.

On a live system, some digital evidence exists in the form of volatile data. The operating system dynamically manages this volatile data. For example, system memory contains information about processes, network connections, and temporary data used at a particular point in time. Unlike nonvolatile data, memory data vanishes and leaves behind no trail after the machine is powered off. You have no way to obtain the original content. Therefore, you have no way to verify the digital evidence obtained from the live system or the dump. The dynamic nature of volatile data makes verifying its integrity extremely difficult.

To produce digital data from a live system as evidence in court, it is essential to justify the validity of the acquired memory data. One common approach is to acquire volatile memory data in a dump file for offline examination. A **dump** is a complete copy of every bit of memory or cache recorded in permanent storage or printed on paper. You can then analyze the dump electronically or manually in its static state.

Programmers have developed a number of toolkits to collect volatile memory data. These automated programs run on live systems and collect transient memory data. These tools suffer from one critical drawback: If run on a compromised system, such a tool heavily relies on the underlying operating system. This could affect the collected data's reliability. Some response tools may even substantially alter the digital environment of the original system and cause an adverse impact on the dumped memory data. As a result, you may have to study those changes to determine whether the alterations have affected the acquired data. Data in memory is not consistently maintained during system operation. This issue poses a challenge for computer forensics.

Maintaining **data consistency** is a problem with live system forensics in which data is not acquired at a unified moment and is thus inconsistent. If a system is running, it is impossible to freeze the machine states in the course of data acquisition. Even the most efficient method introduces a time difference between the moment you acquire the first bit and the moment you acquire the last bit. For example, the program may execute function A at the beginning of the memory dump and execute function B at the end.

▶ **TIP**

Despite the fact that the acquired memory is inconsistent, a considerable portion of it may be useful digital evidence. Moderate the disputes in presenting this evidence by distinguishing usable data from inconsistent data in a memory dump.

The data in the dump may correspond to different execution steps somewhere between function A and function B. Because you didn't acquire the data at a unified moment, data inconsistency is inevitable in the memory dump.

## Understanding the Consistency Problem

To study the consistency problem, you need to understand the basic structure of memory. When a program is loaded into memory, it is basically divided into segments. The structure may not be the same for all hardware and operating systems, but the concept of memory division is consistent. Windows, for example, has four segments (see Figure 12-1):

- **Code (C)**—The code segment contains the compiled code and all functions of a program. The program's executable instructions reside in this segment. Normally, the data stored in the code segment is static and should not be affected while the memory is running. The other three segments contain data that the program uses and manipulates as it is running.

- **Data (D)**—The data segment is used for global variables and static variables. The data in the data segment is quite stable. It exists for the duration of the process.

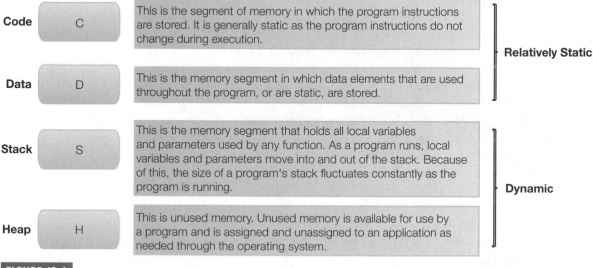

**FIGURE 12-1**

Basic memory structure.

- **Stack (S)**—Memory in the stack segment is allocated to local variables and parameters within each function. This memory is allocated based on the last-in, first-out (LIFO) principle. When the program is running, program variables use the memory allocated to the stack area again and again. This segment is the most dynamic area of the memory process. The data within this segment is discrepant and influenced by the program's various function calls.

- **Heap (H)**—Dynamic memory for a program comes from the heap segment. A process may use a memory allocator such as `malloc` to request dynamic memory. When this happens, the address space of the process expands. The data in the heap area can exist between function calls. The memory allocator may reuse memory that has been released by the process. Therefore, heap data is less stable than the data in the data segment.

When a program is running, the code, data, and heap segments are usually placed in a single contiguous area. The stack segment is separated from the other segments. It expands within the memory allocated space. Indeed, the memory comprises a number of processes of the operating system or the applications it is supporting. Memory can be viewed as a large array that contains many segments for different processes. In a live system, process memory grows and shrinks, depending on system usage and user activities. This growth and shrinking of memory is either related to the growth of heap data or the expansion and release of stack data. The data in the code segment is static and remains intact at all times for a particular program or program segment. Data in the growing heap segment and stack segment causes inconsistency in the data contained in memory as a whole. The stack data has a greater effect than the heap data. Nevertheless, the code segment contains consistent data. Consistent data is usually dormant and not affected when a process is running in memory. When you obtain a process dump of a running program, data in the code segment remains unchanged because the memory segment contains only code and functions of the program.

The global, static, heap, and stack data can be partitioned within a running process. For example, $D_i$, $H_i$, and $S_i$ (where $i = 1, 2, 3, \ldots$) can exist in different segments. In an ideal case, when a snapshot is taken of a process at time $t$, the memory dump is consistent with respect to that point in time. In reality, however, it is impossible to obtain a memory snapshot. Memory dumping takes time. The dumping process spans a time interval.

For a very fast memory dump, the data in $C$ should be consistent, and data in $D$ may be consistent, depending on the program usage. The data in $H$ is likely to be inconsistent because the segment may grow when the program calls it. The data in $S$ is highly likely to be changing due to its dynamic data structure. Variables for the process functions are continually used and reused in this segment. This causes inconsistency in part of the dumped data collected.

The data in $C$ is relatively static and remains consistent in a memory dump. The global and static data in $D$ are less volatile and may remain consistent. Due to the special functionality of heap and stack, the data stored within those segments are more dynamic and may be inconsistent.

## Locating Different Memory Segments in UNIX

Each memory process has its own allocated space in system memory. This space may include both physical and virtual addresses. Locating the heap and stack segments of memory within a logical process dump can help you achieve maximum data validity.

To locate the heap segment, use the system call `sbrk` to reveal the address space of a process. When you invoke `sbrk` with 0 as the parameter, it returns a pointer to the current end of the heap segment. The system command `pmap` displays information about the address space of a process, as well as the size and address of the heap and/or stack segment.

# Tools for Analyzing Computer Memory

When gathering digital evidence, you can't always just pull the plug and take the machine back to the lab. As technology continues to change, you must adopt new methods and tools to keep up. You must know how to capture an image of the running memory and perform volatile memory analysis.

Standard RAM size is now between 2 GB and 8 GB, malware migrates into memory, and suspects commonly use encryption. Therefore, it is no longer possible to ignore computer memory during data acquisition and analysis. Traditionally, the only useful approach to investigating memory was live response. This involved querying the system using application programming interface (API)-style tools familiar to most network administrators. A first responder would look for rogue connections or mysterious running processes. It was also possible to capture an image of the running memory. Until recently, short of using a string search, it was difficult to gather useful data from a memory dump.

The past few years have seen rapid development in tools focused exclusively on memory analysis. These tools, as described in the following sections, include PsList, ListDLLs, Handle, Netstat, FPort, Userdump, Strings, and PSLoggedOn. The following sections show how you use these tools with the following virtual environment scenario:

- A Windows XP, Service Pack 2, virtual machine has an IP address of 192.168.203.132.
- Use Netcat to establish a telnet connection on port 4444, process ID (PID): 3572, with a second machine at 192.168.203.133.
- Install and run MACSpoof, PID: 3008.
- This machine is compromised. The FUTo rootkit and a ProRat server listening on port 5110 are installed on the machine. The Netcat and MACSpoof processes are then hidden using the FUTo rootkit.

The following sections discuss two possible ways to approach the compromised system. The first approach is a live response process using a variety of tools. The second is a volatile memory analysis of a static memory dump, using open source memory analysis tools.

## Live Response

One technique for approaching a compromised system is live response. In **live response**, you survey the crime scene, collect evidence, and at the same time probe for suspicious activity. In a live response, you first establish a trusted command shell. In addition, you establish a method for transmitting and storing the information on a data collection system. One option is to redirect the output of the commands on the compromised system to the data collection system. A popular tool for this is Netcat, a network debugging and investigation tool that transmits data across network connections. Another approach is to insert a USB drive and write all query results to that external drive. Finally, attempt to bolster the credibility of the tool output in court.

During a live interrogation of a system, the state of the running machine is not static. You could run the same query multiple times and produce different results, based on when you run it. Therefore, hashing the memory is not effective. Instead, compute a cryptographic checksum of the tool outputs and make a note of the hash value in the log. This would help dispel any notion that the results were altered after the fact. For example, HELIX is a live response tool from a Linux bootable CD. Use this tool to establish a trusted command shell.

When the data collection setup is complete, begin to collect evidence from the compromised system. The tools used in this exercise are PsList, ListDLLs, Handle, Netstat, FPort, Userdump, Strings, and PSLoggedOn. This is not meant to be an exhaustive list. Rather, these are representative of the types of tools available. The common thread for the tools used here is that each relies on native API calls to some degree. Thus the results are filtered through the operating system.

> **NOTE**
>
> PsList, ListDLLs, Handle, Strings, and PSLoggedOn are all Microsoft Sysinternals Troubleshooting Utilities. They are available as a single suite of tools, available at *http://technet.microsoft.com/en-us/ sysinternals/bb896649.aspx*.

### PsList

Use PsList to view process and thread statistics on a system. Running PsList lists all running processes on the system. However, it does not reveal the presence of the rootkit or the other processes that the rootkit has hidden—in this case, Netcat and MACSpoof.

### ListDLLs

ListDLLs allows you to view the currently loaded dynamic link libraries (DLLs) for a process. Running ListDLLs lists the DLLs loaded by all running processes. However, ListDLLs cannot show the DLLs loaded for hidden processes. Thus, it misses critical evidence that could reveal the presence of the rootkit. The problem is that an attacker may have compromised the Windows API on which your toolkit depends. To a degree, this is the case in the current scenario. As a result, these tools can't easily detect rootkit manipulation. You need a more sophisticated and nonintrusive approach to find what could be critical evidence.

**TIP**

It is useful to show the implications of the tool results. However, remember that simply renaming directories or running `cmd.exe` from a different directory would prevent these disclosures.

### Handle

With Handle, you can view open handles for any process. It lists the open files for all the running processes, including the path to each file. In this case, one of the command shells is running from a directory labeled `...\FUTo\EXE`. This is a strong hint of the presence of the FUTo rootkit. Similarly, there is another instance of `cmd.exe` running from `C:\tools\nc11nt`. The `nc11nt` folder is a default for the Windows distribution of Netcat.

### Netstat

Netstat is a command-line tool that displays both incoming and outgoing network connections. It also displays routing tables and a number of network interface statistics. It is available on UNIX, UNIX-like, and Windows-based operating systems.

Use the Netstat utility to view the network connections of a running machine. Running Netstat with the `-an` option reveals nothing immediately suspicious in this case.

### FPort

FPort is a free tool from Foundstone (*http://www.foundstone.com/us/resources/proddesc/ fport.htm*). FPort allows you to view all open Transmission Control Protocol/Internet Protocol (TCP/IP) and User Datagram Protocol (UDP) ports. FPort also maps these ports to each process. This is the same information you would see using the `netstat -an` command, but FPort also maps those ports to running processes with the PID, process name, and path.

In this scenario, FPort does not reveal the presence of the connections hidden by the rootkit.

### Userdump

Userdump is a command-line tool for dumping basic user info from Windows-based systems. With Userdump, you can extract the memory dumps of running processes for offline analysis. `dumpchk.exe` has a specific metadata format (see *http://support.microsoft .com/kb/315271*). Therefore, you can use `dumpchk.exe` to verify that a usable process memory dump was produced. The Strings utility extracts ASCII and Unicode characters from binary files. In this case, you would apply it to the process dumps to see what evidence you can uncover.

### PsLoggedOn

PsLoggedOn helps you discover users who have logged in both locally and remotely. In this case, only the administrator is logged on.

### OnLine Digital Forensic Suite (OnLineDFS)

In large computer networks, unauthorized activity can have devastating consequences. You need to resolve any such activity quickly. Unfortunately, most organizations simply do not have the staff to examine each local network potentially involved in an attack. In addition, in a geographically dispersed organization, the less time you spend traveling, the more time you have to investigate the incident. To meet the need for remote investigation, Architecture Technology Corporation offers a mobile forensic platform called the OnLine Digital Forensic Suite (OnLineDFS; see *http://www.atcorp.com/Products/odfs.html*). OnLineDFS is a commercial product that allows live investigation of computer systems. It permits you to obtain evidence and perform a thorough investigation remotely.

OnLineDFS is a network appliance that you deploy on an organization's local network. It provides a secure, Web-based investigative interface to an organization's computers. With OnLineDFS, you can investigate machines while they perform their usual functions, without raising the suspicion that they are under investigation.

A live investigation using OnLineDFS involves collecting evidence from one or more targets. During a particular inquiry, you may collect a machine's state, including running processes, a list of who is currently logged in, and networking information such as currently executing servers and which ports they are listening on. During the inquiry, you may also capture memory dumps of physical memory and running processes, examine the Registry on a Windows machine, and copy files from the target to the OnLineDFS network appliance. You can then analyze data acquired during a particular inquiry. Time-consuming operations, such as capturing the physical memory of the target or imaging the entire disk, run as background threads in OnLineDFS and do not tie up the user interface.

OnLineDFS requires administrative privileges on the machine under investigation and uses the operating system and hardware resources of the target. Therefore, you may not be able to use this tool to investigate machines whose operating systems have been completely compromised through the installation of kernel-level rootkits or machines whose administrator account passwords have been maliciously changed. For these kinds of situations, a traditional "dead" analysis is likely required. Keep in mind that in a dead analysis, you lose all contextual evidence, such as what processes were running, who was connected to the machine, and what information is resident only in memory.

## Volatile Memory Analysis

**Volatile memory analysis** is a live system forensic technique in which you collect a memory dump and perform analysis in an isolated environment. Volatile memory analysis is similar to live response in that you must first establish a trusted command shell. Next, you establish a data collection system and a method for transmitting the data. However, you would only acquire a physical memory dump of the compromised system and transmit it to the data collection system for analysis. In this case, VMware allows you to simply suspend the virtual machine and use the .vmem file as a memory image. As in other forensic investigations, you would also compute the hash after you complete the memory capture. Unlike with traditional hard drive forensics, you don't need to calculate a hash before data acquisition. Due to the volatile nature of running memory, the imaging process involves taking a snapshot of a "moving target."

The primary difference between this approach and live response is that you don't need any additional evidence from the compromised system. Therefore, you can analyze the evidence on the collection system.

The following sections discuss the capabilities of two memory analysis tools applied on the memory image example we've been discussing. These tools, The Volatility Framework and PTFinder, are relatively recent additions to the excellent array of open source resources available to digital investigators.

### The Volatility Framework

The Volatility Framework from Volatile Systems (see *https://www.volatilesystems.com/default/volatility*) provides evidence about the attacker's IP address and the connections to the system. In addition, it can help detect rootkits and hidden processes.

The Volatility Framework is a collection of command-line Python script that analyzes memory images. Use it to interrogate an image in a style similar to that used during a live response. Volatility is distributed under a GNU General Public License. It runs on any platform that supports Python, including Windows and Linux.

This exercise uses version 1.1.2 of Volatility. Commands available in this version include `ident`, `datetime`, `pslist`, `psscan`, `thrdscan`, `dlllist`, `modules`, `sockets`, `sockscan`, `connections`, `connscan`, `vadinfo`, `vaddump`, and `vadwalk`. This section explains several of these commands.

You use the `ident` and `datetime` commands to gather information about the image itself—in this case with the image file `WinXP_victim.vmem`:

```
python volatility ident -f WinXP_victim.vmem
```

and

```
python volatility datetime -f WinXP_victim.vmem
```

This `ident` command provides the operating system type, virtual address translation mechanism, and a starting directory table base (DTB). The `datetime` command reports the date and time the image was captured. This provides valuable information and assists with documentation in a forensic investigation. Furthermore, it is useful for creating a timeline of events with other pieces of evidence in the investigation.

Using the `pslist` command produces results similar to those of `SysInternal` `pslist.exe` tool used during live response. Similarly, the `dlllist` command shows the size and path to all the DLLs that the running process uses.

However, when you use the `psscan` option, you see something new. With a PID of 0, `MACSpoof.exe` shows up in the list. This command scans for and returns the physical address space for all the `EPROCESS` objects found.

In the live response scenario, Netstat fails to provide any sign of the Netcat activity. However, using `connscan` shows the connection with 192.168.203.133 on port 4444. The results also indicate a PID of 3572 associated with this connection. The fact that this PID is missing from the other queries could indicate the presence of a rootkit.

With the Volatility Framework, you can also list all the kernel modules loaded at the time the memory image was captured. While the path of the last entry from the `modules` command certainly attracts attention, an even less obvious path would show `msdirectx.sys`, a module that is associated with rootkits.

### PTFinder

PTFinder, by Andreas Schuster, is a Perl script memory analysis tool (see *http://computer.forensikblog.de/en/2007/11/ptfinder_0_3_05.html*). It supports analysis of Windows operating system versions.

PTFinder enumerates processes and threads in a memory dump. It uses a brute-force approach to enumerating the processes and uses various rules to determine whether the information is either a legitimate process or just bytes. Although this tool does not reveal anything new in terms of malware, it does enable repeatability of the results, which is an important benefit in volatile memory analysis.

The "no threads" option on PTFinder provides a list of processes found in a memory dump. PTFinder can also output results in the dot(1) format. This is an open source graphics language that provides a visual representation of the relationships between threads and processes.

## Analysis of Live Response Versus Volatile Memory Analysis

The preceding sections discuss two different incident response approaches. The first approach is the well-known live response, in which you survey the crime scene and simultaneously collect evidence and probe for suspicious activity. The second approach is the relatively new field of volatile memory analysis, in which you collect a memory dump and perform analysis in an isolated environment. Each of these approaches gives you different insight into the environment you're investigating.

Several issues with live response hinder effective analysis of a digital crime scene. The purpose of live response is to collect relevant evidence from the system to confirm whether an incident occurred. This process has some significant drawbacks, including the following:

- **Some tools may rely on the Windows API**—If an attacker compromises the system and changes system files but you don't know it, you could collect a large amount of evidence based on compromised sources. This would damage the credibility of your analysis in a court of law.

- **Live response is not repeatable**—The information in memory is volatile, and with every passing second, bytes are overwritten. The tools may produce the correct output and in themselves can be verified by a third-party expert. However, the input data supplied to the tools can never be reproduced. Therefore, it is difficult to prove the correctness of your analysis of the evidence. This puts the evidence collected at risk in a court of law.

- **You can't ask new questions later**—The live response process does not support examination of the evidence in a new way. This is mainly because you can't reproduce the same inputs to the tools from the collection phase. As a result, you can't ask new questions later on in the analysis phase of an investigation. By the analysis phase, it becomes impossible to learn anything new about a compromise. In addition, if you miss critical evidence during collection, you can never recover it. This damages your case against the attacker.

Volatile memory analysis shows promise in that the only source of evidence is the physical memory dump. Moreover, investigators now collect physical memory more commonly. An investigator can build a case by analyzing a memory dump in an isolated environment that is unobtrusive to the evidence. Thus, volatile memory analysis addresses the drawbacks facing live response as follows:

- **It limits the impact on the compromised system**—Unlike live response, memory analysis uses a simplified approach to investigating a crime scene. It involves merely extracting the memory dump and minimizes the fingerprint left on the compromised system. As a result, you get the added benefit of analyzing the memory dump with confidence that the impact to the data is minimal.

- **Analysis is repeatable**—Because memory dumps are analyzed directly and in isolated environments, multiple sources can validate and repeat the analysis. The scenario described earlier shows this. Two tools identified the hidden malware processes. In addition, thanks to repeatability, third-party experts can verify your conclusions. Essentially, repeatability improves the credibility of an analysis in a court of law.

- **You can ask new questions later**—With memory analysis, you can ask new questions later on in an investigation. The scenario described earlier shows this. The initial analysis of the memory dump with Volatility raised suspicion of a rootkit being present on the system. A live response may have missed this important evidence.

One of the greatest drawbacks with volatile memory analysis is that the support for these tools has not matured. With every release of a new operating system, the physical memory structure changes. Development of memory analysis tools has been gaining velocity recently, but kinks remain. Memory analysis tools must be available in parallel with an operating system for maximum utility.

The development of live forensic acquisition in general presents a remedy for some of the problems introduced by traditional forensic acquisition. With current technologies, however, the most effective analytic approach is a hybrid based on situational awareness and triage techniques. Instead of being used to gather exhaustive amounts of data, live response should move to a triage approach, collecting enough information to determine the next appropriate step. In some situations, greater understanding of the running state of the machine is critical to resolving a case. In such cases, use full memory analysis—and the requisite memory acquisition—to augment and supplement traditional digital forensic examination.

 **TIP**

Live system investigation may be necessary to determine the presence of mounted encrypted containers or full-disk encryption. If you detect either, switch to capturing a memory image for offline analysis as well as capturing the data in an unencrypted state.

**12**

Searching Memory in Real Time

 **CHAPTER SUMMARY**

You have access to a wide variety of tools that preserve and analyze digital evidence. Unfortunately, most current system forensics tools are unable to cope with the ever-increasing storage capacity and expanding number of target devices. As storage capacities creep into hundreds of gigabytes or terabytes, the traditional approach of utilizing a single workstation to perform a digital forensics investigation against a single evidence source is no longer viable. Further, huge data volumes necessitate more sophisticated analysis techniques, such as automated categorization of images and statistical inference.

In the past, many forensic examiners would shut down a system and collect data using a static collection approach. Today, with many examinations focusing more on malware exploitation, examiners need to collect memory data that would be lost if the machine were to lose power. Programmers have developed tools to capture data from live, up-and-running systems. This chapter examines the next generation of live digital forensics tools that search memory in real time.

## KEY CONCEPTS AND TERMS

Computer Forensics Tool Testing (CFTT)

Data consistency

Dead system analysis

Dump

Hardware fingerprinting

Live response

Real time

Slurred image

Virtual machine

Volatile memory analysis

Write blocker

## CHAPTER 12 ASSESSMENT

**1.** _____ is analysis of machines that remain in operation as you examine them.

**2.** _____ is analysis of machines that have been shut down.

**3.** It is not as important to avoid contaminating evidence in live system forensics as it is in dead system forensics.

A. True
B. False

**4.** Which of the following are drawbacks of dead system forensics? (Select three.)

A. It leads to corruption of evidence.
B. It leads to corruption of the original data.
C. It leads to system downtime.
D. It leads criminals to use cryptography.
E. It leads to data consistency problems.

**5.** You can use live system forensics to acquire one type of data that dead system forensics can't acquire. What type of data is this?

A. Binary
B. Virtual
C. Volatile
D. Nonvolatile

**6.** Which of the following is a software implementation of a computer that executes programs as if it were a physical computer?

A. VMware
B. Write blocker
C. Hardware fingerprint
D. Virtual machine

**7.** Which of the following are drawbacks of live system forensics? (Select three.)

A. It leads to system downtime.
B. Slurred images can result.
C. Data can be modified.
D. It leads to data consistency problems.
E. It leads criminals to use cryptography.

**8.** As a result of *not* acquiring data at a unified moment, live system forensics presents a problem with _____.

**9.** What are two possible techniques for approaching a compromised system using live system forensics? (Select two.)

A. Live response
B. Hot swapping
C. Volatile memory analysis
D. Hardware fingerprinting

**10.** The following are some of the benefits of _____: It limits the impact on the compromised system, analysis is repeatable, and you can ask new questions after the analysis.

# PART THREE

# Incident Response, Future Directions, and Resources

# Incident and Intrusion Response

SYSTEM FORENSICS HELPS REDUCE THE OCCURRENCE of security incidents. It also helps minimize the impact of incidents that do occur. A forensic analyst examines how an attack is perpetrated and then develops controls to prevent or mitigate that form of attack. For example, the early Secure Sockets Layer (SSL) protocol safeguarded Internet sessions. However, it was vulnerable to man-in-the-middle attacks. Forensic analyses led to changes in SSL to eliminate this vulnerability.

To prevent and mitigate security incidents, an organization must establish formal incident prevention and intrusion response plans. You write these formal plans using an analytical framework. They should include incident response protocols. They should also assign responsibility for incident prevention and response. This chapter discusses these important forensic investigation processes.

## Chapter 13 Topics

This chapter covers the following topics and concepts:

- How to minimize security threats in an organization
- How to establish an incident response team
- How to define an incident response plan

## Chapter 13 Goals

When you complete this chapter, you will be able to:

- Minimize security threats in an organization
- Establish an incident response team
- Define an incident response plan

# Minimizing Incidents

Many organizations learn about incident response only after experiencing an attack. This approach has some benefits but is costly and disruptive to the organization. For maximum impact, incident prevention and response should be a planned part of an overall risk mitigation strategy.

Successful incident response has two components:

- **Prevention**—An organization must have procedures to minimize the potential for incidents to occur.

- **Incident response**—An organization must be able to react to an incident in a manner that reduces its impact and restores normal operations as quickly as possible.

Of the two components, prevention is the most cost-effective and provides the highest return on investment (ROI). Incident response, however, gets more coverage both within and outside an organization. For example, for years, oil tankers brought oil from Alaska for transfer to the "lower 48." The tankers delivered their cargo without recognition or notice, following controls and safety protocols to navigate the narrow channels without incident. One tanker failure eliminated the years of hard work and dedication by people who had made so many successful oil deliveries routine. That tanker failure also resulted in billions of dollars in cleanup costs and disruption to the lives of individuals affected by the oil spill.

Relating a computer failure to an oil tanker spill might seem like overkill. The reality, however, is that in today's digital world, a computer incident might result in damage and disruption that far exceeds the cost of an oil spill. A successful attack on the electric grid, for example, could cost billions in lost business and disruption, including loss of life. A successful attack on a bank could result in billions of dollars in losses. A successful attack on a navigation system could put more than one tanker "on the rocks."

A basic rule of incident prevention and response is to plan for the worst, test the plan fully, and react to the incident. This rule is based on the assumption that if you plan and test your plan for the worst situation, you will be better prepared to block an attack and mitigate its potential effects when it does occur.

It is impossible to prevent all security incidents. In most cases, it's not even cost-effective to implement all possible security measures. Some incidents result from intentional attacks. Others result from unintentional actions of system users and maintainers. Thus, the goal should be zero incidents. However, although an organization might minimize the number of incidents, the probability of a disruptive event will never be zero.

Given that the potential for a disruptive security event will never be zero, an organization should strive to minimize the potential impact of a security event. Take the following measures to help minimize the number and impact of security incidents in your organization:

- **Establish and enforce security policies and procedures**—Many security incidents are accidents. They may result from information technology (IT) personnel not following or not understanding system operating procedures and controls. IT personnel may make mistakes with change management procedures, system security configurations, or user authentication and privilege assignment. Your policies and procedures should be practical and clear. They should also provide the appropriate level of security. In addition, put metrics in place to determine whether personnel are complying with your security policies.

- **Gain management support for security policies and incident handling**— Senior management should demonstrate this support with approval of reasonable budget requests. Managers should also be vocal in supporting compliance enforcement procedures.

- **Routinely assess vulnerabilities in the environment**—A security specialist with the appropriate clearance and access to sensitive data should perform these assessments. The security specialist should also have no direct responsibility for correcting the deficiencies identified. Individuals who must both identify and correct deficiencies may not identify all deficiencies. They may make tradeoffs based on their assessment of whether management will approve the resources needed for correction. Specialists who are not responsible for remediation tend to identify more risks.

- **Keep systems up to date and routinely check all computer systems and network devices**—Regularly audit systems to ensure that they have all the latest patches. In some situations a patch has the potential to cause more damage than the risk of the patched vulnerability. In this case, organizations use waivers to document why they haven't deployed a patch.

- **Train IT personnel**—Security threats are constantly changing. The only way to ensure that IT staff can stay protected against newer threats is to train them on what they are. Additionally, IT staff need training on how to use recently purchased controls and countermeasures. A brand new sophisticated intrusion protection system isn't useful if it stays in the box.

- **Train end users**—Social engineering is a common tactic in which attackers trick users into giving up valuable information, such as their username and password. The primary reason social engineering succeeds is due to a lack of security awareness by end users. A little training can go a long way.

- **Implement and enforce a password policy**—A password policy will ensure that personnel use strong passwords, and that they change them regularly. You can easily enforce password policies with tools, such as Microsoft Group Policy or third-party tools.

- **Monitor network traffic**—Significant changes in network traffic may indicate a problem. For example, if a worm infects your network, network traffic may increase resulting in decreased performance. If you catch this before it's serious, you may be able to contain the threat. An anomaly-based intrusion detection system (IDS) can automate this process. You start by creating a baseline of normal activity. The IDS then monitors for any changes and sends an alert if the change exceeds a certain threshold.

- **Review logs**—Logs are regularly recording activity that can let you know of a potential issue before it's a serious problem. However, they must be reviewed. Operating systems have logs. Additionally, services and applications, such as firewalls and IDS, all have logs that you can readily review. Either manually review the logs or purchase a third-party tool to automate the review. Most automated tools are preconfigured to look for specific events, and you can modify them to look for other events. They then send an alert to notify administrators of the potential issue.

- **Implement and test a backup policy**—A backup policy identifies what data to back up, how often, and how long to keep the backups. Conduct backups regularly but base the actual frequency on how often the data changes, and how important it is. A *test restore* attempts to restore the backups to verify that backup and restore procedures are sound.

## Events and Incidents

An **event** is any observable occurrence within a system or network. This includes any activity on the network, such as when a user accesses files on a server or when a firewall blocks network traffic. **Adverse events** are events with a negative result or negative consequences. Attacks on systems are adverse events. Adverse events in this book are events that are computer-security related. They are not events caused by sources, such as natural disasters and power failures.

A **computer security incident** is any event that violates an organization's security policies. This includes computer security policies, acceptable use policies, or standard security practices. The following are examples of computer security incidents:

- **Denial of service (DoS) attacks**—A DoS attack could result from an attacker sending specially crafted packets to a Web server that cause it to crash. It could also result from an attacker directing hundreds of external compromised workstations to send many Internet Control Message Protocol (ICMP) requests to an organization's network. When the attack is from multiple sources, you refer to it as a distributed DoS (DDoS) attack.

- **Malicious code**—Malicious software, or malware, is any malicious code, such as viruses, worms, and Trojans. For example, a worm uses open file shares to quickly infect hundreds of systems in an organization. Employees may innocently introduce viruses into a network from their home computer on USB thumb drives. When they plug the USB drive into the work computer, the virus infects it.

- **Unauthorized access**—This includes any time someone accesses files they shouldn't be able to access. The access can be from someone within the organization, such as an employee, or from an external attacker. If you don't lock down shared files with appropriate permissions, users may stumble upon data they shouldn't see. If you don't secure databases used by Web servers, attackers may be able to access sensitive customer data, such as credit card information, from anywhere on the Internet.

- **Inappropriate usage**—Inappropriate usage could take a number of forms. For example, a user might provide illegal copies of software to others through peer-to-peer (P2P) file-sharing services. This same P2P software could cause data leakage resulting in private data from the user's computer being shared on the Internet to anyone else using the same P2P software. Or a person might threaten another person through e-mail.

## Assembling an Incident Response Team

An **incident response team (IRT)** is a group of people who respond to incidents. You can form an IRT as needed in response to an incident. You can also designate one in advance. For example, a small organization may not have a formal IRT. Instead, when an incident occurs, IT professionals respond to the incident as an informal IRT. However, a large organization may have a group of security professionals designated as the IRT.

When an organization sets up an IRT in advance, it ensures the team has the necessary knowledge and skills to respond to incidents. This helps minimize the impact of incidents. Additionally, when a team forms in advance, some team members can be full-time security professionals and work proactively to minimize the occurrence of incidents.

For example, these security professionals can regularly monitor the network for anomalies, since changes in network behavior may indicate a security breach. They can keep up to date with emerging threats, and regularly perform vulnerability assessment and penetration testing.

An incident response team must be equipped to handle incidents. Team preparation includes the following:

- **Training on the proper use and location of security tools**—An organization should preconfigure portable computers with all the tools a team will need during an incident. The IRT should be familiar with the systems and tools before an incident occurs. Properly protect these systems and associated tools when not in use.

- **Assembling relevant communication information**—An organization should have the names and phone numbers of people in the organization who should be notified of an incident. This includes members of the incident response team and those in charge of media relations. The organization also needs details about its Internet service provider (ISP), backup storage provider, and any support contractors. The organization should also know how to contact local and national law enforcement agencies. The organization's legal counsel must be informed of any contacts with law enforcement.

FYI

The **chief information officer (CIO)** is an executive who heads IT in an organization. The CIO is responsible for ensuring that the organization has established and maintains an effective security environment. The **chief technology officer (CTO)** is an executive who focuses on scientific and technical issues in an organization. The CTO is responsible for transforming capital—whether monetary, intellectual, or political—into technology.

- **Placing all appropriate system information in an accessible location**—When a serious incident occurs, the IRT needs access to system information. This includes administrative passwords, network layout diagrams, and router and firewall configuration information. If the team has to search for this information, the incident can cause more damage during the search. The longer the team has to search for this information, the longer the incident has to cause damage. The team needs to secure this very valuable information as well. If the information is in a physical form, such as a binder, keep it in a secure place such as a safe. If it's in an electronic format, such as on a portable computer, safeguard it with permissions and encryption. Additionally, make it clear who is authorized to access this information. For example, the organization may decide that only the incident response team leader, the chief information officer (CIO), chief information security officer (CISO), and chief technology officer (CTO) can access the information.

The incident response team membership and structure depends on the type of organization and its risk management strategy. The incident response team should generally form part or all of an organization's security team. The team's members should include security professionals, network specialists, application maintainers, representatives of the user community, and senior managers. The incident response team should also be responsible for coordinating a response to any incident.

 **NOTE**

The number of members on the incident response team typically depends on the organization's size and complexity. Scale the team to individual incidents.

## Establishing Team Roles

A successful incident response team has several key members:

- **Team leader**—The team leader is generally responsible for the activities of the incident response team. The team leader coordinates reviews of the team's actions. If needed, he or she implements changes in policies and procedures for dealing with future incidents.
- **Incident lead**—The incident lead is responsible for a particular incident or set of related security incidents. This could be the team leader or someone else who may have expertise more relevant to an incident. The incident lead is the focal point for all communications related to the incident. Team members report to the incident lead and the incident lead speaks for the team.

**13**

Incident and
Intrusion Response

- **IT team members**—Team members assist the team leader and/or incident lead in responding to incidents. Team members have expertise in specific IT areas and not all team members will necessarily respond to all incidents.
- **Specialists**—In addition to the primary team members, a team identifies specialists who respond to particular incidents or provide input to the team. These specialists may come from different departments in the organization. Table 13-1 lists some specialist team members and their responsibilities.

## Coordinating a Response

In the event of an incident, the incident response team should coordinate a response and communicate with the associate members of the incident response team. Table 13-2 shows the responsibilities of these individuals during the incident response process.

| TABLE 13-1 Incident response team specialists. | |
|---|---|
| **TEAM MEMBER** | **RESPONSIBILITIES** |
| Legal representative | Many incidents have legal ramifications and need the expertise of a lawyer who understands established incident response policies. The lawyer provides advice on an organization's legal liabilities. He or she provides advice on steps to take before, during, and after an incident if attackers will be prosecuted. |
| Public relations (PR) officer | Communicating effectively to the media is extremely important during a crisis. An organization may be doing all the right things internally, but if the wrong message is communicated externally, then this affects the organization's image and reputation. This can translate to loss of a company's stock value and reduced sales to customers. The public relations officer crafts the message to the media based on management objectives. |
| Human resources (HR) representative | When internal employees are the cause of an incident, the HR representative can advise the team on proper methods for communicating and dealing with the employees. HR reps are experts on HR policies, disciplinary procedures, and employee counseling. |
| Management | Department managers may be a part of the team if the incident directly affects their department. These managers can ensure that the team has adequate resources to respond to the incident. |

**TABLE 13-2** Responsibilities of incident response team members during the incident response process.

| ACTIVITY | ROLE | | | | |
|---|---|---|---|---|---|
| | INCIDENT LEAD | IT TEAM MEMBER | LEGAL REPRESENTATIVE | PR REPRESENTATIVE | MANAGEMENT |
| **Initial assessment** | Assess | Advise | None | None | None |
| **Initial response** | Respond | Implement | Update | Update | Update |
| **Collect forensic evidence** | Implement | Advise | Owner | None | None |
| **Implement temporary fix** | Implement | Implement | Update | Update | Advise |
| **Send communication** | Advise | Advise | Advise | Implement | Implement |
| **Check with local law enforcement** | Update | Update | Implement | Update | Implement |
| **Implement permanent fix** | Implement | Implement | Update | Update | Update |
| **Determine financial impact on business** | Update | Update | Advise | Update | Advise |

## Defining an Incident Response Plan

An **incident response plan** outlines specific procedures to follow in the event of a security incident. It identifies the responsibilities of all members of the team. It also identifies the specific reporting requirements for an incident. Although the team members should be intimately aware of the details of the incident response plan, it's important that all IT staff know the procedures for reporting incidents. For example, if members of the IT staff discover an incident, they should know exactly what to do to raise the alarm.

The incident response plan also identifies the steps to take when an incident occurs. A plan could include the following steps:

1. **Assessment**—Not all events are incidents, and some incidents are more serious than others. The initial assessment verifies the event is an incident and assesses the severity. An IT staff member can carry this out.

2. **Communication**—The incident is reported to the incident response team. The plan identifies whom to notify based on the initial assessment.

3. **Containment**—The team contains the incident to minimize the damage and risk to other systems. For example, if malware has infected a system, the team can remove the network cable to contain the damage to this system alone. It's important to ensure that the team protects evidence for use in court later if necessary.

4. **Evaluation**—The team investigates the incident to determine the type and severity. It may take additional steps, depending on the business and the incident. For example, if the incident resulted in the loss of customer data, the company may be legally responsible to report it to the affected customers.

5. **Recovery**—The incident response team recovers and restores systems. This may be as simple as rebooting the system or may require an extensive rebuild.

6. **Document and review**—Every incident has lessons that the team can learn by evaluating what happened and how the response progressed. Documentation records the details. Later, a review can identify areas to improve. For example, the team could update security policies or modify the response plan.

> **TIP**
>
> Test your incident response plan before an incident. A common way to do so is a tabletop exercise in which key team members sit in a conference room and talk through the steps they'll take. The team leader presents the scenario, and team members logically walk through their response. This method tests the plan without impacting systems and also helps identify areas that the team can improve.

Although these steps are numbered, the team doesn't necessarily have to perform them in the order presented, and there is some overlap between the steps. For example, communication and documentation both occur throughout the incident. Additionally, protecting evidence is important throughout the incident to ensure the evidence is not modified and a chain of custody is maintained.

However, having these steps helps the organization respond to incidents quickly and decisively. It can save time, money, and protect the organization's reputation. The following sections describe these steps in more detail.

## Assessment

Every reported event isn't an incident. One of the first steps to take is to assess the event and determine if it is an actual incident. Many events can occur naturally on a network but be falsely reported as an incident by an automated tool. You don't want to gather the entire IRT for a false alarm.

For example, a common attack is a transmission control protocol (TCP) synchronize (SYN) flood attack. A TCP session is initiated with a three-way handshake using three packets sent back and forth between two systems. The three steps are:

> **NOTE**
>
> The TCP packets have specific bits set known as flags. The SYN bit is short for synchronize. The ACK bit is short for acknowledge.

1. The first system sends a SYN packet.

2. The second system responds with an acknowledge (ACK) packet.

3. The first system then responds with a SYN/ACK packet. This guarantees a connection between the two systems.

However, in a TCP SYN flood attack, the attacker sends the first packet and then withholds the third packet. It's like a practical joker who sticks his hand out to shake hands, and then pulls his hand away as soon as the other person extends her hand to shake. The second person is left hanging. Similarly, the second system is left hanging with resources allocated to complete the TCP handshake.

When a failed TCP handshake happens once or twice, it's not a problem. It sometimes occurs due to network problems. However, if an attacker initiates hundreds of these incomplete sessions, it can cause a system to crash. A network typically has an IDS that detects SYN flood attacks. Depending on the threshold set for the IDS, it might trigger an alarm on normal activity indicating that a SYN flood attack is in progress.

At this point, the incident response team needs to investigate the alarm. Is it an actual attack or is it a false alarm? If an attack is in progress, the team identifies it as an actual incident. However, if it's just a false alarm, the IRT won't take any additional steps.

An initial assessment includes the following actions:

- Determine whether the data indicates an actual incident or a false positive.

- Get a general idea of the type and severity of the attack. Collect enough information to begin detailed research and to contain potential damage.

- Record actions taken. Later use these records to document the incident—whether it was an actual incident or a false positive.

> **▶ TIP**
>
> Investigate all events that are possible incidents. The goal is to complete the initial assessment as quickly as possible. Additionally, responders should err on the side of caution. It's better to act on a false alarm rather than ignore an actual attack.

## Communication

As soon as someone on your team has verified an incident, he or she should let others know about it. This may be a call to the help desk, or a call to the incident response team leader, depending on what the plan dictates. The team leader determines who else to contact. The goal is to ensure that the right team members get on the scene as quickly as possible.

Communication will occur throughout the incident. For example, the initial assessment may have either under assessed or over assessed the incident's impact. As more details come out, they are reported. Once the incident team has responded, the team reports to either the incident response team leader or an incident lead. These leads have the responsibility to ensure that the required details are reported to senior management as necessary.

For example, if an attacker defaced the company's Web site and posted valuable company secrets on the site, the team leader should ensure the information is reported to the CEO. The CEO and other senior management personnel will need to decide how to respond. On the other hand, a simple virus infection of a single system doesn't require notification to the highest levels of management.

Restrict communication of the incident to team personnel. You don't want to tip off an attacker that you're aware of the attack. The attacker could be an unknown internal employee that you'll want to catch in the act if the perpetrator repeats the attack. It could also be an external attacker who may try to attack again. If the attacker thinks no one has detected his or her actions, the attacker is likely to use the same tactics during the next attack.

If the incident requires communication outside the organization, involve the public relations specialist. This ensures the message is properly created to present the company in a positive light, even if a major attack has occurred.

## Containment

> **TIP**
>
> Containment is also known as isolation. You isolate the affected system or network from other systems to contain the incident to the original affected systems.

It's important to contain an incident as quickly as possible. This minimizes the damage. The solution can be as simple as removing the network cable from the affected system to disconnect the system from the network.

A computer worm is an example of a threat you must contain. Many viruses have a worm component. Sometime after a virus activates, it can launch a worm that spreads through a network. If you detect the virus and isolate the system quickly enough, the worm won't spread. Similarly, you can reconfigure routers to prevent a worm from traveling from one subnet to another.

Some incidents are more serious than others. When responding to serious incidents, consider the following:

- **Always protect human life and safety first**—Human lives can't be replaced but things can.

- **Protect data**—Determine the level of protection for data by its value to the company. Some data may be proprietary and deserve the highest level of protection to prevent unauthorized disclosure. Other data may be public and only need protection against unauthorized modification.

- **Protect hardware and software**—This includes protecting systems against unauthorized modification of the system configuration, and against theft of the hardware.

- **Protect service integrity**—Many services require multiple systems to function. If a criminal launches an attack against a database server, it may seem simple to disconnect the database server from the network to isolate it. However, if this server is providing data for multiple servers, isolating it will affect multiple services on the network. Instead, isolate it by modifying the firewall to limit network traffic.

### Classification of Data

Most organizations apply classifications to their data so that it's clear to everyone what data is more important than other data. The government does this with classifications, such as top secret, secret, and unclassified. Organizations may classify the data similarly using the following classifications:

- **Proprietary**—This includes copyrighted, trademarked, and research and development data. It can also include profit and loss statements, and other financial records showing debts and liabilities. If this information is available to competitors, the organization can lose its competitive edge. Financial data can damage a company's reputation if it is publicly available and may adversely affect its credit rating. Data in this category deserves the highest level of protection, since losing control of it can directly affect a company's viability.

- **Internal data**—This includes employee and customer data, such as names and contact information. It can also include additional data, such as credit card data or health-related information, depending on the nature of the business. Losing control of this data can result in legal consequences, such as lawsuits or government fines.

- **Public**—This includes data available on public Web sites or in company brochures. This data is not protected from unauthorized disclosure, but it is protected against unauthorized modification. For example, Web sites are protected so attackers can't modify the content.

While containing an incident, consider some other issues. These include:

- **Protect evidence**—If it's possible that your organization may prosecute the attacker, protect your evidence. Because you rarely know in advance if an incident will go to court, strive to protect all evidence. This includes ensuring that your team doesn't modify the original data and that you use a chain of custody to control the evidence. For example, you may decide to remove the hard drives as evidence. You would copy these with a bit copy tool, and you would only examine the copies. This requires you to rebuild the affected system with new hard drives.

- **Avoid alerting attackers**—If possible, avoid letting the attacker know you're aware of the attack. You may want to continue collecting evidence about the attack to use for prosecution, or you may want to learn more about the attacker's methodologies. If the attacker realizes he or she's been discovered, the criminal may disappear without a trace, and then come back another time with better tactics.

- **Consider costs versus risks**—Containment isn't always an easy choice. For example, consider a Web server that generates $10,000 in revenue per hour. If this server is attacked and you isolate it from the attacker, you may also isolate it from customers and your revenue stream will stop. In the face of a DoS attack from a single attacker, you can modify the firewall to block this attacker. However, if it's a DDoS attack from multiple attackers, it isn't as easy to modify the firewall to block all the attackers, but it may still be a better choice than removing the server from all access.

## Evaluation

Once you've contained an attack, and even while you're trying to contain it, you will be evaluating it. Identify the type of attack, how serious it is, and how many systems it is affecting. This is similar to the initial assessment but more detailed. The primary goal of the initial assessment is to verify that the event is actually an incident. However, later evaluation allows you to look deeper to determine the extent of the incident.

For example, the initial assessment may have indicated the attack was from a single source. However, deeper evaluation may indicate that the attack is from multiple sources. Similarly, you may have originally thought the attack was against a single server but later learn that multiple servers are under attack. Each of these scenarios indicates the attack is more serious than initially thought and may require a different response. For example, you may need to notify additional people in the company, such as upper-level management.

It's common for an incident response plan to include classifications to help the IRT determine severity. For example, an organization could use the following severity levels:

- **Severity level 1**—A successful attack that caused significant disruption of operations. This attack has impacted a significant number of systems, or a system important enough that its failure could impact the mission of the business.

- **Severity level 2**—A successful attack that caused limited disruption of operations. This attack affected one or more systems and requires manual intervention.

**TIP**

Organizations determine severity levels within an incident response plan. The security levels may differ between two organizations.

- **Severity level 3**—An isolated event that was resolved through automated controls, such as antivirus software automatically quarantining a virus, or an intrusion prevention system detecting an attack and thwarting it by modifying the environment.

These classifications can also help identify who should be notified. For example, the CEO may want to be notified of any level 1 incidents, and departmental managers may want to know about any level 2 incidents.

### Collecting Data

You evaluate an attack by examining all the information you have available to you. You normally have quite a bit of information in various logs. These include:

- **System logs**—Look for any suspicious activity, such as the system or individual processes stopping or restarting. Gaps in the logs, or deleted logs, may indicate that the attacker was covering his or her tracks.

- **Security or audit logs**—Look for any unusual audit failures. A series of failures by the same source followed by a success may give you insight into where the attacker was able to access your resources.

- **Application logs**—Logs for applications, such as Web applications or database applications, will give you specific information on what the attacker may have accessed. You'll often need the assistance of the IT personnel who manage the application to identify which logs are relevant.

- **IDS logs**—The IDS logs will often have more details than the router and firewall logs. They are able to analyze these other logs and identify potential attacks. Chapter 11 discusses intrusion detection in more detail.

- **Router and firewall logs**—These logs show what traffic is passing into your network, and what traffic has been blocked. For example, a simple port scan will be logged with the same source and destination IP addresses, but will show different destination ports. Rudimentary port scanners check the ports in sequential order, such as port1 and then port2. Advanced port scanners will randomize the port order. No matter what type of scanning tool is used, the source and destination IP addresses will be the same, and the destination port is different which clearly indicates a port scan.

**TIP**

Attackers frequently use port scans in reconnaissance attacks to determine what services are running on a system. For example, if port 80 is open, the server is probably a Web server running HTTP. The attacker can then use other methods to determine what type of Web server is running. It could be Apache running a Linux system, or Microsoft Internet Information Services (IIS) running on a Microsoft system.

Additionally, many companies use more advanced tools, such as Microsoft System Center Operations Manager (SCOM), to automate the collection of data from these logs. These tools allow you to view a significant amount of data on a single server. You can also configure them to alert you when they detect abnormal activity so you can quickly respond to an attack.

In addition to searching this log data, you can look for other symptoms. These include:

- **Administrator group membership**—Check to see if an attack has modified group membership. For example, the Nimda worm enabled the guest account and placed it into the administrators group on each system it infected. In Microsoft domains, check membership in the Domain Admins and Enterprise Admins groups as well.

- **Unauthorized hardware**—If a criminal has breached your physical security, an attacker may have added hardware that could be a threat. For example, a wireless access point attached to a router can capture and transmit valuable data to an attacker using a wireless laptop in a neighboring parking lot.

- **Unauthorized software**—Attackers may have remotely installed, or tricked a user into installing, rogue software. This could include vulnerability assessment software that can identify the vulnerabilities within your organization. The attacker can use this information to launch new attacks.

- **Changes in performance**—Compare the current performance of systems against the baseline performance. If the performance is significantly different, it could indicate additional rogue processes are running.

This data can help you determine an attack's source. For example, an attacker's IP address will quickly tell you if it is from an internal system, or from the Internet. Internal IP addresses are in one of the private IP ranges and will be much easier to track down to the actual source of an attack. A public IP address lets you know the attack is coming from the Internet, but not necessarily from where on the Internet.

It's important to realize that the attacking IP address may not be the actual source. It's common for attackers to take control of remote systems and use them as zombies to attack when they're commanded to do so. For example, a public IP address may indicate that the source is from a system in the United States, but the actual attacker may be in a foreign country.

This data can also help you determine the goal of the attack. Some attacks are against targets of opportunity. In other words, the attack isn't a personal attack against your organization, but instead you have a vulnerability that the attacker can exploit. On the other hand, it may be a specific attack against your organization for a specific purpose. Some attacks are trying to gather information for monetary gain and will likely be attempted against any similar organization. Other attacks are malicious in nature and attempt to cause damage to a specific organization.

By evaluating what was attacked, what systems were probed, and what files were accessed, you can gain insight into the attacker's motives. For example, the attacker may be focused only on locating and accessing databases. In such a case, you'll want to determine if the attacker accessed any sensitive data.

After collecting the data, you may decide that you need to take other steps. The incident response plan may give specific instructions to follow based on certain attacks. For example, if you detect a DoS attack from a source on the Internet, the plan may direct you to modify the firewall to block all traffic from this IP address.

You also may need to contact other team members, or additional people in the organization. As mentioned previously, team members share new information with the team leader or incident lead. The lead has the responsibility to notify others as needed. This includes ensuring that all personnel on the incident response team have current information.

## Protecting Evidence

In many situations, the organization may decide to prosecute the attacker. However, successful prosecution is dependent on successfully collecting and protecting the evidence. If it is possible that the evidence is tainted, the U.S. justice system protects the accused.

Make sure the evidence is verifiable and protected from modification so your organization can use it as legal evidence.

Because you really never know if your organization will pursue prosecution, protect all evidence. This includes ensuring that you don't modify it during collection. Think about a police show on TV. You may see an inept rookie cop walk through a pool of blood at a crime scene, but you'll never see a seasoned professional do the same thing. Similarly, seasoned IT professionals know that by simply accessing a file on a system, it changes the file. Instead of showing when an attacker accessed the file, it now shows when the IT person accessed it.

In addition to saving the data for prosecution, you'll also save it for later forensic analysis. It's not always possible to do the necessary forensic analysis during the incident. Instead, capture the data and later analyze it in a controlled environment.

If there's a chance that you'll need the data, back it up using a bit copy tool. Many of these tools are available and they are often included in forensic tool kits. A bit copy tool copies the data at the bit level ensuring that it isn't modified.

At least one backup should be on a write-once, read-many media, such as a CD-R or DVD-R. Use this backup only for prosecution of the offender. Create and use another backup for data recovery and forensic analysis. Ensure that no one accesses these backups except for legal or investigative purposes. Also, create detailed documentation about the backups. Include information regarding who backed up the systems, when, how you secured the systems, and who had access to them.

> **NOTE**
>
> In some cases, the benefit of preserving data might not be worth the cost of delaying the response and recovery of the system. Compare the costs and benefits of preserving data against those of faster recovery for each event.

After you make the backups, remove the original hard disks and store them in a physically secure location. Use these disks as forensic evidence in the event of prosecution. Also, use new hard disks to restore the systems.

In addition to creating copies of the data, it's also important to maintain a chain of custody. This shows who handled the data and when. It provides proof to a court that the evidence presented is the same as the evidence collected.

## Notifying External Agencies

Some laws dictate that you must notify external entities if specific breaches occur. Some external agencies may be able to provide assistance in responding to an attack. They may be able to help you recover your systems quicker, or help you identify, thwart, and possibly prosecute the attacker.

Additionally, many state and federal laws require you to notify customers if their private data has been compromised. Personally identifiable information (PII) is protected by many laws. PII includes credit card data, health-related data, and other types of information. If you don't notify the customers of the compromise, your organization may be subject to legal action.

> **NOTE**
>
> Chapter 2 discusses the local, state, and federal law enforcement agencies involved in system forensics. See that chapter for more information on the types of crimes to report to each type of agency.

13

Incident and
Intrusion Response

### Incident Reporting Organizations

The Federal Information Security Management Act (FISMA) of 2002 has imposed significant responsibilities on federal agencies. One of them is that they must report computer security incidents to the **U.S. Computer Emergency Readiness Team (US-CERT)**. The US-CERT provides assistance to federal agencies after an incident is reported. The US-CERT is part of the Department of Homeland Security and is different from the Computer Emergency Response Team (CERT) hosted at Carnegie Mellon University.

While federal agencies must report incidents to US-CERT, civilian organizations can also report incidents and the US-CERT is able to assist them. The US-CERT gathers data on all the reported incidents and is able to analyze the data to identify trends.

All organizations are encouraged to report incidents to US-CERT. They can also report incidents to other organizations including:

- **Information Analysis Infrastructure Protection (IAIP)**—IAIP is part of the Department of Homeland Security (DHS). It is interested in any threats to critical U.S. infrastructures. Organizations can report incidents to IAIP by calling or e-mailing the National Interagency Coordination Center (NICC). See *http://www.nifc.gov/nicc/*.

- **CERT Coordination Center (CERT/CC)**—CERT/CC is located at Carnegie Mellon University. This nongovernmental entity is interested in any computer security incidents involving the Internet. CERT/CC provides an online incident reporting system. See *http://www.cert.org/certcc.html*.

- **Information Sharing and Analysis Centers Council (ISAC Council)**—ISAC Councils are industry-specific private-sector groups that share important computer security-related information among their members. Several ISAC Councils have been formed for industry sectors, such as electricity, financial services, IT, and communications. In addition to reporting incidents, organizations should internally document corrective actions. See *http://www.isaccouncil.org*.

## Recovery

System recovery depends on the extent of an attack. A simple virus scan may detect and remove any malware and the system recovers. Other times, all you need to do is reboot the system, since rebooting a system solves many ills.

However, attacks that require you to save the original disks and make copies require work that is much more extensive to recover a system. For example, you'll need to reinstall the operating system and applications. Many organizations use imaging techniques to speed up this process. The image includes the operating system, the applications, and all the required configuration settings.

Next, you'll restore all the relevant data from a backup. This requires you to have a thorough backup plan with reliable backups. For databases that are frequently modified, you can usually restore the data up to the moment of failure, or up to the moment of the attack.

Before bringing a system back online, make sure as well that it has all current updates and patches. Even if you're using images, updates have probably been applied to the system since the image was first captured. This includes updates to the operating system and any installed applications.

## Document and Review

As the old saying goes, the job isn't complete until the documentation is done. This is as true with security incidents as it is with other jobs. The documentation and review process actually starts as soon as you declare an incident is authentic. During the incident, you are collecting information to contain and resolve the incident. Once you have resolved it and the systems have recovered, you finalize the documentation.

One of the things you'll want to do is document all the information necessary to reconstruct the events. This includes:

- What led up to the event
- What happened during the event
- How effective the response was

### Assessing Incident Damage and Cost

When you're determining the damage your organization has sustained, consider both direct and indirect costs. Incident damage and costs are critical evidence if your organization decides to pursue legal action. These costs could include the following:

- Direct costs related to the loss of business sales
- Costs to restore the organization's reputation and bring back customers
- Costs for time the IRT devoted to responding to, recovering from, investigating, and reviewing the incident
- Costs to recover the systems, including lost productivity, and replacement of any hardware or software
- Legal costs associated with prosecution
- Legal costs in response to lawsuits from customers or employees whose data was compromised

### Reviewing the Response and Updating Policies

The review process also allows you to determine if you need to make changes to the response plan. If the response wasn't effective, you'll want to know why. It could be because team members weren't familiar enough with your plan's steps. For example, a legal chain of custody might not have been established because the team members didn't know how to establish and maintain one.

After the review process, you may have specific recommendations for change. This could be changes to the plan, changes in team membership, changes in training, or some other change. Without the review process, you won't uncover or address problems, and the same mistakes could happen during the next incident.

## CHAPTER SUMMARY

Organizations must reasonably minimize their chances of attack. They should also plan what they will do when they're attacked. This chapter discusses measures that help minimize incidents, including assembling a core computer security incident response team and defining an incident response plan.

## KEY CONCEPTS AND TERMS

Adverse event

Chief information officer (CIO)

Chief technology officer (CTO)

Computer security incident

Event

Incident response plan

Incident response team (IRT)

U.S. Computer Emergency
   Readiness Team (US-CERT)

## CHAPTER 13 ASSESSMENT

1. The ideal time for an organization to learn how to respond to security incidents is after suffering an attack.

   A. True
   B. False

2. It is impossible to prevent all security incidents. Therefore, when a security incident does occur, an organization must _____ its impact.

3. Which of the following is a violation of computer security policies, acceptable use policies, or standard security practices?

   A. Event
   B. Adverse event
   C. Computer security incident
   D. US-CERT

4. The ideal incident response team membership and structure depends on the type of organization and its risk management strategy.

   A. True
   B. False

5. An incident response team should place all emergency system information in a central, offline location. Which of the following is *not* a type of information that falls into this category?

   A. Malicious code
   B. Administrative passwords
   C. Network layout diagrams
   D. Router configuration information
   E. Firewall configuration information

6. Which member of an incident response team is responsible for a particular incident or set of related security incidents?

   A. Team leader
   B. Incident lead
   C. Associate member
   D. Chief information officer

7. The incident response team performs most actions in response to an incident. However, all levels of IT staff should be aware of how to report incidents internally.

   A. True
   B. False

8. An organization's _____ outlines specific procedures to follow in the event of a security incident.

9. An organization should try to let attackers know that the organization is aware of their activities.

   A. True
   B. False

10. _____ assists federal civilian agencies in their incident-handling efforts. It analyzes the information provided by all agencies to identify trends and precursors of attacks.

11. When an organization is determining the damage it has sustained, it should consider both _____ and _____ costs.

13

Incident and
Intrusion Response

# Trends and Future Directions

S YSTEM FORENSICS IS AN EVOLVING FIELD. Forensic specialists must be prepared for changing technology. They must also be prepared for changing legal requirements regarding protecting data. Further, they should know how to conduct investigations using formal, defensible processes. Demonstrating competency in the evolving forensic environment requires forensic specialists to adopt a structured career approach and obtain credentials and certifications. In future hiring decisions, those who have credentials will be more favorably viewed than those who are equally competent but self-taught.

This chapter addresses some trends and future directions in the field of system forensics. It presents a number of thoughts and opinions about how the digital world will evolve. Also, this chapter provides ideas about how that evolution may affect digital forensics and digital forensics specialists.

## Chapter 14 Topics

This chapter covers the following topics and concepts:

- How new hardware technologies affect forensics
- How software trends affect system forensics
- What changes are occurring in the use of technology
- What the legal landscape looks like now and how it might change
- How professionalization and certification will help the field of system forensics

## Hardware Trends

Digital forensics is a new field. However, people have been analyzing digital systems and associated components since the 1950s. At that time, early forensic investigators used tools to store and process data and support decision making. The use of digital systems grew and evolved. So did the need to analyze those systems. Investigators needed to be able to determine what had been done and who was responsible.

One of the earliest uses of digital systems was to compute payroll. One of the earliest digital crimes was taking the "round-off"—the half-cent variance resulting from calculating an individual's pay. A criminal would move that round-off to his or her own account. In this type of fraud, a perpetrator stole very small individual amounts. However, the number of paychecks calculated made the total fraud quite large. This crime showed that digital crime is relatively easy to commit and difficult to detect. The courts frequently sentenced perpetrators to probation instead of prison.

Digital technology provides many benefits and reduces costs in a number of ways. Therefore, the use of digital technology to support business processes and nearly every other facet of modern life has increased. In parallel, criminals have made increasingly innovative use of digital techniques in their activities. The methods of protecting digital systems and associated assets have also grown. However, they haven't grown fast enough to keep pace with the growing number and complexity of attacks. Attackers now realize that there are many ways to illegally obtain benefits from digital systems. They can steal money and identities, and they can even commit blackmail. For example, perpetrators have stolen customer data and held it for ransom.

The field of digital forensics grew out of the need for improved capabilities to analyze digital systems and data. This field is building a new analytical discipline based on techniques that have evolved over the years. It's also merging those techniques with new ones. Many individuals and vendors are developing newer, better forensic tools. These tools let you compete on a more equal footing with those who attack digital assets or use them to commit crimes.

## What Moore's Law Means to System Forensics

In a 1965 paper, Gordon E. Moore, co-founder of Intel, noted that the number of components in integrated circuits had doubled every two years from the invention of the integrated circuit in 1958 until 1965. He predicted that the trend would continue for at least 10 more years. In other words, he predicted, the number of transistors on an integrated circuit would double every two years for the next 10 years. This statement regarding the progression of integrated circuit capacity and capability became known as **Moore's law**.

Moore's law achieved its name and notoriety because it proved to be an accurate representation of a trend that continues today. Specifically, the capacity and capability of integrated circuits has doubled every two years since Moore noted the trend. Further, Moore's law applies to more than just integrated circuits. It also applies to some of the other primary drivers of computing capability: storage capacity, processor speed, and cost.

Moore's law reflects the growing need for increased computing capability and capacity. Only human ingenuity limits new uses for technological solutions. In the 1950s, the UNIVAC I, the first commercial digital computer, was touted as having the capability to meet an organization's total computing requirements. Today, a typical low-end mobile phone has more capability and capacity than the UNIVAC I.

Moore's law also applies to digital forensics. You can expect to conduct investigations requiring analysis of an increasing volume of data from an increasing number of digital devices. Unfortunately, in the forensics world, Moore's law operates as if it's on steroids. For example, digital storage capacity for a particular device might double in a year. The data that you might need to analyze could easily experience double that growth level. For example, a standard point-and-shoot digital camera now takes 5-megapixel photos. High-end cameras take 16-megapixel—or more—photos. A typical Windows XP build consumes roughly 4 GB of disk space. A typical Windows 7 build consumes 8 GB to 10 GB. Although a single copy of a file or data record might be maintained for active use, you must often locate and examine all prior copies of that file.

Because of Moore's law, forensic specialists must develop new techniques, new software, and new hardware to perform forensic assessments. New techniques should simplify documentation of the chain of custody. You will have to determine what techniques have the greatest potential for obtaining needed information. In most investigations, analyzing all available data would be so costly as to be infeasible. Therefore, selectively evaluate data. Such selectivity is not unique to the digital world. It is the same concept that investigators have used for years to follow leads. For example, they often start by interviewing the most likely subjects and follow where the data leads to reach a conclusion. However, the U.S. legal system, helped by advertising and popular television, expects digital forensics to be unconstrained by such mundane factors as time, money, and available technology.

## Device Overload

A common misconception is that a digital forensics specialist will deal only with computers: desktops, laptops, and servers. However, you will also need to know how to deal with any type of digital data from any type of device.

Many types of devices may be able to capture and store data useful in an investigation. The following are some examples:

- **Mobile phones**—Mobile phones today can store e-mail, details about communications sent and received, recorded conversations, photographs, and videos. Smartphones, such as the iPhone and Android, are pocket-sized but have capacity and capability similar to those of a desktop. Further, companies plan to integrate chemical detection and health monitoring capabilities into smartphones. Soon, these phones will be similar to the analyze-anything tricorder used in the science fiction epic *Star Trek*.

- **Cameras**—Cameras have become ubiquitous data collection devices. They are now integrated into laptops and mobile phones. And they're used for crime prevention and data collection. Homeowners, businesses, and governments use cameras for location monitoring and to help enforce the law. London, New York, and Washington have embarked on efforts to install camera surveillance in most public locations. A former mayor of New York noted that from one corner in Times Square, he counted 86 cameras. In such a camera-prevalent environment, you'll need to understand how to identify cameras that might provide useful information. Also, learn how to collect camera data and consolidate data from multiple cameras, in different formats.

- **Copiers, fax machines, and printers**—Every copier made since 2002 has the capability to store copies of the documents copied. Copiers mark the documents they copy with a hidden code to provide an identifier for the copier. Similarly, fax machines and printers store copies of the documents they process. Machine manufacturers are working to develop more secure devices. Know how to search these devices for relevant information.

- **Network components**—A computer network comprises many components, such as routers, firewalls, and servers. These devices transport data and store data. The duration of this storage may be very short—on the order of milliseconds— or it may be long. Some systems store messages in transit for several days for backup. Forensic specialists are beginning to tap the storage maintained in network components as part of their investigative database. The forensic value of these devices will become significantly more critical as organizations move toward cloud processing. In cloud processing, storage on desktops is minimized in favor of centralized storage. You may need to retrieve data as it passes through networks. Cloud processing is discussed further in the section "The Changing Uses of Technology," later in this chapter.

- **Other devices**—Forensic investigations are examining a number of other devices, too. Some examples are standalone global positioning system (GPS) devices, GPS devices built into cars and smartphones, and toll road passes. In addition, you may be required to work with digital gaming devices and digital video recorders (DVRs). Even appliances and vehicles include processors that could become digital evidence. For example, in 2007, New Jersey Governor Jon Corzine was in a car accident in which he was seriously injured. A few days after the accident, a witness— his automobile—contradicted his account of the accident. Most U.S. cars built since 2000 have been equipped with a device known as a motor vehicle event data recorder.

Know how to investigate all these types of devices. Keep up with the constantly changing technology and learn to deal with new devices as they're introduced.

## Software Trends

Several trends in software are affecting forensics. In many cases, amateurs rather than professionals develop software. Applications that can subvert security controls are readily available. Anti-forensics tools are available on the Internet. At the same time, software developers are constantly coming up with new tools to help forensic specialists.

Digital systems cannot work without software. Some of this software is stored in hardware to control the operation of the digital device. Software development once involved strict processes. The organization or individual who developed software was responsible for its proper functioning. Today, software is as likely to be developed by an amateur programmer as by a company. Much software is now developed using a collaborative open source model. In this model, no one person assumes responsibility for system integrity or performance.

The various software development models complicate assignment of responsibility and increase integrity risks. They also expand the number and variety of applications available. As the number of software applications increases, so does the number of applications that are directly useful to forensic specialists. Some software applications are developed specifically to address forensic needs. For example, an Internet search returns more than 100 different Web sites offering forensic software products. Other sites offer tools that you can adapt to support forensic activities. For example, a forensic specialist can use a product developed to retrieve a lost file to explore a disk drive's contents.

When addressing future software trends, look at both the good and bad impacts. The following sections discuss some of these impacts.

### Proliferation of Software Products

As a forensic specialist, you may need to address a huge number of software products of many different formats and types. The number of software products available also increases the amount of data potentially relevant to an investigation.

## Software as a Service

When computing first entered the marketplace, computer manufacturers typically provided software as part of a bundled product. A **bundled product** includes hardware, software, maintenance, and support sold together for a single price. It wasn't long before the industry recognized that it could sell software products individually. This resulted in the rise of companies such as Microsoft.

Another approach to selling software arose. This approach involves selling access to needed software on a time-sharing basis. The price of the software was essentially embedded in a mathematical algorithm, and a user paid for software use based on his or her usage profile. This pricing model continued into personal computer (PC) and server technology.

Then the pricing algorithm was changed to address a number of concurrent users, a number of instances, or some other model. In addition, the idea of buying use of a software product morphed into the concept of **software as a service (SaaS)**—that is, software that a provider licenses to customers as a service on demand, through a subscription model.

The model under which an organization obtains software is important to forensic analysis because it affects four areas of an investigation:

- Who owns the software? Know whom to talk with to obtain information regarding the functionality and patch levels of software.

- How can you get access to the program code? When software is obtained as a shared service, access is usually not possible. In such cases, use alternate techniques.

- What assurance do you have of the safety of a software product? You need to know that a particular software product doesn't contain malware that could alter the investigation.

- How can you keep the status of shared software static until the forensic investigation is complete?

## Forensic Support Software

Many tools available today are designed to support forensic specialists. Also, numerous products have capabilities you can use to support a forensic investigation. Forensic-capable software is becoming increasingly available to specialists. However, such products are also available to other individuals, including criminals. Realize that data may have been manufactured by perpetrators or compromised by individuals seeking to perform their own forensic examination.

 **TIP**

Tools alone do not make a good forensic investigation. Remember to take a disciplined approach and maintain the chain of custody.

**14**

**Trends and Future Directions**

## Proliferation of Software Development Models

Today's software development models expand the types of software products available. They also increase the potential that software will be developed to address a forensic need. However, with open source software, no individual or organization is required to accept product responsibility. This limits the use of much open source software in forensic investigation. It also increases the level of effort required to demonstrate that software included in an investigation can provide supportable evidence.

# The Changing Uses of Technology

When digital technology first entered the work environment, its use was limited. Information technology (IT) began as a centralized environment run by computer specialists. These specialists developed and maintained applications. Technology grew and became integrated as a critical business tool. As it did, government and industry began to push computing capability to the end user. This placed computing capability in the hands of those who needed it. The era of time sharing was born in the mid-1970s. In the 1980s, the desktop computer supplemented time sharing.

Desktops continued the effort to place more computing power in the hands of users. The desktop's advent also started a movement toward cluster computing. **Cluster computing** involves linking computers into local area networks (LANs) to improve performance, availability, and security. Cluster computing also reduces costs. A LAN allows computing power to be placed on the desktop. It also helps centralize and secure data assets. Networking provides centralization of computing and data assets. It therefore makes increased computing capability available to end users. At the same time, it reduces costs and improves security.

Today, cloud computing is reducing costs and expanding capabilities. It can scale up or down to address changes in data volumes. **Cloud computing** involves using the Internet to allow people to access massively scalable technology-enabled services. It includes searching for flights online or using Facebook, neither of which qualify as SaaS.

Today's cloud computing is much like the time sharing of the 1970s and 1980s:

- Both time sharing and cloud computing centralize computing and data resources.
- Both time sharing and cloud computing put access to computing resources on the desktop. The desktop connects to a central facility.
- Time sharing relied on a "dumb" terminal, with all processing performed at the central facility. Cloud computing performs processing at a central site. Users access the cloud through a thin client PC. A PC as a **thin client** uses little of its computing capability, functioning much like a dumb terminal.

Cloud computing presents numerous challenges for forensic specialists. A cloud computing facility can contain an unbelievable volume of programs and data. Understand what data and systems to include in an investigation and what to exclude. You may have to exclude data and systems for a number of reasons:

- **Location**—Cloud computing can have major components or facilities located anywhere in the world. In most cases, the location of cloud capabilities is not really relevant. However, when conducting a forensic investigation, location can be critical. In the United States, individual states have different laws regarding protection of data. States typically honor each other's court orders and e-discovery requests. On the other hand, sometimes you'll collect data from a cloud located in another country. In those cases, be prepared for delay. Different countries can have significantly different legal requirements for protecting data and processing e-discovery requests. Even court-ordered data requests may not be honored without State Department intervention. In planning a forensic investigation, identify when access to needed data may be delayed or restricted. Also, consider those challenges in your investigation plan.

  Distribution of sensitive data is important in conducting a forensic examination. Before cloud computing, data tended to be consolidated within a contiguous storage space. The use of contiguous storage is still promoted. However, in some instances, data is intentionally separated. For example, a user might place all personally identifiable information into a separate file and store it on an encrypted partition. Further, some file structures distribute data across and between sets of disks to improve access speed, especially in shared-access environments. Be aware of special processes used for storing data or segregating sensitive data. Knowledge of these data storage procedures allows you to better focus resources on the storage areas most likely to contain the needed data.

- **Ownership**—Cloud computing may be established to support one or many organizations. If it supports many organizations, the operator of the cloud should have procedures and controls in place that segregate data by client. As a forensic specialist, you may need to determine whether such segregation controls are adequate. If you determine that they're not adequate, you face both technical and legal challenges. The technical challenges are limitations of time and resources. In addition, legal challenges may restrict what data you can collect.

- **Legal procedures**—Legal procedures will change significantly as organizations make use of cloud capabilities. They will also change as governments establish more restrictive requirements to protect individual privacy and trade secrets. For example, government response to a security breach is often to establish new requirements on a system owner. Further, a key characteristic of cloud computing is resource sharing. Specifically, the cloud is established with a very large computing capability. Users consume and pay for the resources they need, when they need them. Unneeded resources are made available for other users. In a shared-resources environment, you'll have to present a much stronger case if you want to perform a full forensic examination of the storage media. For example, searching for deleted or hidden data in unallocated space is more difficult in the cloud than when all resources are dedicated to a single user or organization.

## Collaborative Investigations

**Collaborative computing** is a technique for analyzing problems and developing solutions. It involves using the combined efforts of a number of individuals focused on a particular issue. In the past, such collaboration could be achieved only by co-locating all the individuals involved. Technology has changed that paradigm. E-mail, conferencing software, and shared document preparation allow multiple individuals to coordinate their efforts. Webinars, Web casts, social networks, blogs, and other data sharing approaches have created an environment that promotes collaboration. In the past, a lone investigator performing an investigation in isolation was the norm. This is not the case today.

Use of collaborative investigation techniques involves its own concerns and considerations. Unrestricted collaboration is feasible only if it is limited to specific individuals. These individuals must be vetted regarding their credentials and capability to protect data and follow proper forensic procedures. When individuals are not properly vetted, access to data must be restricted. Independent examiners must be able to support any conclusions reached. All analyses must follow proper procedures for documentation and chain of custody.

## The Changing Legal Environment

Both the federal government and individual states have created laws that address cybercrime. This chapter talks primarily about federal cybercrime laws. It's likely that federal laws will have the most impact on cybercrime. This is because geography or state and national borders don't matter to cybercriminals. The Internet truly blurs these lines. A criminal can easily initiate a cybercrime in one state and harm a victim in another. In addition, cybercrime statutes vary widely between the states. Therefore, federal laws may end up being more comprehensive.

 **NOTE**

It's important to remember that many states criminalize the same behavior that federal cybercrime laws address.

**NOTE**

The Internet Crime Complaint Center (IC3) is a partnership between the U.S. Federal Bureau of Investigation (FBI) and the National White Collar Crime Center. The 2009 "Annual Report on Internet Crime" showed that the total loss linked to online fraud was $559.7 million. You can read the report at *http://www.ic3 .gov/media/annualreport/2009_ IC3Report.pdf*.

### The Computer Fraud and Abuse Act (1984)

Congress passed the **Computer Fraud and Abuse Act (CFAA)** in 1984. It's the first piece of federal legislation that identified computer crimes as distinct offenses. The CFAA provides both criminal and civil penalties. In enacting the CFAA, Congress chose to address computer-related offenses in a single statute. The CFAA limits federal jurisdiction to situations where cybercrime is interstate in nature or when the computers of the federal government are the object of crime.

Congress amended the CFAA with the **Uniting and Strengthening America by Providing Appropriate Tools Required to Intercept and Obstruct Terrorism Act (U.S.A. PATRIOT Act)** in 2001. It amended the CFAA again in 2008. These amendments increased the penalties for CFAA violations. They also lowered the required damage thresholds in light of terrorism and identity theft concerns.

The CFAA criminalizes causing certain types of damage to a protected computer. A protected computer is any of the following:

- A federal government computer
- A financial institution computer
- A computer used in interstate or foreign commerce

The definition of a protected computer is very broad. Under the statute, the Internet is a protected computer.

The CFAA addresses the following types of criminal activity:

- Unauthorized access of national security information
- Unauthorized access to a government computer
- Compromising the confidentiality of a protected computer
- Unauthorized access to a protected computer with an intent to defraud
- Unauthorized access to a protected computer that causes damage
- Intentional transmission of malware, viruses, or worms that damage a protected computer
- Unauthorized trafficking of passwords or other computer access information that allows people to access other computers without authorization and with the intent to defraud
- Extortion involving threats to damage a protected computer

The CFAA doesn't just address intruders or outsider attacks on protected computers. It also takes into account that insiders may exceed the access they have been granted in a protected computer system. Since these people already have access to these systems, their access isn't unauthorized. However, in some cases, they commit a crime if they exceed their scope of authorized access. Under the CFAA, individuals exceed authorized access when they access a computer with authorization but use that access to get or alter information that they aren't allowed to use or alter.

Insiders can be charged under the CFAA with exceeding authorized access if they access national security information inappropriately. They can also be charged if they compromise the confidentiality of a protected computer or exceed their authorization in a protected computer with intent to defraud.

Some sections of the CFAA require the government to show that the intruder caused damage. Under the CFAA, "damage" is any of the following:

- Causes loss of $5,000 or more of total damage during one year
- Modifies medical care of a person
- Causes physical injury
- Threatens public health or safety
- Damages systems used by or for a government entity for administration of justice, national defense, or national security
- Causes or attempts to cause death or serious bodily injury

▶ **NOTE**

The list of what is a well-known cybercrime changes every day. The CFAA is the "go to" act for federal prosecution of cybercrime. It's very broad, and almost any type of Internet-related crime involving computers falls within its scope. Prosecutors often include CFAA charges with other federal criminal charges if a computer is involved in the commission of a crime.

The federal government uses the CFAA to prosecute many different computer crimes. It used the CFAA to charge a 20-year-old University of Tennessee student with unauthorized e-mail access. In late 2008, the student accessed vice presidential candidate Sarah Palin's personal Yahoo! e-mail account. The student then posted her e-mail messages online. A criminal grand jury indicted the student under the CFAA and the federal Electronic Communications Privacy Act (ECPA). In 2010, a jury convicted the student of unauthorized access to a computer and obstruction of justice.

## Computer Trespass or Intrusion

The CFAA is the main federal law addressing cybercrime.

In addition to the CFAA, the federal government has a number of other laws that address computer trespass or intrusion. These laws generally address computers that the U.S. government owns or controls. Some laws, such as the CFAA, expand this definition to include computers used in interstate commerce.

Federal law addresses fraud and related activity in connection with access devices. It outlaws the production, use, or sale of counterfeit or unauthorized access devices. Access devices include any item that can be used to obtain money, goods, or things of value. They include items such as card, plate, code, account number, electronic serial number, mobile identification number, personal identification number, or other telecommunications services. A person who violates this law commits a felony. Such an individual can be imprisoned for 10 to 20 years, depending on the violation's nature.

### State Laws Against Computer Trespass

It's important to keep in mind that states also may have computer trespass statutes that prohibit unauthorized access to computer systems or networks. Depending on the jurisdiction, these crimes have a variety of names. In many states, the mere act of intentionally entering a computer system or network without permission is a crime. In most jurisdictions, first-time computer trespass is a misdemeanor. The penalties for computer trespass may escalate if a person is charged and convicted of more than one offense.

Most trespass statutes address only unauthorized access into a computer system. They stop short of addressing actual computer tampering, access of information, or the injection of computer viruses or worms. These types of crimes, which are malicious in nature, are typically addressed in other statutes.

## Theft of Information

Theft of information via computer networks is on the rise. Most of these crimes take the form of theft of personal identifying information or financial information. Financial gain is nearly always the motive for crimes such as these.

The federal **Identity Theft and Assumption Deterrence Act** (1998) makes identity theft a federal crime. A person who violates the law is subject to criminal penalties of up to 15 years in prison. This period increases to 20 years in special circumstances. Violators can also be fined up to $250,000.

This law recognizes that the victims of identity theft aren't just the businesses that grant credit. A person whose identity is stolen also is a victim. The law also requires the Federal Trade Commission (FTC) to keep a record of identity theft complaints. The FTC must give identity theft victims educational materials to help them repair any damage to their credit and personal data.

 **NOTE**
The FTC's identity theft Web site provides useful information about preventing identity theft. See *http://www.ftc.gov/bcp/edu/microsites/idtheft/*.

The law makes it illegal for anyone to knowingly transfer or use another person's identification with the intent to commit a crime. Under the law, an identification document is any document made or issued by the federal or a state government. Identifying information includes information that is similar to other personal information laws discussed in this book. This information includes name, Social Security number, and driver's license number. It also includes:

- Unique biometric data, such as fingerprint, voice print, retina or iris image, or other unique physical representation
- Unique electronic identification number, address, or routing code
- Mobile telephone electronic serial number
- Any other piece of information that may be used to identify a specific person

The U.S. Secret Service, FBI, U.S. Postal Inspection Service, and Social Security Administration's Office of the Inspector General all have the power to investigate crimes committed under this law.

## Interception of Communications Laws

Federal laws forbid the use of eavesdropping technologies without a court order. Communications covered by the statutes include e-mail, radio communications, electronic communications, data transmission, and telephone calls. The federal **Wiretap Act** (1968, amended) governs real-time interception of the contents of a communication.

 **NOTE**
The Pen Register and Trap and Trace Statute governs access to the real-time interception of headers, logs, and other transmission information.

The Electronic Communications Privacy Act (ECPA; 1986)—which you read about in Chapter 10—governs access to stored electronic communications. This includes access to the contents of a communication and the headers and other transmission information. The ECPA is an amendment to the original Wiretap Act.

14

Trends and Future Directions

The U.S.A. PATRIOT Act amended both the Wiretap Act and ECPA. The PATRIOT Act enhances law enforcement tools to intercept electronic communications to fight computer fraud and abuse offenses.

## Spam and Phishing Laws

Congress created the **Controlling the Assault of Non-Solicited Pornography and Marketing (CAN-SPAM) Act** in 2003. The act covers unsolicited commercial e-mail messages known as spam. Spam is electronic junk mail. Spam is a nuisance to the recipient. The CAN-SPAM Act has both civil and criminal provisions.

The CAN-SPAM Act requires commercial e-mail senders to meet certain requirements. Commercial messages are messages with content that advertises or promotes a product or service. The act also forbids sending sexually explicit e-mail unless it has a label or marking that identifies it as explicit.

Commercial e-mail message senders must meet the following requirements of the CAN-SPAM Act:

- Don't use false or misleading header information.
- Don't use deceptive subject lines.
- Identify the e-mail message as a commercial advertisement.
- Include a valid physical postal address.
- Inform message recipients how they can opt out of future e-mail messages.
- Promptly process opt-out requests.
- Monitor the actions of third parties that advertise on the sender's behalf.

Each separate e-mail sent in violation of the CAN-SPAM Act is subject to penalties of up to $16,000. The FTC enforces the civil provisions of the act. It has also promulgated rules for businesses to follow.

The CAN-SPAM Act also has criminal provisions. It includes penalties for:

- Accessing another person's computer without permission to send spam
- Using false information to register for multiple e-mail accounts or domain names
- Relaying or re-transmitting spam messages through a computer to mislead others about the origin of the e-mail
- Harvesting e-mail addresses or generating them through a dictionary attack
- Taking advantage of open relays or open proxies without permission to send spam

The U.S. Department of Justice enforces the criminal provisions of the CAN-SPAM Act. Criminal penalties include fines or imprisonment of up to five years.

The first conviction under the CAN-SPAM Act occurred in 2004. In that case, the defendant searched for unprotected wireless access hotspots and exploited them to send spam messages. The spam messages advertised pornographic Web sites. Eventually, the court sentenced the defendant to three years' probation and six months of home detention. He also had to pay a $10,000 fine.

Spam e-mail messages can also be phishing attempts. Phishing scams are scams that typically take place via e-mail or instant messaging. They're a form of Internet fraud where attackers attempt to steal valuable personal information from their victims.

The federal government has no anti-phishing law. However, phishing attacks can be prosecuted under a number of federal laws. This includes many of the laws already discussed in this section. For example, if the phishing attackers are attempting to steal personal information, they may be committing identity theft. In such a case, the federal Identity Theft and Assumption Deterrence Act would apply. Phishing attackers also may be committing computer fraud or access-device fraud. Some phishing attacks may be prosecuted under the CAN-SPAM Act.

If a phishing attack includes malicious activity, such as spreading computer viruses, the Computer Fraud and Abuse Act applies. Phishing scams can also violate state fraud and identity theft laws.

## Cybersquatting

**Cybersquatting** is the bad-faith registration of a domain name that is a registered trademark or trade name of another entity. Congress created the **Anti-Cybersquatting Consumer Protection Act (ACPA)** in 1999. It's designed to stop people from registering domain names that are trademarks that belong to other entities.

The ACPA allows entities to sue cybersquatters. To prove their case, the plaintiff must show that the cybersquatter registered the trademark in bad faith with intent to profit from the registration. The ACPA includes nine factors that help a court determine bad faith. Those factors are:

- A person's intellectual property rights in the domain name
- Whether the domain name consists of the legal name of the person
- The person's prior use of the domain name in connection with the sale of goods or services
- The person's noncommercial or fair use of the domain name
- The person's intent to divert consumers from the mark owner's own Web site
- The person's offer to sell the domain name without having used the domain name for the sale of goods or services
- Whether the person gave false or misleading contact information when registering the domain name
- Whether the person registered multiple domain names that are identical or confusingly similar to marks owned by others
- Whether the mark incorporated in the domain name is famous and distinctive

Under the law, a plaintiff can recover damages and ask the court to issue an injunction that stops the cybersquatter from using the contested domain name. The court also can award statutory damages of up to $100,000 per violation. Courts also can award the contested domain name to the winning party.

## Malicious Acts

Common malicious information security activity includes malware, worms, viruses, and Trojan horses. For the most part, the federal government can prosecute these types of activities under the CFAA.

Under the CFAA, the intentional transmission of malware, viruses, or worms that damage a protected computer is a felony. Remember that for the purposes of the CFAA, almost any computer connected to the Internet is a protected computer. The government can charge people who violate this provision of the CFAA with a felony. It can punish violators with up to 10 years in prison.

---

### Well-Known Cybercrimes

Some cybercrimes are popular because they were "first." For example, the Morris worm was one of the first computer worms on the Internet. At the time, it infected and overwhelmed a number of government systems. The creator of the worm was the first person charged with violating the CFAA.

The CFAA was also used to prosecute the creator of the Melissa virus. When it was released, the Melissa virus was one of the fastest-moving and most destructive viruses. David Smith created and distributed the Melissa virus in 1999. The virus caused more than $80 million in damages. Smith was sentenced to 20 months in federal prison in May 2002. He also was fined $5,000.

Other cybercrimes are well known because they're the biggest. For instance, one of the hackers in the TJX Companies, Inc., case received the harshest-ever sentence for a hacking case in March 2010. The federal government had charged him with violating the CFAA, federal laws related to access device fraud, and the Identity Theft and Assumption Deterrence Act.

The federal government has been attempting to expand the use of the CFAA. One area where it has tried to expand the reach of the CFAA is in the area of cyberbullying. In 2008, the Department of Justice indicted Lori Drew for violating the CFAA. The government argued that her activities on a social networking service exceeded her authorization in the use of a protected computer. She exceeded her authorized access by using the site in excess of the use authorized by the site's terms of service agreement. A jury found her guilty of a misdemeanor CFAA violation. That conviction was set aside in August 2009. The judge found that there were several problems in applying the CFAA to the case. The government didn't appeal the judge's reversal.

Learn how the federal government is prosecuting cybercrime by visiting the Department of Justice Computer Crime Web page. The Web page lists notable cybercrime prosecutions. The Web page is available at *http://www.justice.gov/criminal/cybercrime/*.

## Evolving Cybercrime Laws

Not too long ago, a former employee stole customer records from his firm. The judge asked the firm's attorney one question: "Does your client have the customer information?" The attorney replied that his client had the data, but the individual had taken a copy. The judge dismissed the case, saying that if his client still had the data, then it obviously wasn't stolen.

Laws, attorneys, and judges are much more up-to-date today. In the United States, stealing company records is recognized as a crime, even if nothing was physically taken. But there is still much work needed to bring the law and legal procedure current with today's real world. As discussed in the preceding sections, the federal government and individual states have enacted laws that are specific to IT. In the current Congressional session, more than 37 bills are in process that address digital information and information security. As these bills move further along the process, they may be consolidated into fewer bills with a more structured and coordinated set of requirements and responsibilities. Monitor this changing legal environment. Understand how the changes will affect your ability to collect data and document evidence.

One area to expect changes is in the definition of what is sensitive data. Threats to personal identity may result in an expansion of the requirement to protect information related to individuals. This is particularly true, for example, in the health care industry. The federal government is issuing new rules requiring that all health care information be digitized in a manner such that it can be shared. Procedures for documenting digital data as evidence are evolving as well.

## Trends in Professionalization and Certification

According to the U.S. Bureau of Labor Statistics (BLS), the computer forensics and forensic science industries were among the 30 fastest-growing occupations covered in the *2008–2009 Occupational Outlook Handbook*. The BLS forecasts these fields to grow much faster than the average of the overall U.S. economy over the coming decade. Moreover, as demand for the industry continues to grow, salaries and benefits for experience, knowledge, and skill level will also grow.

> **NOTE**
> Specialization can increase an individual's skill in a particular technical area or information domain.

Conducting an effective forensic examination involves both generalists and specialists. Different portions of an investigation may require a variety of specialists. A generalist consolidates the investigation into a cohesive description of how the conclusions of specialists interrelate. This is similar to the medical field, where a general practitioner serves as the primary diagnostician. This general practitioner arranges access to specialists, such as cardiologists and surgeons.

Determining whether an individual is a forensic generalist or specialist or is qualified as either is a difficult task. Organizations typically do not maintain a staff of forensic specialists. Organizations more frequently contract for forensic examinations from specialty firms or ask their general IT staff to conduct investigations using forensic techniques.

Evaluating an individual's competence is as much an art as a skill. It involves determining an individual's knowledge, skills, ability, and past performance. Unfortunately, in a hiring mode, a decision maker generally has only a resume and an interview on which to base a decision. Neither of these information sources is independent or unbiased. Further, contacting references provided by an applicant doesn't provide much help in making a hiring decision. Individuals should be expected to provide positive references, and past employers are reluctant to provide references due to legal liability. Because of these difficulties, professionalization and certification are important.

Federal agencies were a primary driver in establishing the concept of professionalization. Those agencies established standards and guidelines to ensure the skills and experience of individuals. The next step was to provide for education, training, and testing against those standards and guidelines. Agencies grant certification to individuals who show through testing that they have a defined level of competency. Thus, a decision maker can use certifications as criteria on which to base hiring decisions.

The education community has adopted the concepts of professionalization and certification. Technical schools, colleges, universities, and other education providers have supported the professionalization concept. They have developed programs that lead to certification. Educators have also expanded on the concept, offering an increasing number of opportunities to maintain certifications through continuing education, both classroom-based and distance learning.

 **NOTE**

For more information on forensic training programs and certification, see Chapter 15, "System Forensics Resources."

Be aware of the professionalization and certification process. It is no longer sufficient to be a self-taught technician. It is just as important to understand how to properly conduct a forensic investigation as it is to understand the technology. Further, be able to demonstrate knowledge and capability through independent sources—that is, through certification based on a strong, focused continuing educational program.

## CHAPTER SUMMARY

Speculating about where forensic analysis is going is both interesting and challenging. It is interesting because it allows comparison of the thoughts of others to your own. It is challenging because many components are changing concurrently, and it is impossible to cover all issues or estimate their overall impact.

Simply stated, forensic science is changing. The need for individuals trained in forensic techniques is growing. This need will continue to grow as it is driven by changes in technology, expanded use of new technologies, and increasing attacks as individuals and organizations continue to view information databases as profitable targets of opportunity.

## KEY CONCEPTS AND TERMS

Anti-Cybersquatting Consumer Protection Act (ACPA)

Bundled product

Cloud computing

Cluster computing

Collaborative computing

Computer Fraud and Abuse Act (CFAA)

Controlling the Assault of Non-Solicited Pornography and Marketing (CAN-SPAM) Act

Cybersquatting

Identity Theft and Assumption Deterrence Act

Moore's law

Software as a service (SaaS)

Thin client

Uniting and Strengthening America by Providing Appropriate Tools Required to Intercept and Obstruct Terrorism (U.S.A. PATRIOT) Act

Wiretap Act

**14**

Trends and Future
Directions

## CHAPTER 14 ASSESSMENT

**1.** Which of the following laws states that the number of transistors on an integrated circuit will double every two years?

A. Murphy's law
B. The Integrated Circuit law
C. Moore's law
D. The Computer Fraud and Abuse Act (CFAA)

**2.** A digital forensics specialist will deal only with desktops, laptops, and servers.

A. True
B. False

**3.** In a _____, hardware, software, maintenance, and support are provided together for a single price.

**4.** What is the name for software that a provider licenses to customers as a service on demand, through a subscription model?

A. Cluster computing
B. Software as a service (SaaS)
C. Amateur software
D. Thin client software

**5.** Which of the following involves linking computers into local area networks (LANs) to improve performance, availability, and security while reducing costs?

A. Cluster computing
B. Software as a service (SaaS)
C. Cloud computing
D. Collaborative computing

**6.** _____ is a form of on-demand Internet-based computing. Users share resources, software, and information stored on the Internet, using their own computers and other devices.

**7.** What was the first piece of federal legislation that identified computer crimes as distinct offenses?

A. Anti-Cybersquatting Consumer Protection Act (ACPA)
B. CAN-SPAM Act
C. Moore's law
D. Computer Fraud and Abuse Act (CFAA)

**8.** The _____ is a 1999 act designed to stop people from registering domain names that are trademarks that belong to other entities.

**9.** Which of the following is a 2003 act that covers unsolicited commercial e-mail messages?

A. CAN-SPAM Act
B. Anti-Cybersquatting Consumer Protection Act (ACPA)
C. Computer Fraud and Abuse Act (CFAA)
D. U.S.A. PATRIOT Act

**10.** It is no longer sufficient for a forensic investigator to be a self-taught technician. Further, a forensic specialist must be able to demonstrate knowledge and capability through independent sources. Which of the following are methods for demonstrating this knowledge and capability? (Select two.)

A. Professionalization
B. Collaborative computing
C. Certification
D. Good references

# System Forensics Resources

S YSTEM FORENSICS INVESTIGATORS HAVE MANY PLATFORMS and tools to turn
to in their work, whether strengthening a system against attack or dealing
with the consequences of a cyberattack. Add to your knowledge by doing
the following:

- Studying for forensic certifications
- Earning a college or university degree in digital forensics
- Networking with professionals in the field
- Joining user groups and online discussion groups
- Attending lectures, conferences, and events
- Reading books, articles, and Web sites

This chapter discusses resources for system forensics. It begins by looking at
some of the available system forensics training programs and certifications.
It then provides lists of system forensics resources. Finally, it supplies URLs
for forensic organizations and information sources, journals related to system
forensics, and software and hardware forensic tools.

---

### Chapter 15 Topics

This chapter covers the following topics and concepts:

- What system forensics training and certifications are available
- What system forensics user groups exist
- What online system forensics resources are available

# System Forensics Certification and Training

 **TIP**

Before enlisting in a certification program, thoroughly research the program's requirements, cost, and acceptability in your chosen area of employment. Most certification programs require continuing education credits or re-examination of candidates' skills. This can become costly.

Numerous organizations offer **certification** programs for system forensics. These programs usually test a student after completing one or more training sessions successfully. Certifying organizations range from nonprofit associations to vendor-sponsored groups. All these programs charge fees for certification. Some require candidates to take vendor- or organization-sponsored training to qualify for the certification.

Some state and federal government agencies have established their own certification programs. These programs address the skills needed to conduct computing investigations at various levels. In addition, a number of universities and other organizations offer courses in system forensics.

The following sections describe some of the most prominent system forensics training programs and certifications.

## International Association of Computer Investigative Specialists (IACIS)

The International Association of Computer Investigative Specialists (IACIS) is one of the oldest professional system forensics organizations. It was created by police officers who wanted to formalize credentials in computing investigations. Currently, IACIS limits membership. Only law enforcement personnel and government employees working as system forensics examiners may join.

IACIS conducts an annual two-week training course for qualified members. Students learn to interpret and trace e-mail, acquire evidence properly, identify operating systems, recover data, and understand encryption theory and other topics. Students must pass a written exam before continuing to the next level. Passing the exam earns the student Certified Electronic Evidence Collection Specialist (CEECS) status.

Other candidates who complete all parts of the IACIS test successfully receive Certified Forensic Computer Examiner (CFCE) certification. The CFCE process changes as technology changes. Topics include data hiding, determining file types of disguised files, and accessing password-protected files. The program might also ask a student to find evidence and draw conclusions from it. Students must demonstrate proficiency in technical tools and deductive reasoning.

For the latest information about IACIS, visit its Web site, *http://www.iacis.info.*

IACIS requires recertification every three years to demonstrate continuing work in the field of system forensics. Recertification is less intense than the original certification.

## High Tech Crime Network (HTCN)

High Tech Crime Network (HTCN) offers several levels of certification, with different requirements:

- Certified Computer Crime Investigator, Basic
- Certified Computer Crime Investigator, Advanced
- Certified Computer Forensic Technician, Basic
- Certified Computer Forensic Technician, Advanced

HTCN certification is open to anyone in a computing investigations profession.

Unlike IACIS, HTCN requires a review of all related training. This includes training in one of its approved courses, a written test for the specific certification, and a review of the candidate's work history.

The HTCN Web site, *http://www.htcn.org*, specifies requirements for the various certification levels.

## EnCase Certified Examiner (EnCE) Certification

Guidance Software, the creator of the EnCase software, sponsors the EnCase Certified Examiner (EnCE) certification program. EnCE certification is open to the public and private sectors. This certification focuses on the use and mastery of system forensics analysis using EnCase.

For more information on EnCE certification requirements, visit *http://www .guidancesoftware.com.*

## AccessData Certified Examiner (ACE)

AccessData is the creator of Forensic Toolkit (FTK) software. AccessData sponsors the AccessData Certified Examiner (ACE) certification program. ACE certification is open to the public and private sectors. This certification is specific to use and mastery of FTK. Requirements for taking the ACE exam include completing the AccessData boot camp and Windows forensic courses.

For more information on ACE certification, visit *http://www.accessdata.com.*

## Defense Cyber Investigations Training Academy (DCITA)

The Defense Cyber Investigations Training Academy (DCITA) develops and delivers computer investigation training courses for government and law enforcement organizations.

DCITA is accredited through the Council of Occupational Education (COE). DCITA is a government organization dedicated to computer investigations training, development, and delivery. It uses state-of-the-art equipment, classrooms, and technologies to train students in digital forensics techniques. DCITA's training topics include the following:

* How to perform computer search and seizure
* How to investigate network intrusions
* How to forensically analyze computer media
* How to perform basic and advanced forensic examinations

For more information on DCITA training, see *http://www.dc3.mil/dcita.*

## Other Training Programs and Certifications

Besides those already listed, other organizations offer certification programs and related training programs. The following are some of these other organizations and universities that offer certification and training:

* **Computer Technology Investigators Network (CTIN)**—*http://www.ctin.org*
* **CyberSecurity Institute**—*http://www.cybersecurityinstitute.biz*
* **DIBS USA, Inc.**—*http://www.dibsusa.com*
* **Federal Bureau of Investigation Academy**—*http://www.fbi.gov/hq/td/academy/academy.htm*
* **Federal Law Enforcement Training Center (FLETC)**—*http://www.fletc.gov*
* **Florida Association of Computer Crime Investigators, Inc.**—*http://www.facci.org*
* **Forensic Association of Computer Technologists**—*http://www.byteoutofcrime.org*
* **Global Digital Forensics**—*http://www.evestigate.com/computer%20forensic%20training.htm*
* **Henry C. Lee College of Criminal Justice and Forensic Sciences**—*http://www.newhaven.edu/9/*
* **High Tech Crime Institute**—*http://www.hightechcrimeinstitute.com*
* **High Technology Crime Investigation Association (HTCIA)**—*http://www.htcia.org*
* **Indiana Forensic Institute**—*http://ifi-indy.org*
* **Institute of Police Technology and Management**—*http://www.iptm.org*
* **International Society of Forensic Computer Examiners**—*http://www.certified-computer-examiner.com*
* **National Center for Forensic Science**—*http://www.ncfs.ucf.edu*
* **National White Collar Crime Center (NW3C)**—*http://www.nw3c.org*

- **New Technologies, Inc. (NTI)**—*http://www.forensics-intl.com*
- **Paraben**—*http://www.paraben-training.com/pcme.html*
- **Regional Computer Forensics Laboratories (RCFLs) Program**—*http://www.rcfl.gov*
- **SANS Institute**—*http://www.sans.org*
- **Technical Resource Center**—*http://trcglobal.com*
- **Utica College Economic Crime Institute**—*http://www.utica.edu/academic/ institutes/ecii/*
- **Wisconsin Association of Computer Crime Investigators**—*http://www.wacci.org*

## User Groups

A system forensics user group is a good way for you to keep up with the latest tools and trends. Two organizations to consider joining are:

- **High Technology Crime Investigation Association (HTCIA)**—HTCIA enables members to share information, experience, ideas, and knowledge with one another. Members discuss methods, processes, and techniques related to investigations and security in advanced technologies. See *http://www.htcia.org* for more information.
- **Computer Technology Investigators Network (CTIN)**—CTIN provides instruction, presentations, and monthly meetings. It enables discussions on high-tech crime, investigative strategies, and tools. CTIN includes members of federal, state, and local law enforcement. It also includes members from corporate security, educational institutions, and the computer science community. Web site access is available to members only. Membership is free. See *http://www.ctin.org* for more information.

## Online Resources

The following sections provide lists of online system forensics resources. They start with an inventory of forensic organizations and information sources. Then they catalog discussion list servers, journals, and conferences related to system forensics. Finally, they list open source and commercial software tools as well as commercial hardware tools.

### System Forensics Organizations and Information

- **American Academy of Forensic Sciences**—*http://www.aafs.org*
- **Computer Forensics, Cybercrime and Steganography Resources**—*http://forensix.org*
- **Computer Forensics World**—*http://www.computerforensicsworld.com*
- **Department of Defense Cyber Crime Center (DC3)**—*http://www.dc3.mil*
- **Department of Justice Computer Crime & Intellectual Property Section**—*http://www.cybercrime.gov*
- **Digital Forensic Research Workshop**—*http://dfrws.org*

- **Electronic Evidence Information Center**—*http://www.e-evidence.info*
- **Federal Bureau of Investigation Computer Analysis and Response Team**—*http://www.fbi.gov/hq/lab/org/cart.htm*
- **Federal Bureau of Investigation Cyber Investigations**—*http://www.fbi.gov/cyberinvest/cyberhome.htm*
- **Forensic Focus: Computer Forensics News, Information and Community**—*http://www.forensicfocus.com*
- **Forensics Wiki**—*http://www.forensicswiki.org*
- **Global Digital Forensics**—*http://www.evestigate.com/COMPUTER%20FORENSIC%20RESOURCES.htm*
- **High Tech Crime Consortium**—*http://www.hightechcrimecops.org*
- **High Technology Crime Investigation Association (HTCIA)**—*http://www.htcia.org*
- **Information Systems Security Association (ISSA)**—*https://www.issa.org*
- **International Association of Computer Investigative Specialists (IACIS)**—*http://www.iacis.com*
- **International Organization on Computer Evidence**—*http://ioce.org*
- **National Center for Forensic Science**—*http://ncfs.org*
- **National Criminal Justice Computer Laboratory and Training Center**—*http://www.search.org/programs/hightech/*
- **National Institute of Justice Electronic Crime**—*http://www.ojp.usdoj.gov/nij/topics/technology/electronic-crime/welcome.htm*
- **National Institute of Standards and Technology Computer Forensics Tool Testing (CFTT)**—*http://www.cftt.nist.gov*
- **National White Collar Crime Center**—*http://nw3c.org*

## Discussion List Servers

- **Computer Forensic Investigators Digest Listserv (CFID)**—For subscription information, see *http://www.forensicsweb.com* or e-mail jnj@infobin.org
- **Computer Forensics Tool Testing (CFTT)**—For subscription information, see *http://groups.yahoo.com/group/cftt*
- **SecurityFocus: Binary Analysis**—*binaryanalysis@securityfocus.com*
- **SecurityFocus: Forensics**—*forensics@securityfocus.com*
- **SecurityFocus: Honeypots**—*honeypots@securityfocus.com*
- **SecurityFocus: Incidents**—*incidents@securityfocus.com*
- **SecurityFocus: LogAnalysis**—*loganalysis@securityfocus.com*
- **SecurityFocus: Phishing and Botnets**—*phishing@securityfocus.com*
- **SecurityFocus: Real Cases**—*realcases@securityfocus.com*

## Forensic Journals

- *Digital Investigation*—*Digital Investigation* covers cutting-edge developments in digital forensics and incident response from around the globe. It covers new technologies, useful tools, relevant research, investigative techniques, and methods for handling security breaches. See *http://www.elsevier.com*.

- *International Journal of Digital Crime and Forensics (IJDCF)*—*IJDCF* provides state-of-the-art coverage of issues related to digital evidence. *IJDCF* addresses the use of electronic devices and software for crime prevention and investigation. It contains high-quality theoretical and empirical research articles, research reviews, case studies, book reviews, tutorials, and editorials. See *http://www.igi-global.com/ Bookstore/TitleDetails.aspx?TitleId=1112*.

- *International Journal of Digital Evidence (IJDE)*—*IJDE* is a forum for discussion of theory, research, policy, and practice in the rapidly changing field of digital evidence. *IJDE* is supported by the Economic Crime Institute (ECI) at Utica College. See *http:// ijde.org*.

- *Journal of Digital Forensic Practice*—The *Journal of Digital Forensic Practice* is a helpful resource for forensic specialists. Articles in the journal target both the public and private sectors. They present useful information, techniques, and unbiased reviews designed to assist forensic specialists in day-to-day practice. See *http:// www.tandf.co.uk/journals/titles/15567281.asp*.

- *Journal of Digital Forensics, Security and Law (JDFSL)*—*JDFSL* is a unique and innovative publication of the Association of Digital Forensics, Security and Law. The mission of *JDFSL* is to expand digital forensics research to a wide and eclectic audience. See *http://www.jdfsl.org/index.htm*.

- *Journal of Forensic Sciences*—The American Academy of Forensic Sciences produces the *Journal of Forensic Sciences*. This organization is a multidisciplinary professional organization. The academy aims to promote integrity, competency, education, research, practice, and collaboration in the forensic sciences. See *http:// www.wiley.com/bw/journal.asp?ref=0022-1198*.

- *Small Scale Digital Device Forensics Journal (SSDDFJ)*—*SSDDFJ* is an online journal for academics and practitioners. It publishes articles regarding theory, research, and practice in the rapidly changing field of small-scale digital device forensics. *SSDDFJ* is supported by the Cyber Forensics Lab (CFL) at Purdue University. See *http:// www.ssddfj.org/about.asp*.

## Conferences

- **American Academy of Forensic Sciences**—*http://www.aafs.org/default. asp?section_id=meetings&page_id=aafs_annual_meeting*
- **Association of Digital Forensics Security and Law (ADFSL) Conference on Digital Forensics, Security and Law**—*http://www.digitalforensics-conference.org*

- **Black Hat Briefings & Training**—*http://www.blackhat.com/html/bh-link/briefings.html*
- **ChicagoCon—White Hats Come Together in Defense of the Digital Frontier**—*http://www.chicagocon.com*
- **Computer and Enterprise Investigations Conference (CEIC)**—*http://www.ceicconference.com*
- **Department of Defense Cyber Crime Conference**—*http://www.dodcybercrime.com*
- **DFRWS (Digital Forensics Research Conference)**—*http://www.dfrws.org*
- **eDiscovery Summit**—*http://www.ediscoverysummit.org*
- **Forum of Incident Response and Security Teams (FIRST) Conference**—*http://www.first.org/conference*
- **HTCIA International Training Conference and Expo**—*http://www.htcia.org/index.shtml*
- **IACIS Computer Forensic Training Event**—*http://www.cops.org/training*
- **Mobile Forensics World Training Conference**—*http://www.MobileForensicsWorld.org*
- **Open Source Software for Computer and Network Forensics**—*http://conferenze.dei.polimi.it/ossconf/index.php*
- **Regional Computer Forensics Group Conference (RCFG)**—*http://www.rcfg.org*
- **SANS Computer Forensics**—*http://computer-forensics.sans.org/events/*
- **SANSFIRE (SANS Forensics, Investigations, Response, Education)**—*https://www.sans.org/sansfire-2010/*
- **Systematic Approaches to Digital Forensic Engineering (SADFE)**—*http://conf.ncku.edu.tw/sadfe/*
- **Techno Forensics Conference**—*http://www.techsec.com*
- **Techno Security Conference**—*http://www.techsec.com*

## Forensic Tools

Forensic tools can be hardware or software. Software forensics tools can be either open source or commercial. Commercial forensic software ranges in price. Some products cost very little, and others are so costly that only large companies can afford them.

The following sections provide Web addresses for a number of tools. Mares and Company (*http://www.dmares.com/maresware/linksto_forensic_tools.htm*) lists dozens of system forensics tools, both commercial and open source.

### Open Source Software Tools

- **Autopsy Forensic Browser**—Autopsy Forensic Browser is a graphical interface to the command-line digital investigation tools in The Sleuth Kit (TSK). Together, these tools enable investigation of the file system and volumes of a computer. See *http://www.sleuthkit.org/autopsy.*

- **BitPim**—BitPim allows an investigator to view and manipulate data on many mobile phones. See *http://www.bitpim.org.*
- **The Sleuth Kit (TSK)**—TSK is a tool that runs on Windows and UNIX systems, such as Linux, OS X, Cygwin, FreeBSD, OpenBSD, and Solaris. Use it to analyze NTFS, FAT, HFS+, Ext2, Ext3, UFS1, and UFS2 file systems and several volume system types. See *http://www.sleuthkit.org.*

Open source tools are available online at a number of sites. For more information on open source forensic tools and links to open source tools, see the site Open Source Digital Forensics, at *http://www.opensourceforensics.org/index.html.* Also, see the Open Source Computer Forensics Manual, at *http://sourceforge.net/projects/oscfmanual/.*

## Commercial Software Tools and Vendors

- **AccuBurn**—R-AccuBurn-R produces exact copies of disks that have been imaged using CD/DVD Inspector. It supports all types and formats of disks. See *http:// www.infinadyne.com.*
- **ASR Data Acquisition & Analysis**—ASR Data Acquisition & Analysis offers a variety of software: SMART Linux, SMART for Linux, SmartMount (Windows/Linux/ Macintosh), Grok-NTFS (Windows/Linux/Macintosh), and Grok-LNK (Windows/ Linux/Macintosh). These products are customized for forensic work, integrated acquisition, authentication, and analysis. See *http://asrdata.com.*
- **BlackBag Technologies, Inc.**—BlackBag offers several forensic software products, including Mobilyze, SoftBlock, Macintosh Forensic Suite, and MacQuisition CF. Below are some product details (for even more information on Blackbag's tools, see *http:// www.blackbagtech.com*):
  - **Mobilyze** was designed to forensically analyze iPhone, iPod Touch, and iPad devices. The product is capable of analyzing multiple devices simultaneously, easing the time and effort of consolidating findings into one comprehensive report.
  - **SoftBlock** is kernel-based, write-blocking software for Macs that identifies devices when they connect. It can mount a device in a forensically sound read-only manner. It can also mount a device in a conventional read/write configuration. SoftBlock offers flexibility, security, and speed in previewing and analyzing evidence across a number of devices.
  - **Macintosh Forensic Suite** is a unique set of 19 tools that gives forensic examiners a flexible, open analysis environment. The suite is specifically designed for Mac OS X versions 10.1 and higher. The applications speed an examiner's analysis time while ensuring a thorough investigation of the drive.
  - **MacQuisition CF** is an external bootable forensic acquisition tool that safely and easily images Mac drives using the suspect system. MacQuisition provides an intuitive user interface. The tool automatically generates hashes.

**15**

**System Forensics Resources**

- **ComputerCOP**—ComputerCOP has developed two unique forensic tools: Professional and Forensic Examiner. For information on both tools, see *http://computercop.com*:
  - **ComputerCOP Professional** is an automated search tool that allows an examiner to immediately find electronic evidence for trial. Many supervision officers use it to monitor probationers' and parolees' computer use.
  - **ComputerCOP Forensic Examiner** is a field forensic solution. It acts as both an automated forensic search software and a simple-to-connect write blocker.
- **Darik's Boot and Nuke (DBAN)**—DBAN is a self-contained boot disk that securely wipes the hard disks of most computers. DBAN automatically and completely deletes the contents of any hard disk that it can detect. It is a useful utility for bulk or emergency data destruction. See *http://www.dban.sourceforge.net*.
- **DataLifter**—DataLifter is a suite of products designed to assist with computer forensics. DataLifter Forensicware Solution package contains investigative tools and comes in two versions: DataLifter and DataLifter.Net Bonus Tools. Two additional packages, DataLifter Digital Companion and DataLifter File Extractor Pro, are add-ons or major updates to tools already included with DataLifter or DataLifter.Net Bonus Tools. See *http://www.datalifter.com/products.htm*.
- **Digital Detective**—Digital Detective offers Blade, HstEx, and NetAnalysis. For more information on all these tools, see *http://www.digital-detective.co.uk*:
  - **Blade** is a Windows-based data recovery solution. It supports plug-ins that give it advanced data recovery and analysis capabilities.
  - **HstEx** is a Windows-based data recovery solution. It is designed to recover browser artifacts and Internet history. HstEx supports all major forensic image formats.
  - **NetAnalysis** is software for the recovery and analysis of Internet browser artifacts.
- **Digital Intelligence**—Digital Intelligence, Inc., offers forensic hardware and software. Its software products include DRIVESPY, IMAGE, PART, PDBlock, and PDWipe. For information on all these products, see *http://www.digitalintelligence.com*:
  - **DRIVESPY** processes large hard drives, FAT12/16/16x/32/32x partitions, hidden DOS partitions, and non-DOS partitions. It investigates long filenames, file dates, erased files, slack space, and unallocated space.
  - **IMAGE** is a standalone utility that generates physical images of floppy disks. The program is capable of generating highly compressed images for forensic analysis.
  - **PART** is a partition manager. It lists summary information about all the partitions on a hard disk. It also switches bootable partitions and even hides and unhides DOS partitions.
  - **PDBlock** is a write blocker. It provides customary write protection from Interrupt 13 disk access methods.
  - **PDWipe** is a standalone utility capable of quickly wiping large hard drives.

- **Directory Snoop**—This data recovery tool is a cluster-level search tool. It allows Windows users to search FAT and NTFS-formatted disk drives to see what data may be hiding. Directory Snoop can recover deleted files and permanently erase sensitive files. See *http://www.briggsoft.com/dsnoop.htm*.

- **dtSearch**—The dtSearch product line can instantly search terabytes of text across a desktop, network, Internet, or intranet site. See *http://dtsearch.com*.

- **e-fense**—e-fense produces both Helix3 and Live Response. For more information on both of these products, see *http://www.e-fense.com*:

  - **Helix3 Enterprise (H3E)** provides incident response, computer forensics, and e-discovery in one interface. The Helix3 Pro edition software is available to e-fense forum members only.

  - **Live Response** allows a forensic examiner to acquire volatile data, such as Internet history, screen capture, and memory. The examiner can move this data from a suspect system onto a USB thumb drive.

- **Forensic Toolkit (FTK)**—This court-validated digital investigations platform delivers computer forensics analysis, decryption, and password cracking. FTK 3 is fast and provides enterprise-class scalability. See *http://www.accessdata.com/forensictoolkit.html*.

- **Foundstone**—Foundstone is a source for a number of free forensic tools. PatchIt is a file byte-patching utility. DumpAutoComplete is an application that searches for the default Firefox profile of the user who runs the tool and dumps the AutoComplete cache in XML format to standard output. Galleta is an Internet Explorer cookie forensic analysis tool. BinText can extract text from any kind of file and includes the ability to find plain ASCII text, Unicode text, and resource strings. Vision shows all open TCP and UDP ports and maps them to the owning process or application. Pasco is an Internet Explorer activity forensic analysis tool. NTLast is a security audit tool for Windows NT. Rifiuti is a Recycle Bin forensic analysis tool. See *http://www.foundstone.com/us/resources-overview.asp*.

- **Guidance Software**—Guidance Software offers a number of EnCase products, including Enterprise, eDiscovery, Forensic, and Portable. For more information on all these products, see *http://www.guidancesoftware.com*:

  - **EnCase Enterprise** allows the deepest level of visibility into laptops, desktops, file servers, and e-mail servers. Use it to investigate human resources matters or to quickly determine the root cause of suspicious network activity.

  - **EnCase eDiscovery** performs search, collection, preservation, and processing in a forensically sound manner. It collects and processes only potentially relevant data.

  - **EnCase Forensic** gives you the ability to image a drive and preserve it in a forensically sound manner. The EnCase evidence file format is a digital evidence container validated and approved by courts worldwide. EnCase Forensic also contains a full suite of analysis, bookmarking, and reporting features.

  - **EnCase Portable** is a pocket-sized USB data collection and triage solution. Even non-experts can use EnCase Portable so that specialists can focus on case management, processing, detailed analysis, and reporting.

- **ILookPI**—ILookPI is an advanced digital evidence toolset. It includes imaging software and also enables virus/Trojan search and identification. Its analysis features are designed to reduce investigative time while providing focus and clarity. See *http://www.perlustro.com*.

- **L0phtCrack**—L0phtCrack is password auditing and recovery software offered in three versions: L0phtCrack Professional, Administrator, and Consultant. See *http://www.l0phtcrack.com*.

- **M-Sweep**—This tool can repeatedly overwrite ambient computer data storage areas. See *http://www.forensics-intl.com/msweep.html*.

- **New Technologies, Inc. (NTI)**—NTI offers a number of tools and software suites, including AnaDisk, Filter_G, GFE Stealth, SafeBack, TextSearch Plus, and CopyQM Plus. For more information on NTI products, see *http://www.forensics-intl.com/tools.html*:

  - **AnaDisk** software identifies data storage anomalies on floppy diskettes and generic hardware in the form of floppy disk controllers. BIOS are needed when using this software. AnaDisk works at a very low level and makes maximum use of the floppy diskette hardware. The software also has limited search capabilities, and you can use it to copy abnormal diskettes. Apply it as well to write data at a physical sector level and to format diskettes using any number of combinations.

  - **Filter_G** is a forensic English grammar filter utility used to quickly make sense of nonsense in the analysis of ambient data sources, e.g., Windows swap/page files, file slack, and data associated with erased files. Filter_G is a patented fuzzy logic filter that quickly identifies patterns of English language grammar in ambient data files. Use it as a sampling tool. It is particularly useful for evaluating Windows swap/page files.

  - **GFE Stealth**, NTI's forensic graphics image file extractor, is a computer forensics software tool which was designed to automatically extract exact copies of graphics file images from ambient data sources and from SafeBack bit stream image backup files.

  - **SafeBack** creates mirror-image (bit-stream) backup files of hard disks or makes a mirror-image copy of an entire hard disk drive or partition.

  - **TextSearch Plus** is software that quickly searches hard disk drives, zip disks, and floppy diskettes for keywords or specific patterns of text. It operates at either a logical or physical level at the user's option.

  - **CopyQM Plus** essentially turns a PC into a disk duplicator. In a single pass, it formats, copies, and verifies a disk. This capability is useful for system forensics specialists who need to preconfigure CDs for specific uses and duplicate them.

- **Norton Ghost**—Norton Ghost creates full system and file backups, including settings, applications, and files. It also restores from system failures and enables convenient, secure offsite backups. See *http://www.symantec.com/norton/ghost*.

- **Notes the Ripper**—This computer forensic and electronic discovery tool quickly and safely analyzes and extracts data from Lotus Notes NSF files. See *http://www .mykeytech.com*.

- **Ontrack**—Ontrack provides slack space and data recovery tools. See *http:// www.ontrackdatarecovery.com/data-recovery-software.*

- **Paraben Forensic Tools**—Paraben Forensic Tools produces a number of tools, including Device Seizure and P2 Commander. For more information on these tools, see *http://paraben.com/catalog/*:
  - **Device Seizure** is a forensic investigation tool for handheld devices.
  - **P2 Commander** is a comprehensive digital forensic tool. It examines e-mail and chat logs. Use it as well for file sorting and Internet file analysis.

- **pdd**—Pdd (Palm dd) is a Windows-based tool for memory imaging and forensic acquisition of data from the Palm OS family of PDAs. Pdd preserves the crime scene by obtaining a bit-by-bit image or snapshot of the Palm device's memory contents. See *http://www.grandideastudio.com/portfolio/pdd.*

- **Process Monitor**—Process Monitor is an advanced monitoring tool for Windows that shows real-time file system, registry, and process/thread activity. It combines the features of two legacy utilities, Filemon and Regmon, and adds an extensive list of enhancements. See *http://technet.microsoft.com/en-us/sysinternals/bb896645.aspx.*

- **SnapBack Exact**—This server-based backup and restore program for Windows servers features full open file management, remote administration, and backup scheduling. It copies an actual byte-by-byte copy of a server hard drive to tape while the backup is running and files are open and being modified. See *http://www .snapback.com.*

- **Tech Assist, Inc. (Tools That Work)**—Tech Assist offers a variety of forensic software products, including BringBack, ByteBack, and Omniquad Detective. For information on all these tools, visit the Web at *http://www.toolsthatwork.com.*
  - **BringBack** enables easy-to-use and highly successful file recovery for Windows and Linux operating systems. It also works on digital images stored on memory cards and more.
  - **ByteBack Data Recovery Investigative Suite** allows forensic examiners to recover data, repair logical damage, and verify the integrity of an investigation.
  - **Omniquad Detective** is a Windows-driven search-and-report utility. It can make searching for images and keywords simple and fast.

- **Technology Pathways Tools**—Technology Pathways offers the ProDiscover Family of tools, including Forensics and Incident Response. For more information on these tools, see *http://www.techpathways.com*:
  - **ProDiscover Forensics** is a Windows application for the collection, analysis, management, and reporting of evidence. It supports all Windows-based file systems in addition to file systems such as Sun Solaris UFS and Linux Ext 2/3.
  - **ProDiscover Incident Response** turns the ProDiscover Forensics workstation product into a client/server application. It allows disk preview, imaging, and analysis over any TCP/IP network. It also allows live disk preview, imaging, and analysis. In addition, it includes advanced tools for incident response to cyberattacks.

- **ThumbsDisplay**—This tool examines and reports on the contents of Thumbs.db files used by Windows. ThumbsDisplay prints a full-page version of thumbnail images without any other graphics programs being required. See *http://www.infinadyne.com/ forensicsoftware.html*.

- **ThumbsPlus**—This tool provides database and thumbnail organization, image viewing and editing, and folder and file organization. See *http://www.cerious.com/ thumbnails.shtml*.

- **Visual TimeAnalyzer**—Visual TimeAnalyzer automatically tracks all computer use and activities, including working time and pauses. It presents detailed, richly illustrated reports. See *http://www.neuber.com/timeanalyzer/*.

- **X-Ways Software Technology AG**—X-Ways produces a number of products, including Evidor, X-Ways Forensics, and WinHex. For more information on all these products, see *http://www.x-ways.net*:

  - **Evidor** searches text on hard disks and retrieves the context of keyword occurrences on computer media. It examines the entire allocated space as well as currently unallocated space and slack space. That means it even finds data from files that have been deleted if the files still exist physically.

  - **X-Ways Forensics**—X-Ways Forensics is an advanced work environment for system forensics examiners. It's integrated with the WinHex hex and disk editor.

  - **WinHex** is a system forensics, data recovery, and IT security tool that includes a hex editor, disk editor, and RAM editor.

- **Zdziarski's forensic guide for the iPhone**—Jonathan Zdziarski's forensic technique for iPhones provides a way to make a bit-by-bit copy of the original media. By analyzing the image this method provides, discover a wealth of information that other tools can't provide. Site access is freely available to full-time, active-duty law enforcement or military personnel tasked with mobile forensic imaging as part of their duties. See *http://www.iphoneinsecurity.com*.

## Commercial Hardware Tools and Vendors

- **DIBS USA, Inc.**—DIBS USA, Inc., produces a range of computer forensics hardware and software. Its products are specifically designed to copy, analyze, and present computer data in a forensically sound manner. DIBS Mobile Forensic Workstation is for on-site collection and analysis of suspect computer data. DIBS Advanced Forensic Workstation is for laboratory-based collection and analysis of suspect computer data. DIBS Rapid Action Imaging Device (RAID) enables fast copying of suspect hard drives. See *http://www.dibsusa.com*.

- **Forensic Computers, Inc.**—Forensic Computers, Inc., offers forensic workstations, hardware, accessories, and software. It sells write-protection kits, forensic bridges, adaptors, hardware accelerators, hard disk drive erasure tools, and more. See *http:// www.forensic-computers.com/index.php*.

- **ForensicPC.com**—ForensicPC.com sells forensic workstations and forensic computer systems, including laboratory and portable stations. It also offers forensic acquisition devices, drive bays, tools, and kits. In addition, if offers write blockers and forensic software. See *http://www.forensicpc.com.*

- **FRED (Forensic Recovery of Evidence Device)**—Digital Intelligence, Inc., produces devices, write blockers, networks, and the FRED family of forensic workstations. FRED workstations are integrated forensic processing platforms available in mobile, stationary, and laboratory configurations. These systems are designed for both the acquisition and examination of computer evidence. Digital Intelligence, Inc., products enable you to easily duplicate evidence directly from hard drives and other media in a forensically sound manner. See *http://www.digitalintelligence.com.*

- **Intelligent Computer Solutions**—Intelligent Computer Solutions produces a wide variety of forensic products. Image MASSter Solo-4 is a high-speed, handheld hard drive duplication device. RoadMASSter-3 is a portable forensic station. Intelligent Computer Solutions also produces multi-drive duplicators, write protectors, and hard drive encryption products. See *http://www.ics-iq.com.*

- **Kazeon**—Kazeon offers both software forensics products and hardware devices. The Information Server product line creates a content and metadata index, applies classification rules and policies, and enables automated or manual searching, reporting, and action on resulting data sets. Information Center allows corporations with distributed information to create groups of clusters to deliver administrators a data management capability across all Information Server installations. Information Center also allows a unified search and unified reporting capability across clusters. See *http://www.kazeon.com.*

- **Logicube**—Logicube provides hard drive duplication and computer forensics systems. Logicube's hard drive cloning systems offer high-speed solutions for copying hard drives, drive formatting, data recovery, and disaster recovery. Logicube's products include Echo Plus, SuperSonix, OmniClone Xi series, OmniSCSI, and OmniSAS hard drive duplicators. See *http://www.logicube.com.*

- **MOBILedit**—MOBILedit! Forensic is a mobile phone investigation tool. It extracts all content from a device and generates a forensic report ready for courtroom presentation. See *http://www.mobiledit.com.*

- **MyKey Technology, Inc.**—MyKey Technology, Inc., produces NoWrite FPU, a FireWire write blocker. It also produces NoWrite FlashBlock II, a write-blocker add-on for compact flash and digital media. See *http://www.mykeytech.com.*

- **Paraben Forensic Tools**—In addition to forensic software, Paraben provides cell phone cable kits, hard drive lockdown devices, signal blocking bags, and other forensic hardware to support investigations. See *http://paraben.com/catalog/.*

- **Secure Kit for Forensics**—This software and hardware solution provides law enforcement, corporate security, and forensic consultants with logical data extraction of the content stored in a mobile phone. Susteen also provides Secure View Mobile, a standalone mobile forensics solution to extract mobile phone data at the touch of a button. See *http://www.susteen.com.*

- **UFED (Universal Forensic Extraction Device) System**—CelleBrite UFED is a stand-alone device for use in the field as well as in the forensics labs. UFED can extract vital data, such as phonebook, pictures, videos, text messages, and call logs from 2,500 models of handsets sold worldwide. UFED system supports almost all mobile phones on the market today, including smartphones and PDA devices. UFED easily stores hundreds of phonebooks and content items onto an SD card or USB flash drive. Extractions can then be brought back to the forensics lab for review and verification using the reporting/analysis tool. See *http://www.cellebrite.com.*

- **WiebeTech**—WiebeTech produces a variety of forensic products. USB WriteBlocker is for in-line USB write-blocking. RTX400-QR is a RAID in a portable enclosure. Forensic UltraDock is a quad-interface, write-blocking imager. Forensic Notebook DriveDock provides write-block access to 2.5-inch notebook drives via FireWire. HotPlug lets a forensic specialist move a computer to battery power and transport it elsewhere without ever shutting it down. WiebeTech also offers forensic field kits. See *http://www.wiebetech.com.*

## CHAPTER SUMMARY

This chapter discusses a variety of system forensics resources. It begins by discussing training and certifications available in the field of system forensics. It also lists other system forensics resources, such as user groups, conferences, and list servers. It provides URLs for forensic organizations and information sources, journals related to system forensics, and software and hardware forensics tools.

## KEY CONCEPTS AND TERMS

**Certification**

## CHAPTER 15 ASSESSMENT

**1.** A number of free system forensics certification programs are available.

A. True

B. False

**2.** EnCE stands for _____.

**3.** Which of the following is a government organization dedicated to computer investigations training, development, and delivery?

A. IACIS

B. HTCN

C. EnCE

D. DCITA

**4.** Being a member of a _____ is a good way for a forensic specialist to keep up with the latest tools and trends.

**5.** The field of system forensics is so young that not many resources exist.

A. True

B. False

# Answer Key

**CHAPTER 1** System Forensics Fundamentals

1. F   2. A   3. Clues   4. B   5. A, B, and D   6. C   7. B   8. A
9. Disk forensics   10. Live system forensics   11. Software forensics

**CHAPTER 2** Overview of Computer Crime

1. DoS/DDoS attacks   2. A and C   3. B   4. Hacking   5. C and D   6. A
7. A   8. B   9. C   10. B   11. D   12. Federal crimes

**CHAPTER 3** Challenges of System Forensics

1. C   2. A, C, and D   3. A   4. Data analysis plan   5. D   6. C
7. Locard's exchange principle   8. A   9. B   10. B, C, and D

**CHAPTER 4** Forensics Methods and Labs

1. Forensically sound   2. C   3. B   4. Business case   5. B   6. B
7. A, B, and C   8. C   9. B, C, and E   10. B   11. A   12. B and C
13. 150   14. C   15. B

**CHAPTER 5** System Forensics Technologies

1. Department of Defense (DoD)   2. D   3. B   4. B   5. A   6. Fuzzy logic tool
7. B   8. B   9. B   10. EnCase   11. C   12. C   13. D   14. A   15. C

**CHAPTER 6** Controlling a Forensic Investigation

1. D   2. Live analysis school of thought   3. B   4. B   5. B   6. A
7. A, C, and D   8. B   9. C   10. Unallocated space   11. Fourth   12. A

**CHAPTER 7** Collecting, Seizing, and Protecting Evidence

1. A   2. C   3. B   4. Five rules of evidence   5. B   6. D   7. B
8. A, C, and D   9. B, D, and E   10. A   11. Chain of custody   12. B

**CHAPTER 8** Understanding Information-Hiding Techniques

1. Covert channel   2. ADS   3. A   4. Rootkit   5. B   6. C   7. A   8. A
9. B   10. D   11. B, C, and E   12. B   13. B   14. Extraction   15. A, D, and F

**CHAPTER 9** Recovering Data

1. A   2. Hard disk or Hard drive or Hard disk drive   3. B   4. C and D
5. A   6. B   7. A   8. D   9. A   10. B   11. Mirroring   12. A

**CHAPTER 10** Investigating and Scrutinizing E-mail

1. Mail server  2. An e-mail client  3. A, B, and E  4. B  5. C  6. A  7. B
8. "Received:"  9. A, C, and D  10. A  11. Spam  12. C

**CHAPTER 11** Performing Network Analysis

1. Network  2. B  3. D  4. A  5. C
6. An IDS or An intrusion detection system  7. B  8. B  9. B and D
10. B  11. Router  12. OSI reference model or Open Systems Interconnection reference model

**CHAPTER 12** Searching Memory in Real Time with Live System Forensics

1. Live system forensics  2. Dead system analysis  3. B  4. A, C, and D
5. C  6. D  7. B, C, and D  8. Consistency  9. A and C
10. Volatile memory analysis

**CHAPTER 13** Incident and Intrusion Response

1. B  2. Minimize  3. C  4. A  5. A  6. B  7. A  8. Incident response plan
9. B  10. US-CERT  11. Direct, Indirect

**CHAPTER 14** Trends and Future Directions

1. C  2. B  3. Bundled product  4. B  5. A  6. Cloud computing
7. D  8. Anti-Cybersquatting Consumer Protection Act or ACPA
9. A  10. A and C

**CHAPTER 15** System Forensics Resources

1. B  2. EnCase Certified Examiner  3. D  4. User group  5. B

# Standard Acronyms

| | |
|---|---|
| **3DES** | triple data encryption standard |
| **ACD** | automatic call distributor |
| **AES** | Advanced Encryption Standard |
| **ANSI** | American National Standards Institute |
| **AP** | access point |
| **API** | application programming interface |
| **B2B** | business to business |
| **B2C** | business to consumer |
| **BBB** | Better Business Bureau |
| **BCP** | business continuity planning |
| **C2C** | consumer to consumer |
| **CA** | certificate authority |
| **CAP** | Certification and Accreditation Professional |
| **CAUCE** | Coalition Against Unsolicited Commercial Email |
| **CCC** | CERT Coordination Center |
| **CCNA** | Cisco Certified Network Associate |
| **CERT** | Computer Emergency Response Team |
| **CFE** | Certified Fraud Examiner |
| **CISA** | Certified Information Systems Auditor |
| **CISM** | Certified Information Security Manager |
| **CISSP** | Certified Information System Security Professional |
| **CMIP** | common management information protocol |
| **COPPA** | Children's Online Privacy Protection |
| **CRC** | cyclic redundancy check |
| **CSI** | Computer Security Institute |
| **CTI** | Computer Telephony Integration |
| **DBMS** | database management system |
| **DDoS** | distributed denial of service |
| **DES** | Data Encryption Standard |
| **DMZ** | demilitarized zone |
| **DoS** | denial of service |
| **DPI** | deep packet inspection |
| **DRP** | disaster recovery plan |
| **DSL** | digital subscriber line |
| **DSS** | Digital Signature Standard |
| **DSU** | data service unit |
| **EDI** | Electronic Data Interchange |
| **EIDE** | Enhanced IDE |
| **FACTA** | Fair and Accurate Credit Transactions Act |
| **FAR** | false acceptance rate |
| **FBI** | Federal Bureau of Investigation |
| **FDIC** | Federal Deposit Insurance Corporation |
| **FEP** | front-end processor |
| **FRCP** | Federal Rules of Civil Procedure |
| **FRR** | false rejection rate |
| **FTC** | Federal Trade Commission |
| **FTP** | file transfer protocol |
| **GIAC** | Global Information Assurance Certification |
| **GLBA** | Gramm-Leach-Bliley Act |
| **HIDS** | host-based intrusion detection system |
| **HIPAA** | Health Insurance Portability and Accountability Act |
| **HIPS** | host-based intrusion prevention system |
| **HTTP** | hypertext transfer protocol |
| **HTTPS** | HTTP over Secure Socket Layer |
| **HTML** | hypertext markup language |
| **IAB** | Internet Activities Board |
| **IDEA** | International Data Encryption Algorithm |
| **IDPS** | intrusion detection and prevention |
| **IDS** | intrusion detection system |

| | |
|---|---|
| **IEEE** | Institute of Electrical and Electronics Engineers |
| **IETF** | Internet Engineering Task Force |
| **InfoSec** | information security |
| **IPS** | intrusion prevention system |
| **IPSec** | IP Security |
| **IPv4** | Internet protocol version 4 |
| **IPv6** | Internet protocol version 6 |
| **IRS** | Internal Revenue Service |
| **(ISC)²** | International Information System Security Certification Consortium |
| **ISO** | International Organization for Standardization |
| **ISP** | Internet service provider |
| **ISS** | Internet security systems |
| **ITRC** | Identity Theft Resource Center |
| **IVR** | interactive voice response |
| **LAN** | local area network |
| **MAN** | metropolitan area network |
| **MD5** | Message Digest 5 |
| **modem** | modulator demodulator |
| **NFIC** | National Fraud Information Center |
| **NIDS** | network intrusion detection system |
| **NIPS** | network intrusion prevention system |
| **NIST** | National Institute of Standards and Technology |
| **NMS** | network management system |
| **OS** | operating system |
| **OSI** | open system interconnection |
| **PBX** | private branch exchange |
| **PCI** | Payment Card Industry |
| **PGP** | Pretty Good Privacy |
| **PKI** | public-key infrastructure |
| **RAID** | redundant array of independent disks |
| **RFC** | Request for Comments |
| **RSA** | Rivest, Shamir, and Adleman (algorithm) |

| | |
|---|---|
| **SAN** | storage area network |
| **SANCP** | Security Analyst Network Connection Profiler |
| **SANS** | SysAdmin, Audit, Network, Security |
| **SAP** | service access point |
| **SCSI** | small computer system interface |
| **SET** | Secure electronic transaction |
| **SGC** | server-gated cryptography |
| **SHA** | Secure Hash Algorithm |
| **S-HTTP** | secure HTTP |
| **SLA** | service level agreement |
| **SMFA** | specific management functional area |
| **SNMP** | simple network management protocol |
| **SOX** | Sarbanes-Oxley Act of 2002 (also Sarbox) |
| **SSA** | Social Security Administration |
| **SSCP** | Systems Security Certified Practitioner |
| **SSL** | Secure Socket Layer |
| **SSO** | single system sign-on |
| **STP** | shielded twisted cable |
| **TCP/IP** | Transmission Control Protocol/Internet Protocol |
| **TCSEC** | Trusted Computer System Evaluation Criteria |
| **TFTP** | Trivial File Transfer Protocol |
| **TNI** | Trusted Network Interpretation |
| **UDP** | User Datagram Protocol |
| **UPS** | uninterruptible power supply |
| **UTP** | unshielded twisted cable |
| **VLAN** | virtual local area network |
| **VOIP** | Voice over Internet Protocol |
| **VPN** | virtual private network |
| **WAN** | wide area network |
| **WLAN** | wireless local area network |
| **WNIC** | wireless network interface card |
| **W3C** | World Wide Web Consortium |
| **WWW** | World Wide Web |

# Glossary of Key Terms

**802.11 standards** | A set of wireless local area network (LAN) standards for computer communication in the 2.4, 3.6, and 5 GHz frequency bands.

## A

**Adverse event** | An event with negative consequences, such a system crash, network packet floods, unauthorized use of system privileges, unauthorized access to sensitive data, and execution of malicious code that destroys data.

**Algorithm** | A step-by-step procedure that a computer follows to solve a problem.

**Alternate data streams (ADS)** | In Microsoft's NTFS (NT File System), metadata associated with a file system object. ADS can be used to hide data.

**Ambient computer data** | Data stored in the Windows swap file, unallocated space, and file slack. It includes e-mail fragments, word processing fragments, directory tree snapshots, and potentially almost anything that has occurred on the subject computer. Ambient computer data can be a valuable source of computer evidence. Also known as residual data.

**American Society of Crime Laboratory Directors (ASCLD)** | An organization that provides guidelines for managing a forensics lab. ASCLD also certifies computer forensics labs.

**Anonymizer** | An e-mail server that strips identifying information from an e-mail message before forwarding it with the mailing computer's IP address.

**Anonymous remailing** | Sending an e-mail message to an anonymizer to strip identifying information from an e-mail message before forwarding it with the mailing computer's IP address.

**Anti-Cybersquatting Consumer Protection Act (ACPA)** | A 1999 act designed to stop people from registering domain names that are trademarks that belong to other entities.

**Anti-forensics** | Attempts to adversely affect the existence, amount, and quality of evidence from a crime scene or to make the analysis and examination of evidence difficult or impossible to conduct.

**Artifact** | Data that an attacker leaves behind when compromising a system—such as code fragments, trojaned programs, running processes, or sniffer log files.

## B

**Backdoor** | A difficult-to-detect way to bypass normal authentication, gain remote access to a computer, obtain access to plaintext, and so on. A rootkit may install a backdoor to enable an attacker to access the system, regardless of changes to system accounts or other access control techniques.

**Backup** | A copy of data that can be used to restore data if it is lost or corrupted.

**Backup server** | A server that is used to manage the policies, schedules, media catalogs, and indexes associated with the systems it is configured to back up.

**Backup window** | The period of time when backups can be run.

**Batch file** | A text file that contains a series of commands intended to be executed by the command interpreter. When a batch file is run, another program reads the file and executes its commands.

**Bit stream backup** | A backup that involves the copying of every bit of data on a computer hard disk drive or another type of storage media. A bit stream backup exactly replicates all sectors on the storage device, so all files and ambient data storage areas are copied. Bit stream backups are sometimes referred to as *mirror image backups* or *evidence-grade backups*, and they differ substantially from standard file backups and network server backups. Making a bit stream backup is referred to as *imaging*.

**Black-box system forensic software tools** | Tools that are used to check that the output of a program is as expected, given certain inputs. These tools do not actually examine the program being executed.

**Block-level incremental backup** | A backup of only the blocks that have changed since the last backup.

**Bluetooth** | A popular wireless protocol for connecting devices over short distances. The most popular use of Bluetooth is to create PANs of devices that communicate with a computer or device.

**Boot process** | A process that starts an operating system when the user turns on a computer system.

**Botnet** | A collection of software robots that create and send out spam extremely quickly.

**Bundled product** | Hardware, software, maintenance, and support provided together for a single price.

**Business case** | A reasoned proposal for making a change, such as a plan that justifies acquiring newer and better resources to investigate computer forensics cases.

## C

**Campus area network (CAN)** | A network that is larger than a LAN but generally smaller than a MAN. CANs are useful to connect the LANs across multiple buildings that are all in fairly close proximity to one another.

**Carrier file** | The data that is used to hide secret data in steganography. Today, multimedia files, such as pictures or sound, are most commonly used as carrier messages to hide secret data. A carrier file is also called a *cover file* or *carrier message.*

**Certification** | A designation that recognizes a person's qualification to perform a job or task. Many certifications are earned based on experience and passing an exam. Professional bodies provide certification to safeguard the public interest.

**Chain of custody** | Continuity of evidence that makes it possible to account for all that has happened to evidence between its original collection and its appearance in court, preferably unaltered.

**Chief information officer (CIO)** | An executive who heads information technology (IT) in an organization.

**Chief technology officer (CTO)** | An executive who is focused on scientific and technical issues in an organization. A CTO is responsible for the transformation of capital—whether monetary, intellectual, or political—into technology.

**Clean room** | An environment that has a controlled level of contamination, such as dust, microbes, and other particles. The level of contamination is specified by the number of particles per cubic meter at a specified particle size. Data recovery experts use a clean room to protect media while making repairs to salvage the data.

**Cloud computing** | Using the Internet to allow people to access massively scalable technology-enabled services. Cloud computing includes searching for flights online or using Facebook, neither of which qualify as SaaS.

**Cluster** | A fixed-length block of data—one to 128 sectors—in which DOS- and Windows-based computers store files. Clusters are made up of blocks of sectors.

**Cluster computing** | Linking computers into local area networks (LANs) to improve performance and availability while reducing costs.

**Collaborative computing** | A technique for analyzing problems and developing solutions using the combined efforts of a number of individuals focused on a particular issue.

**Compression** | The process of encoding information with fewer bits than the unencoded information would use.

**Computer Forensics Tool Testing (CFTT)** | A project of the National Institute of Standards and Technology (NIST) that focuses on developing standards to ensure reliable results during forensic investigations. The project seeks to help forensic tool providers improve their products, keep the justice system informed, and make information available to government agencies and other organizations.

**Computer Fraud and Abuse Act (CFAA)** | Passed in 1984, the first piece of federal legislation that identified computer crimes as distinct offenses. The CFAA criminalizes the act of causing certain types of damage to a protected computer.

**Computer-generated information** | Records that are produced by a computing device. This information includes logs, content analysis, packet captures, reconstructed artifacts, and so on. The admissibility of computer-generated records depends on their authenticity.

**Computer security incident** | A violation or an imminent threat of violation of computer security policies, acceptable use policies, or standard security practices.

**Configuration management** | A process in which an organization records all updates it makes to its workstations.

**Connection** | Two Internet Protocol (IP) addresses that are communicating with each other, as well as two port numbers that identify the protocol or service.

**Consistency checking** | A data recovery technique that involves scanning the logical structure of the disk and checking to make sure it is consistent with its specification.

**Controlling the Assault of Non-Solicited Pornography and Marketing (CAN-SPAM) Act** | A 2003 act that covers unsolicited commercial e-mail messages. The act has both civil and criminal provisions. Each separate e-mail sent in violation of the CAN-SPAM Act is subject to penalties of up to $16,000.

**Covert channel** | A technique for passing information between computers on a network, without being detected by a firewall or an intrusion detection system. Packet crafting and protocol bending are two covert channel techniques.

**Criminal intent** | The mental state of mind of a defendant in committing a crime.

**Cyber Crimes Center (C3)** | A part of U.S. Immigration and Customs Enforcement (ICE) that identifies and apprehends Internet child pornographers.

**Cybercrime** | Criminal activity that pertains to the wrongful taking of information or the causing of damage to information.

**Cybercriminal** | An individual who uses a computer or network technology to plan or perpetrate a violation of the law.

**Cybersquatting** | The bad-faith registration of a domain name that is a registered trademark or trade name of another entity.

**Cyberstalking** | A crime that involves using the Internet, e-mail, or other electronic communications devices to repeatedly harass or threaten another person.

**Cyberterrorist** | An attacker or a group of attackers that use a target country's computers and information, usually through the Internet, to cause physical harm, severely disrupt the country's infrastructure, or create panic.

**Cyberwarfare** | The use of computers and the Internet to conduct warfare in cyberspace.

## D

**Data** | Raw numbers, pictures, and other "stuff" that may or may not have relevance to a particular event or incident under investigation.

**Data analysis plan** | A plan that lists the types of data to be collected and describes the expected sources for the data. It should also list any anticipated problems as well as recommended strategies to deal with those problems.

**Data consistency** | The validity, accuracy, usability, and integrity of data. This is an issue in live system forensics. When data is not acquired at a unified moment, it is inconsistent.

**Data recovery** | The process of salvaging data from damaged, failed, corrupted, or inaccessible primary storage media when it cannot be accessed normally. It involves evaluating and extracting data from damaged media and returning it in an intact format. Data recovery can also be the process of retrieving and securing deleted information from a storage media for forensic purposes or spying.

**Dead man's switch** | A switch an attacker plants that destroys any evidence when the system detects that it's offline.

**Dead system analysis** | Forensic analysis of machines that have been shut down.

**Demonstrative evidence** | Information such as a chart that helps explain other evidence to a judge and jury.

**Denial of service (DoS)/distributed denial of service (DDoS) attack** | An attack in which an attacker deprives people of the services they are entitled to access or provide.

**Department of Defense (DoD)** | The department of the U.S. federal government that coordinates and supervises agencies and functions of the government related to national security and the U.S. armed forces.

**DFRWS framework** | A framework for ensuring forensic soundness that has six classes: identification, preservation, collection, examination, analysis, and presentation. Each of these classes has several elements. The Digital Forensics Research Workshop (DFRWS) created this framework in 2001.

**Differential backup** | A backup in which only files that have changed since a backup was last made are backed up to the backup facility.

**Digital Forensics Research Workshop (DFRWS)** | A nonprofit volunteer organization that aims to enhance the sharing of knowledge and ideas about digital forensics research. The DFRWS sponsors annual conferences, technical working groups, and challenges to help drive the direction of research and development. In 2001, the DFRWS developed a framework for digital investigation that is useful today.

**Digital watermarking** | A technique that allows the addition of copyright notices or other verification messages to digital audio, video, or image signals and documents.

**Disaster recovery plan** | A plan that helps a lab restore its workstations and file servers to their original condition after a catastrophic failure occurs.

**Disk forensics** | The process of acquiring and analyzing data stored on physical storage media, such as computer hard drives, smartphones, and removable media. Disk forensics includes the recovery of hidden and deleted data. It also includes the process of identifying who created a file or message.

**Documentary evidence** | Written evidence that must be authenticated, such as a printed report or a log file.

**DoD Cyber Crime Center (DC3)** | A U.S. federal government agency that sets standards for digital evidence processing, analysis, and diagnostics. It is involved with DoD investigations that require computer forensic support to detect, enhance, or recover digital media.

**Dump** | A complete copy of every bit of memory or cache recorded in permanent storage or printed on paper.

## E

**Electronic Communications Privacy Act (ECPA)** | A federal act that extends legal protection against wiretapping and other forms of unauthorized interception to e-mail, mobile telephones, pagers, computer transmissions, and communications provided by private communication carriers. It also explicitly allows employers to monitor communications by employees using the employers' equipment.

**E-mail attachment** | A file such as a picture, document, audio file, program, or video that is attached to an e-mail message.

**E-mail body** | An area of an e-mail message that contains the content of the communication.

**E-mail client** | A software program used to compose and read e-mail messages.

**E-mail forensics** | The study of the source and content of e-mail as evidence. E-mail forensics includes identifying the sender, recipient, date, time, and origination location of an e-mail message.

**E-mail header** | An area of an e-mail message that contains addressing information and the route that an e-mail takes from sender to receiver. It is an abbreviated record of the e-mail message's journey.

**E-mail log** | A record of each e-mail message that passes through a computer in a network.

**E-mail tracing** | Examining e-mail header and other information to determine the route the e-mail has traveled and the sender's identity. E-mail tracing programs and services can be used to resolve problems with sexually harassing e-mail, cyberstalking, and other unwanted Internet and intranet communications.

**Embedded file** | In steganography, the data that is to be kept a secret. An embedded file is also called an *embedded message*.

**Embedding** | In steganography, the process of hiding data. Also known as *running the steganography algorithm*.

**Event** | Any observable occurrence in a system or network. Examples of events include a user connecting to a file share, a server receiving a request for a Web page, a user sending e-mail, and a firewall blocking a connection attempt.

**Event-based digital forensic investigation framework** | A model for forensic investigation that has five phases: readiness, deployment, physical crime scene investigation, digital crime scene investigation, and presentation. The Center for Education and Research in Information Assurance and Security (CERIAS) at Purdue University created this model in 2004.

**Evidence** | Information that supports a specific finding or determination. Evidence may be conclusive or interpretive.

**Evidence dynamics** | Anything that changes or destroys digital evidence between the time the evidence is created and when the case goes to court. An action that changes the evidence could be either accidental or deliberate.

**Evidence storage container** | A container that stores evidence and is secured so that no unauthorized person can easily access the evidence. Also known as an evidence locker.

**Evidence storage room** | A room that stores large computer components, such as computers, monitors, and other peripheral devices. It may or may not be located within the lab itself.

**Exculpatory evidence** | Evidence that clears or tends to clear someone of guilt.

**Extortion** | An attempt to gain money or something else of value by threatening, coercing, or intimidating a victim.

**Extraction** | In steganography, the recovery of an embedded message.

**Federal Rules of Evidence (FRE)** | A code of evidence law that governs the admission of facts by which parties in the U.S. federal court system may prove their cases. The FRE provides guidelines for the authentication and identification of evidence for admissibility under sections 901, 902, and "Searching and Seizing Computers and Obtaining Electronic Evidence in Criminal Investigations."

**File allocation table (FAT)** | A table that stores associations between files and the clusters assigned to them.

**File slack** | A form of fragmentation that pertains to any space left over between the last byte of the file and the first byte of the next cluster. File slack is a source of potential security leaks involving passwords, network logons, e-mail, database entries, and word processing documents. Also known as slack space.

**Firewall** | A set of hardware and software components that protect system resources from attack by intercepting and checking network traffic.

**Flash memory media** | A computer memory chip or card that retains its data without being connected to a power source.

**Footprinting** | The process of collecting data about a specific network environment, usually for the purpose of finding ways to attack the target.

**Forensic soundness** | A state in which data is complete and materially unaltered.

**Fourth Amendment to the U.S. Constitution** | An amendment that guards against unreasonable searches and seizures. The Fourth Amendment specifically requires that search and arrest warrants be judicially sanctioned and supported by probable cause.

**Fraud** | A crime that involves intentional deception for personal gain or to cause other damage to an individual or a company.

**Freezing the scene** | A data collection method that involves taking a snapshot of a system in its compromised state and notifying the necessary authorities.

**Fuzzy logic tool** | A tool used to identify unknown strings of text by searching for values between "completely true" and "completely false."

## G

**Global area network (GAN)** | A collection of interconnected LANs, CANs, MANs, and even WANs that spans an extremely large area.

**Graphical user interface** | An interface for issuing commands to a computer using a pointing device (mouse) that manipulates and activates graphical images on a monitor.

## H

**Hacking** | Illegal intrusion into a computer system without the permission of the computer owner or user.

**Hardware fingerprinting** | Checking to determine what hardware is present on a system.

**Hearsay** | Evidence presented by a person who was not a direct witness. Hearsay is generally inadmissible in court and should be avoided.

**Honeypot** | A trap set for cybercriminals that involves a system or data that is attractive to the hackers.

**Honeypotting** | A data collection process that involves creating a replica system and luring the attacker into it for further monitoring.

**host protected area (HPA)** | An area on a hard drive where data can be hidden. The HPA was designed as an area where computer vendors could store data that is protected from user activities and operating system utilities, such as delete and format.

**Human-generated information** | Information created by humans. It includes e-mail messages, text messages, word processing documents, digital photos, and other records that are transmitted or stored electronically.

**Hypertext Transfer Protocol (HTTP)** | A protocol that is involved in requesting and transmitting files over the Internet or another network; a protocol used for most Web browser/Web server communication.

## I

**Identity theft** | A crime in which someone wrongfully obtains and uses another person's personal data in some way that involves fraud or deception. Criminals typically commit identity theft for economic gain. Also known as identity fraud.

**Identity Theft and Assumption Deterrence Act** | A federal 1998 act that makes identity theft a federal crime. A person who violates the law is subject to criminal penalties of up to 15 years in prison. This period increases to 20 years in special circumstances. Violators can also be fined up to $250,000.

**Image backup** | A backup that creates copies or snapshots of a file system at a particular point in time.

**Imaging** | The process of creating a complete sector-by-sector copy of a disk drive. Also known as making a bit stream backup.

**Incident response plan** | A document that outlines specific procedures to follow in the event of a security incident.

**Incident response team (IRT)** | A group of people with responsibilities for dealing with any security incident in an organization.

**Incremental backup** | A backup that transfers only the data that has changed since the last backup.

**Incriminating evidence** | Evidence that shows, or tends to show, a person's involvement in an act, or evidence that can establish guilt.

**Information** | Data that has been processed and assembled so that it is relevant to an investigation.

**Intellectual property theft** | A crime that involves stealing trade secrets, material that is copyrighted, or other information to which an individual or a company has a right.

**Internet forensics** | The process of piecing together where and when a user has been on the Internet.

**Internet Message Access Protocol (IMAP)** | A protocol that allows an e-mail client to access e-mail on a remote mail server.

**Internet Protocol (IP)** | The primary network protocol used on the Internet. On the Internet and many other networks, IP is often used together with Transport Control Protocol (TCP) and referred to as TCP/IP.

**Internet Protocol (IP) address** | A numeric label that identifies a device and provides a location address. A forensic investigator may be able to identify IP addresses from a message header and use this information to determine who sent the message.

**Intrusion detection system (IDS)** | Software that automates the process of monitoring events occurring in a computer system or network and analyzing them for signs of possible incidents and attempting to stop detected possible incidents.

**Jailbreaking** | A hacking process by which iPhone firmware is overwritten to install third-party applications or unlock the device. The jailbreaking process makes modifications to the user data partition and is therefore forensically unsound.

## K

**Kerckhoffs' principle** | A theory which states that a system will be secure even if everything about it except the key is public knowledge.

**Kernel module rootkit** | A type of rootkit that installs itself into the application programming interface (API). The rootkit then intercepts system calls by acting as a "man in the middle," deciding what information and programs the user does and does not see.

## L

**Lab manager** | An individual who performs general management tasks for a computer forensics lab, such as promoting group consensus in decision making, maintaining fiscal responsibility for lab needs, and enforcing ethical standards among staff members.

**Live analysis school of thought** | A segment of the forensics world that recommends leaving a suspect computer turned on and working on it immediately after securing it.

**Live response** | A live system forensics technique in which an investigator surveys the crime scene and simultaneously collects evidence and probes for suspicious activity. The purpose of live response is to collect relevant evidence from a system to confirm whether an incident occurred.

**Live system forensics** | An area of systems forensics that is used to search memory in real time. Live system forensics is typically used for working with compromised hosts and to identify system abuse.

**Local area network (LAN)** | A network that covers a small physical area, such as an office or a building. LANs are common in homes and businesses and make it easy to use resources such as printers and shared disks.

**Locard's exchange principle** | A basic concept of forensic science, which states that "with contact between two items, there will be an exchange." In other words, every contact leaves a trace.

**Log file** | A record that a network device keeps of a person's activities on a system or network. Network security devices such as firewalls and intrusion detection systems (IDS) generate logs. Routers, VPNs, and other devices also produce logs.

**Logical analysis** | Analysis using the native operating system, on the evidence disk or a forensic duplicate, to peruse the data. Logical analysis looks for things that are visible, known about, and possibly controlled by the user.

**Logical damage** | Damage to a file system that may prevent it from being mounted by the host operating system. Logical damage is caused primarily by power outages that prevent file system structures from being completely written to the storage medium. However, problems with hardware and drivers, as well as system crashes, can have the same effect.

## M

**Mail relay** | A server typically used within local networks to transmit e-mail messages among local users. Mail relays are often used in e-mail aliasing: They forward mail for multiple e-mail addresses to a single address.

**Mail server** | A device and/or program that routes an e-mail to the correct destination. A server that functions as an electronic post office, sending and receiving electronic mail. Most of the time, the mail server is separate from the computer where the mail was composed. Also referred to as a mail relay.

GLOSSARY

**Malware** | Malicious software that is designed to infiltrate a computer system without the user's consent. Malware includes computer viruses, worms, Trojan horses, spyware, some types of adware, and other malicious and unwanted software.

**Master boot record (MBR)** | On a drive that uses a DOS partition, a reserved space at the beginning of the drive. The MBR often contains the boot code needed to start loading the operating system. The MBR contains 62 sectors of empty space where data can be hidden.

**Means** | The ability to commit a crime.

**Metadata** | Data about data. In a computer file, metadata provides information about a file. This information includes the means of creation, the purpose of the data, the time and date of creation, the creator or author of data, where the data was created, and what standards were used.

**Metropolitan area network (MAN)** | A network that connects two or more LANs but does not span an area larger than a city or town. MANs are used to connect multiple buildings or groups of buildings spread around an area larger than a few city blocks.

**Mirroring** | Physical replication of all data, with two copies of the data kept online at all times. The advantage of mirroring is that the data does not have to be restored, so there are no issues with immediate data availability.

**Moore's law** | A trend in which the number of transistors on an integrated circuit doubles every two years.

**Motive** | A reason a suspect commits a crime.

### N

**Network** | A collection of computers and devices joined by connection media. In a typical enterprise network environment, network components work together to make information and resources available to many users.

**Network forensics** | An area of system forensics that focuses on investigating network intrusions, abuse, and often crimes that cross jurisdictions.

### O

**Obscured data** | Data that is difficult to collect and analyze because it is encrypted, compressed, or in a proprietary format.

**Open Systems Interconnection (OSI) reference model** | A tool for understanding communications systems. The OSI reference model divides networking into seven layers. Each layer contains similar functions that provide services to the layer above it and receive services from the layer below it.

**Opportunity** | The chance to commit a crime.

**Order of volatility** | A list of evidence sources, ordered by relative volatility.

### P

**Packet crafting** | A covert channel technique that involves embedding data in packet headers.

**Peer-to-peer (P2P) network** | A network in which each user manages his or her own resources and configures who may access the user's computer resources and how. On a P2P network, each computer is configured individually.

**Personal area network (PAN)** | A network that consists of one or more workstations and its network devices, such as printers, PDAs, network disk systems, and scanners. A PAN refers to the networked devices one person would likely use and normally does not span an area larger than an office or cubicle.

**Phishing** | A crime that involves using e-mail or Web sites to get confidential information by deceptive means.

**Physical analysis** | Offline analysis conducted on an evidence disk or forensic duplicate after booting from a CD or another system. Physical analysis looks for things that may have been overlooked, or are invisible, to the user.

**Physical damage** | Damage to storage media that occurs on a physical level, such as broken tapes or CDs or hard disks damaged by fire or water. Physical damage always causes at least some data loss. In many cases, the logical structures of the file system are damaged as well.

**Piracy** | Theft of material that is copyrighted through the illegal copying of genuine programs or counterfeiting of products that are intended to pass as originals.

**Pirate** | To defeat copy protection in order to copy software or other files.

**Post Office Protocol (POP)** | A protocol that local e-mail clients use to retrieve e-mail from a remote server.

**Pretty Good Privacy (PGP)** | A widely used encryption program for protecting the privacy of e-mail and other computer files. PGP uses two keys and an NIST-certified algorithm. It makes encrypted data practically impossible to decipher without the appropriate key.

**Protocol bending** | A covert channel technique that involves the use of a network protocol for some unintended purpose.

**Public-key cryptography** | A form of encryption that uses a pair of cryptographic keys: one public, the other private. The public key is freely distributed and is used to encrypt the information to be sent. The recipient holds the private key and uses it to decrypt the received information.

**Public key steganography (PKS)** | A form of steganography in which the sender and receiver share a secret key, called the stego key. Only a possessor of the stego key can detect the presence of an embedded message.

## R

**Real evidence** | A physical object that can be touched, held, or directly observed, such as a hard drive or removable media. *Also:* Any evidence that speaks for itself, without relying on anything else. An example is a log produced by an audit function.

**Real time** | The actual time during which a process takes place.

**Rootkit** | A program or a combination of several programs designed to hide or obscure the fact that a system has been compromised.

**Router** | A hardware or software device that forwards data packets across a network to a destination network.

**Rules of evidence** | Rules that govern whether, when, how, and why proof of a legal case can be placed before a judge or jury. The rules vary depending on the type of court and the jurisdiction.

## S

**Safe shutdown school of thought** | A segment of the forensics world that believes a suspect computer should be carefully shut down immediately when the computer is secured.

**Sandboxing** | A data collection method that involves limiting what an attacker can do while still on the compromised system, so the attacker can be monitored without much further damage.

**Script kiddy** | A rather unsophisticated hacker who uses a point-and-click tool rather than program software.

**Search warrant** | A court order that allows law enforcement personnel to collect equipment or data from that equipment. Search warrants are typically used by law enforcement officers.

**Sector** | The smallest unit of storage on a computer. A sector is composed of bits and is generally a power of two bytes in size. A "regular" disk sector is 512 bytes.

**Security through obscurity** | A principle that attempts to provide security through the use of secrecy of design, implementation, and so on. A system that relies on security through obscurity may have security vulnerabilities, but its owners or designers believe that the flaws are not known, and that attackers are unlikely to find them.

**Server-based network** | A network in which a central server manages which users have access to which resources through a database called a *directory*. This is the best option when an organization has 10 or more network users.

**Shadow data** | Fringe data that remains on the physical track of storage media after deletion, sweeping, or scrubbing.

**Simple Mail Transfer Protocol (SMTP)** | A protocol that mail servers use to send and receive mail messages. E-mail clients use SMTP to send messages to a mail server for relaying.

GLOSSARY

**Simple steganography** | A form of steganography that is based on keeping the method for embedding a secret. Also called *pure steganography.*

**Slurred image** | An image that results from acquiring a file system while it is being updated or changed by a program in process. A slurred image is similar to a photo of a moving object.

**Sniffing** | Monitoring network data using a self-contained software program or a hardware device. Sniffers examine network traffic, making a copy of the data without redirecting or altering it. Some sniffers work only with TCP/IP packets, but the more sophisticated tools can work with many other protocols.

**Software as a service (SaaS)** | Software that a provider licenses to customers as a service on demand, through a subscription model.

**Software forensics** | An area of systems forensics that is most often used to examine malicious code. Also known as malware forensics.

**Spam** | Unsolicited or undesired electronic messages.

**Spamming** | Abusing electronic messaging systems to send unsolicited, unwanted bulk messages indiscriminately.

**Spoliation** | Withholding, hiding, alteration, or destruction of evidence relevant to a legal proceeding, whether intentional or negligent.

**Spoofing** | Making an e-mail message appear to come from someone other than the real sender or location.

**Steganalysis** | The process of detecting messages hidden using steganography. In other words, steganalysis is about separating cover messages from stego messages.

**Steganalysis software** | Tools that can detect the presence of steganography.

**Steganography** | The process of hiding secret data within nonsecret data.

**Stego key** | In secret key steganography, the secret key that the sender and receiver share. Only a possessor of the stego key can detect the presence of an embedded message.

**Stego message** | In steganography, the message that results from the embedding process.

**Storage area network (SAN)** | An architecture in which a network separate from the traditional LAN connects all storage and servers. In a SAN, the devices appear to be locally attached to the operating system.

**Subpoena** | A court order than requires the person or organization that owns the equipment to release it for analysis. Subpoenas are typically used in civil actions or court proceedings.

**System forensics** | The collection, preservation, analysis, documentation, and presentation of digital evidence so that it is admissible in a court of law.

**System forensics evidence** | Evidence gathered from computers, digital media, or electronic devices, such as a mobile phone or digital camera.

**System forensics specialist** | An individual responsible for system forensics.

### T

**TEMPEST** | Special computer-emission shielding used to shield sensitive computing systems and labs and prevent electronic eavesdropping on any computer emissions.

**Temporary data** | Data that an operating system creates and overwrites without the computer user taking a direct action to save this data.

**Testimonial evidence** | Information that is used to support or interpret real or documentary evidence. *Also:* Any evidence supplied by a witness. Documents from a word processing program written by a witness may be considered testimonial.

**Thin client** | A PC that uses little of its computing capability, functioning much like a dumb terminal.

**Topology** | A network design that specifies the devices, locations, and cable installation as well as how data is transferred in the network.

**Trade secret** | A plan, method, technology, or other sensitive information that is owned by an individual or a company. Theft of these secrets damages a business's competitive edge.

**Transmission Control Protocol/Internet Protocol (TCP/IP)** | A set of protocols used to send messages between computers over the Internet. IP handles delivery of the data. TCP keeps track of the individual units of data, called packets, in a message.

## U

**Unallocated space** | The unused portion of the hard drive that is not allocated to any volume. Unallocated space is also called free space.

**Uniting and Strengthening America by Providing Appropriate Tools Required to Intercept and Obstruct Terrorism (U.S.A. PATRIOT) Act** | A law that amended both the Wiretap Act and the ECPA. The Patriot Act enhances law enforcement tools to intercept electronic communications to fight computer fraud and abuse offenses.

**Unused space** | The space that is left on a hard drive or disk when a file is deleted. The computer considers that spaced unused and available for reuse.

**U.S. Computer Emergency Readiness Team (US-CERT)** | Part of the National Cyber Security Division of the Department of Homeland Security that assists civilian agencies in their incident-handling efforts.

## V

**Virtual machine** | A software implementation of a computer that executes programs as if it were a physical computer. For example, a Mac user might use a virtual machine to run Windows on the Mac. VMware and VirtualBox are commonly used virtual machine software programs.

**Volatile data** | Data from running processes on a live computer. Volatile data is memory that is highly sensitive to system usage, such as registers, memory, and cache. Such data is lost whenever a system is used. It should be collected first to minimize corruption or loss.

**Volatile memory analysis** | A live system forensics technique in which an investigator acquires a physical memory dump of the compromised system and transmits it to the data collection system for analysis.

**Voluntary surrender** | Permission from a computer or equipment owner to search and/or seize equipment as part of an investigation.

## W

**Wide area network (WAN)** | A network that connects multiple LANs and can span very large areas, including multiple countries. WANs provide network connections among computers, devices, and other networks that communicate across great distances. For example, the Internet is a WAN.

**Wireless local area networks (WLANs)** | A local area network that links devices wirelessly.

**Wiretap Act** | An amended 1968 act that governs real-time interception of the contents of a communication.

**Write blocker** | A piece of hardware or software that allows a system to read data from an external drive at full speed. At the same time, it blocks any write commands to the external drive to prevent unauthorized modification or formatting of the drive being examined.

## Z

**Zero-knowledge analysis** | A file system repair technique in which a recovery specialist assumes very little about the state of the file system to be analyzed, uses any hints that any undamaged file system structures might provide, and rebuilds the file system from scratch.

**GLOSSARY**

# References

Bace, Rebecca. *An Introduction to Intrusion Detection Assessment*. Herndon, VA: ICSA Labs, 2005.

Berghel, Hal. *Hiding Data, Forensics and Anti-Forensics*. Berghel.net, 2007.

Berghel, Hal, David Hoelzer, and Michael Sthultz. "Data Hiding Tactics for Windows and UNIX File Systems." Identity Theft and Financial Fraud Research and Operation Center, May 26, 2006. http://www.berghel.net/publications/data_hiding/data_hiding.php (accessed June 1, 2010).

Berinato, Scott. "The Rise of Anti-Forensics." *CSO*, June 8, 2007. http://www.csoonline.com/article/221208/The_Rise_of_Anti_Forensics (accessed May 20, 2010).

Biggs, Maggie. "Forensics Tools Can Help Stop Threats to Ever-Expanding Networks." *Government Computer News*, August 19, 2009. http://gcn.com/articles/2009/08/24/it-forensics-tools-tech-strategies.aspx (accessed June 15, 2010).

Blumberg, Andrew J., and Peter Eckersley. "On Locational Privacy, and How to Avoid Losing It Forever." Electronic Frontier Foundation, August 2009. http://www.eff.org/files/eff-locational-privacy.pdf (accessed June 11, 2010).

Blunden, Bill. *The Rootkit Arsenal: Escape and Evasion in the Dark Corners of the System*. Boston: Wordware Publishing, Inc., 2009, pp. 496–498.

Braid, Matthew. *Collecting Electronic Evidence After a System Compromise*. Bethesda, MD: The SANS Institute, 2005.

Burnette, Michael W. "Forensic Examination of a RIM (BlackBerry) Wireless Device." June 2002. http://www.rh-law.com/ediscovery/Blackberry.pdf (accessed June 11, 2010).

Carrier, Brian D., and Eugene H. Spafford. *An Event-Based Digital Forensic Investigation Framework*. West Lafayette, IN: Center for Education and Research in Information Assurance and Security (CERIAS), Purdue University. Presented at DFRWS 2004.

CBS News. "Cyberbully Mom Guilty of Lesser Charge." *CBS News*, November 26, 2008. http://www.cbsnews.com/stories/2008/11/26/national/main4635346.shtml (accessed May 14, 2010).

Chisum, W. Jerry, and Brent E. Turvey. "Evidence Dynamics: Locard's Exchange Principle and Crime Reconstruction." *Journal of Behavioral Profiling* Vol. 1, No. 1, January 2000.

Chuvakin, Anton. "Linux Data Hiding and Recovery." Guardian Digital, Inc., 2010. http://www.linuxsecurity.com/content/view/117638/49/ (accessed May 21, 2010).

Clarke, Richard A., and Robert K. Knake. *Cyberwar: The Next Threat to National Security and What to Do About It*. New York: HarperCollins, 2010.

Committee on Identifying the Needs of the Forensic Sciences Community and National Research Council. *Strengthening Forensic Science in the United States: A Path Forward*. Washington, DC: National Academies Press, 2009, pp. 5–41.

Computer Forensic Services. *Data Analysis & Recovery.* Minnetonka, MN: Computer Forensic Services, Inc., 2006.

"Computer Forensics Recruiter Provides Career Information in the Computer Forensics Field with the Best and Latest Education Resources and Schools." *Information Engineer Technology News,* March 7, 2010. http://www.informationengineer.org/2010/03/06/computer-forensics -recruiter-provides-career-information-in-the-computer-forensics-field-with-the-best-and -latest-education-resources-and-schools.html (accessed July 8, 2009).

Computer Forensics UK Ltd. *DIVA Computer Evidence—Digital Image Verification and Authentication.* Warwickshire, England: Computer Forensics UK Ltd., 2005.

Corbin, Kenneth. "Massive Cyber Spy Ring Seen Operating in China." *Internetnews.com,* April 8, 2010. http://www.internetnews.com/security/article.php/3875471/Massive-Cyber -Spy-Ring-Seen-Operating-in-China.htm (accessed June 11, 2010).

———. "Report Alleges Vast Cyber Crime Syndicate in China." *eSecurity Planet,* April 7, 2010. http://www.esecurityplanet.com/news/article.php/3875281/Report-Alleges-Vast-Cyber -Crime-Syndicate-in-China.htm (accessed May 14, 2010).

Cornell University Law School. *Computer Fraud and Abuse Act.* Cornell University Law School, January 5, 2009. http://www.law.cornell.edu/uscode/18/1030.html (accessed June 11, 2010).

Dignan, Larry. "How Databases Connect to the Arrest of Faisal Shahzad." *Tech Republic,* May 4, 2010. http://blogs.techrepublic.com.com/datacenter/?p=2579&tag=nl.e040 (accessed May 20, 2010).

Economy Watch. "Porn Industry, Porn Trade, Adult Entertainment Industry." *Economy Watch,* n.d. http://www.economywatch.com/world-industries/porn-industry.html (accessed May 20, 2010).

Federal Bureau of Investigation. *2008 Computer Crime and Security Survey.* Washington, DC: FBI, 2008.

Furuseth, Andreas Grytting. *Digital Forensics: Methods and Tools for Retrieval and Analysis of Security Credentials and Hidden Data.* Trondheim, Norway: Norwegian University of Science and Technology, Department of Computer and Information Science, 2007. http://pogostick. net/~andreas/ (accessed June 14, 2010).

Gamradt, Derek. *Data Backup + Recovery.* Englewood, CO: StorNet, 2005.

Graham, Robert. "FAQ: Firewall Forensics (What Am I Seeing?)," version 0.3.0. LinuxSecurity. com, January 15, 2000. http://www.linuxsecurity.com/resource_files/firewalls/firewall -seen.html (accessed June 11, 2010).

Gonzalez, Alberto R., Regina B. Schofield, and David W. Hagy. *Investigations Involving the Internet and Computer Networks,* NCJ 210798. Washington, DC: U.S. Department of Justice, Office of Justice Programs, National Institute of Justice, January 2007. http://www.ncjrs.gov/pdffiles1/ nij/210798.pdf (accessed June 15, 2010).

Grubb, Tom. "The Five A's That Make Cybercrime so Attractive." *Security Week,* April 26, 2010. http://www.securityweek.com/content/five-a%E2%80%99s-make-cybercrime-so-attractive (accessed May 14, 2010).

Hansche, Susan, John Berti, and Chris Hare. *Official (ISC)² Guide to the CISSP Exam.* Prattville, AL: (ISC)², 2003.

Hoog, Andrew, and Kyle Gaffaney. "iPhone Forensics." viaForensics, June 2009. http://viaforensics.com/services/iphone-forensics/ (accessed June 11, 2010).

Internet Crime Complaint Center (IC3). "2009 Internet Crime Report." Internet Crime Complaint Center, n.d. http://www.ic3.gov/media/annualreports.aspx (access June 11, 2010).

Kakutani, Michiko. "The Attack Coming From Bytes, Not Bombs." *The New York Times*, April 26, 2010. http://www.nytimes.com/2010/04/27/books/27book.html (accessed May 20, 2010).

Kerr, Orin S. "Computer Records and the Federal Rules of Evidence." U.S. Department of Justice, March 2001. http://www.justice.gov/criminal/cybercrime/usamarch2001_4.htm (accessed May 26, 2010).

Kruse, Warren G., and Jay G. Heiser. *Computer Forensics: Incident Response Essentials.* Indianapolis: Addison-Wesley, 2002.

Law, Frank Y. W., K. P. Chow, Michael Y. K. Kwan, and Pierre K. Y. Lai. *Consistency Issue on Live Systems Forensics.* The University of Hong Kong, 2009. http://www.cs.hku.hk/cisc/forensics/papers/Consistency.pdf (accessed June 15, 2010).

Lee, Jiyun Cameron. *Working with Computer Forensics Experts—Uncovering Data You Didn't Know Existed Can Help Make Your Case.* Chicago: American Bar Association, July 2006.

Lessing, Marthie, and Basie von Solms. *Live Forensic Acquisition as Alternative to Traditional Forensic Processes.* Johannesburg: University of Johannesburg Academy for Information Technology, 2009.

McKemmish, Rodney, quoted in Ray, Indrajit, and Sujeet Shenoi. *Advances in Digital Forensics IV.* Boston: Springer, 2008, pp. 3–15.

Microsoft. *Responding to IT Security Incidents.* Redmond, WA: Microsoft Corporation, 2007.

Morris, Jamie. "Forensics on the Windows Platform, Part Two." Symantec, February 11, 2003. http://www.symantec.com/connect/articles/forensics-windows-platform-part-two (accessed June 11, 2010).

National Center for Missing & Exploited Children. *2008 Annual Report.* Alexandria, VA: National Center for Missing & Exploited Children, 2008. http://www.missingkids.com/en_US/publications/NC171.pdf (accessed May 20, 2010).

National Institute of Standards and Technology Boulder Laboratories. "General Information." NIST Boulder Laboratories. http://www.boulder.nist.gov/geninfo.htm (accessed June 11, 2010).

New Technologies, Inc. "Computer Evidence Defined." New Technologies, Inc., 2008. http://www.forensics
-intl.com/def3.html (accessed June 11, 2010).

———. *Computer Evidence Processing Steps.* Gresham, OR: New Technologies, Inc., 2005.

O'Connor, Thomas R. *Cybercrime: The Internet as Crime Scene.* Fort Campbell, KY: Austin Peay State University Center, 2005.

———. *Digital Evidence Collection and Handling.* Fort Campbell, KY: Austin Peay State University Center, 2006.

———. *Disaster Data Recovery and Computer Forensics.* Fort Campbell, KY: Austin Peay State University, 2008.

Phillips, Amelia. *The Investigator's Office and Laboratory.* Des Moines, WA: Highline Community College, 2007.

Pidanick, Ryan. "An Investigation of Computer Forensics." *Information Systems Control Journal,* Vol. 3, 2004. http://www.itgi.org/TemplateRedirect.cfm?template=/ContentManagement/ContentDisplay.cfm&ContentID=19743 (accessed June 11, 2010).

Rehman Technology Services, Inc. *Computers.* Mount Dora, FL: Rehman Technology Services, Inc., 2005.

Richard III, Golden, and Vassil Roussev. In Kanellis, Panagiotis, Evangelos Kiountouzis, Nicholas Kolokotronis, and Drakoulis Martakos. *Digital Crime and Forensic Science in Cyberspace.* Hershey, PA: Idea Group Publishing, 2006. http://rcirib.ir/digital_books/PDF%20Books/Digital%20Crime%20And%20Forensic%20Science%20in%20Cyberspace-Panagiotis%20Kanellis-1591408725-Idea%20Group%20Pub.pdf (accessed June 15, 2010).

Robbins, Judd. *An Explanation of Computer Forensics.* Incline Village, NV: National Forensics Center, 2006.

Rogers, Larry. "Cybersleuthing: Means, Motive, and Opportunity." Software Engineering Institute, June 2000. http://www.sei.cmu.edu/library/abstracts/news-at-sei/securitysum00.cfm (accessed May 20, 2010).

Rogers, Marc. "A New Hacker Taxonomy." 1999. http://homes.cerias.purdue.edu/~mkr/hacker_doc.pdf (accessed May 20, 2010).

Savage, Marcia. "CSI for the CISO." *Information Security,* Vol. 10, No. 8, September 2007.

Scarfone, Karen, Tim Grance, and Kelly Masone. *Computer Security Incident Handling Guide.* Gaithersburg, MD: National Institute of Standards and Technology, 2007.

Sommer, Peter. *Computer Forensics: An Introduction.* London: Virtual City Associates, 2003.

Sremack, Joseph C. *Formalizing Computer Forensic Analysis: A Proof-Based Methodology.* Raleigh, NC: North Carolina State University, Department of Computer Science, 2005.

Symantec. "Cybercrime's Financial and Geographic Growth Shows No Slowdown during the Global Economic Crisis." Symantec, April 20, 2010. http://www.symantec.com/about/news/release/article.jsp?prid=20100419_02 (accessed May 20, 2010).

"Tracing Email." USUS: The Usually Useful Internet Guide for Journalists, 2005. http://www.usus.org/elements/tracing.htm (accessed June 15, 2010).

Tsoutsouris, Damian. *Computer Forensic Legal Standards and Equipment.* SANS Institute InfoSec Reading Room, 2001.

U.S. Department of Justice. http://www.justice.gov (accessed June 13, 2010).

———. "1999 Report on Cyberstalking: A New Challenge for Law Enforcement and Industry." USDOJ, February 7, 2003. http://www.justice.gov/criminal/cybercrime/cyberstalking.htm (accessed June 11, 2010).

———. "Identity Theft." U.S. Department of Justice, n.d. http://www.justice.gov/criminal/fraud/websites/idtheft.html (accessed May 20, 2010).

U.S. Department of Labor. *2008–2009 Occupational Outlook Handbook.* Indianapolis: JIST Publishing, 2008.

U.S. General Accounting Office. "Computer Attacks at Department of Defense Pose Increasing Risks." Washington, DC: GAO, May 1996. http://www.pbs.org/wgbh/pages/frontline/shows/hackers/risks/dodattacks.html (accessed June 11, 2010).

U.S. Immigration and Customs Enforcement. "Cyber Crimes Center." U.S. Immigration and Customs Enforcement, April 13, 2010. http://www.ice.gov/partners/investigations/services/cyberbranch.htm (accessed June 11, 2010).

Vacca, John R. *Computer and Information Security Handbook.* Burlington, MA: Morgan Kaufmann, 2009.

———. *The Essential Guide to Storage Area Networks.* Upper Saddle River, NJ: Prentice Hall, 2002.

———. *Guide to Wireless Network Security.* Philadelphia: Springer, 2006.

———. *Practical Internet Security.* New York: Springer, 2006.

———. *Public Key Infrastructure: Building Trusted Applications and Web Services.* Boca Raton, FL: Auerbach, 2004.

Vacca, John R., and Scott R. Ellis. *Firewalls: Jumpstart for Network and Systems Administrators.* Burlington, MA: Elsevier Digital Press, 2005.

Vogon International Limited. *Vogon Forensics Bulletin*, Vol. 3, Issue 3, 2001.

Waits, Cal, Joseph Ayo Akinyele, Richard Nolan, and Larry Rogers. *Computer Forensics: Results of Live Response Inquiry vs. Memory Image Analysis.* Pittsburgh: Carnegie Mellon University, Software Engineering Institute, 2008.

Walker, Don. *Computer Forensics: Techniques for Catching the "Perp" Protect Company Data.* Austin, TX: Publications & Communications, Inc., 2005.

Weiguand, Shen. "Checking Information Warfare Epoch Mission of Intellectual Military." *Jiefangjun Bao*, February 2, 1999, p. 6.

Wiechmann, Fred J. "Processing Flash Memory Media." New Technologies, Inc., 2008. http://www.forensics-intl.com/art16.html (accessed June 11, 2010).

WikiSTC. "Alternate Data Streams." WikiSTC, 2006. http://www.wikistc.org/wiki/Alternate_data_streams (accessed June 13, 2010).

Zwaniecki, Andrzej. "Low-Risk, High-Profit Opportunities Drive Up Cybercrime." U.S. Department of State, September 28, 2009. http://www.america.gov/st/peacesec-english/2009/September/20090921193606saikceinawz0.926037.html (accessed May 14, 2010).

# Index